2003

Transition to Democracy in Eastern Europe and Russia

Transition to Democracy in Eastern Europe and Russia

Impact on Politics, Economy and Culture

Edited by Barbara Wejnert

Westport, Connecticut
London

Library of Congress Cataloging-in-Publication Data

Transition to democracy in eastern Europe and Russia : impact on politics, economy and
    culture / edited by Barbara Wejnert.
        p. cm.
    Includes bibliographical references and index.
    ISBN 0–275–97234–8 (alk. paper)
        1. Democratization—Europe, Eastern.   2. Europe, Eastern—Politics and
    government—1989–   3. Europe, Eastern—Social conditions—1989–
    4. Democratization—Former Soviet republics.   5. Former Soviet republics—Politics and
    government.   6. Former Soviet republics—Social conditions.   I. Wejnert, Barbara.
    JN96.A58T725   2002
    947'.0009'049—dc21   00–052871

British Library Cataloguing in Publication Data is available.

Library of Congress Catalog Card Number: 00–052871
ISBN: 0–275–97234–8

First published in 2002

Praeger Publishers, 88 Post Road West, Westport, CT 06881
An imprint of Greenwood Publishing Group, Inc.
www.praeger.com

Printed in the United States of America

The paper used in this book complies with the
Permanent Paper Standard issued by the National
Information Standards Organization (Z39.48–1984).

10 9 8 7 6 5 4 3 2 1

Copyright Acknowledgments

The editor and publisher gratefully acknowledge permission for use of the following material:

"Landscape" from VIEW WITH A GRAIN OF SAND, Copyright © 1993 by Wislawa Szymborska,
English translation by Stanislaw Baranczak and Clare Cavanagh copyright © 1995 by Harcourt,
Inc., reprinted by permission of the publisher.

Krynski, Magnus J. and Robert A. Maguire (trans.): SOUNDS, FEELINGS, THOUGHTS: SEV-
ENTY POEMS BY WISLAWA SZYMBORSKA. Copyright © 1981 by Princeton University Press.
Reprinted by permission of Princeton University Press.

Every reasonable effort has been made to trace the owners of copyright materials in this book, but
in some instances this has proven impossible. The editor and publisher will be glad to receive information leading to more complete acknowledgments in subsequent printings of the book and in the
meantime extend their apologies for any omissions.

With love to
Richard, Cyprian, and Cami

Contents

Preface   ix

I. Introduction   1

1. Integration of the Processes and Components of
    Transition to Democracy
    Barbara Wejnert   3

II. Impact on Politics   27

2. McCarthyism Has a New Name—Lustration:
    A Personal Recount of Political Events
    Jan Kavan   29

3. The Contribution of Collective Protests to the Softening
    of Communist Regimes in East Central Europe
    Barbara Wejnert   65

4. A Line of Blood: How December 1970 Prepared
    Polish Workers for Political Transition in 1989
    Jack M. Bloom   91

III. Impact on Economy   109

5. Transitional Economies and Income Inequality:
    The Case of Estonia
    Nancy Brandon Tuma, Mikk Titma and Rein Murakas   111

6. Fiscal Policy and Capital Formation in Transition
    Economies
    Grzegorz W. Kolodko   141

7.   Privatization Politics in Russia: Success or Failure? Privatization
     and the Development of Corporate Governance Structure
     Alexei Makeshin   173

IV. Social Problems and Policy Issues   **183**

8.   *Nouveaux Riches* Versus *Nouveaux Pauvres*:
     Policymaking in Transition Economies
     Grzegorz W. Kolodko   185

9.   Vision of the Polish Working Class:
     A Well-Ordered Economy
     Juliusz Gardawski   221

10. A Country in Transition: Health Crisis in Ukraine,
     with a Focus on Tobacco and Alcohol
     Lara A. Romaniuk   241

11. Polish Women During Transition to Democracy:
     A Preliminary Research Report
     J. Mayone Stycos, Barbara Wejnert and Zbigniew Tyszka   259

V. Impact on Culture   **279**

12. Cultural and Civic Movements Prefiguring the
     Breakdown of the Socialist Regime in Yugoslavia
     Stjepan Gredelj   281

13. The Artist's Freedom and Democracy
     Maria Nowakowska Stycos and Grazyna Borkowska   309

14. The Politics of Architecture and the Architecture of Politics
     Sergei Zherebkin and Barbara Wejnert   325

VI. Concluding Remarks   **339**

15. The Impact of Democratic Transitions on Politics, Economy
     and Culture: Lessons from Eastern Europe and Russia
     Barbara Wejnert   341

Selected Bibliography   349

Index   355

About the Editor and Contributors   365

Preface

The idea for this book germinated during my visits to the former Soviet bloc countries as a U.S. Agency for International Development (USAID) advisor, visiting professor and researcher. Having lived for many years in communist Poland and being a former member of a student chapter of the Polish Solidarity movement, principles of democracy and human rights and the opportunity for economic development were among my main life concerns. Initially, the issue of democratization and democratic movements became the central focus of my research, with my doctoral dissertation on the Solidarity movement, and more recently with comparative, empirical research on world democratic transitions over the past two centuries.

Considering my professional and personal background, I joyfully welcomed the victory of the first free democratic elections, the initiation of democratic reforms and the downfall of communism in Eastern Europe and Russia. However, during my first visits to post-communist states, I saw rapidly emerging problems of everyday life, such as joblessness, homelessness, poverty and an increasing gap between the wealthiest and the poorest citizens. The economic difficulties experienced by citizens overlap with rapid changes in other aspects of life: an enormous increase in the crime rate; drugs and prostitution; shortening of life expectancy due to stress enhanced by alcohol, drug and nicotine addiction; a collapse of strong family systems and community support networks and the Westernization of culture that has led to a partial loss of cultural distinctiveness and identity. No wonder many industrial workers expressed to me that Solidarity, which was a symbol of the democratic movement, betrayed them. The societal expectation of better living conditions for many, if not the majority, has yet been realized.

In addition, my exposure to East European and Soviet scholars, government members and policymakers supplement evidence of societal confusion, shock and disillusionment. I realize that democratization is a long process that starts with democratic political changes and democratic elections, but it takes many decades for its institutionalization. It requires experience, knowledge and skills of domestic politicians and suitable preexisting economic, political and cultural structures. Hence, democracies cannot be implemented solely by outside advisors or necessarily be isomorphic with the structures of established democracies. It was then that I decided that a publication focusing on the complexities of democratic transitions, the multilevel changes resulting from transition to democracy and the diversity of democratization's outcomes could shed light on the political, economic and cultural processes at work in newly democratic countries. To comprehensively address these complicated and often perplexing issues, I chose to prepare an interdisciplinary volume that incorporates both scholarly and practically oriented studies. The volume is divided into four sections that reflect fundamental structures of society and transition: political institutions, economic institutions, social and policy issues and culture. Each section contains a selection of chapters written by scholars and practitioners that address diverse issues relevant to the central theme of the section.

At this point, I would like to express my thanks to professor Metta Spencer for her interest in this volume, her critical comments on a number of the contributions and for her solicitation of three chapters which are included in this book. Furthermore, I owe gratitude to many people for putting me in contact with East European scholars and politicians, especially Dr. Larysa Kobelyanska, Director of the Gender Unit, Development Program of the United Nations in Ukraine, and my Polish, Russian and Ukrainian colleagues, professors Zbigniew Tyszka, Stefan Jurga, Anna Wachowiak, Irina Zherebkina and Ella Plisovska. I must also mention the endless editorial help of Ms. Patricia Heines and Danica Anderson on numerous sections, as well as the editorial assistance of my editor at Greenwood Press. Finally, I want to thank my husband Richard and my sons Cyprian and Camille for their support and patience without which this book would not have been possible.

Barbara Wejnert

I

Introduction

1

Integration of the Processes and Components of Transition to Democracy

Barbara Wejnert

Over the last four decades, democracy as a form of government has seen un-precedented growth. The number of democratic states has more than doubled since the mid-1970s; by the mid-1990s, 60 percent of the world's population lived in countries with some form of democratic system (Gurr, Jaggers & Moore 1990; Jaggers & Gurr 1995; Karatnycky 1995; Starr 1991). These same dec-ades, however, have also seen a significant change in the nature of decisions to adopt democratic forms of government. Prior to the 1970s, most adoptions of democracy were individual decisions made simultaneously by sovereign states located in disparate geographical regions. Since then, democracy has most often been adopted within geographically proximate, structurally similar and often interconnected countries, taking a form of a regional adoption and exemplifying a process of diffusion. Prime examples of such regional adoption and diffusion are Southern Europe in the 1970s (Cotta 1992; Gunther 1992; Higley & Gunther 1992; O'Donnell, Schmitter & Whitehead 1988; Pridham 1990; Tarrow 1989), Latin America in the 1980s (Higley & Gunther 1992; O'Donnell, Schmitter & Whitehead 1988; Przeworski 1988), and Soviet-block states in the 1990s (Havel 1985; Ost 1992; Szelenyi 1996; Wejnert 1994).

To address the issue of democratic transition, this book proposes and illus-trates a dual-level conceptual framework that concentrates on objectification of the fundamental and unique roles of various mechanisms and components of transition using examples of democratic changes in the former communist states. The first of these levels is an integrative framework of the diverse social *proc-esses of transition*. Here, the chapters examine the effects of international fac-tors, domestic factors, and diffusion on the articulation of transition from com-munism. The second level is a similarly integrative framework of the interrela-tion of three distinct social *entities of economy, polity* and *culture* as recorded at a time-point when the polity-economy-culture are inserted into the processes of social change.

Unlike pioneering investigations of social science that analyze polity, economy and culture in the context of joint accumulation of knowledge about social reality (Durkheim 1895, 1897; Engels 1884; Weber 1904, 1949), until the most recent decades culture was generally treated as a distinct entity vis-à-vis economy and polity as dual entities, rather than treating all three as distinct yet interrelated dimensions collectively contributing to the assessment of societal life. The author of this volume believes that the symbiosis of the culture products with the social processes of polity and economy unfolds the social reality of the transformation of regimes even more precisely and comprehensively then when assessing only economy and polity. Thus, the polity, economy and culture are the three essential dimensions that need to be taken into account for the appraisal of social reality during the time of societal transition, including transition from totalitarian, communist regimes to some form of democracy.

In contrast to most books devoted to democratic transitions in Eastern Europe and Russia, which focus mainly on economic or political changes, this volume offers a unique portrayal of the multilevel, simultaneous impact of the transitions on a broad spectrum of societal life, from economy and politics to health, culture and art. This broad perspective and the dual dimensional framework of analysis allows for a comprehensive appraisal of interrelations between societal components (polity, economy and culture), and the mechanisms causing their change, illustrating post-communist reforms more accurately. Such an approach adds to an understanding of the complexity of processes involved in a regime's democratization, an approach which the author hopes will be applicable as a conceptual tool for future analyses of democratic transitions.

The conceptual framework informs and ties together the unique collection of papers that this book encompasses. The chapters are written by Eastern European, Russian and American scholars, as well as prominent political figures from democratically-elected East European governments; such as Jan Kavan, vice-prime minister of the Czech Republic, and Grzegorz Kolodko of Poland, former finance minister and the designer of the post-communist "therapy" economic plan. The collection of both theoretical and practically-oriented papers is further enriched by the interdisciplinary character of the book, as represented by the diversified approaches of political science, sociology, economics, social policy studies, health science, literary and art critique.

TWO OBJECTIVES OF THE BOOK

The first objective of this book concentrates on social processes; that is, mechanisms of change for the three components of social reality, analyzing their fundamental and particular roles specifically in relation to the transition from communism. This could be summarized by saying that the diverse variables in the processes of transition can be grouped into three major sets that focus on the contribution of *international factors*, *domestic factors* and *diffusion effects* in the process of democratization. The manner in which these three sets influence the process of democratization is explored in those chapters that assess the contribution of all variables to lines of influence (international factors, domestic factors and diffusion effects) on the democratic transition and offer a framework for

Figure 1. 1
Conceptual Framework for Integrating Processes and Components of Democratic Transition

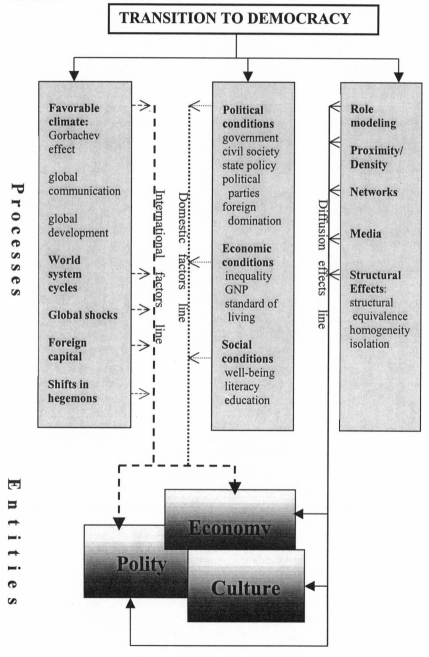

conceptually organizing the effects of the diverse set of variables represented in the process of democratization. This framework is illustrated in Figure 1.1.

The first set of processes conceptualizes democratization as being associated with the influence of international factors, inviting discussion of variables concerning favorable international climate, global development, global shocks, foreign capital and world system cycles. A second type of processes concerns the influence of domestic factors, which incorporate processes that modulate democratization via structural characteristics of the political and economic environment of potential democracies. This component may be viewed as encompassing three sets of variables: economic, political, and social characteristics. Finally, the third type of democratic transition processes involves the characteristics of diffusion; that is, diffusion effects. This component incorporates four sets of variables—role modeling; proximity and density; organizational networks; and media that, taken together, are integrated with how the combination of structuralization effects (the structural equivalence of the communist bloc, its relative homogeneity, and the isolation from the rest of the world) influence each country's likelihood of adopting a democratic system. The processes of transition from communism are assessed according to their contributory role to changes of structural entities of the polity-economy-culture.

The second objective of this book concentrates on entities of transition and includes the systemic appreciation of *polity*, *economy* and *culture* in the appraisal of transitional processes, in place of a mere systematic (i.e., ordered) examination of culture, economy and polity as discrete variables. These three differentiated components of social reality, when interconnected, articulate what is happening in society, within and across time. This unifying approach has critically informed recent academic debates on such topics as the integration of culture into social science (Ferrarotti 1993; Mukherjee 1998; Wood 1999), interactor theories (Berger, Eyre & Zelditch 1989) and the concept of microfoundations within macrosociology (Collins 1981). In this conceptual setting, this volume discusses the transition from communism to democracy in former Soviet bloc countries with a particular concentration on the specific time frame of the late 1980s and the 1990s.

PROCESSES OF TRANSITION

While factors accounting for transitions from communism and their outcomes appear to be diverse, they are concordant with recent scholarly interpretations of democratization processes. One example of this interpretation is Schwartzman's (1998) work on the effects of international (external) and domestic (internal) factors. Similarly, salient examples include Wejnert's (2001) conceptual taxonomy of diffusion variables and work around concepts of Blau's (1977) group interactions perspective.

Influence of International Factors

According to most interpretations, the international conditions influencing democratic transition concern a *favorable international climate* which creates appropriate conditions for worldwide acceleration of democracy; *world system cycles*; *global shocks* in the world economy; and *shifts in global hegemons* that mainly affect peripheral states (Bunce 1991; Huntington 1991; Wallerstein 1984, 1991; Whitehead 1988).

The strongest determinant of the favorable international climate related to the democratization of the communist bloc is the *Gorbachev effect,* which led to elimination of the world thread of communism. Gorbachev's liberal policy of competition among candidates during elections and elections by secret ballot was initially announced in his address delivered at the Central Committee Plenum discussing progress on reforms in the Soviet Union in January 1987 (Bunce 1990). Although Gorbachev quickly withdrew from this radical stance after disapproval by the party hierarchy, the introduction of democratic concepts had already occurred and it underlined future political statements by Gorbachev. Consequently, in 1988, Gorbachev restated the need for leniency toward democratic movements in Eastern Europe, responding to the Polish communist party request that the Central Committee of the Soviet communist party assist them in an anti-Solidarity campaign (Zakowski 1991). It was "the Gorbachev Era Opportunity Structure" that improved chances for imposition of political and economic reforms in communist countries (Sedaitis & Butterfield 1991), and convinced the former Soviet states that the USSR would not intervene during implementation of democratic reforms (Holmes 1997). In this volume the influence of the Gorbachev effect on Eastern European democratization is briefly examined in Wejnert's chapter "The Contribution of Collective Protests to the Softening of Communist Regimes in East Central Europe." I argue that Gorbachev's policy was one of the preconditions that, together with collective protests, led to the softening of communist regimes at the end of the 1980s.

The second factor that contributed to the favorable climate was the expansion of global communication systems, such as fax, Internet and satellite TV, and the expansion of global transportation (Huntington 1991; Markoff 1996). The prevalence of global transportation and communication, which transmitted knowledge about political events around the world, made it difficult to withhold information about democracy from the masses, and thus triggered comparable democratization processes in non-democratic countries (Huntington 1991).

And the third factor of favorable climate concerns global economic development. According to this approach, global economic development induced industrialization in the developing world and enlarged the middle and working classes. These classes tend to hold to democratic principles and demanded economic equality, which in turn promoted the spread of democratic ideas and increased the rate of democratization (Huntington 1991; Rouquie 1988; Rueschmeyer, Stephens & Stephens 1989; Stepan 1988; Therborn 1977). The large working class that was created following rapid industrialization in the post-Second World War period was the main force in promoting democratic reforms in the Soviet bloc states (Ost 1990; Sedaitis & Butterfield 1991).

Moreover, economic development provided a basis for the enlargement of urban populations (Stephens 1989) and increased literacy rates (Lipset 1959; Huntington 1991), both of which play a critical role in democratization. Literate and urbanized societies are prime areas for the origination of democratic regimes. Bloom's chapter on the role of the urban working class in the democratization of Poland, explicate this issue in respect to Eastern European transitions to democracy. Author broadly examines the role of the Polish workers' movement in the pro-democracy protests of December 1970, which contributed to the establishment of the Solidarity movement in 1980, and consequently to the democratization of Poland in June 1989.

The notion of a favorable international climate is supported in the literature by the concept of *world system cycles,* which hypothesizes that the world economic system develops through a cyclical process of periods of economic accumulation followed by periods of stagnation. Exit from economic stagnation requires reorganization of peripheral economies to better respond to crisis, which in turn influence political processes (Wallerstein 1979, 1984, 1991). Peripheral countries, while converging to a new economic system, often select democracy because it organizes the growing working class into citizens, allowing for peaceful transition (Whitehead 1988). They also choose democratic regime because democratization causes the country to lose its peripheral status and integrate more readily into the global economy. It is understandable, then, that in the late 1980s developing countries of the Soviet bloc responded to deteriorating living conditions and economic crisis with pro-democratic reforms. These processes are examined by Grzegorz Kolodko, Lara Romaniuk and Nancy Tuma et al. who argue that the economic conditions during communist rule were a significant contributor to the growing societal demands for democratic reforms at the end of the 1980s and in the early 1990s (see chapters 5, 6, 8 and 10).

Furthermore, as many interpretations suggest, *global shocks* in economic systems, with worldwide political reverberations and foreign interventions, have accounted for strong impact on rates of democratization throughout the world. In particular, the global economic effect of the oil crises in 1970 and 1978 led to deterioration of living conditions in countries that were highly dependent on Western economies. This resulted in the implementation of democratic systems in formerly totalitarian Latin American nations (Higley & Gunther 1992; Huntington 1991). In this book, Stjepan Gredelj discusses the deteriorating economic conditions in Yugoslavia ignited by the global oil crises. The author argues that "petrodollar" loans were the force behind the micro-self-management that formed a conservative coalition between the ruling oligarchies and manual laborers corrupted by excessive consumption (granted using foreign petrodollar loans). The working classes were rewarded with petrodollar loans that resulted in ever-increasing income and benefits while at the same time being less productive. The immediate costs of this initiative were covered using the accumulating foreign loans that became the main source of funds for both investment and consumption during the 1970s. These long-term expenses came due for payment in the 1980s, and the Yugoslavian economy started to collapse as a result of the significant foreign currency debt (about 20 billion dollars) and the total dependence on future-development investments supported by expensive short-term foreign loans received after the 1970s global oil crisis. The immediate societal reactions were the withdrawal of support for the communist regime and demand for democratic reforms; this was especially visible after the death of Tito.

Gredelj's chapter sheds light on an additional factor of the international conditions facilitating democratic changes: *foreign capital*. The author discusses the influence of funds from the United States and Western Europe on Yugoslavian political decisions and economic reforms. Such financial aid often coincided with foreign intervention in the promotion of democratic ideas. Similarly, direct foreign intervention of the United States, accompanied by economic aid, has facilitated the establishment of democracies in a number of South East Asian and African countries (Schwartzman 1998). Direct intervention by the United Kingdom in its former colonies aided in democratization by transferring British representative institutions to the newly independent states (Crenshaw 1995; Strang 1990).

In particular, the *shift in hegemonic powers* opened opportunities for direct intervention of hegemons on peripheral states (Wallerstein 1984,1991). By the end of the 1950s, colonial powers had collapsed and capitalistic development—with the need for inexpensive labor and export of capital to less-developed countries—became the driving force of world economy. This caused hegemonial power to shift from the United Kingdom to the United States in the 1960s, and to Japan and West Germany by the end of the 1970s. In Third World countries, this development led to the rise of a new class of capitalists, as well as urban migration, proletarianization of peasants and the creation of alliances between the new capitalists and wageworkers. The consequence of shifts in global hegemons was the abolishment of the Yalta agreement between the United States and the Soviet Union, which divided control over some parts of the world between those superpowers (Wallerstein 1991). When taken together, the cumulative effect of such changes created the conditions that made liberation of the former communist states of Eastern Europe possible.

All these processes, together with foreign intervention, were cornerstones in the foundation of opposition to totalitarian regime oppression that led directly to democratization in less developed countries, including former communist states (Schwartzman 1998).

Influence of Domestic Factors

Systematic and complex analyses of domestic *political conditions* as foundations for democratic transitions present studies on governmental institutions, civil society and state policies. A few examples of analyses of political processes include Bloom's studies of changes in American political institutions in the later twentieth century (Bloom 1987), Vaclav Havel's explanation of the power of civil society in non-democratic states (Havel 1985), Theda Skocpol's analysis of the influence of social movements and civil society on the origin of social policy in the United States (Skocpol 1992) and Wejnert's (1988) study on the impact of Solidarity movement on political structures. Correspondingly, one of this book chapter's examines the impact of collective protests on the softening of communist regimes and the eventual replacement of such regimes by democratic systems (see chapter 3).

Similarly important examples include the analysis of states as promoters of economic development and social redistribution (Evans, Rueschmeyer & Skocpol 1985; Rueschmeyer, Stephens & Stephens 1989), and studies of the impact of state authority and the state–society relationship (Bermeo 1992b; Dahl 1971, 1990; Migdal 1988). Other studies on democratization indicate that fragmented multi-party political systems rarely tolerate democracy adoption (Dahl 1971, 1990), and that occupation or domination of a country by a foreign power inhibits democracy adoption (Dahl 1971; O'Donnell, Schmitter & Whitehead 1988; Ryan 1995). Hence, fragmentation of political parties and domination by foreign powers act as political variables in democratization.

A variable contributing to the set of *economic factors* is social and economic inequality, most frequently measured by the Gini index of inequality (Lipset 1959; Russett et al. 1964). This measurement determines the level of equal and open opportunities for all citizens to participate in democratic processes, indicating the degree of inclusiveness of minorities and regional groups in political processes—the very essence of democracy. Countries with high levels of social inequality are the least likely to tolerate democratization processes (Dahl 1971; Russett et al. 1964).

A broad range of other economic factors, such as the well-being of citizens, standard's of living, allocation of property and property rights are considered to be additional determinants of democratic transitions (Havel 1985; Nee & Stark 1989; Przeworski 1988). Studies on democratization indicate that the gross national product (GNP) is a significant contributor; countries with a GNP lower than 4 percent of the overall mean GNP had the greatest difficulty overcoming problems of democratic restructuring (Dahl 1971; Lipset 1959; Russett et al. 1964). In each country, the level of development closely corresponds to the type of economy that existed prior to the potential adoption of democracy. This indicates that in the case of communist-bloc countries, those with a higher GNP will more quickly and smoothly undergo democratic transition. It also suggests that the societal cost of transition will be lower, and hence, the progress of democratization more quickly visible. Kolodko's paper on social inequalities across the former communist bloc, Tuma, Mikk & Murakas's paper on Estonia and Alexei Makheshin's paper on privatization and social inequalities in Russia address this issue very clearly. Authors emphasize that the preexisting economic conditions in former communist states had significant influence on the temporal rate of democratization and democratization's outcomes. These chapters provide strong evidence of the mutual interaction and interdependence of social inequalities and democratization processes, and the functional dependence of success in democratization movements on social inequalities.

The highly public aspect of democratic politics depends on a society's reading and writing abilities. Thus, important social variables are a country's well-being, level of education (estimated by the percentage of children enrolled in primary and secondary schools) and level of literacy. The lower the literacy and education level, the more difficult it becomes for a country to adopt democracy; an illiteracy rate higher than 80 percent, with schooling unavailable to more than 60 percent of children, inhibits democracy adoption (Dahl 1971; Merritt & Rokkan 1966). Several of the chapters discuss the role of education in the process of transition from communism. Lara Romaniuk's study on the Ukraine, for example, focuses on the correlation between education and alcohol and tobacco addiction; Mayone J. Stycos, Barbara Wejnert and Zbigniew Tyszka's paper analyzes the impact of education on labor force participation, which in turn, determines Polish women's well-being. And Stjepan Gredej's paper concerns the involvement of intellectuals in promoting democratic movements in Yugoslavia.

The above analyses, while providing important insights into factors involved in transitions to democracy, are still concerned primarily with global and domestic structural influences and ignore communication channels that have enhanced interconnectedness and interactions between democratic and non-democratic entities. Studies that focus on mutual communication and connectedness consider the democratic changes to follow a pattern of waves of democratization. A wave of democratization is a group of transitions from nondemocratic to democratic regimes that occur within a specified period of time and that significantly outnumber transitions in the opposite direction during that time period. A wave also usually involves liberalization or partial democratization in political systems that do not become fully democratic (Huntington 1991:15). Thus Southern Europe (Spain, Portugal and Italy) in the 1970s can be seen as the first wave, Latin America in the 1980s as the second wave, and East Central Europe and the Soviet Union in the 1990s as the third wave (Huntington 1991; Jaggers & Gurr 1995; Tarrow 1992). Grounding for addressing these relational issues can be found in the theory of *diffusion*.

Diffusion Effects

The most important result of the transition from communism has been the rapid integration of former communist countries with the developed world, which has brought significant changes in the lifestyle, culture, economy and social policies of former communist societies (DeSoto & Anderson 1993; Kolodko 1996; Ziolkowski, Pawlowska & Drozdowski 1994). The rate and outcomes of transitions from communism, however, vary among Soviet-type states (Bermeo 1992a; Bruszt & Stark 1991; Piccone 1990; Stark 1992, 1996). This indicates that each country responded to the possibility of convergence with the democratic world and to international and domestic pro-democracy stimuli in different ways. Given this, the conventional view on the impact of external and internal influences is insufficient for explaining the timing and outcomes of decisions concerning when and how to proceed toward democratization. An alternative approach might look to *processes of diffusion* as an additional explanation for transitions from communism, using a framework of diffusion models (Wejnert, in press).

Diffusion is "a sociologically-grounded account of change emphasizing the channels along which practices flow" (Strang & Soul 1996: 265). Diffusion refers to the *spread* of some sort of practice within a social system, where the spread denotes flow or movement from a source to an adopter, paradigmatically via communication and influence. This process enhances an actor's probability of adopting a new practice, where an *actor* may be any social entity, including individuals, groups, organizations or national polities. Studies of diffusion generally assess the introduction and adoption of innovative practices or ideas. Consequently, diffusion of democracy could be defined as accounting for change toward a democratic system that emphasizes the channels along which the transition to democracy flows. It refers to the spread of democracy in the world from democratic to non-democratic countries, occurring typically via communication, modeling and interactive influence.

Thus, a powerful stimulus in the adoption of new ideas or practices in diffusion processes is *role modeling*. In the case of democratic transitions, Western practices have been perceived as "modern" and therefore symbolize socioeconomic advancement and elevated status (Whitehead 1988). For less-developed countries moving toward economic prosperity, characteristics of modernity and Western culture have been some of the strongest stimuli eliciting adoption of new practices (Fukuyama 1992; Pellicani & Volpacchio 1991).

Fukuyama and others, for example, cite such a process as contributing to the triumph of Western cultural values and norms across post-communist Eastern Europe (Fukuyama 1992; Karnoouh 1991; Koralewicz & Ziolkowski 1993). The diffusion of computer-controlled machinery during the 1980s in Hungary (Oakley, Hare & Balazs 1992) and the spread of satellite TV antennas in newly democratic Bulgaria (Bakardjiva 1992) have also been attributed to this effect. In spite of the inefficiency of these technologies for Hungarian and Bulgarian consumers, and the degradation of national cultural roots through the influence of Western mass-culture (Koralewicz & Ziolkowski 1993; Szelenyi 1996), these practices were still broadly adopted.

Several papers in this volume indicate that modeling on Western practices was one of the strongest catalysts for the spread of ideas to communist countries. For example, Stjepan Gredelj's chapter discusses the copying of cultural models of rock music and punk rock culture by Yugoslavian youth. Despite disapproval of the type of music and its culture by the older generation, and general negative stereotyping of rock music and its fans, this aspect of Western culture was adopted and soon became a symbol of struggle against the communist regime. Sergei Zherebkin and Barbara Wejnert and Maria Nowakowska Stycos and Grazyna Borkowska also analyze the cultural synergy between the West and the former Soviet states before and after the 1990 transition. Zherebkin and Wejnert's paper focuses on aspects of Western modernism and Western-style commercial architecture that was imported from the West to Russia; while Nowakowska Stycos and Borkowska cover the influence of Western culture on Polish poetry and literary styles, vividly visible in the post-communist time.

A second category of diffusion variables concerns the effects of *spatial factors*, such as proximity and density, on the probability of practices being transmitted from one country to another. In the simplest view of proximity, distance is the critical variable. Hence, practices are thought to spread automatically between countries that are geographically close. Proximity is important because it can facilitate imitative behavior and also affect the frequency of communication and interaction between countries, which enhances the spread of information and ideas.

Moreover, the density of countries that have already adopted democracy may be an important dimension of spatial effects (Blau, Land & Redding 1992; Knoke 1982) because each adopter of new practices also subsequently serves as a transmitter, influencing other potential adopters who are in close proximity (Brown 1989; Strang 1990; Walker 1969). Of course, the effects of density are themselves a function of the proximity of social units, indicating that spatial effects are best viewed as a joint function of these two variables (Wejnert 2001). Because the communist bloc in East Central Europe was composed of neighboring countries with the highest possible density of communist states, we should assume that density and proximity affected adoption of democracy as soon as the democratic transition was initiated. Indeed, this becomes clear when considering the timetable of events in 1989-1990 presented in Wejnert's paper on democratic movements. As soon as a democratic government was elected in Poland, a number of nearby communist countries went through a similar transition within months, with Czechoslovakia and East Germany—direct neighbors of Poland—and Hungary leading the way. Furthermore, the Ukraine and Lithuania, Soviet republics sharing borders with Poland, were early initiators of democratization processes within the Soviet Union.

A third category of diffusion variables concerns *network connectedness*. Although democratization appears to be significantly influenced by structural features of a country's domestic environment and international system, timing of adoption has typically depended on the communication and interaction between democratic and nondemocratic countries, and within blocs of nondemocratic countries. Accordingly, a major focus in diffusion research has been the variables mediating communication processes between members of social groups interacting within organizational, political and economic networks (Coleman, Katz & Menzel 1966; DiMaggio & Powell 1983; Rogers 1962, 1983, 1995; Rogers & Shoemaker 1971; Ryan & Gross 1943; Valente 1995; Weimann & Brosius 1994). A number of well-institutionalized factors influenced communication processes and mutual interactions in the communist-bloc countries, including the political, military and economic unification of the communist world under the watchful eye of the Soviet Union; the Council of Mutual Economic Assistance (CMEA), an umbrella of the Warsaw Pact; and multiple bilateral cultural, economic and political treaties sponsoring frequent membership meetings. Within such channels of influence, countries could affect the rate of democratization in other countries via multiple roles. As Wejnert (2001) explains, they could, for example, take on an *informative* role, where members learn of the newest developments. Their role could be *conductory*, involving the facilitation of contact with former adopters; such facilitations could include meetings with representatives of countries that have already adopted democracy. Countries could also play an *inductive* role, where some members would induce changes on other members using economic or political restraints.

Two variables have been shown to be particularly strong in shaping network influence. The *structural equivalence* of members in the network, particularly in terms of comparable economic and social status, where the level of perceived equivalence affects homogeneity of behavior and adoption rate more than, for example, a firm's level of cohesion (Mizruchi 1993; Palmer, Jennings & Zhou 1993); and the *density* of adopters within an organization, discussed above, where greater density of adopters lessens the perceived risk of new adoptions occurring (Hannan & Freeman 1987; Wejnert 2001).

As others have pointed out, institutionalized models (such as models of democracy) may spread more rapidly between structurally equivalent countries, even when the structural equivalence is based on higher-order variables such as common ideology, politics or economics; the global trend toward democracy is reinforced by such links (Starr 1991; Uhlin 1995). The economic and political equivalence of countries promote inter-group associations (within the structurally equivalent bloc) but inhibit intercourse with other countries (outside the bloc). As would be predicted by Blau (1964, 1977), in the case of the Soviet-type countries, the structural equivalence and the relatively small number of communist states as compared to the whole world facilitated a higher rate of inter-group associations, and the rate of internal associations significantly exceeded the rate of such associations within noncommunist states, as well as the rate of interactions between communist and noncommunist countries. This created strong bonds and inter-group reliance within the communist bloc that, in turn, led to isolation from the rest of the world.

Furthermore, the massive disparity between Soviet-bloc states and Western democracies in terms of diversity in social hierarchy, stratification and ideological foundation inhibited any substantial interaction between, or interconnectedness of, the Eastern and Western parts of Europe. And because divergence from the West—economically, politically, culturally and socially—was dictated by communist ideology, states' boundaries were consolidated, and barriers between insiders (the communist states) and outsiders (the West and the rest of the world) were strengthened. Thus, the impact of structural equivalence on the diffusion of innovative ideas appears to involve a process of imitation within a network, especially after one member of the relatively homogenous network successfully adopts a new idea (Wejnert 2001).

Significant connectedness between members of the former communist bloc, along with the high frequency of interaction and communication, enhanced the rate of democratic transition as soon as one of the members in the bloc initiated democratic reforms. Indeed, as explained in Wejnert's essay in this book, former communist countries adopted democratic practices after the success of the first Polish democratic election in June 1989, after which the temporal rate of adoption of democratic reforms throughout the communist bloc increased exponentially. Future analyses of democratic transition variables, however, should help to explain the variation evident with respect to factors such as the rate of adoption of democracy between countries within the same interconnected bloc, for example, between Poland, which initiated democratic reforms, and Albania, which was the last of the Eastern European states to proceed with democratic transition.

Finally, the fourth category of the diffusion variable and a topic that has received considerable attention in the area of diffusion is *media*. A detailed analysis of media as a significant channel in communication processes is beyond the scope of this discussion. The main focus here is the manner in which media exposure interacts with the characteristics of countries and organizational networks to influence democratization. For example, political authorities in communist states closely controlled access to politically undesirable news (Wejnert 1996) and deliberately restricted access to ideas carried by domestic democratic movements. Limited societal exposure to media information was supposed to limit the spread of democratic movements. However, as Bloom discusses in his analyses of the December 1970 protests in shipyards of Gdansk, Gdynia and Szczecin, protesting shipyard workers sent messages using networks of railroad workers to Silesian miners about strikes and military actions in shipyards. This innovative communication channel that was developed in the workers milieu because of censorship of the press, helped spread the strategy of protest actions and within weeks eventuated in the organization of cross-national strikes.

In addition, political authorities markedly affected the adoption of democracy under communist systems because access to modern communication technology was unavailable in most societies of the former Soviet-bloc states. For political reasons, and fear of exposure to Western ideology, such items as satellite antennas, fax machines, cellular phones and computers were not available to citizens of those countries. Changes in availability, as well as political conditions, eventually led to the spread of communication technology in the 1990s (Bakardjieva 1992).

Analysis of each of these processes—influence of international factors, domestic factors and processes of diffusion, along with their respective sets of variables—is associated with different concepts and methods involving diverse principles and determinants of democratic transition. Consequently, the literature concerned with each of these processes tends to analyze democratic transitions in isolation from the insights of the others. As a means of correcting this situation, the consideration of each of these components is intended to establish the basis for their integration into a subsequent complete model. It is consideration of this integration effect that binds together the papers contributing to this volume.

Moreover, the transition from Communism to some form of democracy in 1989-90 crosscut the socio-economic and political variance between communist states and the rest of the world, inducing rapid convergence with the world economy, politic and culture. Introduction to the market economy and exposure to the Western style of life—and presumably also to higher standards of living—placed individuals at the intersection of a web of group affiliations of the former communist alliances and new Western democratic networks (Brown, Hormats & Luers 1992). This weakened the hold of the old communist social and political structures on their former followers, which, in turn, widened the opportunities for change and increased societal freedoms. The importance of convergence with the Western world together with other processes of democratic transition and their impact on political, economic and cultural institutions of former communist countries are presented in following discussion.

STRUCTURAL ENTITIES OF TRANSITION

As most authors agree, though democracy was perceived as a system that would guarantee an equally high standard of living for all citizens, the connectedness of democratic freedom with economic liberty has led to social inequality and social discomfort, a problem that has been broadly discussed by scholars studying democratic transitions (e.g., Dahl 1971, 1982; Held 1987; Sandel 1996). As many authors in this book suggest, the ongoing political and economic unification with Western Europe has exposed former Soviet-bloc societies to the lifestyle of Western democracies accompanied by a higher standard of living. But democratization and transition toward a market economy have also been associated with changes in employment levels, family relationships, redistribution of financial resources, restructuring of individual lifestyles, the emergence of a new class system and the quality of life in the post-communist as compared to the communist period. Hence, the variables of change can be categorized into three entities of *polity, economy* and *culture*.

The integration of these components in an appraisal of post-communist transition is a fundamental strategy that helps to overcome the obvious limitations of econo/polity-centric visions of social reality. However important the economy and polity may be, they do not challenge the central assertions of a comprehensive examination of societies and this is particularly true for former communist societies. It is also true, however, that the bi-focal approach—incorporating only two principle social components (polity and economy)—has received the greatest attention in most of the literature devoted to examination of the post-communist transformations. This may be due to the fact that the economy and polity have in the past, as noted earlier, been considered to be the most essential, and hence most visible, components of society. Also, most studies have tended to focus on a limited set of variables of democratic transition at any one time, making it difficult to comprehensively appraise the pre and post-communist societal structures. Figure 1.1, along with the discussion below, demonstrate that the studies in this volume identify an expanded array of variables that significantly influence the probability of democratization, and the outcomes of post-communist reforms. The depicted variables are integrated in the second level of the proposed conceptual framework forming categories of structural entities of transition (see Figure 1.1).

Polity-Centered Entity

During the transition years prior to the democratic elections of the 1990s, the communist countries took a journey on what seemed to be an evenly paced road toward a developed communist system. Any twists and turns on this road were due only to explorations of different paths communist governments and ruling communist elites might devise for control over public activity and to buffer citizens against their political rights and material wants. In an era when many industrialized nations were launching competitive market economies and democratic rights for their citizens, the communist regimes sought to help not working people but small ruling elites of Party nomenclature secretly covering this political strategy with ideological propaganda.

Within this perspective, the growing civil movements and dissatisfaction that eventually led to replacements within the top administrative rank of communist regimes and to those regimes softening (see chapter 3), explicates the issue of civil resistance to communist rule and their political goals. This rigorous analysis shows that executive changes were regularly made in response to civil protests, which provide quantitative exemplification of prior qualitative analysis of the power of social movements in softening and restructuring powerful totalitarian regimes (e.g., Tarrow 1998).

Examination of workers' strikes and demonstrations against communist regimes is also the topic of Jack Bloom's paper, which recounts the December 1970 events in Polish shipyards. He draws on interviews with eyewitnesses and protesting workers to offer a general overview of the impact of these historical happenings on future development of the nationwide Solidarity movement and its role in breaking the communist regime in 1989.

In a similar vein, Stjepan Gredelj investigates public reactions to the Yugoslavian regime's communist propaganda and its economic tactic of borrowing capital from foreign investors in order to divert societal attention from problems of political and economic privileges of communist nomenclature, growing poverty, social inequalities and the potential increase in unemployment. Such a strategy of manipulation, often using nationalistic ideology and lies, eventuated in the origination of cultural protest movements, which their organizers, mostly youth's and intellectuals, perceived to be by far the safest and easiest way to express their discontent with the politics of ruling elites.

Ideological manipulation and unfair political and economic maneuvering has in many cases culminated in the illegitimacy of ruling regimes and their eventual collapse. Along the way, it has also led to the implementation of policies of social justice and to retributions paid to victims of communist political and economic oppressions, such as the forced collectivization of farms, the nationalization of industry and private property and political persecutions. Jan Kavan's analysis of the *lustration* policy in former Czechoslovakia at the time of the presidency of Vaclaw Havel, the first elected president in the post-communist period, provides a personal recount of post-communist retributive justice initiated by the newly democratic government. Here the goals, purpose and mistakes made in the implementation of the lustration policy, and their impact on societal sense of justice and fairness, are discussed in great detail. Kavan also briefly compares the Czechoslovakian situation to other forms of retroactive justice in former communist states.

Within a broader, organizationally grounded analysis of political development, this book also explains the politics of policymaking. This approach makes it possible to understand the types of distinct social policies that former communist and post-communist states have elaborated. In most countries, social policies have not developed simply in tandem with capitalistic industrialization or urbanization; they have not been straightforward responses to the demands that emerging social classes place on governments. Similarly to other countries (Skocpol 1992), communist governmental institutions, electoral rules, political parties and prior public policies—all of these, and their transformations over time—created many of the limits and opportunities within which social policies were devised and changed by politically involved actors over the course of each nation's history. The new post-communist governments and governing entities supporting them either have not responded or are unable to respond to societal demands concerning peoples' well-being and/or emerging social problems. Some of the unanswered policy-related problems are examined in this book (see the chapters by Romaniuk, Stycos, Wejnert & Tyszka, Gardawski, and Kolodko). Accordingly, these authors argue that most of these problems need immediate attention of policymakers if the democratization processes are to be sustained in post-communist states.

The list of such problems is long and complex, including, for example, poverty, development of an underclass, change in workers attitude toward the market economy, uncontrolled aggressive advertisement of alcohol and tobacco sales by foreign industry that enlarges alcohol and tobacco consumption, speedily rising gaps in income and living conditions and disparities in economic development of rural as compared to urban communities. In this context, Lara Romaniuk's chapter considers problems of health that are frequently addressed by many scientists concerned with shortening of life expectancy in former Soviet states (Stone 2000). Romaniuk specifically emphasizes tobacco and alcohol addictions and their impact on mortality rates and complicated health problems. Stycos, Wejnert and Tyszka address issues related to the welfare and well-being of women living in rural communities, their rising unemployment and worsening living conditions in post-communist as compared to communist times. And Kolodko, the former Polish finance minister, explores social security/social equality policies incorporated in the presented strategy for economic development. This strategy that emphasizes economic justice and economic therapy is addressed to the newly developed post-communist states and is intended to help solve many economic and social policy problems.

One of the recently arising problems, for example, is the negative attitude of workers toward market competition and market economy. Gardawski's study of Polish workers' attitudes toward the market economy scrutinizes the problem of societal approval of post-communist reforms. Workers in his study that were aggregated by income, residence, social class and social position only partly approved post-communist change. As Gardawski argues, the strongest indicator of workers' approval of market reforms is shown by workers income combined with duration of their employment. It seems, then, that the political situation is inevitably assessed through the prism of societal economic conditions. It is to this economic component of transition that I now turn.

Economy-Centered Entity

Continuing the road metaphor, the former communist region was a laggard on the otherwise universally traveled global road toward a competitive market economy, modernity and high quality of production. It also lagged in the creation of suitable economic living standards comparable to Western democracies. Integrated with the communist political ideology and centrally planned economy, the tendency toward self-sufficiency cut communist states off from the fast-developing Western world and its technological innovations. Strategies of mutual economic assistance within the communist bloc inhibited exposure to principles of global markets, international investments and international finances. Although exposure to global corporatism is not always the most beneficial to local national economies in the developing world (because it often produces large economic disparities and social inequalities), on average it provides higher living standards, and a better quality and greater quantity of consumer goods. Because of the latter, most developing countries strive to be incorporated into Western markets (Stone 2000).

As a result, in most of the former communist countries, economic demands to improve living conditions have led to protest confrontations, withdrawal of legitimacy from ruling regimes, economic reformations of communist centrally planned systems (e.g., in Hungary and Yugoslavia), and requests for privatization and market competition. The market orientation of post-communist states, however, has collided with social inequalities, complex monetary problems, necessity of reconstructing banking systems and reformation of state fiscal policies (Pellicani 1990). Several chapters in this book address these complex situations and the subsequent difficulties experienced by transitional economies and new capital formations.

The chapter written by Grzegorz Kolodko, for example, comprehensively and comparatively analyzes fiscal policies and capital formation in transitional economies across former communist states. Focusing on the monetary situation, the author analyzes major obstacles in reformation of state budgets, monetary funds and transformation of local currency into international currency, all necessary preconditions of potential foreign investment in former communist states and joint membership in the European Union.

Tuma, Titma and Murakas, who emphasize the transitional economy of Estonia, focus on the distinct characteristics of the preexisting economic conditions of the 1980s that allowed fast progress into market transformation and achievement of a higher, on average, living standard than in any other former Soviet Union state. These authors also discuss the primary contributor to growing social inequalities, that of income inequality.

Alexei Makeshin proposes an interesting argument in his discussion of the complexity of privatization politics in Russia. The main observation of the author is that the Soviet system cannot be readily marketized without first being dismantled. Its future prospects are in at least one respect even worse that those of other Third World societies attempting to industrialized. Unlike in the latter, where it is merely a matter of standard industrialization, the former USSR will have to first deindustrialize, that is, dismantle most of the existing industrial system, before even beginning to re-industrialize on the basis of a depoliticized instrumental rationality. The existing politicized class of managers are unwilling to change its political views and, at the same time, are incapable of efficiently managing newly constructed industrial plants that need to compete with Western-style management. This study, supported by research data, is in accord with observations of political economists such as Piccone (1990), who argue that the managerial staff and communist protectionism of managers by the Communist Party is one of the greatest barriers of success of post-communist economic reforms.

The comprehensive analysis of changes in social reality and the attempt to articulate a micro-macro connectedness, which has been a focal concern of many major thinkers in the history of social sciences, is the topic of the last section of the book, which includes papers on the impact of transition from communism on the transformation of culture. The inclusion of chapters that discuss the formation of culture as a function of political and economic conditions provides empirical groundwork for the recently growing scholarly dispute over interconnectedness and dependence of cultural products on political and economic structures.

Culture-Centered Entity

Culture does not change on its own because "by definition, culture is not capable of self-revision or self-production: it registers the worldview which may or may not change over time" (Mukherjee 1998:41). Emphasis on changes in the manifestation of culture caused by political and economic transformations represents an example of a re-focused conceptual trend that considers incorporation of the three basic elements of societal life—culture, politics and economy—in an analysis of social change (Piscatori 1991). As Jameson vividly explains, "no satisfactory model of a given mode of production can exist without a theory of the historically and dialectically specific and unique role of 'culture' within it" (1984:XV).

Several authors in this volume attempt to reconstruct culture and cultural effects in order to see democratization processes more comprehensively. Recognizing the intense dependence of culture on both the central ideological communist view prior to the 1990s and the rational, materialistic, market economy view combined with notions of democratic freedom in the post-communist period, the authors pose questions about the impact of political and economic reforms on manifestations of culture in the communist and post-communist societies.

The interrelation of democracy and artistic freedom is explored in chapter 13 by Nowakowska Stycos and Borkowska, who discuss the impact of political transitions on poetry and writing in former communist states. After presenting a general notion that democratic transitions affected the themes and style of writing and created opportunities for new journals or literary centers in the 1990s, the authors comment that the relationship between political freedom and the realm of art is not an easy one. It might have clearly marked a difference in the writings of young writers by provocatively turning away from traditional myths and literary themes. But did democracy change the writing practices of mature artists, those who made their debut twenty or thirty years before the democratic change and who have been continually widening the scope of their artistic work in communist times? Analyzing the literary output of two Polish writers, Nobel prize winner Wieslawa Szymborska and the younger, well-known poet Ewa Wolska, the authors conclude that democratization processes did not lead to change in the highly reputable literature and poetry that crossed political boundaries prior to political changes, suggesting that a mature poet's freedom is not directly dependent on political freedom.

Tendencies and changes in music and the artistic expressions of film producers are the main focus of Gredelj's chapter on cultural movement and trends in Yugoslavia. Introducing a problem concerning the limits of artistic expression, the author analyzes the emergence of the "Black Wave" in Yugoslavian art as a protest against limited freedom of expression. The Black Wave trend became a leading force in the anti-communist movement. This undesirable label—the "Black Wave"—initially referred to the basic tone of discussions on painting of that time. However, it is primarily remembered as an official evaluation of the most important and most revolutionary period of development in Yugoslav cinematography (between 1960 and 1970). The Black Wave cinematography, together with imported Western punk culture, become the main strategy of protest against communist totalitarianism, lasting until the early 1980s.

The chapter on "Politics of Architecture and Architecture of Politics" by Zherebkin and Wejnert offers an analysis of changes in architectural forms and monuments as a function of political and economic situations. In this framework, the architectural forms of the communist and post-communist periods in the Soviet Union operated, according to the authors, as articulated segments of societal structures, and thus played a significant role in holding together configurations of Soviet-type societies. Zherebkin and Wejnert's essay offers an analysis of how architectural forms and monuments can be understood as artifacts that articulate and portray the social, economic and political reality of the developing communist society of the Soviet Union from its establishment in 1917 to its rupture in 1990. In this conceptual notion the paper provides an analysis of the diversified architectural styles in appendage to their personification and reflection of social reality of different stages of the communist system's development, and concludes with a discussion of the impact of democracy and market economy on the social realities of post-communism as mirrored by architectural forms.

In each case the transition to democracy affected cultural unification with Western culture but with differing results. In the Ukraine, for example, democratization led to the transformation of art (Zherebkin & Wejnert's paper), and influenced trends in music in Yugoslavia (Stjepan's paper), but it did not effect the mature, highly reputable Polish literature and poetry examined by Nowakowska-Stycos & Borkowska.

CONCLUSION

It is the interconnectedness of the processes of democratic transition with structures of polity, economy and culture that makes this book a unique volume devoted to post-communist change. This approach of comprehensive modeling of the transitional processes is in contrast to dualistic theoretical extremism, which assigns explanatory power predominantly to either selected processes of democratization, or components of transition, or separately *micro*-processes of culture and *macro*-processes embedded in economic and political contexts. The theoretical framework of synergy between components of social reality and between components and processes of their change provides direct links between macro- and micro-theory, an issue that is the emerging central theoretical problem in contemporary social sciences (Ritzer 1992). In this sense, the model explored in this volume extends current attempts to rediscover a micro-macro connectedness (as in the work of Giddens, Collins, Coleman, Habermas, and Alexander), which has been a focal concern of such major thinkers in the history of social sciences as Weber, Simmel, Marx, and Durkheim.

An additional strength of this book is the framing of the central conceptual discourses of all chapters that are examined comparatively in the distinct periods of pre- and post-Communist collapse. Similar time frames are employed to portray structural components of communist and post-communist societies. The collection of interdisciplinary writings on diverse topics related to democratization and their comparative, historical assessment make the book applicable to students of many disciplines: political science, international studies, sociology, social policy, history and history of art, to name a few. This cross-disciplinary approach, a comprehensive assessment of changes guided by a conceptual framework extends the understanding of democratization beyond the simple notion of an adoption of a political system that concerns: "the right of all citizens to have a share of political power, the right of all citizens to vote and participate in politics" (Fukuyama 1992: 10).

REFERENCES

Bakardjieva, Maria. 1992. Home Satellite TV Reception in Bulgaria. *Journal of Communication, 7*, 477- 489.

Berger, Joseph, Dana Eyre & Morris Zelditch. 1989. Theoretical Structure and the Micro/Macro Problem. In J. Berger, M. Zelditch & B. Anderson (Eds.), *Sociological Theories in Progress: New Formulations* (pp.11-32). Newsbury Park, CA: Sage.

Bermeo, Nancy. 1992a. *Liberalization and Democratization: Change in the Soviet Union and Eastern Europe.* Baltimore: John Hopkins University Press.

_____. 1992b, April. Democracy and the Lessons of Dictatorship. *Comparative Politics*, 273-291.

Blau, Judith R., Kenneth C. Land & Kent Redding. 1992. The Expansion of Religious Affiliation: An Explanation of the Growth of Church Participation in the United States, 1830-1930. *Social Science Research, 21*, 329-352.

Blau, Peter. 1964. *Exchange and Power in Social Life.* New York: Wiley.

_____. 1977. A Macrosociological Theory of Social Structure. *American Sociological Review, 83*, 26-54.

Bloom, Allan. 1987. *The Closing of the American Mind.* New York: Simon & Schuster.

Brown, J. F., Robert D. Hormats & William H. Luers. 1992. *Western Approaches to Eastern Europe.* New York: Council of Foreign Relations Press.

Brown, Richard. 1989. *Knowledge Is Power: The Diffusion of Information in Early America, 1700-1865.* New York: Oxford University Press.

Bruszt, Laszlo & David Stark. 1991. Remaking the Political Field in Hungary: From the Politics of Confrontation to the Politics of Competition. *Journal of International Affairs, 45*, 201-245.

Bunce, Valerie. 1990, Summer. The Struggle for Liberal Democracy in Eastern Europe. *World Policy Journal, 7*, 395-431.

Coleman, James S., Elihu Katz & Herbert Menzel. 1966. *Medical Innovations: A Diffusion Study.* New York: Bobbs-Merrill.

Collins, Randall. 1981. On the Macrofoundation of Macrosociology. *American Journal of Sociology, 86*, 984-1014.

Cotta, Maurizio. 1992. Elite Unification and Democratic Consolidation in Italy: A Historical Overview. In John Higley & Richard Gunther (Eds.), *Elites and Democratic Consolidation in Latin America and Southern Europe.* Cambridge, UK: Cambridge University Press.

Crenshaw E. M. 1995. Democracy and Demographic Inheritance: The Influence of Modernity and Proto-Modernity on Political and Civil Rights. *American Sociological Review, 60,* 702-718.

Dahl, Robert. 1971. *Polyarchy: Participation and Opposition.* New Haven: Yale University Press.

_____. 1984. *Dilemmas of Pluralist Democracy: Autonomy vs. Control.* New Haven: Yale University Press

_____. 1990. *After the Revolution? Authority in a Good Society.* New Haven: Yale University Press

DeSoto, Hermine & David Anderson. 1993. *The Curtain Rises: Rethinking Culture, Ideology, and the State in Eastern Europe.* Atlantic Highlands: Humanities Press.

DiMaggio, Paul J. & Walter W. Powell. 1983. The Iron Cage Revisited: Institutional Isomorphism and Collective Rationality in Organizational Fields. *American Sociological Review, 48,* 147-160.

Durkheim, Emile. 1895. *The Rules of Sociological Method.* New York: Free Press.

_____. 1897. *Suicide.* New York: Free Press.

Engels, Friedrich. 1884. *The Origin of Family, Private Property and the State.* New York: International Publishers.

Evans, Peter B., Dietrich Rueschmeyer & Theda Skocpol (Eds.). 1985. *Bringing the State Back In.* Cambridge, UK: Cambridge University Press.

Ferrarotti, Franco. 1993. Culture and Photography. Reading Sociology Through a Lens. *Politics, Culture and Society, 7,* 74-95.

Fukuyama, Francis. 1992. *The End of History and the Last Man.* New York: Avon Books.

Glenny, Misha. 1991. *The Rebirth of History: Eastern Europe in the Age of Democracy.* New York: Penguin Books.

Gunther, Richard. 1992. Spain: The Very Model of the Modern Elite Settlement. In John Higley & Richard Gunther. (Eds.), *Elites and Democratic Consolidation in Latin America and Southern Europe.* Cambridge, UK: Cambridge University Press.

Gurr, Robert Ted, Keith Jaggers & Will H. Moore. 1990. The Transformation of the Western State: The Growth of Democracy, Autocracy, and State Power Since 1800. *Studies in Comparative International Development, 25,* 73-108.

Hannan, Michael T. & John Freeman. 1987. The Ecology of Organizational Founding: American Labor Unions, 1836-1985. *American Journal of Sociology, 92,* 910-943.

Havel, Vaclav. 1985. *The Power of the Powerless.* Armonk, NY: M.E. Sharpe, Inc.

Held, David. 1987. *Models of Democracy.* Stanford, CA: Stanford University Press.

Higley, John & Richard Gunther (Eds.). 1992. *Elites and Democratic Consolidation in Latin America and Southern Europe.* Cambridge, UK: Cambridge University Press.

Holmes, L. 1997. *Post-Communism.* Oxford, UK: Oxford University Press (Polity).

Huntington, S. 1991. *The Third Wave: Democratization in the Late Twentieth Century.* Norman: University of Oklahoma Press.

Jaggers, Keith & Ted R. Gurr. 1995. Tracking Democracy's Third Wave with the Polity III Data. *Journal of Peace Research, 32,* 469-482.

Jameson, F. 1984. Postmodernism or the Cultural Logic of Late Capitalism. *New Left Review, 146,* 53-93.

Karatnycky, Adrian. 1995, February. Democracies on the Rise, Democracies at Risk. *Freedom Review,* 5-10

Karnoouh, Claude. 1991. The End of National Culture in Eastern Europe. *Telos, 89,* 133-140.

Kolodko, Grzegorz. 1996. *Poland 2000: The New Economic Strategy.* Warsaw, Poland: Poltext.

Koralewicz, Jadwiga & Marek Ziolkowski. 1993. Changing Value Systems. *Sisyphus, 9,* 123-139.

Knoke, David. 1982. The Spread of Municipal Reform: Temporal, Spatial, and Social Dynamics. *American Journal of Sociology, 87,* 1314-1339.

Lipset, Seymour M. 1959. Some Social Requisites of Democracy: Economic Development and Political Legitimacy. *The American Political Science Review,* 68-105.

Markoff, J. 1996. *Waves of Democracy.* Thousand Oaks, CA: Pine Forge.

Merritt, Richard L. & Stein Rokkan (Eds.). 1966. *Comparing Nations: The Use of Quantitative Data in Cross-National Research.* New Haven: Yale University Press.

Migdal, Joel. 1988. *Strong Societies and Weak States.* Princeton, NJ: Princeton University Press.

Mizruchi, Mark S. 1993. Cohesion, Equivalence, and Similarity of Behavior: A Theoretical and Empirical Assessment. *Social Networks, 15,* 275-307.

Mukherjee, Ramkrishna. 1998. Social Reality and Culture. *Current Sociology, 46,* 29-39.

Nee, Victor & David Stark. 1989. *Remaking the Economic Institutions of Socialism: China and Eastern Europe.* Stanford, CA: Stanford University Press.

Oakley, R. P., P. G. Hare & K. Balazs. 1992. Computer Numerically Controlled Machinery Diffusion Within the Hungarian Economy. *Science and Public Policy, 19,* 241-250.

O'Donnell, Guillermo, Phillippe C. Schmitter & Laurence Whitehead (Eds.). 1988. *Transitions from Authoritarian Rule.* Baltimore: John Hopkins University Press.

Ost, David. 1990. *Solidarity and the Politics of Anti-Politics.* Philadelphia: Temple University Press.

_____. 1992. Labor and Social Transition. *Problems of Communism, 3,* 48-51.

Palmer, Donald A., P. Devereaux Jennings & Xueguang Zhou. 1993. Late Adoption of the Multidivisional Form by Large U.S. Corporations: Institutional, Political, and Economic Accounts. *Administrative Science Quarterly, 38,* 100-131.

Pellicani, Luciano. 1990. Preconditions for Soviet Economic Development. *Telos, 84,* 43-58.

Pellicani, Luciano & Florindo Volpacchio. 1991. The Cultural War Between East and West. *Telos, 89,* 127-132.

Piccone, Paul. 1990. Paradoxes of Perestroika. *Telos, 84,* 3-33.

Piscatori, James (Ed.). 1991. *Islamic Fundamentalisms and the Gulf Crisis.* Chicago, IL: The American Academy of Arts and Sciences.

Pridham, Geoffrey. 1990. *Securing Democracy: Political Parties and Democratic Consolidation in Southern Europe.* New York: Routledge.

Przeworski, Adam. 1988. Social Problems in the Study of the Transition to Democracy. In Guillermo O'Donnell, et al. (Eds.), *Transitions from Authoritarian Rule.* Baltimore: John Hopkins University Press.

Ritzer, George. 1992. *Contemporary Sociological Theory.* New York: McGraw Hill.

Rogers, Everett M. 1962. *Diffusion of Innovations.* New York: The Free Press.

_____. 1983. *Diffusion of Innovations,* 3d ed. New York: The Free Press.

_____. 1995. *Diffusion of Innovations,* 4d ed. New York: The Free Press.

Rogers, Everett M. & F. Floyd Shoemaker. 1971. *Communication of Innovations: Cross-Cultural Approach.* New York: The Free Press.

Rogers, Everett, J. R. Ascroft & N. Roling (Eds.). 1970. *Diffusion of Innovations in Brazil, Nigeria and India.* Unpublished report. East Lansing, MI: Michigan State University.

Rouquie, A. 1988. Demilitarization and the Institutionalization of Military-Dominated Polities in Latin America. In Guillermo O'Donnell, et al. (Eds.), *Transitions from Authoritarian Rule.* Baltimore: John Hopkins University Press.

Rueschemeyer, Dietrich, Evelyne Huber Stephens & John Stephens. 1989. *Capitalist Development and Democracy*. Chicago, IL: Chicago University Press.

Russets, Bruce .M., et al. 1964. *World Handbook of Political and Social Indicators*. New Haven: Yale University Press.

Ryan, Joseph E. 1995. Survey of Freedom Methodology. *Freedom Review*, *26*, 10-14.

Ryan, B. and Neal Gross. 1943. The Diffusion of Hybrid Seed Corn in Two Iowa Communities. *Rural Sociology*, *8*, 15-24.

Sandel, Michael J. 1996. *Democracy's Discontent: America in Search for a Public Philosophy*. Cambridge, MA: Harvard University Press.

Schwartzman, Kathleen. 1998. Globalization and Democracy. *Annual Review of Sociology*, *24*, 159- 81

Sedaitis, Judith S. & Jim Butterfield. 1991. *Perestroika From Below: Social Movements in the Soviet Union*. Boulder, CO: Westview Press.

Skocpol, Theda. 1992. *Protecting Soldiers and Mothers*. Cambridge, MA: Harvard University Press.

Stark, David. 1992. Path Dependence and Privatization Strategies in East Central Europe. *East European Politics and Societies*, *6*, 17-53.

_____. 1996. Recombinant Property in East European Capitalism. *American Journal of Sociology*, *10*, 993-1027.

Starr, Harvey. 1991. Democratic Dominoes. *Journal of Conflict Resolution*, *35*, 356-381.

Stepan, Alfred. 1988. Paths Towards Redemocratization: Theoretical and Comparative Considerations. In Guillermo O'Donnell, et al. (Eds.), *Transitions from Authoritarian Rule*. Baltimore: John Hopkins University Press.

Stephens, John D. 1989. Democratic Transition and Breakdown in Western Europe, 1870-1939. *American Journal of Sociology*, *95*, 1019-77.

Stone, Richard. 2000. Stress: The Invisible Hand in Eastern Europe's Death Rates. *Science*, *288*, 1732-1733.

Strang, David. 1990. From Dependency to Sovereignty: An Event History Analysis of Decolonization 1870-1987. *American Sociological Review*, *55*, 846-860.

Strang, David & Sarah Soul. 1998. Diffusion in Organizations and Social Movements: From Hybrid Corn to Poison Pill. *Annual Review of Sociology*, *24*, 265-290.

Stycos, Mayone J., Barbara Wejnert & Zbigniew Tyszka. 1999. Polish Women and Quality of Life: A Preliminary Research Report. *Sociology of Family Annals*, *11*, 29-50.

Szelenyi, Szonja. 1996. Interests and Symbols in Post-Communist Political Culture: The Case of Hungary. *American Sociological Review*, *61*, 466-477.

Tarrow, Sidney. 1989. *Democracy and Disorder*. Oxford: Clarendon Press.

_____. 1991, March. Understanding Political Change in Eastern Europe. *Political Science & Politics*, 12-20.

_____. 1998. *Power in Movement: Social Movements and Contentious Politics*. Cambridge, MA: Cambridge University Press.

Therborn G. 1977. The Rule of Capital and the Rise of Democracy. *New Left Review*, *103*, 3-42.

Uhlin, Anders, 1993. Indonesian Democracy Discourses in a Global Context. The Transnational Diffusion of Democratic Ideas (Working Paper No. 83). Clayton, Australia: Monash University, The Center of Southeast Asian Studies.

_____. 1995. Democracy and Diffusion. Transnational Lesson-Drawing Among Indonesian Pro-Democracy Actors (Working Paper No. 87). Lund University, Sweden: Lund Political Studies

Usselman, Steven W. 1991. Patents Purloined: Railroads, Inventors, and the Diffusion of Innovation in 19th–Century America. *Technology and Culture*, *32*, 1047-1075.

Valente, Thomas W. 1993. Diffusion of Innovations and Policy Decision-Making.

Journal of Communication, 43, 30-45.

_____. 1995. *Network Models of the Diffusion of Innovations.* Cresskill, NJ: Hampton Press.

Walker, Jack. 1969. The Diffusion of Innovations Among the American States. *American Political Science Review, 63,* 880-899.

Walker, John. 1992. Book review on Sport and Society in Latin America: Diffusion, Dependency and the Rise of Mass Culture. *International Review for the Sociology of Sport, 27,* 195-196.

Wallerstein, Immanuel. 1979. *The Capitalist World Economy.* Cambridge, UK: Cambridge University Press.

_____. 1984. *The Politics of the World Economy.* Cambridge, UK: Cambridge University Press.

_____. 1991. *Geopolitics and Geoculture.* Cambridge, UK: Cambridge University Press.

Weber, Max. 1904. *The Protestant Ethic and the Spirit of Capitalism.* New York: Scribner's.

_____. 1949. *The Methodology of the Social Sciences.* New York: Free Press.

Weimann, Gabriel & Hans-Bernd Brosius. 1994. Is There a Two-Step Flow of Agenda-Setting? *International Journal of Public Opinion Research, 6,* 323-341.

Wejnert, Barbara. 1988. The Student Movement in Poland: 1980-1981. *Research in Social Movements, Conflicts and Change, 10,* 173-183.

_____. 1994. Did Democracy Diffuse in Eastern Europe? Paper presented at the annual meeting of the American Sociological Association, Miami.

_____. 1996. Family Studies and Politics: The Case of Polish Sociology. In Marvin Sussman & Roma Stoval Hanks (Eds.), *Intercultural Variations in Family Research and Theory: Implication for Cross-National Studies* (pp. 233-257). Binghamton, NY: Haworth Press.

_____. 2002. A Conceptual Framework for Integrating Diffusion Models. *Annual Review of Sociology, 28.*

Whitehead, Laurence. 1988. International Aspects of Democratization. In Guillermo O'Donnell, et al. (Eds.), *Transitions from Authoritarian Rule* (pp. 3-47). Baltimore: John Hopkins University Press.

Wood, Julia T. 1999. *Gendered Lives: Communication, Gender and Culture.* Belmont, CA: Wadsworth Publishing Company.

Zakowski, Bronislaw. 1991. *Zakowski Pyta Geremek Odpowiada.* Warsaw, Poland: Panstwowe Wydawnictwo Naukowe.

Ziolkowski, Marek, Barbara Pawlowska & Rafal Drozdowski. 1994. *Jednostka Wobec Wladzy.* Poznan, Poland: Wydawnictwo Naukom.

II

Impact on Politics

2

McCarthyism Has a New Name— Lustration: A Personal Recount of Political Events

Jan Kavan

In Czechoslovakia at the time of breaking with communism new law was passed that allowed screening of public officials for evidence of their former collaboration with the Czechoslovak Secret Service (StB). In the process of this law implementation, however, wide extension of the screening was introduced. The list of categories of people to whom the law applied extended beyond high ranking Communist Party officials to district officials, officers of the Peoples' Militia, as well as its ordinary members and former students of some Soviet schools, and allowed to screen not only ministers, Parliament members and top civil servants but also most public officials, applicants for license to run private businesses, and so forth. The published list of alleged StB collaborators contained 150,000 names of accused people. Some 365,000 citizens have been checked (lustrated) under "The Lustration Act," 10,950 (3% of the total) have been lustrated with positive record. 656 out of those 10,950 appealed to the court and won their lawsuits against the Ministry of the Interior. The Ministry won 65 lawsuits (10%). Most of the accused were found innocent but the publication of the list of alleged StB collaborators caused numerous tragedies.

In the last decade of the twentieth century, the new Czech politicians introduced an unusual term into the vocabulary of people interested in the politics of postcommunist societies: *lustration*. The Czechoslovak Secret Service (StB) had been using the term lustrace for decades, but only as part of its almost impenetrable internal jargon. The Latin, *lustrare*, means to purify, to cleanse, to illuminate. The StB had been using it in the sense of screening and exposing agents. In the 1990s this practice was justified as "a democratic polity's attempt to deal with evildoers who were acting on behalf of the state under a previous nondemocratic regime" (Waller 1994). Supporters defended it as "a defensive screening procedure aimed at eliminating ex-agents of the former Communist secret police from the top echelons of power of a new and thus still fragile, democratic republic" (Waller 1994). Opponents argued that it became "an instrument of a political struggle against current political opponents rather than against the shadows of the past" (Palous 1993). It was perceived as a residue and hangover of Bolshevik mentality, which became part of the policies of "anticommunists with Bolshevik face." Many of those who experienced lustration personally viewed it as an act of revenge, a witch-hunt that violated fundamental legal principles as well as several international human rights covenants and agreements.[1]

What do these different approaches tell us about the way a postcommunist society attempts to come to terms with its past? What can we learn about the nature of these societies and about the struggle for the political character of the new states? In this chapter I portray with detail the implementation of this law using as a case study accusations that I had to face. As a target of lustration, my case received the widest publicity in the foreign press. It was, however, far from unique. Thousands of others could recount their experience, though, of course, each case has some of its own specific circumstances.

I argue here that the aims of lustration law could not have been achieved by the law as it was passed and implemented. It is understandable that people would want to know who the collaborators were and to also prevent former top Communist officials from infiltrating the new democratic system. However, many of the officials, who remained loyal to one of the most hard-line Communist parties in Europe right up to its collapse in November 1989, were soon comfortably perched on luxurious jobs for international organizations or enjoying unprecedented power as the new top capitalists. Comparison of their fate with my own and others who were wrongly accused underlines the bitter irony of the situation. Turncoats have once again profited from a dramatic turn of history. Let me now explain the development of these events.

DENAZIFICATION: A MODEL FOR LUSTRATION?

The lustration witch-hunt against former Communists was unleashed in 1991 and soon began to resemble McCarthyism. Increasingly a comparison was made between this form of decommunization and the denazification after World War II. Both were supposed to be attempts to purge a society of something evil.

I was not yet born at the time of the Nuremberg Trials but the literature available has convinced me that the process was fully respected and the real perpetrators of the monstrous crimes were punished. I recall the anger I felt as a young schoolboy when I finally comprehended that the Nazis exterminated my Czech grandmother and almost all my father's numerous relatives because the family was Jewish. My sense of justice was sustained by the fact that the murderers did not go unpunished.

Later I read reports about inconsistent denazification: Some "small fry" lost their jobs in various occupation zones while some "big fish" elsewhere kept their freedom and jobs because they were deemed useful in the new struggle against the rising Soviet danger. Still, I concluded that the policies, flawed and imperfect as they may have been, nevertheless fulfilled their main purpose. More recently I came across arguments that supported the lustration process by reference to the denazification process, which allegedly rooted-out lesser functionaries, who had served the Nazi regime, even if they had not actually committed crimes themselves (Weigel 1992). Looking at the history books more carefully, I learned that some "who gave the orders for murders, deportation, plunder and slavery had not just survived; they had, in many instances, returned to their desks and were again in a position to give orders" (Bower 1983:14). Professor Robert Gordon recently argued that denazification was less a punitive program than the crucial prerequisite to positive reconstruction: Key offices in the key institutions had to be staffed with people committed to the values of the new order. Such people, of course, did not have to have anti-Nazi credentials. So denazification may offer some useful comparisons to lustration—but denazification was ineffectual. "As of 1950," asserts Gordon, "former Nazi party members were still in, or returned to, high positions in the civil service, judiciary, universities and industry. Some victims of denazification received compensation in the civil courts; most importantly, a statute was passed...giving all those civil servants dismissed since 1945 a legal right to reinstatement and back pay" (Gordon 1994).[2]

My father fought the Nazis in the Czechoslovak army in the West. He became a Communist because he believed in the party's promises and its undertaking to ensure that there would never again be a Holocaust. But two years after the Communists seized power he was recalled from the embassy in London, where he had been posted in 1946, and sentenced to twenty-five years in Stalinist jails as "an imperialist agent," a "traitor" and a "Zionist." In the search for an internal enemy a couple of hundred were executed and many thousands imprisoned. My father was relatively lucky because he was still alive when, several years later, the Communist party reversed some of its policies at the onset of slow de-Stalinization. However, he left the prison very ill and died at the age of 46, eight years before the reformist Prague Spring of 1968 finally exposed the horrors of the Stalinist trials.

My English mother taught me—and my experience as "a son of a traitor" only underlined it—that genuine socialism is incompatible with injustice. As a teenager I realized that many people of my father's generation knew the truth about the Stalinist fifties but had been cowed into silence by fear. I concluded then that through their ostrich behavior many of my father's generation shared responsibility for the judicial murders. Therefore, as a radical student of the late sixties, I despised such indifference. When the Party confronted me in 1966 with a choice between silence, which would ensure my smooth career, and the defense of student leader Jiri Muller, who was persecuted for his belief in pluralism, my response was unhesitating. From then on my clashes with the Communist state became regular and increasingly intense. Twenty-five years after the fact I discovered that the StB had opened a file on me in 1964 and began to "assemble information" which eventually led them to put me on a list of "enemies of the state and socialism".[3]

THE RETURN OF INDIFFERENCE

In 1968 during several stormy Prague Spring public meetings I disagreed with those reformists who wanted the new Party leadership magnanimously to expose those responsible for the past crimes and let them suffer only public moral condemnation. I demanded that those guilty of judicial murders should stand trial.

After the Warsaw Pact invasion, I helped to organize, together with other radical students, opposition against the so-called normalization. Unfortunately, many reformist Communist Party leaders feared the consequences of resistance more than capitulation. It was against their compromises and the ensuing public apathy that Jan Palach (one of the protesting radical students) sacrificed his young life. My initial pride that we (students) were resisting as much as we could gave way to shame and a feeling that we, too, shared a responsibility for his death. Palach held up a merciless mirror to all of us and asked whether we had done our utmost to fight apathy and indifference. On the radio on behalf of the student union I promised "a torch of positive deeds so mighty that in its light Palach's friends will see that there is no need for their sacrifice." [4] I remained faithful to that resolution.

This was so, notwithstanding my controversial meetings in 1969-70 with Frantisek Zajicek, an education officer at the Czechoslovak Embassy in London, who—as I was told in 1991—was also an StB agent. At that time I was the president of the Union of Czechoslovak Students in the Unite Kingdom. Before it was dissolved by the government for opposing the normalization at the end of August 1969, the fiercely independent Student Union (SVS) in Prague asked me to be in contact with this diplomat. I did talk to him about the Czech and Slovak students in England—their need for scholarships and their desire to be allowed to finish studying there without jeopardizing their return home. I told him absolutely nothing about the emerging underground opposition in Czechoslovakia with which I was already in close contact. In fact, at that time (1969) I was setting up a communication channel between the West and the opposition, which soon became its main lifeline. For the majority of the groups it would remain their only one for more than a decade.

The allegation that I was to face in the 1990s did not suggest that I did any harm to anyone. My "crime" was simply to have talked to a diplomat not knowing that he is an StB agent, for I was supposed to have guessed that he was also an StB employee, despite his professed pro-Dubcek sympathies. His pretence made sense to me at that time, for I knew a large number of pro-reform officials who had not yet been purged at that time. Indeed, Zajicek's recall to Prague in the summer of 1970 because of his support for the Prague Spring only confirmed my impression.

By the summer of 1970 Zajicek was no longer able to arrange for me, or for any other Czech student, a further extension of the official permission for study abroad and I was therefore confronted with a traumatic dilemma: to become an emigré and feel that I was betraying my friends or to return and face the consequences.[5] Unable to make up my mind, I decided to go back to Prague and consult my friends. I am British by birth and thus entitled to a British passport. Under British law it is possible to change one's name as often as one wishes by the simple procedure of a deed poll. I therefore changed my name quite legally (obviously without informing anyone about it), changed my appearance, got a new British passport, and returned home. The trip was illegal from the Czechoslovak government's point of view but legal according to British and international law. To minimize risk, I met only my most trusted friends, who mostly advised me to stay abroad and help the opposition from there, or more precisely, as Jiri Muller put it "to meet our needs, as we will define them." And this is what I did for twenty years until November 1989 when, as the first Czech emigré, I returned to Prague to join the Civic Forum.[6]

Whatever the opposition requested—tons of books and periodicals, video equipment, duplicators—I arranged to be smuggled into Czechoslovakia. On their return trips to London my specially adapted camper vans brought out dissident manuscripts and Charter 77 documents [Charter 77 was a human rights movement launched in January 1977 by dissidents such as Vaclav Havel], thousands of meters of clandestine films for Western TV stations and hundreds of samizdat publications for Western research institutions and university libraries. The vans also brought out materials such as the documentation used to obtain the Nobel Prize for Czech poet Jaroslav Seifert, documents needed by Amnesty International to help Czechoslovak political prisoners, and legal and political analysis that my press agency, Palach Press presented to international legal and human rights organizations, governments and political leaders. Palach Press publicized all the materials smuggled out of Czechoslovakia virtually all over the world, including Havel's seminal essay "Power of the Powerless" and Dubcek's "Open letter to the Czechoslovak Federal Assembly," which we published in 1975 simultaneously in thirty-five countries.

I was also able to publicize daily news items about the work of the opposition and its persecution. I set up a charitable organization that raised funds for Czech samizdat publishing houses and financed their translations of Western scholarly books for the underground university seminars.[7] I helped to link up opposition movements across East European borders and published the articles written by leaders of the opposition, in a quarterly journal I helped to launch: *The East European Reporter.*[8] [After 1989, the list of honorary editors read like a list of political leaders: Vaclav Havel, Jiri Dientsbier, Jaroslav Sabata, Petr Uhl, Jacek Kuron, Adam Michnik, Miklos Haraszti and Janos Kis among others]. I also helped to forge links between East European human rights activists, especially Charter 77, and a section of the West European peace movement which understood that peace did not depend on military disarmament alone but had to be secured by eradicating the causes of political and social tensions. As

Charter 77 leaders said, the main such cause was the undemocratic legacy of the last war, the division of Europe and the subsequent Cold War. [9]

A number of English friends helped me for the full twenty years. Among them were: April Carter, Michael Randle, Richard Molineux, George Joffe, Trevor Roberts, Peter Gowan, Heather Allan, Austrian feminist Erica Fischer, and Czech emigre and former political prisoner Ales Machacek. Most of those people were leftist activists, including Trotskyists (who proved to be disciplined and reliable drivers of the smuggling campers), peace activists, left-of-center liberals and human rights activists. Shortly after I was accused in 1991 the fact of my collaboration with leftist activists was interpreted by some former Czech conformists as "evidence" that I belong to the "enemy side."

However, by uniting dissident movements on both sides of the Iron Curtain, I believed in those years that the mutually reinforcing cycle of arms race and totalitarian repression could be broken. I therefore appealed to those Westerners who wanted to see democracy prevail and the communist bloc system end to lend their full support to the East European independence movements rather than to put their faith in reformists-from-above, such as Gorbachev. One day I would be suspect in my country precisely because I rejected the Cold War black-and-white thinking.

I worked closely with leading Western journalists and experts on Eastern Europe. Many of them defended me when I later faced absurd accusations. For two decades I demanded that Western journalists report the persecution of East European dissidents. Along with Vaclav Havel, I believe that the activities of seemingly small and powerless groups should not be treated only as examples of moral courage on the fringe of society but that they represent significant political news in their own right because they illustrate important, though not yet very visible, shifts in the society which are crucial pointers to the shape of the future (Kavan 1988). Some journalists understood, many did not. The situation was the same or even worse among the politicians. Many leading politicians, despite their declared anti-communism, were then convinced that the Soviet Empire was a permanent feature of the world scene and that dissidents, whom they claimed to admire, could only endanger trade, peace and stability.

They were proven wrong. In October 1989 hundreds of thousands exposed the weakness and the rotted power base of Czechoslovak communism simply by jingling their key rings and shouting, "We do not want to be the last!" The Communist government, deserted by the Kremlin, negotiated its own demise and a peaceful, "velvety" transfer of power.

The victorious Civic Forum acknowledged my contribution to the collapse of the repressive regime and in the first free parliamentary elections I was elected on its Prague slate as a deputy of the Federal Assembly.

REVOLUTION: UNFINISHED OR BETRAYED?

The euphoria of the first few weeks was soon replaced by an understandable disillusionment. Revolutions always raise expectations; people expect "liberte, egalite, fraternite," along with material abundance and perhaps even a guarantee of good weather. Most of my parliamentary colleagues believed in the almost miraculously curative powers of the "absolutely" free market. Instead, there were mountains of problems with which we were not fully equipped to deal. My then parliamentary colleague Milos Zeman, who is today the prime minister and leader of a minority Social Democratic government, pithily compared us to a sprinter who enthusiastically raced from the starting line only to find out after 100 meters that he is running in a marathon (Zeman 1991).

Some of the students whose demonstration's acted as a catalyst for the No-vember 1989 "Velvet Revolution" felt that the revolution was betrayed. Many of the Communists simply transformed their political control into ownership and thus into decisive economic power. Their new influence and ostentatious wealth aroused anger and envy. Among those who profited most from the post commu-nist freedoms, who formed the prominent core of the new capitalist elite, mem-bers of the former Communist nomenclature are especially conspicuous. They threw away their party cards when these ceased to be convenient tickets to power but an obstacle to it (Mink & Szurek 1993).

The Communists negotiated their downfall, both in Czechoslovakia and at the Polish round tables. Theoretically they could have resorted to violence but they refrained. It was unclear whether a gentleman's agreement was reached on the non-use of violence in exchange for the protection of the communist part-ners of the dialogue. This puzzle later fueled many conspiratorial theories. Natu-rally, the former dissidents, who always stressed moral values and their abhor-rence of violence, were inclined to respond positively to the promise of a peace-ful solution. Despite the heterogeneous nature of the dissident movement itself, and even greater divergences within the ad hoc formed Civic Forum, a consen-sus seemed to exist on this issue.

I recall that an open letter by Petr Uhl to Vasil Bilak, smuggled to Palach Press in June 1988, had forced me to think—for the first time—how we should deal with the Communists in a postcommunist society. Petr Uhl, a leading hu-man rights activist, spent nine years in communist prisons (today he is the gov-ernment's commissioner for human rights); Vasil Bilak was a leading Commu-nist hard-liner. Uhl reminded Bilak that for him and his comrades, the Charter 77 activists represented the only guarantee of safety in the future because the opposition genuinely believed in respect for law and human rights, while the silent conformist majority would be far less magnanimous. The hard-liners ig-nored the warning.

Vaclav Havel stuck to his '"velvet" approach. Many former dissidents—currently government leaders—indignantly denied that they were too soft on the Communists by refusing to punish them for their crimes. They did, however, underline the need to observe the law, which had been, all along, their guiding principle.

In the pre-election spring months of 1990 the first public row concerning the archive files of the former StB hit the headlines. Vilem Sacher, the then

Minister of Interior and a leading politician of the Peoples' Party (a Christian party, formerly allied with the Communists), who warned about the unreliable and explosive nature of these files, was alleged to have locked in his personal safe files on the current Parliament members. Rumors abounded that files were pilfered, hidden, vanished or used to blackmail former collaborators. To reassure the public, the Civic Forum announced that it would subject all its parliamentary candidates to a thorough lustration to ensure that it had not been infiltrated by the former StB. I wholeheartedly agreed.

The lustration system solved a puzzle that had tormented me since April 1981, when my smuggling system suffered its only major setback during the twenty years I maintained it. One of my literature-smuggling campers was caught on the Austrian-Czechoslovak border. A week later, a garage was found in Czechoslovakia, full of samizdat books and personal archives, waiting for the French couriers to take them to London. This discovery led to the arrest of several dissidents, seven of whom spent almost a year in prison, before they were released under pressure of an international campaign that we had organized. The lustration of the Civic Forum members of the Parliament, who were co-opted to the Federal Assembly in early 1990, exposed the man who had betrayed the arrival of the van and the whereabouts of the hiding place. Ukrainian-born former political prisoner Pavel Murasko had managed at the end of 1980 to infiltrate the distribution group of Dr. Jirina Siklova, my main Prague contact at that time. Murasko acknowledged his guilt, left the Parliament the same day and took up a university job in Eastern Slovakia.

Committee for Public Safety

During the fall of 1990 conspiracy theories proliferated. The feared Communist powerhouse had collapsed like a pack of cards when confronted by a peaceful demonstration of a quarter of a million people shouting "Finally we have come! Now's the time!" This change must have perplexed the majority, who had stayed at home during the earlier Charter 77 demonstrations. If it was so easy, why were they so afraid to help the dissidents? Had their cowardice kept the Communists in power? To counter such unpleasant questions, they claimed that it was easy only because the Communists were never really defeated! They had simply reached a deal with the dissidents. A similar deal was allegedly reached at the Polish round tables. The revolution or a *coup d'etat* was just a sham for public consumption.

As a result, the parliament set up a special commission to investigate the events of 17 November 1990 and to expose the assumed conspiracy between the dissidents and the Communists. Finding nothing, it turned itself into a Committee for Public Safety and began to search for the hidden internal enemy within the parliament's own ranks. We gave them the green light to do so. In January 1991 most members of the Parliament (MPs) voted to empower the 17th November Commission to ascertain if any MPs were "registered" as StB collaborators. I voted for the resolution because I agreed with its main motivation: To expose those StB agents who had escaped discovery during the first lustration and who could be blackmailed to sabotage our democratic transformation. The resolution, however, did not specify the methods for checking the StB files or the criteria defining collaboration. It allowed no appeal procedure, no rules of due process.

PERSONAL INVOLVEMENT

Within weeks, I was astonished to hear rumors that the Commission had unearthed information linking me to the StB. At first I regarded it as a bad joke. Then I began to wrack my memory for some event in my life that, if distorted by the StB, could have misled the Commission. (My father and his friends also responded to the accusation in the 1950s by examining their past for inadvertent transgressions. Obviously the notion that one's "own side" judges one an enemy is so painful that one seeks normal explanations.) My formerly dissident friends told me that Jiri Ruml, the Commission's chairman, disliked me for my leftist political views and also because he regarded me as "a dangerous adventurer". The irony that this was a former hard-line Communist, who earned praise in the 1950s for his reports on the Stalinist trials, which included my father's, was not lost on me.

I earned the label of "an adventurer" by my illegal visits to Czechoslovakia. I have already mentioned my August 1970 trip to Prague. For eighteen years I occasionally changed my name by the cheap and simple British method of a deed poll declaration and traveled to Hungary, Poland, East Germany, Rumania and Bulgaria where I met Czech dissidents and established links with the local opposition. I did not risk going to Czechoslovakia again until Christmas of 1987 and then twice in 1988, after my English mother and grandmother died and no one would have been crushed if I were captured. There I met Havel, Dienstbier, Uhl, Sabata, Muller, Siklova, Jan Ruml and other dissidents and solved problems in our communications without endangering anyone.[10]

Suspicious Interrogations

I eventually began to speculate that the rumors about my suspect past had nothing to do with my trips to Prague but were linked to the circumstances of my return to Czechoslovakia. The speed of the events in mid-November 1989 had left me no time for the complex procedure of changing my name, appearance, and passport again, and I was not prepared to wait in London when such major events were unfolding in Prague. I therefore took the first available flight as soon as I heard that Jakes, the Communist general secretary, was forced to step down. Everything I had worked for seemed about to be realized. I simply had to be there, even though I guessed that the details of my British passport could then be known to the StB.

I landed in Prague late on the morning of November 25, 1989. As soon as I presented my passport I was escorted from the line to wait in a tiny empty office. Two hours later StB officers arrived and questioned me until 2 a.m. the following morning. The entire interrogation was openly videotaped. There were the usual techniques: the nice guy offering coffee and the tough one issuing threats. They asked me about Palach Press and my previous visits. Whom do I want to see? What do I think about the current situation? In the background the television relayed sounds of a demonstration. It was eerie. When the guard took me to the bathroom, I overheard conversation in front of the TV set: "It's worse than in 1968," one confided. They sounded both arrogant and nervous. At midnight the interrogators told me that my friend Petr Uhl was being released from prison. Soon afterwards they let me go but warned that I should not mention the interrogation to anyone.

The next day I informed Petr Uhl and several other dissident friends about the interrogation but their minds were preoccupied with the historic events taking place virtually every hour. Uhl, whose advice I asked about how to behave if picked up again by the StB, later admitted that he listened to me only out of respect for my past work, but attached little importance to the incident.

Two days later one of the same StB men woke me at 7 a.m. in my hotel and drove me to a villa where two other secret policemen were waiting. The second round of questioning was shorter and less hostile than the one at the airport. Half- way through similar questions they even gave me a choice between whisky and champagne. I was told later that I should have refused the offer indignantly, but I was simply astonished. My only thought at that moment was that the whisky would lower my guard and therefore I chose champagne, which does not have that effect. I wanted to avoid unnecessary confrontation, for they still controlled the border and I needed to return to London to close my affairs of the past years, before settling in Prague. I was carefully not to give them any political information. Everything else seemed totally unimportant.

Later I wondered if the StB had embellished their report of the interrogation, so I asked Petr Uhl whether his friends on the Commission could set the record straight and dispel the rumors. He soon found out that the Commission did indeed have a videotape. This reassured me, for surely viewing it carefully would clarify any misunderstanding. However, all the airport videotapes disappeared and the only tape left was, apparently, filmed secretly in the villa by a camera hidden in a TV set. The only shot from it I have seen to date (together with millions of Czechoslovak TV viewers) was that of me drinking champagne with the StB officers.

I was finally summoned to the Commission on 22 February, 1991. The tape was not mentioned, as the record of the interrogation contained nothing that could have been used against me. It proved useful only to the journalists. The shock of what I was told was that much greater. I was tersely informed by Stanislav Devaty that I was registered in 1969 as "a secret collaborator-confidential contact (DS)," that I had been in close contact until the summer of 1970 with StB agents Zachystal and Zajicek [I found out later that Zachystal was Zajicek's code name, the Commission having created two people out of one by inattentive reading of the file]. Moreover, he said, I had passed reliable information to the StB and acted under their instructions. I was told that if I did not resign my seat within fifteen days I would be publicly denounced. I asked to see the evidence for such preposterous claims and was told that it sufficed that he had seen it; I asked about an appeal and was told there was none. I asserted that I had never signed any promise to collaborate. They agreed that this was true but apparently it made no difference. I offered to call witnesses to disprove the accusation and was told that the Commission was not a court and not concerned with the question of guilt or innocence; it was simply to establish who was registered as a collaborator (agent). This subtle distinction was never made clear to the public, though it was later highlighted by the courts, which slowly cleared the names of some of the accused and explained that to be registered as an agent need not mean to be an agent. The Commission plainly conveyed to the public their unshakable opinion that all the denounced MPs were guilty.

First Commission, First Vote

Only later did I learn how deeply my case had divided the Commission. Its members argued past midnight before "Black Friday"—22 March, 1991, when the verdict was broadcast live to a nationwide television audience. By a margin of one, they had decided that the file the StB created on me indeed contained the fact of my registration as a collaborator! The majority agreed with alleged fact; the minority did not.

Admittedly the StB file is ambiguous, as I was later able to ascertain when I was finally allowed to read it. Its sinister StB jargon is misleading but contains no evidence of my conscious collaboration. Furthermore, the Commission was able to question Zajicek, and one other StB officer, who both testified that I was not a collaborator and that the file was created without my knowledge. The Commission was also told by the Ministry of the Interior (though at the very last minute) that the "DS" mark on my file denoted a category of people who had strong reasons "not to collaborate with any section of the Ministry of Interior."[11] which grouped all intelligence and counterintelligence organizations. Despite this information the Commission chose to quote some sentences from the file, taken out of context, to back up their assertion that I was indeed registered as a collaborator. I was surprised and angered by this reliance on the veracity of the StB files but the legal and political consequences became clear to me only several months later when the Parliament discussed the lustration law.

I refused to resign because to me that would have been an acknowledgment of guilt. And what should I feel guilty about? For talking, as a 23 year old student, to an StB agent, whom I believed to be a diplomat sympathetic to the reform? It may have been a mistake but it had no harmful consequences. Or should I apologize for living in the West while others suffered under communism? Or should I feel sorry that, together with other radical students, I offered critical support to the Dubcek's reformists in 1968? The Prague Spring reforms did not make us absolutely free but they were a step in the right direction. For my generation Prague Spring offered the first taste of freedom to think and act independently. Or should I reject my unconventional but efficient ways of helping the opposition? Or part with my peace and anti-Cold War Western friends?

Or recant my criticism of Western shock therapy models or of the widespread consumer-oriented indifference?

Several people advised me to quietly take the fall for the sake of our fragile democracy. They were worried that my defense would be misused by the "enemies of the revolution." "You have bad luck," admitted a former dissident and at that time Czechoslovak ambassador to the United States, Rita Klimova, "but you, of all people, given your past work, should understand, that the interests of the country are far more important than those of an individual." The spokesperson for the 17th November Commission, Dr. Petr Toman, a young lawyer, chillingly explained that even if an innocent person is accused, he or she "should quietly resign, because to contest the accusation would create doubts about the whole screening process, which would help the real agents" (Nagorski 1991). He clearly believed, as Czech Stalinists did in the 1950s, that individuals could be sacrificed for the greater good of the cause. My father also returned from his British exile to be accused by his own party of collaborating with the enemy. And during his incarceration the interrogators argued that he should sign a monstrous confession for the greater good of the Party.

In my parliamentary response to the accusation I continued to defend the general lustration principle but appealed to all concerned to "act sensitively, justly and legally," lest a possible witch-hunt could stain the noble ideals of November 1989. I noted that many journalists had decided in advance that anyone named by the Commission was a proven dangerous StB collaborator, irrespective of what any future court might adjudicate.

TRIAL BY MEDIA

In addition to the pressure imposed by the Commission, a vicious media campaign began, which took a nonchalant attitude toward facts that would have contradicted the conclusions already reached. I was stunned by its disrespect for truth and the right of reply, made possible by the virtual absence of libel laws. Some right-wing journalists tried to spread blatant lies, including the notion that I had been a top StB agent and had manipulated the entire dissident movement for twenty years.

According to one allegation (Dolezal 1991), I had informed the diplomat about the activities of my father, who had died 10 years earlier (Sustrova 1992). According to another story, I was responsible for the 1981 capture of my van and the subsequent arrests of my friends (Kuras 1991a). Falsified alleged quotations were published in the journal Respect (Kuras 1992). Neither my reply nor the response of my friends, who offered documentary evidence to disprove these absurd allegations, were ever published.[12] Three years later the former deputy director of the post-1989 Secret Service (FBIS) revealed that it had supplied StB materials, including the StB file on me in violation of the law, to the journal.

I was also made guilty by association. A leading right-wing daily, Cesky Denik mentioned that in the late 1960s I had met West European radicals such as Rudi Dutschke, who founded the Green Party, and Danny Cohn-Bendit, who had since become a Frankfurt city councilor for the Greens. The story connected me to Regis Debray and his textbook on terrorism, though I never met Debray, and concluded with a reference to my discussions with the American Students for a Democratic Society (SDS) (I had one brief talk in 1968 with Tom Hayden and another student). This enabled the daily to write about me and in the same breath with "not too successful terrorists" and "even mountains of corpses." Political desire to project my image as an outcast was unmistakable.

Some journalists justified this campaign by the need to counterbalance the positive coverage I have been receiving in English-speaking countries and also the growing international criticism of the lustrations. Other knowledgeable observers attributed the 1992 media campaign against me to the unfolding election struggle between the two parties that emerged from the break-up of the Civic Forum. The more dominant rightist Civic Democratic Party (ODS) enjoyed the support of many journalists. It championed capitalist market economy to be achieved by radical shock therapy. People still associated capitalism with the negation of communism and, most importantly, with prosperity and furthermore, prosperity for all, and thus were prepared to make certain sacrifices. The only potential Achilles heel of the ODS was the number of the former nomenclature elite among its members and its striking lack of dissident credentials.

The Civic Movement (OH), on the other hand, boasted a star-studded dissident leadership but projected an image of hesitant intellectuals who were unable to deal with the tough, hard-nosed decisions needed to promote market economy. Their talk about capitalism with a human face was unconvincing. However, the elections were not won on a complex economic argument but on the issue of anti-communism.

ANTI-COMMUNIST DISSIDENTS DEFEATED BY ANTI-COMMUNIST AUTHORITARIANS

By the end of 1991 it seemed impossible to uphold economic and political liberalism at the same time. If the new power elite were perceived to have facilitated the re-emergence of the old communist elite in new clothes, it might provoke the disillusioned and envious population to accept a demagogic populist nationalism that would embrace anti-communist authoritarianism and reject the political principles of liberalism. If, on the other hand, the new elite chose to prevent the old elite from leading the liberalized economy, it ran the risk of defeating economic liberalism, for the reforms clearly required investment capital and managerial know-how, which the technocratic nomenclature of the old regime could immediately provide but which would not otherwise be readily available.

The ODS managed to solve this dilemma by both keeping the cake and eating it. It facilitated the former communist elite's acquisition of economic power. It elevated this elite's well-known opportunism into a virtue, smoothly incorporating it into its own new political structures, and then placed authoritarian anti-communism firmly on its flag. To do so they needed scapegoats who could be perceived as having made such a deal with the communists while it was still theoretically possible to prevent it—that is, immediately after the Velvet coup d'etat or, as the conspiratorial theorists suggest, long before it took place. For scapegoats to be believable they had to be people who appeared "soft" on the communists, for example by defending human rights for all without any discrimination. They also had to be infiltrated by the hated StB. The former human rights dissidents, most of whom were associated with the Civic Movement, were the most obvious choice. The new "Jacobins" [13] used my case to throw a shadow of doubt on Charter 77 and the entire former dissident human rights movement by exposing the alleged link between the victims and their persecutors.

The ex-dissident leaders of the OH realized how the campaign against me could harm them and in early 1992 several of them began to defend me publicly and openly. Petr Pithart, the first Czech premier after November 1989, explained that he had to defend me in order to defend the dissent itself. He noted that, had I been an StB collaborator, then

everything we organized here, everything that was sent, from medicines through tons of books to money, everything was under the control of the StB. This would clearly discredit the dissent. I maintain that such an idea is absurd. I personally was in charge of the communication between the opposition and the West arranged through Jan Kavan between 1972 and the end of 1976. These suggestions hint to the ordinary Czech that only fools or agents could have joined the dissidents. Wise and prudent people could do nothing but wait and indeed they waited till November 17, 1989. Now people expect absolution for having waited so long. The myth that the dissidents were controlled by the StB is exactly what the most radical people, who were silent before November, want to hear today. (Premier haji dissent 1992: 1)

The media, who also needed to justify their past conformism, enthusiastically obliged. Their earlier admiration for the courageous dissidents quickly vanished. The OH voice became almost inaudible. It was further weakened by lack of unity and a clear strategy for opposing the emerging authoritarian anti-communism. This became apparent in the clash about the lustration law, described below, and showed that some OH politicians became paralyzed by fear that the public would perceive them as being soft on the communists. The radicals, who discovered their anti-Communist courage after the Communist party became a political corpse, were avengers. They needed new legitimacy as well as clear space to carry out a radical transformation of the society. They could achieve it by discrediting the former dissidents. To do so they complemented the StB label by the alleged dominance of Charter 77 and the former opposition by the 1968 Prague Spring communist reformists. This was pure myth, though it has to be admitted that the dissidents were joined by a number of Communists expelled from their party after the 1968 invasion. These were courageous people, who openly rejected the Soviet occupation. In the eyes of the rightist hawks, however, they represented a link to communism, albeit a reformist one. The same hawks chose to overlook the fact that the post-1992 rightist government included a very high percentage of people who remained in the Communist party until early 1990.

In Poland, Adam Michnik responded to the newly discovered anticommunist courage succinctly saying: "I was not such a coward then to need to be so brave now."[14] His Czech colleagues' feelings of moral superiority toward the avengers and their clear conscience compelled them to watch the rush to exorcise the past with bemused feebleness. In the clash with the avengers these ex-dissident moral absolutists understandably stressed the need for a rule of law but they defended themselves ineffectually. Some did not even notice the growing gap between them and the majority of the population, whose own experience was, of course, much closer to the conformists, who were attempting to drown their bad conscience by radical outbursts. Vaclav Havel, in an interview with the Polish newspaper *Gazeta Wyborcza*, said:

They (people who were conformists and did not cooperate in the past either with the communists or the opposition) consider the opposition fought the communists for so long that they got their own hands dirty during the fight, and their role is now laid out. In addition they hold it against the opposition that some of them were previously members of the communist party, in the 1950s or 1960s, and they hold that all communists are the same, whether from the 60s or the 80s. Meanwhile, public opinion tends to identify with the non-dissident politicians for the simple reason that the majority of people were neither dissidents nor members of the communist establishment. (Interview with Vaclav Havel 1991: 2)

As Michnik responded unambiguously "dissidents are in a way pangs of conscience for people who were conformists and now practice the rhetoric of de-communization" (Michnik 1991).

MUZZLED MEDIA

The 1992 election campaign crystallized the entire society politically including the nominally independent media. The muzzling of the media can be seen in the very incident that was originally known as "Commission gate," the first major scandal since 1989 that exposed the contempt held by some leading parliamentarians.

What happened? Stanislav Devaty, the radical driving force behind the parliamentary lustrating 17th November Commission, ostensibly motivated by the desire to inform Western journalists about my case, enabled U.S. journalist Don McNeil of Boston's *Christian Science World Monitor* to film the carefully selected extract of me "drinking with StB officers" in November 1989. Devaty even showed him my StB file, although it was classified as strictly confidential, and quoted from it on camera. He must have known he was violating the law. At a Prague press conference McNeil offered to show the video to the twenty-five Czech journalists present. Only one—a journalist from the ex-Communist party *Rude Pravo*, accepted the offer and then wrote about it. He soon stopped because, as he later explained, "I didn't want to put a gun into the hands of those who say that *Rude Pravo* is attacking the government [and our reporters are] plotters attempting to discredit the commission" (Kaval 1993).

Initially, television coverage challenged Devaty and his friends on the Commission to explain why, as MPs, they could simply trample on the law at will. The response was disproportionate. Parliamentary business was interrupted and the defense of Devaty became deafening. Television news reporters quickly shifted into reverse. The drinking shots were transmitted in the main news slot to every household and the journalists found me guilty. To protect the lustration process and to fight against the StB agents, it was said to be sometimes necessary to ignore the law. A very popular weekly discussion program enabled Petr Toman, the Commission's press spokesperson, to accuse me of collaboration with the StB and even to quote sentences from the confidential StB file which, taken out of context, suggested my guilt. The moderators allowed neither me nor any of my supporters to reply. The media called me "the agent," though I had never been officially accused of being an agent. Editorials in some major newspapers even suggested that friends from the parliamentary club Social Democratic Orientation, which I belonged to, and I staged the incident in order to discredit the 17th November Commission and the leading right-wing politicians associated with it. In the face of all this, supervising prosecutor Vladimir Nechanicky stated in a television interview that a criminal act may have been committed, that Devaty's conduct should be investigated and that the StB files should not be used or quoted from until their veracity was confirmed by the courts. Nechanicky did not survived as the supervising prosecutor for long.

Jan Urban, the former Charter 77 spokesperson who brought the Civic Forum to its victory in the June 1990 elections, published a correct account of this event in the daily *Lidove Noviny* and began to ask difficult questions: How did the Commission acquired the cassette? If the content of the cassette is such that it cannot be included in any formal accusations against me, then why is it publicized at all? If, on the other hand, it is really important, then why is it not made available to the district court, which is dealing with my case? However, the editors of *Lidove Noviny* soon told Urban to drop the story, for, as he pointed out "some politicians took all this as an attack on the right. There was a fear behind this decision that the right would take *Lidove noviny* as a leftist paper" (Kayal 1993: 269).

Urban explained elsewhere that "because this society is still so Bolshevik— in the sense that an opponent means an enemy—many people are afraid to talk openly and give Jan Kavan the possibility of defending himself for fear that they would be accused of defending a leftist" (Mitchell 1992). Urban faced this danger, and so did two dozen other former dissidents, including several who were then still government ministers, though aware that the opinion polls predicted their defeat. They issued a joint statement and made clear that during my many years of work for the opposition "nothing has ever leaked out". And they condemned the media campaign against me as "incompatible with the principles of civic and journalist ethics and the rule of law."[15] But it was too late for me and for them.

I received letters suggesting that I should hang myself; some of my parliamentary colleagues wanted me to feel excommunicated from the community of decent people. I relied on the help of my ex-dissident friends, who were maligned for expressing their solidarity with me. Although this was nothing new for them, as Drahuse Probostova said, "it was much easier under the old regime. It was simple; black and white; us and them. We knew why they had to persecute us and we helped each other effectively. But today it is more difficult, we are supposed to be finally free but there is so much struggle for power, envy, distrust, lack of solidarity without presumption of innocence, we will never have a legal state."[16]

Being silenced at home, I appealed for help to those who had helped me before 1989 to publicize the plight of dissidents. Well-known journalists such as William Shawcross, Neal Ascherson, Christopher Hitchens, Edward Mortimer, Richard Davy and others immediately responded. I also welcomed expressions of solidarity from leading British parliamentarians, including the then shadow cabinet ministers (today some of them are members of the Labour government); from more than a hundred Russian, Bulgarian, Polish and Hungarian parliamentarians, including many former leading dissidents; from Joan Baez and her California-based human rights group Humanitas, from Senator Paul Simon and others.

But this Western support infuriated the lustration supporters. Some of their responses illustrated their misunderstanding of democracy. *Respekt's* columnist Ben Kuras thundered that "Well functioning democracy is a dictatorship of the parliament and its expressed wishes have to be perceived as a law, which no one has a right to disobey. By asking for the protection of the courts proved that their stay in the Parliament is very risky for the citizens and for democracy" (Kuras 1991b). To interpret willingness to criticize illiberal procedures as subversion of "our fragile democracy" illustrated well the prevailing low level of political culture.

LUSTRATORS RESIST LEGAL LEASH

The major struggle between the avengers and the liberals, which included most of the former dissidents, took place in October 1991 when the Parliament finally attempted to rein in the wild lustrations by a proper legal framework. However, the liberals were caught unprepared. They did not understand that this was the first crucial battle in a long struggle that would determine the character of the future state.

The Parliament—thinking that it was guided by the denazification experience—charged its own lustrating commission with only one criterion: the list of agents and informers compiled by the communist secret police; the so-called registers. The Parliament thus unwittingly gave the Commission free interpretation of its tasks and powers. Their "wild" lustrations and disregard for legal procedures evoked the memory of the communist revolutionary justice of the post-war years. A law became necessary. The dissident-dominated government had to weigh the domestic criticism that it was too soft on the StB and the former Communist officials against foreign criticism that its proposed legislation was too harsh, curtailing some rights to which all citizens are entitled. The deputy prime minister at that time (and again today) was Pavel Rychetsky, a lawyer and a former dissident. He acknowledged that the government's draft was on a tight-rope. A mechanism was needed that could be used to purge all those guilty of the Communist regime's crimes versus the need to conform to our own Bill of Human Rights and Freedoms and to international legal norms.

I thought that the government managed to balance these objectives rela-tively well. Suppressing some of my moderate civil rights objections to one or two paragraphs, I was prepared to vote for the bill. I still considered a legal mechanism, even an imperfect one, desirable to protect the government from being infiltrated or blackmailed by the StB. On the other hand, the long-term imprisoned Petr Uhl admitted that my case converted him from a supporter of lustrations to a cautious skeptic. He warned against coming to terms with past injustices by committing new wrongs. The main reason why I raised my hand for the government's proposal was its precondition that evidence would have to be found that former Communist officials or people registered as collaborators actually participated "in the suppression of human rights." I believed that indi-vidual evaluation, hopefully by courts employing proper rules of evidence, would minimize the danger of new injustices.

It was all in vain. The rightists managed to reverse approval of the human rights preamble.[17] In an unprecedented move a second vote was taken, two MPs changed their minds and the precondition was defeated by a margin of one vote.[18] The resulting bill replaced the need for individual evaluation by the prin-ciple of collective guilt and it institutionalized the presumption of guilt based solely on the evidence of the StB files or on the posts held in the Communist party hierarchy, though not in the hierarchy of the state, which was an absurd distinction in a communist state.

Now thousands of others would go through the same experience as I had gone through, but this time it would be sanctioned by law. Jeri Laber of the U.S. Helsinki Watch, who helped us in the opposition consistently for many years, summarized it eloquently: "Supporters of the lustration law have thus put their faith in the secret police, who were known to have lied consistently and to have misled and abused the population; in this it appears the police still rule, reaching out from the grave" (Laber 1992).

After being defeated on this crucial clause, the government's supporters were thrown into disarray. The parliamentary mathematics were clear: if all members of Parliament of the pro-government Civic Movement voted against the entire bill in the final vote, the law would be scupper and a new version would have to be negotiated. About half of these MPs protested against the ma-nipulation by ignoring the final vote, but a dozen of the others voted with the

Right to save the bill. These liberals were so afraid that they would not be perceived as sufficiently anticommunist that they stopped behaving as liberals. [American liberals, who remember the McCarthy atmosphere, should understand this.] Others joined the Communists, the Social Democrats, the Movement for Democratic Slovakia (which later formed an independent Slovak government) and some individual Christians in opposing the law but were defeated in all three chambers of the Parliament by margins of single figures (Kavan 1991).

It was sad to see Jiri Dienstbier, then a top government minister, well-known in the West for his past Charter 77 human rights activities, rush out of the chamber just before the vote. It seemed that he did not want to vote either against his own conscience or against the raging "Jacobins," whose majority was, however, far from assured. They had to summon the then federal Prime Minister Marian Calfa (minister in the Communist government till November 1989), who dashed to the chamber to cast his vote against the decision of his own government. Calfa, I was told by parliamentary colleagues, succumbed to the threat, that the lustration law could cover former heads of Communist party branches. This criterion would purge Calfa as well as Economy Minister Vladimir Dlouhy out of the government, as until 1989 they had been the head of the Communist Party branch in the government and in the Forecasting Institute of the Academy of Sciences, respectively.

"Regain your senses! Wake up!" Petr Uhl pleaded in vain from the parliamentary rostrum for the defence of the rights for which the dissidents had spent decades struggling. Milos Zeman, in a somber tone, read out the June 1990 prophetic words of the Polish democrat Adam Michnik,

All revolutions—whether bloody or not—unfold in two stages. In the first, struggle for freedom prevails, in the second, struggle for power and for revenge against supporters of the old regime. . . . The logic of revenge creates a new atmosphere. It leads to the purges of yesterday's enemies. . . . Then comes the turn of the opponents of revenge who were yesterday's leaders of the opposition and, finally, their defenders. The atmosphere of revenge and hatred is followed by the ordinary mechanism of revenge which we know well and which was the same during the Jacobin terror as during the Islamic revolution in Iran. We lack democratic culture and democratic institutions, traditions of democratic coexistence with others. (Michnik 1990: 2).

The Right: Lustration Neither Witch-hunt Nor Justice

The warning fell on deaf ears. The Czech hawks were on the ascendancy. Having held the classical Cold War view for decades, they believed that history has proven them right, and they even began to receive some Western support. They saw lustration not as a witch-hunt but as an application of principles employed by the Allies in postwar Germany. Some even suggested that NATO should admit formerly communist countries only if they first defended themselves internally by lustration. Some commentators, for example Weigel, were convinced that the aim of the lustration law was not revenge:

Its aim was to secure and consolidate the transitions to democracy and the free economy. . . restoring public confidence in the basic fairness of the machinery of governance. . . does not ban former Communists and collaborators from employment . . . it does not forbid anyone from running for the parliament . . . it does not forbid anyone from publishing. [The law only] bans former high-ranking Communists, and former StB members and collaborators, from employment for a period of five years in key sectors of the society. (Weigel 1992: 1)

I do not know of any evidence that the lustrations restored public confidence. Opinion polls in the Czech Republic placed lustration at the very bottom of peoples' concerns. The controversy surrounding cases like mine has shaken any earlier confidence beyond repair. Other post-communist countries that planned to copy the Czech model abandoned such attempts. In Poland, the determination of the Olszewski's government to persevere with this folly led to its downfall.

Weigel's belief that the law bans only "high-ranking Communists," repeated frequently by all defenders of the lustration law, does not stand up to a closer look. What about any of the thousands of people who, during the last forty one years, became members of the People's Militia or officials of a Communist party district committee or studied for three months at one of the Soviet security schools? It is not clear what danger these people pose to democracy today. On the other hand, Communist government ministers and other top officials of the state (but not the Party), who misused their power to violate basic civil rights of their opponents, were not touched by the law. And freedom to publish or run for the Parliament? Article 21, which provides for the lustration of journalists and leading politicians, in practice means that "positively lustrated" individuals would not be able to publish (except in the Communist press) or run for Parliament (except on the Communist ticket).

True, five years does not sound very long. In fact, since then the application of the law has been extended to ten years. But I fail to see why, for example, the head of a local post office or a neighborhood bank should be perceived as "key sectors" and banned from such employment. How can they sabotage the transition to market economy? Czech lustration supporters argue that individuals are not punished but prevented from occupying certain positions, "just as all thieves are disqualified as bank managers, so people who were actively involved in the destruction and oppression of one social group by another—the so-called class struggle—are disqualified from the administration of a democratic state" (Kavan 1991). This argument overlooks the fact that the reason why thieves are prevented from becoming bank managers is that each one of them was individually convicted of theft, in a court of justice, whereas lustration did not prove guilt of anything.

The lustration law does not allow individual evaluation of responsibility. People are guilty simply because they belonged to a particular group or a category. The assumption is that because a person has an attribute that is sometimes associated with a wrongful act, that person has in fact committed that act. Alexander Dubcek, whom history will remember as the symbol of a defiant attempt to replace Soviet-style totalitarian communism by "socialism with a human face" would not, under the terms of the law, be allowed to run a local state bank or to obtain a license to become a taxi driver, auctioneer or antique dealer. These restrictions would, however, not apply to the thousands who persecuted Dubcek supporters after the Soviet tanks crushed the reform—from the journalists, who vilified them, and the employers, who sacked them, to the prison warders, who beat them up, to the government ministers, who issued the orders.

The lustration law can be used against people who became targets of StB interest because of their opposition to the regime, while at the same time the names of thousands of top-level agents, and especially their controllers and other superiors, remain unknown because their names were not included in the StB files.[19]

No provision in the law allows discrimination, let alone punishment, of those "whose past behavior shows that they will in fact undermine the transition to democracy" (Havel 1985: 35-37), irrespective of the suffering they may have caused to dissidents and other opponents of the old regime. If they did not hold official positions in the Communist party, or if there are no StB files on them (and obviously, there will be none), they could both enjoy the fruits of any past misdeeds and occupy any position they wanted in the new establishment. The law clearly has not achieved, and could not achieve, what it formally purported to do. It is a failure. As courts began to clear the names of some of the alleged collaborators, top officials dismissed these court adjudications by asserting that within five years they will produce evidence to substantiate the accusations. Therefore, whoever had been accused remains, for all practical purposes, guilty despite being cleared by the courts.

THE INDEPENDENT MINISTERIAL COMMISSION

I voted against the final version of the law. Ironically, the law's only exception to the blanket collective guilt was contained in Article 2c which described "a conscious collaborator" as "a person listed in the StB files either as a confidant, candidate of secret collaboration or a secret collaborator-confidential contact," but warned that such people need not have known that they were in contact with StB employees, let alone knowingly implemented their instructions. A body ominously called the Independent Commission of the Ministry of Interior was established to review such cases individually. As the only known "confidential contact" in the country I was entitled to such a review.

I would have preferred a full assessment of the StB files by a proper court but at that time I believed that an independent commission would be able to do justice to the task, especially when I learned that Jaroslav Basta, a former political prisoner, known for his integrity, was appointed its chairman. Basta had been sacked from his post as the deputy director of the post-1989 secret service for making public his criticism of the practices prevailing in this important new institution. "Making public" meant informing President Havel in person. Today Basta is a minister without portfolio in charge of intelligence services.

Nine out of the fourteen commission members were appointed by the ministries dealing with security and military matters. I knew that the commission was a far cry from the impartial tribunal envisaged by the European Convention on Human Rights and that European Commission President Antonio La Pergola, Secretary General of the Council of Europe Catherine Lalumiere and the International Labor Organization, all agreed that the commission could not be really independent of the government, and in particular of the Ministry of Interior (Helsinki Watch 1992: 12).

Minister Twists and Turns

To ask Basta's commission to review my case I needed written proof that I was indeed registered as a "secret collaborator-confidential contact," as accused by the parliamentary commission. I therefore formally asked the Ministry of Interior to lustrate me. To my surprise, the ministry's officials obtained my StB file, ignored all political pressures, and examined it strictly under the terms of the lustration law. They found no evidence that I was ever registered as a collaborator under any category and duly prepared a certificate of "negative lustration," that is, a clean bill of health, which the federal Minister of Interior Jan Langos signed and issued on 24 February 1992. The result was a major uproar. Newspaper headlines screamed that this marked the death of the entire lustration process which had been discredited beyond salvation.

Someone was not telling the truth: Either the parliamentary commission or the Ministry of Interior responsible for applying the law to millions of citizens. After two days, Langos, publicly reversed his decision, a step for which there is no provision in the law [20] and violated Article 19 of the lustration law by disclosing on television details from my StB file. He claimed that his employees only "examined the file's numbers and codes" and did not look inside it where, according to him, I was "consistently described as a secret collaborator confidential contact" (Prorok 1992). The minister lied. Petr Uhl, who became well acquainted with my file, accused him of lying but the minister ignored him (Dengler 1992). The head of the ministerial division that prepared my negative certificate was replaced.

A few weeks later the minister claimed that his employees had searched through my file but, finding no evidence of conscious collaboration, cleared me. According to the minister, "they were supposed to concern themselves only with the fact of registration" (Homolka 1992). He publicly promised to make the StB file available to me and allow me to publish it to prove my innocence. He failed to keep this promise. I received a new "positive" certificate, also signed by Minister Langos.

There was no explanation. But the new certificate only referred to the controversial "C" category of "a conscious collaborator" it enabled me to submit my case to Basta's independent commission to determine whether I was a conscious collaborator or not.

Second Commission, Second Vote

I did so on 13 March, 1992. The lustration law requires that the independent commission must review a case within 60 days. Employers were allowed to sack the recipients of positive certificates after 30 days. Being found innocent later did not provide ground's for reinstatement.[21] The commission was sometimes unable to meet the 60-day legal deadline. In my case it took the commission seven months to reach its verdict. Its work began at the height of the campaign against me, when in the public eye the lustration law stood or fell with my guilt or innocence. Nevertheless, the commission heard only one of the fifteen witnesses I proposed: William Shawcross, a leading British journalist and writer.

Shawcross' testimony was crucial because, according to the StB file, Zajicek asked me to obtain from Shawcross a copy of an important document and to find out how it was smuggled from Czechoslovakia. The file acknowledges the fact that I never passed this document to the diplomat but explains it by asserting that Shawcross began to suspect me of working for the StB and thus never gave it to me. The parliamentary commission accepted this strange story. Shawcross testified that he never suspected me and he gave me the document for my mother to translate into English. The documentation was published in the United Kingdom and the United States and my mother (Rosemary Kavan) was acknowledged as the translator of *The Czechoslovak Political Trials, 1950-1954: The Suppressed Report of the Dubcek Government's Commission of Inquiry* (Pelikan 1971).

The fact that I did not pass it on to Zajicek, though I had it in my possession, was for Shawcross proof that I did not collaborate. He added that almost all Czech opposition documents he published during the last twenty years were smuggled from Czechoslovakia by my couriers. Chairman Jaroslav Basta regarded this testimony as decisive in convincing him of my innocence (in Probostova 1992). Nevertheless, aware of the political pressures his commission was under, he urged me to await the Constitutional Court's ruling, which was widely expected to abolish the category of "conscious collaborator" and thus no further proceedings against me would be legal. I refused the offer because I wanted to win on the merits of my case, not by default. I therefore demanded a verdict from his commission.

The commission reached its finding in October 1992 without asking me any relevant questions concerning the core accusations and without questioning Zajicek at all. One member simply looked at him and then reported to the commission: "I would not have even gone for a cup of coffee with such a disgusting-looking secret policeman" (in Probostova 1992). The verdict again reached by a majority vote was guilty of being a conscious collaborator in 1969-70. Shocked, I asked which piece of evidence led to such an incredulous conclusion. I was told that the commission is not required to find any concrete proof. There were contradictory interpretations of my StB file but the majority believed that, twenty-three years earlier, I must have been "intelligent enough to realize that Mr. Zajicek was an StB agent." And that was it. The commission did not have to

explain its judgments or conduct any conversation with me. I knew how my far-
ther must have felt at his "trial."

Basta, who voted with the minority for my innocence, advised me to appeal
to the Prague City Court. He explained that his commission had not a single
witness to back up its verdict. The only witness besides Shawcross the commission heard had been a representative of the Czechoslovak intelligence service,
who testified that the ministry's "specialists analyzed the file and concluded that
Mr. Kavan was innocent" (in Probostova 1992). I did appeal, but the Prague
City judge did not even look at the documentation on my case, since the legal
category concerned was by then abolished. He concluded that the City Court's
right to consider appeals against the commission's past verdicts was no longer
within its jurisdiction.

Final Verdict

I was shattered. The only appeal procedure stipulated by the lustration law
had been closed. From then on I was left with only one way how to clear my
name and that was to pursue my civil case against the Ministry of Interior,
which I had started in March 1991 in the Prague 7 District Court. In September
1994 the district court, after three-and-half years of deliberations (during which
the Ministry of Interior was unable to produce a single witness against me) finally reached an unequivocal verdict: Jan Kavan was not a conscious collaborator, he did not know that Zajicek was an StB officer, he did not supply him with
information in any conspiratorial manner and he never fulfilled any of Zajicek's
instructions. Mass media paid very little attention to this fact, as compared with
the headline publicity received by my accusation. In November 1994 the Ministry of Interior appealed against the verdict and its lawyers promised to produce
new evidence. They produced none, not even any new arguments, but I had to
wait further sixteen months for the Prague City Court to reject the appeal and
thus to finally and irrevocably clear my name from all shadows of accusations. I
was therefore able to stand in the parliamentary elections few months later. In
the Social Democratic primaries in Prague I finished sixth, which was perceived
to be a great success after years of vilifications. I narrowly missed being elected
to the Parliament as Prague elected only the first five Social Democrats. Then
suddenly in August I was asked by the Social Democrats of the Prostijov district
in central Moravia to run on their behalf for the Senate, the new upper chamber
of the Parliament. Part of my father's family came from Prostijov but almost all
had died in Nazi concentration camps. In November 1996 I was elected to the
Senate in the first past-the-post electoral system. At the end of 1997 the rightist
government coalition collapsed and following early new elections in June 1998,
the Czech Social Democratic party was able to form a minority government. I
became foreign minister. In December 1999 I was named vice-premier for foreign affairs, defense and security. However, media attacks continued. Some of
the major media responded to the court verdict with the assertion that I was
found not guilty only because of a lack of evidence that was presumably destroyed.

I have often wondered about the lustration law and about the link between freedom of press and the ability of journalists to write objectively. Drahuse Probostova who was one of the few journalists that did not succumb to the temptations of witch-hunts, conducted an interview with chairman Jaroslav Basta soon after the Independent Commission of the Ministry of Interior found me guilty. Basta then asserted her that my StB file "does not provide evidence about Mr. Kavan but about the work of Frantisek Zajicek . . . who tried very hard to prove to his superiors that he was important" (in Probostova 1992). Basta admitted that the jargon used in the file may have convinced some people that I could have been a collaborator, but he did offer another explanation.

There was a conflict of totally different life experiences. Kavan lived through 1968 and the members of the Commission did not, or they remember it differently from him. They could not understand Mr. Kavan's way of thinking. Furthermore, they are, as they would themselves say, right wing. The lustration law, or any other law, should have first hit the communist nomenclature, then the StB, and only then the alleged collaborators, who were probably victims of the regime rather than its supporters . . . As it is, the lustration law punishes innocent, honest people. It tarnishes their character. This causes them a lot of pain (in Probostova 1992).

Basta finally reminded the readers of a trade union daily paper that the lustration issue was raised exactly at the moment when Parliament began discussing the responsibility of the Communist nomenclature for the state of the country:

In my view, this was a classic political maneuver, whereby people's attention was diverted from the main issue to a less important question, which is, however, more attractive and more easily tackled. To find out which members of the communist nomenclature now own what, i.e. the price we have paid to the communists for our freedom, is much more difficult. The Poles say that the former communist nomenclature in their country now includes the richest people in the land and that this was the price Poland had to pay. Similar developments are taking place in Czechoslovakia, in Hungary, in Germany, in Bulgaria. You take people's attention away from this reality by starting scandals like Mr. Kavan's case (Probostova 1992).

Jaroslav Sabata, former Charter 77 spokesperson and a minister in Petr Pithart's Czech government (1990-92), also believed that my case was intended to divert attention from the real nature of the political change. As a former leading dissident and a political prisoner he felt that what the dissidents stood for was being targeted. Sabata recalled the arguments of the late philosopher Jan Patocka, written in March 1977, after people criticized him for helping to launch Charter 77. The human rights challenge provoked the hard-line forces of the regime, which at that time had been sufficiently moderate to make a decent life possible. Patocka argued that such forces have to be resisted, and that there were values worthy of sacrifice. To remain faithful to this principle even after November 1989, Sabata insisted, meant to "fight on the Kavan's case to the very end. The case of Jan Kavan represents a great internal drama of the Czech dissent. On this case the Czech dissent can prove its moral strength" (Vysatova 1993:1).

It was Vaclav Havel who shaped Patocka's appeal "to live in truth" into the guiding force of the dissident movement. At the same time he understood that most ordinary citizens found absolute moral criteria difficult to aspire to, as they felt compelled to make daily compromises with the regime. On the now famous example of the conformist greengrocer, Havel illustrated how the dividing line ran through each person, for everyone was both a victim and a supporter of the system. No one had unlimited responsibility and guilt, nor was anyone completely absolved (Havel 1985). In his first presidential speech on New Year's Day 1990, he stressed that we were all "though naturally to varying degrees— responsible for keeping the totalitarian machinery in motion. None of us were mere victims. We were all its co-creators" (Michnik 1991: 2).

Havel had been critical of the lustration law from the day it was passed. He immediately sent his criticism of many aspects of the law to the Parliament, especially of the sweeping collective guilt clause. In an interview he granted to his Polish friend Adam Michnik, Havel called the act harsh and unjust. He argued eloquently against witch hunts, persecutions, fanaticism and the creation of an atmosphere of fear (Michnik 1991). When, in the fall of 1991, we met openly for three hours in a Prague restaurant, he reminded me that his "highly critical attitude to the lustration is well known."[22] (He then told me that he would publicly respond to my case when he was no longer a president or after the courts issued their final verdicts. I fully understood and accepted these reservations. Unfortunately, as far as the public is concerned, Havel has remained silent to date.)

Havel acknowledged that when he was pondering whether or not to sign the lustration law he was aware that "from the viewpoint of fundamental human rights, it is a highly questionable law." He admitted that some of his former dissident friends urged him not to sign it and return it to the Parliament. He turned down the advice because it would have been "a typically dissident-like, morally pure, yet immensely risky act of civil disobedience." He therefore signed it, knowing that the bill "will be valid with my name on it, and that a number of people will be unfairly treated". This experience enabled him to discover that "truly moral politics is not simple, or easy" (Havel 1991).

Havel's decision to sign the bill made it even easier for the lustration supporters to suggest that preoccupation with morality has to be left to philosophers or moralist ex-dissidents. The lustration law harmed innocent people, in addition to those who were simply weak. This is not to say that the lists do not include some real informers, who did harm their fellow countrymen. However, I shall never learn who was sent to spy on me in London and, much more importantly, the public will never learn the names of top officials directly responsible for the major acts of persecution, for ordering long-term imprisonment of political opponents or causing the death of some of them.

The StB files cannot provide the answers. They were always incomplete, for the Secret Service was not allowed to recruit Communist party officials, let alone to open files on really top agents. Besides, only a tiny fraction (10 %) of the files have survived the selected destruction of the archives in 1989. It was acknowledged that all so-called live files were destroyed, that is, files of agents who were still active in 1989, as well as files of the main targets, that is, files of leading dissidents, including—I was told—my own.[23]   But no one ever explained the criteria for deciding which parts to burn and which parts to leave for the new regime to use in reinterpreting history. Finally, though I am not suggesting that the files are forged (at least mine was not), their credibility cannot be strong enough to justify their use as the sole evidence of anyone's wrongdoing.

Vaclav Havel has even asserted that only a minority of people registered in the StB files were active informers and "a large percentage is represented by people, who were persecuted in a way, which cannot be even imagined by the majority of those, who managed to slip through the previous regime without the StB finding them worthy of any notice." [24]

DISCREDITING OPPOSITION TO THE COLD WAR AND TOTALITARIANISM

In 1993 Havel was once again confronted with the dilemma of whether to sign a law that enshrined the principle of collective guilt, which he has condemned on numerous occasions. The ""Law Concerning the Illegitimacy of the Communist Regime" (known as the anticommunist law) states that "The Communist Party of Czechoslovakia, its leaders and its members, are responsible for the way our land was governed in the years 1948-1989, for the conscious violations of human rights and freedoms, for the moral and economic decline accompanied by judicial crimes and terror against dissidents..." and so forth (Law Concerning the Illegitimacy of the Communist Regime 1993). Havel, however, signed it, as he explained, because for moral reasons a law that explicitly rejects the evil of the past was needed. The past is thus exorcised by a law that concludes: "The Communist Party of Czechoslovakia was a criminal organization . . . just like other organizations based on its ideology; its activity was aimed at suppressing human rights and the democratic system" (Law Concerning the Illegitimacy of the Communist Regime 1993). The law condemns the regime as illegitimate and makes no distinction between the hard-line Stalinists guilty of judicial murders and setting up concentration camps and the reformists, who attempted to democratize the regime and give it *a human face*.

Resistance to the regime, the law promulgates, "even if in cooperation with a democratic foreign power, was legitimate, just, morally justified and is worthy of respect." This does not seem to apply to former Communists, though many have spent years in prison for their opposition to the regime. One of them, Jaroslav Sabata, emphasized that the law attempted to delegitimize the leftist resistance to totalitarianism by making it part of the same "criminal system." Sabata underlined the common denominator between the anticommunist and the lustration laws: Both laws were formulated by people whose views corresponded to those that prevailed during the height of the Cold War. At that time, Sabata recalled, it was argued that "communism can be defeated only by violence or war" (Vysatova 1993). In time, a leftist opposition emerged, including reformist Communists, asserting that a radical change can take place peacefully. Sabata pointed out examples of radical changes being achieved peacefully both in 1968 (before the invasion) and in the 1989 "velvet, negotiated, revolution," but acknowledged that Czech political life after 1989 was dominated by supporters of the Cold War opposition. "Both laws are part of an endeavor," Sabata concluded, "to discredit any opposition, any democratic alternative, to the right-wing attempt to restore classical capitalism, which was not the aim of the dissident movement" (Vysatova 1993: 1). It has to be admitted that the anticommunist law has no teeth and can thus besmirch the moral integrity of the reformists but it cannot punish the hard-line Stalinists.

Sabata's observation served as a reminder of the confusion that can be caused by terminology. Sabata included the Dubcek reformist Communists among the "leftist opposition" to understandably distinguish them from both the Stalinists and their right-wing opponents. This should not detract from the fact that during the Prague Spring the reformists also provoked criticism from the democratic left, primarily for their undue reliance on a top-down structure, despite their greater democratization and decentralization than their predecessors.

It would be over-simplification to argue that the opponents of the lustration law and my supporters were all recruited from the noncommunist left, while the supporters of the law and my opponents are all on the right, though this is true of the majority. To be more accurate, the former group also included ex-dissidents who did not regard themselves as leftists; who always rejected the hawkish Cold War perception of the world; and who never expressed themselves in terms of communism or anticommunism but rather in terms of a respect for human dignity, basic civil and human rights, peace, "living in truth" and transcendent moral norms.

It may be useful for ardent Czech lustrators to group together Dubcek and the Stalinists who invited the troops that smashed his reforms, or top StB officers with everyone whose names they placed in their files. It may be also useful for authors such as Weigel to group together Harry Truman, Ronald Reagan and the Cold War with Vaclav Havel and dissident intellectuals, and counter pose them, as Weigel did, to the Ford Foundation, the MacArthur Foundation, the Carnegie Corporation and those American intellectuals and peace activists who were critical of the Cold War. It may serve their arguments but it does not square with the truth.

The Greatest Success of the Secret Police

While almost the entire former nomenclature elite was able to transform itself into the new capitalist elite, it is also necessary to note the interesting inter-penetration of the old and new bureaucracies. The lustration law does not apply to bureaucrats and thus allowed them smoothly to transfer their loyalties from one regime to another. The public attention directed toward the former dissidents and "registers" of alleged StB's collaborators helped to sustain the legitimacy of this genealogical link between the old and new bureaucracies. Even the StB's repressive nature was not allowed to detract from the alleged truthfulness of their files. This suggests that even bad structures can employ honest bureaucrats. The individuals who have been vilified were not essential to the networks, whose members could be and mostly were re-employed and whose expertise was badly needed. Thus a comparison to the practical results of the denazification process may not be so far-fetched, after all.

The processes described in this chapter could not have taken place but for the absence over many decades of any experience of democracy, of dialogue, of negotiations. Instead, the tradition was to perceive problems as conflicts in which there was a recognizable enemy. That adversarial mind-set construes opposing interests as subversive and illegitimate. This legacy continues to foster suspicion, distrust, intolerance and witch-hunts.

It is extremely important to use the media, the educational process and democratic political means to promote and strengthen a budding legal system. Surprisingly, none of the liberals, while they were in power, or President Havel, drew attention to the serious injury inflicted on this legal system by the decommunization laws. Yet Havel himself was brought to court as a defendant in December 1993. In one of his most eloquent speeches he explained that "only someone really cynical or fanatical will fail to understand what it means for a person who was persecuted throughout his life by the communist regime, and spent even a number of years in prison, to find his or her name on a list of collaborators—without ever committing anything. Everyone around him ceases to talk to him. The world collapses for such a person" (Havel 1993: 1). The results, Havel confirmed, was that innocent people lost their jobs and careers, families divorced, people were ostracized and some even committed suicide, including several children of accused fathers. Lustration practices were "the successors of the communist ideology of hate, revenge and totalitarian contempt for the law." He went on to describe angrily the unofficial publication of the StB's list of alleged collaborators as "one of the greatest successes of the StB, which has managed for many years to poison the atmosphere of a democratic state, to mobilize all the rabble whose greatest joy is to harm others . . . and to throw in doubt those basic values which are the foundations of a legal and democratic state" (Havel 1993).

LET THE COURTS DECIDE!

No legal and democratic state can be built on the rotten foundations of past covered-up crimes, be it in Chile, El Salvador or the Czech Republic. I admire President Nelson Mandela's appeal for "national reconciliation," for "healing of the wounds and bridging the chasms that divided black and white South Africans" (President Mandela Appeal 1994:A8). But I am convinced that drawing a symbolic thick line under a past steeped in cruel injustices does not bring justice

Transition to Democracy in Eastern Europe and Russia

for all. It would mean to have to live with the painful tumor of the past unexposed iniquities and result in tensions that may cast a deep shadow over any noble endeavors of reconciliation.

Whereas Havel has consistently maintained that we are all co-responsible for the past, he has admitted that there were "varying degrees," within days of becoming president he specifically underlined that "independent courts should impartially consider the possible guilt of those who were responsible for the persecutions, so that the truth about our recent past might be fully revealed" (Havel 1990:57). We should have heeded this appeal then, and he should have persevered with this idea, which would have made clear to the public that to be critical of the lustration law did not mean to whitewash those who committed crimes and harmed their fellow citizens.

Reluctantly, I finally concluded that it was impossible to formulate any lustration law, which would not violate international human rights covenants and agreements, or harm innocent people and be able, at the same time, to weed out those responsible for the Communist oppression.[25] People who committed the crimes that the anti-communist law ascribes to the entire Communist party should be brought to court and confronted with the evidence against them under the rules of due process. Only courts should have the power to establish guilt.

Democracy can never be built by undemocratic or illiberal means. History should have taught us that. The past is not only about informers, thieves and criminals but also about our indifference, selfishness and cynicism. We have to challenge the bad old habits not by lustration or anticommunist laws but by patient struggle to overcome the communist legacy of intolerance, disrespect of laws and a distrust of civil society. We need an active participation of decent teachers, journalists and politicians. To establish institutions of civil society is difficult and slow but essential. Human rights dissidents in the 1980s argued that a nascent civil society can be created if we behave as if we were already free. Today we can strengthen the existing fragile civil society by behaving as if we were already living in a fully functioning and well-established democracy. The developments of the last few years are a telling testimony to the fact that democracy in the Czech Republic is irreversible, though more time is needed for citizens to get democracy into their bloodstreams, to develop more democratic mindset and a high level of political culture to become a dominant feature of the society.

NOTES

The chapter was written in August 1984 in Amherst College, Amherst, MA and updated in December 1999, Prague.

1. For the best analysis of how the Czech lustration law violates international agreements see the Memorandum submitted by Helsinki Watch (USA) (International Helsinki Federation for Human Rights and Project on Justice in Times of Transition of the Center for Human Rights and Humanitarian Law of the Washington College of Law) to the Czechoslovak Constitutional Court in December 1992.

2. Quoted from Robert W. Gordon's lecture "Undoing Historical Injustice," delivered at Amherst College on 9 March 1994. Professor Gordon in this context commented acidly that "for all practical purposes, former membership in the Nazi party became a requirement for joining the civil service."

3. KS MV Prague [Ministry of the Interior, Prague region] report, dated 17 June 1970, states that information about me was collected since 1964 because of my student activities in a group led by Jiri Muller and Lubos Holecek. [This is stated in the "KATO" file, see below note 12]. Presidium of the Central Committee of the Communist Party approved on 8 January 1971 a list of "enemies of the state and socialism," which included my name. The list was published in *Lidove Noviny* on 28 July 1992.

4. *Mlada Fronta*, 21 January 1969; the text was written on behalf of the student union (SVS) by three student leaders Lubos Holecek [see preceding note], Karel Kovanda [currently Czech Ambassador to the UN], Jan Kavan and law lecturer Petr Pithart [Czech Premier 1990-92].

5. On 19.June 1970 Zajlcek was informed by his StB superiors that on my return to Prague I should be subjected to the same measures that are be taken against other "representatives of the right wing student movement, for example, Muller, Holecek." [Muller was sentenced to five and half years imprisonment in 1972 for his opposition activities, Holecek was killed in 1973 in a mysterious hit—and—run accident by an employee of the prosecutor's office.]

6. The Civic Forum, set up on 19 November 1989, included Charter 77 leaders such as Vaclav Havel, Jiri Dienstbier and others, representing the entire ideological spectrum of the dissident movement from Petr Uhl on the left to Vaclav Benda on the right. The dissidents were joined by technocrats, primarily from the Prognostic Institute of the Academy of Sciences, including a banking and financial expert Vaclav Klaus [the current prime minister], who was not a member of the Communist party but never incurred the party's displeasure and Vaclav Dlouhy, the head of the Communist party branch at the institute [current minister of Trade and Industry, and according to opinion polls, the most popular Czech politician]. Both Klaus and Dlouhy revealed in 1990 their pro-capitalist sympathies while another member of the same institute, Milos Zeman, displayed social democratic convictions. Representatives of the students and workers had to be included in the Civic Forum as well but, as the need for their active support diminished, their views were taken less seriously (Wheaton & Kavan 1992:127-151).

7. The charity, registered in the United Kingdom, was called the Jan Palach Information and Research Trust. Different aspects of these varied projects were supported by different U.S. foundations but for some of the work we were never able to raise sufficient funds and for other tasks, in particular translations of information about less well-known prisoners or legal documents or some essays by people other than Vaclav Havel (for example, future Foreign Minister Jiri Dienstbier, we failed to raise anything. We were therefore always struggling with debts. From that point of view the November revolution came at a most inopportune time. Firm promises of financial help were withdrawn as no longer necessary and as a result I am still burdened with a heavy debt that I am repaying, in installments, from my Czech salary in the 1990s.

8. Cooperation between the East Europeans was facilitated by the London-based East European Cultural Foundation that I was vice-president of and is described in Kavan (1988).

9. Prague Appeal (Charter 77, Document No.5/85), *Palach Press Bulletin* 26, October 1985; *East European Reporter* Vol. l, no.1, April 1985.

10. Given my British passport, place of birth in Britain, British name without any indication that it was changed by deed poll) and the Czechoslovak policy at the time not to harass bona fide hard currency tourists by any tough questions, it was virtually impossible that a routine check by passport and customs officials could reveal my true identity. Jiri Ruml and his commission acquired a notebook, which belonged to an StB officer Mr Chovanec, that— I was told by the commission's spokesperson Petr Toman— confirmed my impression that the StB discovered my trips only after I completed them all.

11. The description of the category "secret collaborator confidential contact" (TS DS) was provided to the Parliament by minister of Interior Jan Langos at the request of Petr Uhl, MP in April 1991. Petr Toman informed me that he was given the same description a day before the Commission reached its verdict. According to Article 6 of the Procedures for Intelligence Work of the State Security's Division 1, this category denotes people who do not want to collaborate with the Ministry of Interior but for ideological, patriotic, selfish or personal reasons do not refuse collaboration with other bodies of the Czechoslovak state administration. Jaroslav Basta, appointed by the Prague 7 District Court as the court's expert, stressed that this wording made the inclusion of this category into the lustration law under the category of "a conscious collaborator," who had to be aware that he was in contact with employees of the Ministry of Interior, "logical and legal nonsense." Basta also pointed out that the TS DS category was only created in 1983, while I was supposed to belong to it in 1969. See Basta's "Expert's Evaluation" submitted to the Prague court on 25 November 1993. This same information was made available to Dr. Robert P. Beschel, Jr., for his case study "Jaroslav Basta and the Difficult Case of Jan Kavan," which was published in 1995 by Project Liberty of Harvard University's John F. Kennedy School of Government.

12. Drahuse Probostova, a respected journalist and former dissident, who worked closely with me for more than twenty years submitted to Ivan Lamper, the chief editor of *Respekt*, a testimony based both on her own experience and on those of several leading dissidents, whom she specifically interviewed for the rejected article.

13. This "Jacobin" tendency is explained within the context of the youth and dissident movements before and after 1989 in Libor Konvicka and Jan Kavan, "Youth Movements and the Velvet Revolution," *Communist and Post-Communist Studies*, vol. 27, no. 2 (Butterworth Heinemann, Oxford, UK, June 1994), especially pp.166-167. The "Jacobin" metaphor became widely used to denote people who perceived the "revolution as incomplete or betrayed and desired to safeguard its continuation by a new crusade against the enemy within the revolution's own ranks.

14. Quoted by Konstanty Gebert, former Polish dissident known under the pen name of David Warszawski, in HCA dossier "What Has Happened to Us?," p.18.

15. Statement by twenty-four former dissidents, including J. Dientsbier, P. Pithart, I. Dejmal, P. Uhl, J. Siklova, and J. Sabata was released by the Czechoslovak Press Agency (CSTK) on 18 March, 1992. The reporter was Stanislav Holec.

16. Quoted from an interview with Drahuse Probostova, recorded by Mary Hrabik Samal, a US journalist and a writer, for a book on women dissidents, shortly before Probostova succumbed to cancer in August 1993.

17. The rightist ODS MPs wanted to extend the list of categories of people to whom the law would apply beyond high ranking Communist Party officials to district officials, officers of the Peoples' Militia, as well as its ordinary members and former students of some Soviet schools, and to be allowed to screen not only ministers, MPs and top civil servants but also most public officials, applicants for license to run private businesses, and so forth. They made a deal with the MPs of the liberal OH whereby the liberals

would vote for this wide extension of the screening net in exchange for the rightists' support for the preamble that would guarantee individual assessment of all the cases. The deal reached in the corridors was not binding, but a number of ODS MPs voted for the preamble which was therefore passed and then number of OH MPs voted for a longer list of categories (which passed). But at that point some of the rightists reneged on the deal and forced a new vote on the preamble, which was then defeated.

18. Case-by-case evaluation was subsequently rejected by the Constitutional Court which, ironically, concluded that: "The demand for individual assessment of the work of secret collaborators, which was submitted by the group of MPs [99 MPs signed the request to the Constitutional Court to abolish the law as unconstitutional] was, in fact, deliberately obstructed by the orders and procedures of the StB leading bodies, that is, by the deliberate destruction of almost 90 percent of all files." [In counterintelligence struggle against internal enemy only 2,189 files were found out of the original 20,337]. Ruling by the Constitutional Court of the Czech and Slovak Federative Republic No.1/92, of 26 November 1992, p. 27. The Court, at the same time, clearly believed that the remainder of the files could be trusted because the court trusted "the system of evidence and control of the agency's network, which was unequivocally laid down and confirmed by testimonies of witnesses." Constitutional Court Ruling, op. cit. p. 26. It may be important to recall that the judges were appointed by the Parliament for a short seven-year term and, as leading U.S. lawyers warned, "the possibility of reappointment could well lead to the judges' excessive dependence on the political bodies that appoint and reappoint them." Quoted from paper excerpted from "Constitutional Reform in Czechoslovakia—E Duobus Unum?" by Lloyd Cutler and Herman Schwartz, presented by Lloyd Cutler at a conference on Western Assistance to East-Central Europe, held in Bardejov, Slovakia, June 1991, p.30.

19. One estimate by Roman Zelenay, former Slovak chairman of the Chamber of Nations of the Federal Assembly [killed in a car accident, 1993] was that "at least 16,000 top-level agents were not listed in any registers." Engelberg' "The Velvet Revolution Turns Rough," *The New York Times Magazine*, 31 May, 1992, *supra* note 9 at p.49. The Czechoslovak Constitutional Court also acknowledged that former General Prosecutor Dr. J. Setina submitted to it evidence of collaboration with the StB of persons not formally registered in the StB archives. Constitutional Court, *op. cit.* p. 23. Similarly, for example, in Poland, former Prime Minister Jan Olszewski argued that there were agents who were so important that it was too risky to let their files be handled by the employees of the archives.

20. This reversal of my lustration within 48 hours compelled some politicians to compare my case with that of Dreyfus. "This is a state performance, where everything is turned upside down, only in order to defend the already taken decision. It was the same in the Dreyfus' case in France" said Lawrence Weschler interviewed by Karel Jezdinsky, Radio Free Europe, New York, 22 October, 1992.

21. This fact was given by the Constitutional Court as its main reason for abolishing Article 2C of the lustration law. See Constitutional Court Ruling, pp. 30-35.

22. This private meeting in a public restaurant in the center of Prague was arranged by Petr Uhl and attended also by his wife, Anna Sabatova, former Charter 77 spokesperson. Havel confirmed the intended public impact of the meeting with "a positively lustrated MP" in the above mentioned interview with Michnik.

23. My StB "Kato" file refers to my "very thick file in the possession of Division 2" [counterintelligence] where I was treated as a "person hostile to the state". A Ministry of Interior official informed me that the file was destroyed, together with many others, in

December 1989, probably to protect StB agents assigned to try to cover my activities until December 1989.

24. Quoted from President Vaclav Havel's speech delivered in court in response to charges of libel submitted by Petr Cibulka, chief editor of *Necenzurovane Noviny*. The full text was published as "Trvam na tom, ze zverejnenl seznamu udajnych spolupracov-niku StB zpusobilo cetne tragedie" [I maintain that the publication of the list of alleged StB collaborators caused numerous tragedies], *Rude Pravo*, 15 December, 1993. Cibulka's list contained 150,000 names of the people accused of cooperation with the StB. Some 365,000 citizens who have kept positions under "The Lustration Act" have been checked (lustrated). 10,950 (3% of total number) have been lustrated with positive record. 656 out of those 10,950 appealed to the court and won their lawsuits against the Ministry of the Interior. The Ministry won 65 lawsuits (10 percent).

25. International covenants on political and civil rights and on social, economic and cultural rights were ratified by Czechoslovakia and became a part of its own legal code (as Law 52, No.120/1976) in November 1976. The hypocrisy of this move helped to give birth to the human rights movement (Charter 77), which demanded that the communist government fulfills its legal obligations and respect the two covenants. In 1991 the Czechoslovak Parliament elevated them, together with the European Convention on Human Rights and some other international covenants dealing with human rights, to the highest level in the country, even above the constitution. The Czech Parliament, two years later, reduced them to the level of the constitution but still kept them superior to other ordinary legislation.

REFERENCES

Bower, Tom. 1983. *Blind Eye to Murder. Britain, America and the Purging of Nazi German—A Pledge Betrayed*. London, UK: Granada Publishing.

Dengler , Robert. 1992. Davam v sfizku svou cest [I place my honor at stake]. Interview with Uhl, Petr. *Rude Pravo* (2 April).

Dolezal, Jiri X. 1991(April). "I Politicke procesy budou!!!" [There will be political trials] *Forum*, 15.

Gordon, Robert W. 1994. Undoing Historical Injustice. Lecture delivered at Amherst College on 9 March.

Havel, Vaclav. 1985. *The Power of the Powerless, Citizens against the State in Central-Eastern Europe*. London, UK: Hutchinson (copyright Palach Press).

Havel, Vaclav. 1990. New Year Day's Speech (translation by Jan & Lesley Cullk) *East European Reporter, 1* (Winter), 56.

Havel, Vaclav. 1991. Letni Premltanf [Summer Reflections]. *Odeon, 4*, 100.

Havel, Vaclav. 1993. Trvam na tom, ze zverejnenl seznamu udajnych spolupracovniku StB zpusobilo cetne tragedie [I maintain that the publication of the list of alleged StB collaborators caused numerous tragedies]. *Rude Pravo* (15 December) [Havel's 1993 court speech].

Helsinki Watch (USA). 1992. Memorandum, International Helsinki Federation for Human Rights and Project on Justice in Times of Transition of the Center for Human Rights and Humanitarian Law of the Washington College of Law to the Czechoslovak Constitutional Court, December.

Homolka, Lubos. 1992. Interview with Jan Lagos. *Smer* (7 April), 3.

Interview with Vaclaw Havel. 1991. *Gazeta Wyborcza* (1 December), 2.

Kavan, Jan. 1988a. From the Prague Spring to a Long Winter. In Jiri Pehe (ed.), *The Prague Spring: A Mixed Legacy* (pp. 120-127). New York: Freedom House.

Kavan , Jan. [paul Edwards, pseudonym]. 1988b. Why East and East Must Meet. Interview with Vaclav Havel. *East European Reporter*, *3*, 2.

Kavan, Jan. 1991. Inside Parliament. *Prague Post* (10 October), 2.

Kayal, Michele. 1993. The Unfinished Revolution: The Czech Republic's Press in Transition. In James M.Cox, Jr., (ed.), *Creating a Free Press in Eastern Europe*. Athens, GA: Center for International Mass Communications, Training and Research, College of Journalism & Mass Communications, The University of Georgia.

Kuras, Benjamin. 1991a. Operace Delta. *Respekt*, *33*, 8.

Kuras, Benjamin. 1991b. Poslanci a presumpce neviny [Parliamentarians and the presumption of innocence]. *Respekt, 11*, 1.

Kuras, Benjamin. 1992. Kavan-KATO, Tajny spolupracovnik-Duvernystyk [Kavan-KATO, Secret collaborator-confidential contact]. *Respekt, 9*, 5-6.

Laber, Jeri. 1992. Witch Hunt in Prague. *The New York Review of Books* (5-8 April), 23.

Law Concerning the Illegitimacy of the Communist Regime. 1993. Prague.

Michnik, Adam. 1990. *Liberation*, Paris, France.

Michnik, Adam. 1991. Interview with Vaclav Havel. *Gazeta Wyborcza* (1 December), 1.

Mink, George & Jean-Charles Szurek. 1993. Strategy of Adaptation and Conversion of Former Communist Elites. *Sociologicky Csopis, 29*, 295- 308.

Mitchell, Mitch. 1992. Ex-Dissidents Dissent on Kavan-Bashing. *Prague Post* (30 March), 1-2.

Nagorski, Andrew. 1991. A Witch Hunt. *Newsweek* (14 October) [quote of Petr Toman].

Palous, Martin. 1993. Bez pameti a svedomi [Without a memory and a conscience]. In *Co se s nami stalo?* [What Has Happened to Us?], a dossier of contributions to a seminar on lustrations organized by the Citizen's Assembly in the Czech Republic (HCA) and the Czechoslovak Helsinki Committee in Prague, 21 November 1992. Prague: HCA, pp. 25-26.

Pelikan, Jiri. 1971. *The Czechoslovak Political Trials, 1950-1954: The Suppressed Report of the Dubcek Government's Commission of Inquiry*. (Translated by Rosemary Kavan). Stanford, CA: Stanford University Press.

Premier haji dissent [The Premier defends dissent]. 1992. *Metropolitan* (22 March) (extensive interview with Petr Pithart).

President Mandela Appeal for National Reconciliation. 1994. *New York Times* (11 May), A8.

Probostova, Drahuse. 1992. Interviewed with Jaroslav Basta. *Rude Pravo*, Prace, Prague, 29 October.

Prorok, Roman. 1992. Interview with Jan Lagos. *CSTK Report*, 27 February.

Sustrova, Petruska. 1992. The Lustration Controversy. *Uncaptive Minds, 5* (Summer), 132.

Vysatova, Romana. 1993. *Jaroslav Basta and the Difficult Case of Jan Kavan*. Report prepared by Dr. Robert P. Beschel Jr., for Project Liberty at Harvard University's John F. Kennedy School of Government.

Waller, Michael. 1994. Delay NATO Expansion—But for the Right Reason. *The Wall Street Journal*, 10 January.

Weigel, George. 1992. Their Lustration—And Ours. *Commentary, 94* (October).

Wheaton, Bernard & Zdenek Kavan. 1992. *The Velvet Revolution, Czechoslovakia 1988-1991*. Boulder, CO: Westview Press.

Zeman, Milos. 1991. Nase post-totalitnl krize a jej mozna vychodiska [Our post-totalitarian crisis and its possible solutions]. *Alternativy* (Fall).

3

The Contribution of Collective Protests to the Softening of Communist Regimes in East Central Europe

Barbara Wejnert

An examination of the potential of the "powerless" can be only begun with an examination of the nature of power in the circumstances in which these powerless people operate

—Vaclav Havel
The Power of the Powerless (1985, p.25)

Democratic transition in the former communist-bloc countries reopened scholarly dispute comparing the relative predictability of political transformations by the changes in global, international climate versus each country's internal conditions. Some researchers emphasized macropolitical and economic context assuming the impact of international circumstances on democratic reforms, whereas others focus more on domestic conditions of grass-root political mobilization and reformation from above by a state mechanism.

Although it is generally recognized that political change is an outcome of multifactorial rather than unitary influences, the goal of this discussion is to focus on domestic conditions with specific emphasis on differences among East Central European countries in the strength of anti-communist collective protests and the strength of regimes that may have affected the temporal rate of transitions from the communist system. Using data on indicators of political mobilization in East Central Europe between the end of 1940s and 1982 from the *World Handbook of Political and Social Indicators* (Taylor & Jodice 1982), data from the *World Polity III* (Jaggers & Gurr 1995) and *Cross-Nation Indicators of Liberal Democracy, 1950-1990* (Bollen 1998) supported by the description of democratic transition in 1989-1990, I hypothesize that during the Soviet era: (1) there were visible differences in the degree of mobilization of political opposition among countries of East Central Europe, (2) frequent changes in the top

governmental positions were a consequence of the mobilization of political opposition, (3) changes among the top political cadre contributed to the weakening
of the regimes, and hence, (4) countries that had a stronger tradition of collective protests sooner shed off their communist governments.

In this chapter, I first present an overview of the international and domestic
factors that contributed to democratic transition in East Central Europe, and
then, concentrating on domestic conditions, I analyze interactions between collective protests and regimes' weakening.

THE CONTRIBUTION OF INTERNATIONAL FACTORS TO DEMO-CRATIC TRANSITION IN EAST CENTRAL EUROPE

According to some researchers, democratic reforms in East Central Europe can
only be understood within the framework of external, global conditions, because
these conditions would have a permissive effect on the influences of domestic
conditions in communist states (Banac 1992; Bunce 1990; Jowitt 1992; Szelenyi
1992). For instance, changes in international relations and international political
circumstances intensified exposure to principles of freedom and equality, and to
the existence of economic co-dependency in the world. Thus, the international
political and economic trends influenced the economy and politics of each
former communist country lighting a path for transition from communism; for
example, Gorbachev's politics (Bunce 1990; Holmes 1997); East-West détente
(Banac 1992; Burawoy & Lukacs 1992; Pridham 1990); the snowballing affect
of world-wide democratization (Huntington 1991); expansion of global
communication system's (Huntington 1991); and shifts in world hegemons
(Wallerstein 1991). These international factors were viewed as permissive in
nature modulating the degree to which domestic conditions could express
themselves and exert an influence on an existing authoritarian regime (Pridham
1990; Schwartzman 1998).

At the most general level, transformation in global political and economic
conditions during the second half of the twentieth century stimulated democratic
movements, which, in turn, rapidly sensitized the masses and political dissidents
to democratic ideas. Furthermore, international conditions supported communist
regimes and members of communist governments in their attempts to initiate
democratic reforms.

Particularly important as a permissive or disinhibitory factor on domestic
forces were Gorbachev's policies, because these policies reduced significantly
the degree of threat and control exerted by the central authoritarian power in the
Soviet bloc. For example, in January 1987 during a Central Committee Plenum
to discuss progress on reforms in the Soviet Union, Gorbachev introduced a new
slogan into the reform debate, *dimocratizatsia*, by which he meant competition
among candidates during elections and elections by secret ballot. After disapproval by the Party hierarchy, Gorbachev quickly withdrew from this radical
stance. But it was too late: The introduction of democratic concepts had already
occurred, and it underlined future political statements by Gorbachev. Thus,

when in 1988 the Polish Communist Party requested that the Central Committee of the Soviet Communist Party assist them in an anti-Solidarity campaign, Gorbachev restated the need for leniency toward democratic movements in Eastern Europe (Zakowski 1991). Sedaitis and Butterfield (1991) suggest that it was the Gorbachev era opportunity structure that improved chances for imposition of political and economic reforms in communist countries. Holmes argues that Gorbachev's criticism of socialism and his own proposed reforms, "helped to undermine the legitimacy of communists everywhere" (1997, p. 26). Political liberalization in the Soviet Union and the Gorbachev era were, then, precipitating factors that led to a breakdown of authoritarian regimes in former communist states (Bunce 1990).

Regimes of East Central Europe were also vulnerable to fluctuations of interest and support provided to communist allies by the Soviet Union. The "compromised integrity of the communist Moloch was exacerbated by the dependence of the East European communist parties on a powerful but capricious Soviet Union that provided their political and economic livelihood" (Bunce 1989:235). For instance, as a result of Gorbachev's policies and of Gorbachev's critical speech of April 1987 (which legitimized the independence of all Communist parties and called for reforms throughout the bloc), several Communist parties replaced their top political executives. In Czechoslovakia, Husak was replaced by Milos Jakes as general secretary of the Party in December 1987; in Hungary, the relative hard-liner Karoly Grosz, leader of the Communist party from 1956, replaced Janos Kadar. With these changes communist regimes began to be perceived to be in a weakened state; this weakness created difficulties in implementing policies and signaled an increasing incapability to exercise political power (Banac 1992; Havel 1985; Sedaitis & Butterfield 1991; Szelenyi 1992).

In addition to Gorbachev's policies changes in the international political sphere provided opportunities to initiate democratic reforms in communist countries. Among such factors were peace movements in Western Europe (Rochon 1988), East-West economic and political détente, and more open Soviet-American relations, promoted by the Gorbachev effect, that broadened cooperation between the two superpowers (Bunce 1990). Particularly influential was global economic development and the economic need of the Soviet-bloc countries to collaborate with Western democracies. For example, the organization of the European Community (EC), as well as the elimination of the politics of separate East and West European economies within the framework of trading relations, channeled the merging of East Central Europe and the Soviet Union into a capitalistic world (Harris 1997; Lovenduski & Woodall 1987). Some of the communist countries became successful rivals of industries in the capitalist world market, and complemented capitalistic economies as subcontractors (e.g., Hungary, German Democratic Republic, and Poland) and as producers of raw materials and agriculture products indirectly demanded by the world market (e.g., Asian regions of the Soviet Union) (Kulluk 1993). At the end of the 1980s, the reunification of Germany became a critical issue in Western politics (Graf, Hansen & Schulz 1987). Thus, a combination of international events, led perhaps by the strong permissive effect of Gorbachev's politics but supported by other ideological and philosophical trends, and an increasing hegemony of Western economic systems, coalesced and to different degrees coincided with the expression of domestic forces in East Central European countries.

THE CONTRIBUTION OF DOMESTIC CONDITIONS TO DEMOCRATIC TRANSITIONS IN EAST CENTRAL EUROPE

Overview

Internal socio-political structures, differentially affecting each country's readiness for incorporation of democratic reforms also heavily influenced the 1989-1990 transitions toward democracy in East Central Europe. Domestic conditions of either weakening political regimes associated with development of political opposition and grass roots collective protests (Sedatis & Butterfield 1991, Tarrow 1991a, 1991b), or broader opportunity for open parliamentary negotiation which shifted the source of changes from collective protests to state-based influence (Bruszt & Stark 1991; DeSoto & Anderson 1993; Stark 1992, 1996) allowed for the introduction of democratic reforms. On one hand, democratic mobilization would be seen as influencing communist regimes' readiness and agreeability to accept political and economic reform. On the other, the state would be seen as an agent that, although influenced by the society that surrounds it, shapes social and political processes, thereby influencing political cleavages and collective action (DeSoto & Anderson 1993; Evans, Rueschemeyer & Skocpol 1985; Kitchelt 1986).

The most important domestic factors were a weakening of the ruling elite and their illegitimacy, economic crisis and deteriorating living conditions. Accordingly, analyses of the transformation of East Central Europe from communism to some form of democratic system uncovered *political, economic* and *social processes* that were already present and embedded in those societies, and that challenged in different ways the weakening communist regimes (Bunce 1990; Havel 1985, 1988; Janos 1970).

Contribution of Political Processes

As the literature suggests, two political processes—*regimes' liberalization* and *dissidents' activity*, were among the most influential contributors to post-communist transitions (Dahl 1991; Tarrow 1991a). Despite popular notions about the authoritarian, repressive nature of communist regimes, these regimes varied in the degree of their liberalization and in their attitudes toward political opposition (Bunce 1990; Przeworski 1991; Wejnert 1988). It is believed that the variability in the degree of liberalization was partly due to internal conflicts and divisions that plagued the authoritarian power of Communist parties (Banac 1992; Havel 1985). Thus, on the basis of qualitative assessment, compared to

Poland and Hungary, Czechoslovakia and East Germany were two of the more hard-line Stalinist countries (Bunce 1990), while the Yugoslavian regime was considered to be one of the the the most liberal (Vodopivec 1992; Woodward 1995). The more liberal regimes were less punitive toward the developing civil society and its democratic mobilization, thus themselves setting up more suitable conditions for a transition from communism. At the same time, the regimes that were perceived as strong, measured for example by the severity of sanctions against political opponents, prevented or significantly limited grass-root actions aimed at democratic reforms; for example, the Ceausescu regime in Romania and the Brezniev regime in former Soviet Union (Beck 1993; Bunce 1990). The degree of liberalization could be considered the foundation for potential development of collective protests.

Organized networks of political dissidents and their antigovernment activity constituted another set of determinants of communist regimes' agreeability to accept democratic reforms (Marody 1991; Opp & Gern 1993; Zakowski 1991). Indeed, Tarrow (1991a, 1991b) has proposed that political changes may be viewed as a wave of mobilization of collective action in response to generally expanding political opportunities, which lower the costs and risks of collective action yet secure higher potential gains. Evolving grass root mobilization strengthened political opposition, thus helping in the enactment of democratic reforms. The 1980s violent and non-violent protest demonstrations and ethnic conflicts constituted the foundation of social and political changes in the former Soviet Union (Beissinger, 1990), accounting for *perestroika from below* (Sedaitis & Butterfield 1991). From this perspective, the political changes in Eastern Europe could be seen as consequences of waves of mobilization for collective action that were present in those countries prior to the beginning of democratic initiatives (Tarrow 1998). What was most threatening to authoritarian regimes, then, was not the breakdown of legitimacy, since this process started prior to the 1989 reforms, but "the organization of counterhegemony: collective projects for an alternative future" (Przeworski 1991:54).

Contribution of Social and Economic Processes

Several investigators have emphasized the impact of development in Eastern Europe and the economic situation of the 1970s and 1980s on the formation of democratic movements (Huntington 1991; Przeworski 1991; Sanford 1992; Stark & Bruszt 1998). Increasing industrialization, urbanization and literacy levels contradicted the economic crises, poor living conditions and poverty, leading to growing public awareness of social inequalities and economic deprivation, and setting nations on the path to demand democratic reforms. The unequal distribution of scarce goods and benefits that was magnified by social inequalities and special privileges of the ruling elite, abused the psychological state of citizens. Eventually, such conditions awakened a psychological need for freedom from authoritarian repression (Goldfarb 1991; Vladislaw 1987), or, as is put in the poetic words of Vaclav Havel, "communism exhausted itself, had proven to be inhuman, its dream of utopia fully dissipated and bankrupt" (Havel 1988:42). Eastern European democratization, thus, had its roots in despair and an awakening imperative for change that would guarantee social equality and social freedoms (Havel 1988), a view congruent with Dahl's (1989) concept of citizens' frustration taking a form of public opposition to monocratic regimes.

A parsimonious account of pre-transitional economic conditions in East Central Europe was presented by Stark and Bruszt (1998). Comparing changes in several Soviet-bloc countries, authors described various paths of extrication from monocratic state socialism. Depending on the geopolitical and economic situation, the paths produced differences in the institutional outcomes of the 1990s transitions. Analysis of the democratization processes of the former Soviet-bloc, conducted by students of global democratization theory, emphasized such domestic social economic factors as an increase in literacy level and mass communication made it difficult to withhold from the general public information about democracy (Huntington 1991; Markoff 1996), and the development of a middle class *intelligencia* that was more likely to sense democratic principle (Rueschmeyer, Stephens & Stephens 1992).

From the broad spectrum of domestic determinants I have selected two factors in order to assess their contribution to and affect on the democratization processes in East Central Europe. Those factors are a) the strength of *political opposition* and b) the strength and harshness of *communist regimes*. I hypothesize that the interaction between the former and the latter significantly determine the potential and the feasibility of democratization processes in East Central European countries. Taken together, these factors serve as an indicator of domestic agreeability to political change signaling the development of a political opposition, its preparation to overthrow communist rulers, the availability of educated leaders to direct an alternative government, and the degree of punitiveness and stability that symbolize the strength of communist regimes.

THE SOFTENING OF POLITICAL REGIMES AS A FUNCTION OF AN INCREASING DEMOCRATIC MOBILIZATION

The strength of political opposition most frequently is measured as a function of a few conducive components: (a) the organization of strikes and anti-regime demonstrations, (b) the organization of anti-regime protest actions, (c) the organization of *coup detat*, (d) development of dissident organizations, and (e) education of kindred-spirit through alternative schooling and samizdat books (Jepperson 1991; Opp & Gern 1993; Szelenyi 1991; Wejnert 1988). Similarly, the strength and harshness of a political regime most generally can be indexed to the stability of the ruling elite, its irreplaceability and its control over societal life; and the severity of prosecution of political opposition (see Figure 3.1).

More specifically, the strength of regime is a function of the following variables: (a) the length and number of terms the same elite has served in political offices; (b) the scope and depth of control over activities of members of society, for example, by the exertion of censorship and control over media; (c) the severity of sanctions issued against members of the political opposition; and (d) the number of political prosecutions (Dahl 1990; Held 1987; Migdal 1988).

Figure 3.1
A Framework for Conceptual Organization of the Effects of the Diverse Variables Represented in the Process of Transition to Democracy

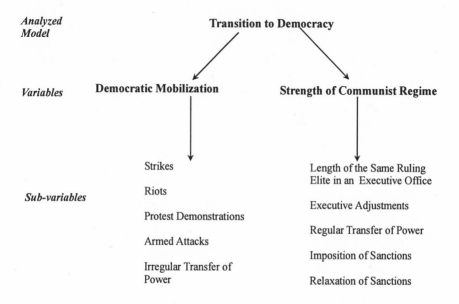

Analyzed Model	**Transition to Democracy**	
Variables	**Democratic Mobilization**	**Strength of Communist Regime**
Sub-variables	Strikes Riots Protest Demonstrations Armed Attacks Irregular Transfer of Power	Length of the Same Ruling Elite in an Executive Office Executive Adjustments Regular Transfer of Power Imposition of Sanctions Relaxation of Sanctions

My hypothesis is that, in countries of the former Soviet-bloc the organization of protest actions, strikes and demonstrations, supported by an erosion of authoritarian power, are indicators of the growing strength of political opposition that, in turn, leads to the softening of communist regimes and determines their aggreeability to democratic changes.

METHODS AND DATA

To test the above hypothesis I employ qualitative and statistical analyses of indicators of political changes in East Central Europe collected from Taylor and Jodice (1982), Jaggers and Gurr (1996) and Bollen (1998). The literature suggests that the variable of *democratic mobilization* can be measured by sub-categories of mobilization, such as strikes, demonstrations, riots and sit-ins (e.g., Tarrow 1989, Turner & Killian 1987). For the purpose of this analysis I selected strikes, riots, protest demonstrations, armed attack aimed at the existing regime and irregular transfer of political power associated with violence (e.g., *coups d'etat*). Moreover, each category of variable was weighted according to the degree of organization of a particular action for the announced purpose of protesting against the established regime and the degree of violence associated with the collective protests. The weights of each variable were determined using the literature (Gamson 1990; Miller 1985; Morris & Meuller 1992; Tarrow 1989; Turner & Killian 1987) and the description of variables included in Taylor and Hudson's *World Handbook of Political and Social Indicators* (1972). Hence, each collective protest action was assigned a scalable, weighted rating. Once the scales were defined, each country was assessed on the same attribute rating scales to estimate the degree to which that country's political opposition was mobilized in terms of organized grass roots protest actions.

Furthermore, using literature describing the degree of regimes' liberalization (Bermeo 1991; Burton, Gunther & Higley 1992; Dahl 1982, 1998; Doyle 1983; Migdal 1988), I measured the *strength of each Communist regime* using sub-variables of the length and number of terms the same elite served in political offices, executive adjustments within the same elite, regular transfer of political power from one political group to another via conventional legal or customary procedures (e.g., elections), and the imposition and relaxation of sanctions for political activity. The description of these variables is provided in the appendix.

In a manner similar to that used in measuring political mobilization, the degree of a regimes' strength was assessed using assigned scalable, weighted ratings as determined by an analysis of variables provided in the *World Handbook* (Taylor & Hudson 1972) and by an analysis of relevant literature (Evans, Higley & Gunther 1992; Held 1987; Migdal 1988). The weights were assigned according to the degree of liberalization of a regimes' policy toward political opponents and scope of changes in the top executive positions. Once the scales were defined, each country was assessed on the same scale to estimate the degree of strength of political regimes.

I observed the influence of democratic mobilization on the strength of communist regimes from the time of their solidification (which is somewhat later than origination) at the end of 1940s until 1990, and assessed the association among those variables across different countries of East Europe using data from Taylor and Jodice (1982) supported by *World Polity* data (for years 1948-1982) and data from Bollen (for years 1982-1990).

To test whether the differences in the degree of democratic mobilization and the degree of strength of communist regimes are statistically significant, I used the t-test for the communist regimes and democratic mobilization variables for countries that introduced democratic transition first (i.e., Poland and Czechoslovakia), and last (i.e., Romania and Albania). Next, using cross-lagged correlation I examined whether the predictability of introducing democratic changes was higher when influenced by variables of communist regime (e.g., political sanctions, frequent changes in governmental offices) or when influenced by democratic mobilization (e.g., a mobilized grass roots activity).

FINDINGS

Figure 3.2 shows the number of collective protests that were organized in various East Central European countries from 1948 through 1982. Clearly, there is substantial diversity among the countries of East Central Europe in the degree of democratic mobilization, expressed by various forms of collective protests. The countries that experienced active political opposition during communist rule, indicating the development of strong mobilization, were Poland, Czechoslovakia and Hungary, while in the remaining states of Bulgaria, Albania and Romania few political protests of substance were organized. A different situation existed in East Germany, where active political opposition accelerated in the beginning of the 1950s; this opposition was a result of the forceful establishment of the communist system in the Eastern part of Germany prior to the solicitation of communism (Graf, Hansen & Schulz 1993; Lovenduski & Woodall 1987; Naimark, 1991). In Yugoslavia, on the other hand, the regime's policy of self- management and openness toward Western countries successfully suppressed democratic mobilization until the end of the 1970s (Gligorov 1992).

Data on the number of protest demonstrations, the most frequently organized collective protests (see Figure 3.3), stress even further the diversity of strength of political opposition in Eastern European countries. It also provides additional documentation of the strength of Polish, Hungarian and Czechoslovakian political opposition, as compared to the weakness of opposition in Albania, Bulgaria and Romania.

The strengthening of political dissident groups had a strong impact on the stability of the political regimes of East Europe. This is shown in Figure 3.4, which illustrates the correlation between executive regime adjustments and democratic mobilization for each former communist country from the establishment of the communist system (the end of 1940s) through the post-Solidarity period (1982), that is, when a network for diffusion of democracy was established and chances for democratization increased (Wejnert 2001) until the beginning of post-communist period (1990).

Contrary to popular belief in the irreplaceability of authoritarian regimes and their immunity to influences of dissident groups, the data depict the regimes' susceptibility to leverage and challenge by political opponents. Such a covariation is especially visible in states experiencing significant uprisings in the post-World War II era, where executive adjustments closely vary with the emergence of protest actions. This was certainly the case in Poland, which was the first country to initiate democratic changes. Here, prior to 1989, communist rulers frequently were forced to shuffle party *aparatchics* [privileged political elite) and to transfer party officials from one position to another (see Figure 3.4). As a result of worker protests in 1956, 1970 and 1976, student uprisings in 1968, and the national Solidarity movement in 1980-1981, the Polish Communist party was repeatedly forced to make policy changes and personnel replacements in top political positions.

Figure 3.2
Mean Values of Collective Protests in East Central European Countries per Year, 1948-1982

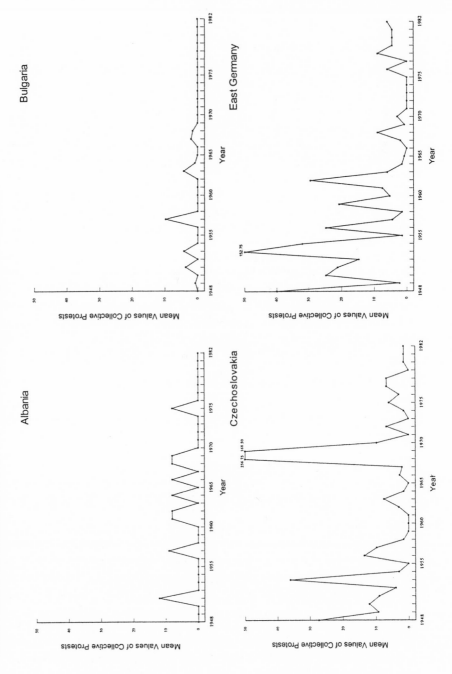

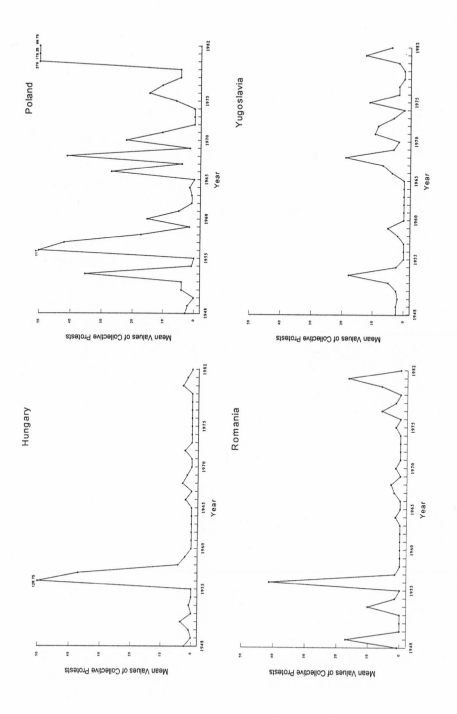

**Figure 3.3
Yearly Number of Demonstrations in East Central European Countries, 1948-1982**

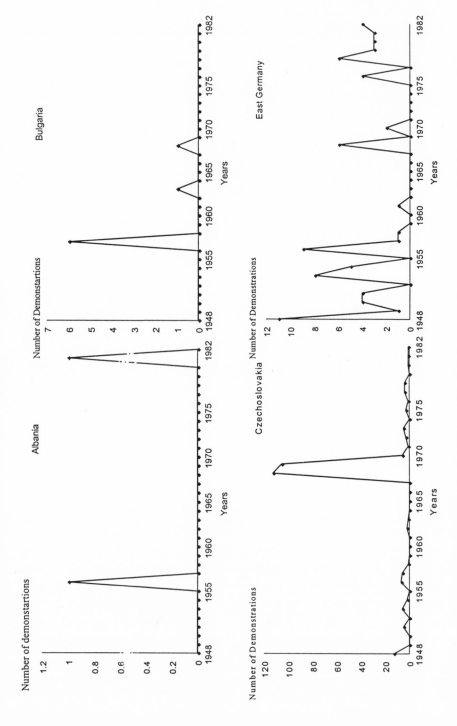

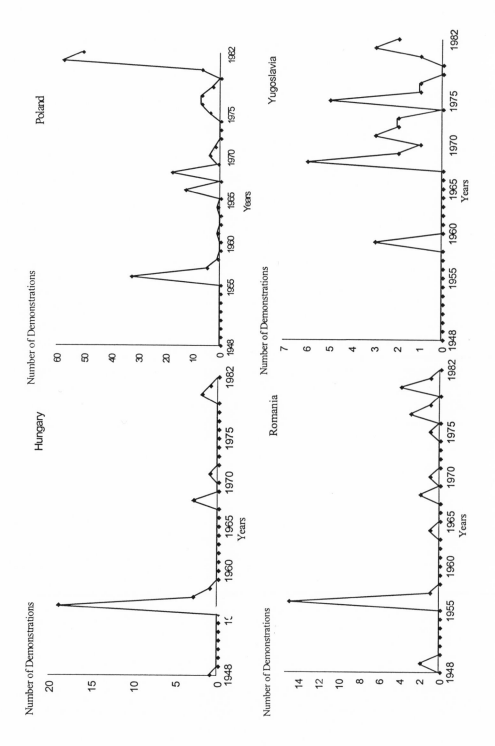

Figure 3.4
Number of Regime Adjustments as a Function of Collective Protests in East Central European Countries, 1948-1982

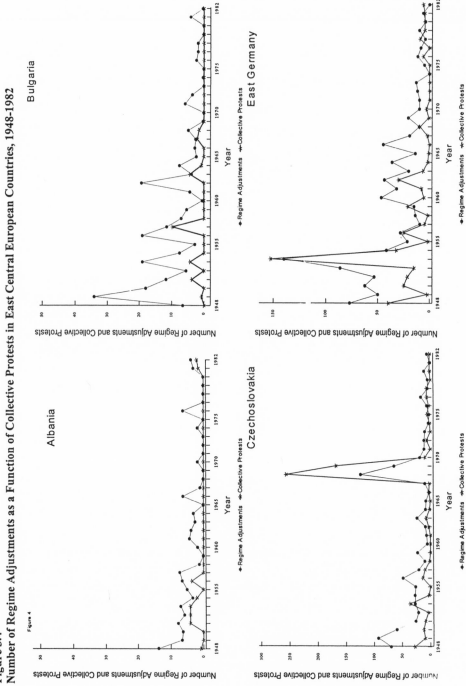

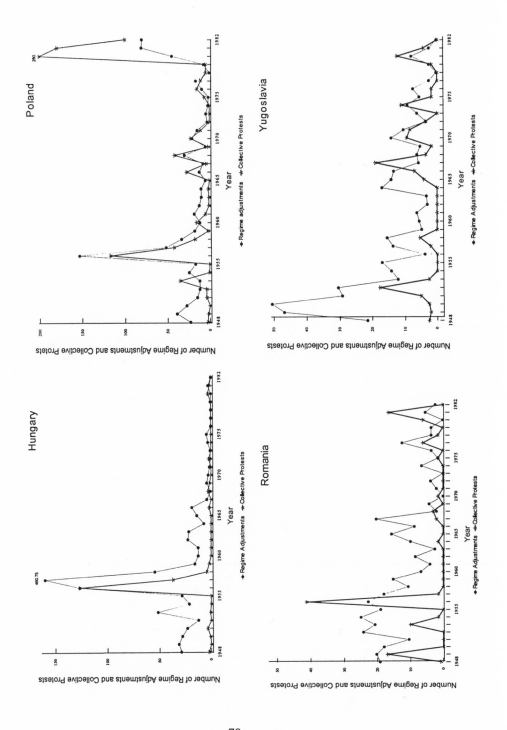

79

Similarly in Czechoslovakia (see Figure 3.4), the Prague Spring of 1968 ended with a brief victory when party reformer Alexander Dubcek assumed political leadership. After a brutal Soviet intervention, other communist hard-liners, Antonin Novotny and Gustav Husak, replaced the Stalinists Klement Gottwald and Antonin Zapotocky that occupied the leadership positions in the Communist party before Dubcek's appointment. Although changes within political regimes can be observed in all East European countries, in countries that experienced major political opposition (see Figure 3.2: Poland and Czechoslovakia) the number of executive adjustments is much higher. The masses took advantage of regime instability by organizing grass roots protests. "It is not accidental, therefore, that periods of elite instability also tended to be periods of mass instability in Eastern Europe" (Bunce 1990:405). Such a situation not only weakened the strength of the ruling elite but also strengthened the power of dissident groups pondering the replacement of communist politicos by other elite. Consequently, suitable conditions for democratic change had begun to stabilize. Thus, the strength of political opposition was related to the strength of the existing political regime or, put differently, to a regime's vulnerability to political and economic reforms. Furthermore, the weakening communist regimes perpetuated development of democratic mobilization adding to their destabilization.

Although changes within political regimes can be observed in all East European countries, in countries that experienced major political opposition (see Figure 3.2: Poland and Czechoslovakia) the number of executive adjustments is much higher. The masses took advantage of regime instability by organizing grass roots protests. "It is not accidental, therefore, that periods of elite instability also tended to be periods of mass instability in Eastern Europe" (Bunce 1990:405). Such a situation not only weakened the strength of the ruling elite but also strengthened the power of dissident groups pondering the replacement of communist politicos by other elite. Consequently, suitable conditions for democratic change had begun to stabilize. Thus, the strength of political opposition was related to the strength of the existing political regime or, put differently, to a regime's vulnerability to political and economic reforms. Furthermore, the weakening communist regimes perpetuated development of democratic mobilization adding to their own destabilization.

It seems, as well, that the weakening of political regimes, indexed by the number of executive adjustments, transfers of power and relaxation of sanctions, and increasing strength of political opposition groups jointly influence the *temporal rate* at which a society experiences democratic change (see Figure 3. 4 and Table 3.1). For instance, Poland experienced the most frequent and substantive political strikes and anti-communist demonstrations among East European countries, thereby building a network and structure of dissident groups, and gaining experience in the organization of democratic movements. Hungary, Czechoslovakia, and East Germany had a smaller but still substantial number of political strikes and demonstrations.

The democratic transition emerged first in Poland, followed by Czechoslovakia and Hungary, while East European countries lacking dissident activity fell behind. For example, Romanian and Albanian opposition was created after democratic transition took place in most of the former communist Eastern Europe (Beck 1993). Moreover, in the aftermath of transition the communist states that lacked political opposition networks did not have an alternative political elite and, thus, communist rulers were succeeded by ex-communists who renamed themselves as social democrats (e.g., Bulgaria and Romania) (see Table 3.1). Whereas in states with well-developed political opposition communist political elite were replaced by coalitions between the political opposition and the ex-communists (see Table 3.1).

Table 3.1

Democratic Transition by East European Countries

Country	Date of Transition from Communism	Year of Democratic Mobilization	Time & Type of Opposition Movement	Type of Post-Communist Government
Poland	6/1989	1956, 1968, 1970, 1976, 1980-1981	6/1976- KOR 8/1980-Solidarity	Coalition: Solidarity & ex-communists
Czechoslovakia	9-10/1989	1968	1977-Charter 77	Coalition: Civic Forum & ex-communists
Hungary	8-9/1989	1956	Kadar's reformers	Communist reformers
East Germany	10-11/1989 (with German unification)	1953	9/1989-New Forum	Unification with West Germany
Bulgaria	12/1989-6/1990	no major movement	4/1989-Podkrepa	Ex-communists
Yugoslavia	11/1989 state disintegration	no major movement		Separate governments for each new state
Romania	12/1989-1/1990	1970 small scale miner's protests		Ex-communists
Albania	2/1990	no major movement		Ex-communists

As shown in Table 3.1, the difference in temporal rate of democratic transition between Poland and Romania or Albania was approximately one year. The statistical significance of this difference was tested by a student's t test, in which political protests and executive adjustment for each of those two sets of countries were summed across years and compared. These comparisons are clear: Poland-Czechoslovakia is characterized by significantly greater political protest actions ($t=4.75$, $p<.01$, 2-tailed) and changes in executive positions ($t=3.91$, $p<.01$, 2-tailed) than Romania.

This supports the premise that the preexistence of strong political mass movements was one of the strong determinants of the temporal rate of democratic transition. Importantly, when the existence of strong opposition coincided with instability, conflict, and frequent personnel shuffling within the communist regime, democratic reforms also occurred more quickly (e.g., as in Poland), and often the country became an initiator of diffusion of democracy (Wejnert 1993) and a model within a block of countries (Kolodko 1996, 2000).

Mere observation of Figure 3.4 is not completely adequate to determine whether political protests predict executive adjustments or vice versa. This question can be addressed by use of cross-lagged correlational analysis. In this analysis, the number of political protests per unit of time (per quarter of a year) is correlated with the number of executive adjustments per quarter, where the latter variable is lagged by one or more quarters to see if protests predict (correlate with) subsequent time periods of executive adjustments. The *best* time-lag association is shown by the highest correlation coefficient. The analysis is then reversed, with executive adjustments predicting protests that are now time lagged. Comparison of the magnitude of correlations across the two versions of analysis indicates the better prediction model (i.e., the higher coefficients indicating the better prediction scheme).

Table 3.2
Cross-Lag Correlations Between the Number of Political Protests and Number of Executive Adjustments for East Central European Countries+

Number of Lags++	P	C	EG	H	Y	A	B	R
			Protests Predicting Adjustments					
1	06	41***	04	06	10	04	05	05
2	23**	11	11	04	06	10	11	12
3	04	19*	15	06	08	05	06	11
4	05	19*	07	08	05	05	00	08
5	03	02	08	03	11	05	00	07

Number of Lags	P	C	EG	H	Y	A	B	R
			Executive Adjustments Predicting Protests					
1	04	03	04	04	03	05	09	06
2	13	14	04	00	01	10	14	01
3	14	01	15	07	02	04	12	03
4	03	09	01	01	11	05	03	08
5	05	01	06	11	12	05	07	01

Notes: P- Poland, C-Czechoslovakia, EG-East Germany, H-Hungary, Y-Yugoslavia, A-Albania, B-Bulgaria, R-Romania.
+ Correlation coefficients after lag of one are partial correlation coefficients. Data values computed separately for each country. Decimal points are omitted.
++ Each lag represents one quarter of a year.
* $p = <.02$,   ** $p = <.007$, *** $p = <.0001$

Table 3.2 shows the correlation coefficients for each version of the cross-lagged correlation analysis as a function of number of lags (quarters) for each country. The only significant correlation occurred for Poland and Czechoslovakia, and, as Table 3.2 illustrates, the best prediction model is "protests forecasting adjustments" (but not vice versa), where the number of protests predicts executive adjustments over approximately a half-year period (three months for Czechoslovakia, six months for Poland). As shown in Table 3.2, no adequate prediction is possible for Bulgaria or Romania, because the number of protests was insignificant.

The exception is Hungary, where the number of protests was significant in 1956. However, protests did not generate significant frequent executive adjustments in this case, because the communist party initiated substantial policy reforms at the end of the 1950s that prevented further protest actions, creating the so called *goulash communism* (Przeworski 1991). East Germany, on the other hand, experienced a significant number of protests, but only as a reaction towards initial implementation of the communist system in the first years of the 1950s.

DISCUSSION AND CONCLUSIONS

Overall, as shown in Figure 3.2, 3.3, and 3.4 and in Table 3.1, both the grass roots mobilization, as indexed by a history of political protest and the establishment of political opposition groups, and the strength of political regimes created circumstances that either expedited, delayed, or postponed origination of democratic reforms (Bunce 1990; Opp & Gern 1993; Wejnert 1988, 1993; Wejnert & Spencer 1996). Developed political opposition was a necessary factor contributing to democratic transition; however, it was not a sufficient factor in and of itself. Severity of sanctions, frequency of changes in top political positions, and stronger prosecution of anti-communist opposition were all effective indicators of the regimes' agreeability to democratic reforms. Hence, communist regimes played an important role in the transition to democracy, both directly through undertaking preventive measures to control the development of a political opposition or through implemented reforms (Bruszt & Stark 1991, Woodward 1995), and indirectly through their instability which provided opportunities to mobilize the opposition (Sedaitis & Butterfield 1991).

Moreover, societies in which the internal structures were not prepared for the upcoming political and economic reforms were less vulnerable to democratic changes and, hence, were the last to establish, and probably the least likely to maintain, democratic reforms (Kornai 1992; Szelanyi 1991). For instance, states such as Romania, Albania and Bulgaria, in which there were no substantial collective protests from the post-Stalinist period to 1989, no prior integrated network of political opponent groups, and/or no establishment of alternative political opposition groups at the end of 1980s experienced later-occurring periods of transition.

The political outcome of the transition process also appears to be related to these domestic conditions. For instance, when communist rulers were eventually replaced in states lacking a political opposition network; that is, experiencing the paucity of an alternative political elite, they were succeeded by ex-communists who renamed themselves as social (e.g., Bulgaria and Romania) or liberal (Russia) democrats in the aftermath of transition. Therefore, states with internal conditions providing less fertile ground for political transition showed either no or delayed change and, even when change occurred, the internal conditions were such that change was more cosmetic than substantive (see Table 3.1). In societies that had a history of political opposition and of previous protests, communist rulers were replaced by coalitions between the political opposition and the ex-communists (see Table 3.1). The domestic circumstances conditioned by mobilized citizenry and the presence of weakening regimes increased the agreeability to and rate of democratic transition in East Central Europe. From this perspective, Tarrow's thesis of the *power in social movement* (Tarrow 1998) gains a new cogent meaning.

Taken together, as the literature suggests, rather than being the product of any one of the factors just discussed, the process of democratization in East Central Europe may be more accurately viewed as the dynamic interplay of multiple influences, where changes in external factors interact with an internal national environment of malleable political institutions. Factors affecting the domestic environment may be viewed as the necessary conditions which determine the probability (and temporal rate) that shifting international influences will initiate a democratic political process. For methodological purposes, the sets of permissive international conditions and network of the domestic variables could be approached as creating the basis for a multilevel analysis of democratization, at the country level (the domestic factors) and the global world level (the international factors). Combining both types of analysis would make it possible to measure the complexity of processes of democratization. Future analysis might consider undertaking such task.

APPENDIX: DESCRIPTION OF VARIABLES OF DEMOCRATIC MO-BILIZATION AND STRENGTH OF REGIMES

Political Strike is defined as a work stoppage by a body of industrial or service workers or a stoppage of normal academic life by students to protest against a regime, government leaders and/or a government policy or action. Strikes that were included in the data set were judged to have assumed a primary political significance. A political strike may have lasted for many days or weeks and was counted as a single event. An additional strike is scored, however, at junctures in which the character of the strike changes, for example, each time a new category of strikers joins the strikes, or each time a new political goal is enunciated.

Protest Demonstrations are indexed as a non-violent gatherings of people organized for the announced purpose of protesting against a regime, government or one or more of its leaders; or against its ideology, policy, intended policy, or lack of policy; or against its previous action or intended action. This variable is intended to encompass peaceful protest outside the formal structures of government and, therefore, excludes election meetings, rallies and boycotts.

Riots are violent demonstrations or disturbances involving a large number of people. "Violence" implies the use of physical force and is usually evinced by the destruction of property; the wounding or killing of people by authorities, the use of riot control equipment such as clubs, gas, guns or water cannons; and by the rioter's use of various weapons.

Governmental Sanction is an action taken by the authorities to neutralize, suppress or eliminate a perceived threat to the security of the government, the regime or the state itself. The category encompasses a diversity of governmental activities, but they share the characteristic of constituting specific responses to a perceived security problem at the national level. The category includes the following types of action: censorship; restriction on political participation, such as banning of a political party, the arrest of opposition politicians or arrest of persons reportedly involved in political protest actions, and exiling or deportation of persons for political action; and espionage.

Relaxation of Sanctions is an event in which government modifies or eliminates restrictions on political action or expression of the type classified as governmental sanctions.

Executive Adjustment is defined as a modification in the membership of a national executive body that does not signify a transfer of formal power from one leader or ruling group to another. National executive bodies include cabinets, councils of ministers, presidential offices and ruling party councils in states in which authoritarian power is wielded by a single party. Modification in the membership of such a body, short of major executive transfer, typically includes "reshuffles" or "shakeups" in which one or a small number of people are removed from or added to the membership. Executive adjustments always involve the movement of people into or out of the executive; they do not include acts such as the redistribution of ministerial portfolios within an executive body.

Regular Executive Transfer is a change in the office of national executive from one leader or ruling group to another which is accomplished through conventional, legal or customary procedures and is unaccompanied by actual or directly threatened physical violence. The office of national executive refers both to individual leaders, such as presidents and prime ministers, and also to collegial executive bodies, such as cabinets composed of one or more parties or groupings.

Irregular Executive Transfer is a change in the office of national executive from one leader or ruling group to another that is characterized by actual or threatened violence and by abnormal procedures. The office of national executive refers both to individual leaders, such as presidents and prime ministers, and also to collegial executive bodies, such as cabinets composed of one or more parties or groupings.

NOTE

This research was supported in part by grants from the National Endowment for the Humanities, Summer Fellowship for University Scholars, 1994. My thanks to Valerie Bunce, David Stark, Sidney Tarrow, David Strang, Nancy Tuma and Roy Liedke for helpful criticisms and suggestions at various stages of this research.

REFERENCES

Banac, Ivo. 1992. Introduction. In I. Banac (ed.), *Eastern Europe in Revolution*. Ithaca, NY: Cornell University Press.

Beck, Sam. 1993. The Struggle for Space and the Development of Civil Society in Romania, June 1990. In H. G. DeSoto, & D. G. Anderson, *The Curtain Rises: Rethinking Culture, Ideology and the State in Eastern Europe*. Atlantic Highlands, NJ: Humanities Press International.

Beissinger, Mark. 1990. *Protest Mobilization Among Soviet Nationalities*. Report submitted to the National Council for Soviet and Eastern European Research, August.

Bermeo, Nancy. 1991. *Liberalization and Democratization*. Baltimore: Johns Hopkins University Press.

Bollen, Kenneth A. 1998. *Cross-Nation Indicators of Liberal Democracy, 1950-1990*. Chapel Hill: University of North Carolina (ICPSR 2532).

Brown, J. E., Robert D. Hormats, William H. Lures & Ivo John Lederer (Eds.). 1992. *Western Approaches to Eastern Europe*. New York: Council on Foreign Relations Press.

Brus, Wlodzimierz. 1989. Evolution of the Communist Economic System: Scope and Limits. In V. Nee & D. Stark, *Remaking the Economic Institutions of Socialism. China and Eastern Europe*. Palo Alto, CA: Stanford University Press.

Bruszt, Laszlo & David Stark. 1991. Remaking the Political Field in Hungary: From the Politics of Confrontation to the Politics of Competition. *Journal of International Affairs*, *45*, 1, 201-245.

Bunce, Valerie. 1990. The Struggle for Liberal Democracy in Eastern Europe. *World Policy Journal*, *7* (Summer).

_____. 1989. Soviet Decline as a Regional Hegemon: Gorbachev and Eastern Europe. *Eastern European Politics and Society, 3*, 235-267.

Burawoy Michael & Janos Lukacs. 1992. *The Radiant Past*. Chicago: Chicago University Press.

Burton, Michael, Richard Gunther and John Higley. 1992. Introduction: Elite Transformations and Democratic Regimes. In J. Higley & R. Gunther, *Elites and Democratic Consolidation in Latin America and Southern Europe*. Cambridge, UK: Cambridge University Press.

Dahl, Robert. 1982. *Dilemmas of Pluralist Democracy. Autonomy vs. Control*. New Haven: Yale University Press.

_____. 1989. *Polyarchy. Participation and Opposition*. New Haven: Yale University Press.

_____. 1990. *After the Revolution? Authority in Good Society*. New Haven: Yale University Press.

_____. 1998. *On Democracy*. New Haven: Yale University Press.

Deacon, Bob (Ed.). 1992. *The New Eastern Europe*. London: Sage Publications.

DeSoto, Hermine G. & David G. Anderson. 1993. *The Curtain Rises. Rethinking Culture, Ideology and the State in Eastern Europe.* Atlantic Highlands, NJ: Humanities Press International.

Doyle, Michael. 1983. Kant, Liberal Legacies, and Foreign Affairs. *Philosophy and Public Affairs, 12,* 205-236.

Evans, Peter, Dietrich Rueschemeyer & Theda Skocpol (Eds.). 1990. *Bringing the State Back In.* Cambridge, UK: Cambridge University Press.

Gamson, William. 1990. *The Strategy of Social Protest.* Belmont, CA: Wadsworth Publishing Company.

Garner Roberta Ash & Mayer Zald. 1987. The Political Economy of Social Movement Sectors. In M. Zald & J. D. McCarthy, *Social Movements in an Organizational Society.* New Brunswick, NJ: Transaction Books (pp. 293-317).

Gligorov, Vladimir. 1992. Balkanization: A Theory of Constitution Failure. *East European Politics and Societies, 6,* 283-303.

Goldfarb, Jeffrey. 1991. *Beyond Glasnost. The Post-Totalitarian Mind.* Chicago, IL: University of Chicago Press.

Graf William, William Hansen & Brigide Schulz. 1987. From the People to One People: Social Bases of the East German 'Revolution' and Its Preemption by the West German State. In A. Desoto, J. Lovenduski & J. Woodall. *Politics and Society in Eastern Europe.* Bloomington, IN: Indiana University Press.

Havel, Vaclav. 1985 [1979]. The Power of the Powerless. In V. Havel, et al., *The Power of the Powerless: Citizens Against the State in Central-Eastern Europe.* Edited by John Keane and translated by Paul Wilson. Armonk, NY: M.E. Sharpe.

_____. 1988. Cards on Table. In B. Gwertzman & M. Kaufman, (Eds.), *The Collapse of Communism, The Correspondents of New York Times.* New York: Times Books.

Harris, Geoffrey. 1997. Rola Parlamentu Europejskiego w Procesie Rozszerzania Unii Europejskiej. *Studia Europejskie, 1,* 37-56.

Held, David. 1987. *Models of Democracy.* Palo Alto, CA: Stanford University Press.

Higley, John & Richard Gunther. 1992. *Elites and Democratic Consolidation in Latin America and Southern Europe.* Cambridge, UK: Cambridge University Press.

Hirschman, Albert O. 1982. *Shifting Involvements: Private Interest and Public Action.* Princeton, N. J.: Princeton University Press.

Holmes, L. 1997. *Post-Communism.* Oxford, UK: Polity.

Huntington, S. 1991. *The Third Wave: Democratization in the Late Twentieth Century.* Norman: University of Oklahoma Press.

Jaggers, Keith & Ted Robert Gurr. 1995. Tracking Democracy's Third Wave with the Polity III Data. *Journal of Peace Research, 32,* 4, 469-482.

Janos, Andrew. 1970. The One-Party State and Social Mobilization: East Europe Between the Wars. In S. Huntington & C. Moore (Eds.), *Authoritarian Politics in Modern Society.* New York: Basic Books.

John, Bell. 1991. Bulgaria. In S. White (Ed.), *Handbook of Reconstruction in Eastern Europe & the Soviet Union.* Harlow, Essex, U.K.: Longman Current Affairs.

Jowitt, Ken. 1992. The Leninist Legacy. In I. Banac (Ed.), *Eastern Europe in Revolution.* Ithaca, NY: Cornell University Press.

Kitchelt, Herbert. 1986. Political Opportunity Structures and Political Protest: Anti-Nuclear Movements in Four Democracies. *British Journal of Political Science, 16,* 57-85.

Kolodko, Grzegorz W. 1996. *Poland 2000. The New Economic Strategy.* Warszawa: Poltext Press.

_____. 2000. *Post-Communist Transition: The Thorny Road.* Rochester, NY: University of Rochester Press.

Kornai, Janos. 1992. The Postsocialist Transition and the State. *American Economic Review, 82,* 1-21.

Kriesberg, Louis. 1988. Peace Movements and Government Peace Efforts. *Research in Social Movements, Conflicts and Change, 10,* 57-75.

_____. Louis. 1998. *Constructive Conflicts:From Escalation to Resolution.* Lanham, Md: Rowman & Littlefield Publishers.

Kulluk, Fahrunnisa. 1993. From the National Question to Autogestion and Perestroika: Controversies in Theoretical and Political Approaches to Nation(ist) Movements. In H. DeSoto & D. Anderson (Eds.), *The Curtain Rises: Rethinking Culture, Ideology and the State in Eastern Europe.* Atlantic Highlands, NJ: Humanities Press International.

Kuran, Timur. 1990. Now Out of Never. The Element of Surprise in the East European Revolution of 1989. In N. Bermeo (Ed.), *Liberalization and Democratization.* Baltimore: John Hopkins University Press.

Laba, Roman. 1991. *The Roots of Solidarity.* Princeton, NJ: Princeton University Press.

Leibfried, Stephan & Paul Pierson. 1992. Prospect for Social Europe. *Politics & Society, 20,* 333-367.

Lovenduski, Joni & Jean Woodall. 1987. *Politics and Society in Eastern Europe.* Bloomington: Indiana Univeristy Press.

Markoff, J. 1996. *Waves of Democracy.* Thousands Oaks, CA: Pine Forge.

Marody, Mira. 1991. New Possibilities and Old Habits. *Sisyphus, 7,* 33-40.

Migdal, Joel. 1988. *Strong Societies and Weak State: State-Society Relations and State Capabilities in the Third World.* Princeton, NJ: Princeton University Press.

Miller, David. 1985. *Introduction to Collective Behavior.* Belmont, CA: Wadsworth Publishing.

Morris, Aldon D. & Carol McClurg Mueller. 1992. *Frontiers in Social Movements Theory.* New Haven: Yale University Press.

O'Donnell, Guillermo, Philippe C. Schmitter & Laurence Whitehead. 1988. *Transitions from Authoritarian Rule. Comparative Perspective.* Baltimore: John Hopkins University Press.

Opp, Karl-Dieter & Christiane Gern. 1993. Dissident groups, Personal Networks, and Spontaneous Cooperation: The East German Revolution of 1989. *American Sociological Review, 58,* 659-680.

Ost, David. 1990. *Solidarity and the Politics of Anti-Politics.* Philadelphia: Temple University Press.

Piven, Fox Frances & Richard A. Cloward. 1979. *Poor People's Movements: Why They Succeed, How They Fail.* New York: Vintage Books.

Pridham, Geoffrey (Ed.). 1990. *Securing Democracy: Political Parties and Democratic Consolidation in Southern Europe.* New York: Routledge Press.

Przeworski, Adam. 1991. *Democracy and Market.* Cambridge, UK: Cambridge University Press.

Rochon, Thomas. 1988. *Mobilizing for Peace: the Antinuclear Movements in Western Europe.* Princeton, NJ: Princeton University Press.

Rueschmeyer, Dietrich, Evelyne Huber Stephens & John Stephens. *Capitalist Development and Democracy.* Chicago, IL: Chicago University Press.

Sanford, George. 1992. The Polish Road to Democratization: from Political Impasse to the "Controlled Abdication" of Communism Power. In G. Sanford (Ed.), *Democratization in Poland, 1989-1990*. New York: San Martin's.

Schwartzman, Kathleen. 1998. Globalization and Democracy. *Annual Review of Sociology, 24,* 159-181.

Skocpol, Theda. 1992. *Protecting Soldiers and Mothers: The Political Origin of Social Policy in the United States*. Cambridge, MA: Harvard University Press.

Sedaitis, Judith & Jim Butterfield (Eds.). 1991. *Perestroika from Below*. Boulder, CO: Westview Press.

Stark, David. 1989. Coexisting Organizational Forms in Hungary's Emerging Mixed Economy. In V. Nee & D. Stark, *Remaking the Economic Institutions of Socialism: China and Eastern Europe*. Stanford, CA: Stanford University Press.

_____. 1992. Path Dependence and Privatization Strategies in East Central Europe. *Eastern European Politics and Societies, 6,* 17-53.

_____ 1996. Recombinant Property in East European Capitalism. *American Journal of Sociology, 101,* 993-1027.

Stark, David & Laszlo Bruszt. 1998. *Postsocialist Pathways*. Cambridge, UK: Cambridge University Press.

Szelanyi, Ivan. 1991. Eastern Europe in an Epoch of Transition: Toward a Socialist Mixed Economy. In N. Victor & D. Stark. *Remaking the Economic Institutions of Socialis: China and Eastern Europe*. Palo Alto, CA: Stanford University Press.

_____. 1992. Social and Political Landscape, Central Europe, Fall 1990. In I. Banac (Ed.), *Eastern Europe in Revolution*. Ithaca, NY: Cornell University Press.

Tarrow, Sidney. 1989. *Democracy and Disorder*. New York: Oxford University Press.

_____. 1991a. "Aiming at the Moving Target": Social Science and the Recent Rebellions in Eastern Europe. *Political Science and Politics, 3,* 9-10.

_____. 1991b. Understanding Political Change in Eastern Europe. *Political Science and Politics, 3,* 12-20.

_____. 1998. *Power in Movement: Social Movements and Contentious Politics*. New York: Cambridge University Press

Taylor, Charles & David Jodice. 1982. *World Handbook of Political and Social Indicators #III: 1948-1982. Quarterly Event Data*. Ann Arbor, MI: Inter-university Consortium for Political and Social Research.

Taylor, Charles & Michael Hudson. 1980. *World Handbook of Social and Political Indicators*. New Haven: Yale University Press.

Turner, Ralph & Lewis M. Killian. 1987. *Collective Behavior*. Englewood Cliffs, NJ: Prentice Hall.

Vladislaw, Jan (Ed.). 1987. *Vaclaw Havel: or Living in Truth*. London: Faber and Faber.

Vodopivec, Peter. 1992. Slovens and Yugoslavia, 1918-1991. *East European Politics and Societies, 6,* 220- 242.

Wejnert, Barbara. 1988. Student Movement in Poland in 1980-1981. *Social Movements, Conflict and Change, 10,* 173-183.

_____. 1993. *Did Democracy Diffuse in Eastern Europe?* Paper presented at the annual meeting of the American Sociological Association, Miami, August 1993.

_____ (in press). A Conceptual Framework for Integrating Diffusion Models. *Annual Review of Sociology, 28.*

Wejnert, Barbara & Metta Spencer. 1996. *Women in Post-Communism*. Greenwich, CT: JAI Press.

Woodward, S. .1995. *Balkan Tragedy*. Washington DC: The Brookings Institution.
Zakowski, Bronislaw. 1991. *Zakowski Pyta Geremek Odpowiada*. Warsaw: PWN.

4

A Line of Blood: How December 1970 Prepared Polish Workers for Political Transition in 1989

Jack M. Bloom

In December 1970, Poland's police and army fired upon workers who were striking in response to sharp increases in the prices of consumer goods, especially food. In all likelihood, hundreds were killed and thousands—perhaps tens of thousands—injured. This catastrophe not only brought down the government led by the Communist Party Secretary, Wladyslaw Gomulka, who had previously been lifted to power by worker strikes in 1956; it also destroyed the last shred of ideological legitimacy for the regime. This chapter first explores what happened during the traumatic events of December 1970, as they were remembered by workers participating in them.[1] Second, it examines the impact of these events on the Solidarity movement in 1980.

THE END OF GOMULKA'S REGIME

During his long reign, Gomulka had grown increasingly isolated, and this isolation was reflected in his policies. The economy was stagnating and his proposed solutions required sacrifices to be borne by already-burdened workers in the form of longer hours, production speed-ups and some 200,000 laid off (Blazynski 1979, p. 4). Expenditures for safer working conditions, sanitary installations and social facilities in the factories had virtually ceased. Housing construction lagged and the waiting period for an apartment increased on average to about fifteen to twenty years. Expenses for schools, roads and housing were lifted from the state and put back in the hands of communities and individuals (Laba 1991, pp. 16-17; Pelczynski 1980a, pp. 401-402). Gomulka's policy of self-sufficiency and independence from the West made things worse when disastrous harvests hit in 1969 and 1970. Imports of grain for livestock were severely curtailed, forcing a cut in the animal population, which meant meat prices had to be substantially raised (Blazynski 1979, p. 7). Meat at that time began to play the crucial role as the strategic "political" grocery (Kasprzyk 1988, interview).

Making things more difficult was that the economic stagnation had persisted for so long that the living standards of the population had also deteriorated for a decade or more. By 1968, Gomulka had already been weakened by a student movement and its brutal suppression. Opposition was growing within the bureaucracy even as discontent simmered below. "That Gomulka had to leave, there was no doubt. Quietly, Party activists, even Party Secretaries on the *powiat* (local district) level discussed it. There was talk about factions in the Central Committee. The leading players and the wider circle of activists, including the secret police and the First Secretaries of the Basic Party Organizations, the managers of various departments in the city council, the directors of larger companies knew that 'something was wrong' in the Central Committee," recalled Adam Sucharski, later a colonel in the secret police (Sucharski 1997, interview).

Overnight, on 12 December 1970, after more than a decade of relative price stability, the price increases were announced. They took effect immediately just before Christmas, averaging 17.5 percent (though the range was between four percent and thirty-seven percent) (Blazynski 1979, p. 4; Laba 1991, p. 19; Pelczynski 1980b, pp. 401-403). In Poland, a large bulk of one's salary went to pay for food—on average, around 58 percent. The price rises brought that figure closer to 70 percent, and created a precipitous drop in real wages just before the holiday celebrations (Majkowski 1985, p. 75). Coupled with the stagnant standard of living, this move threatened many of the hard-won gains of the postwar period. Especially hard hit were the lower-paid workers, who spent a greater percentage of their earnings on food. Some workers faced what one sociologist called "a specter of hunger" (Szczypinski as cited in Laba 1991, p. 19). While prices were lowered for some manufactured goods, like televisions and stereos, these goods were luxuries and many workers could not afford them anyway (Singer 1981, p. 157). Other consumer goods, like clothing, went up substantially (Blazynski 1979, p. 7). Together, these policies led to an increase of class differences in the supposedly classless society.

The price rises ignited the glowing embers of discontent that already lay strewn about, and provided workers the occasion to give voice to their accumulated hostilities (Rakowski 1973, pp. 30-31). Walesa described "a climate of uncertainty everywhere" (Walesa 1987, p. 56). He recalled that people "were fed up with this kind of special privilege . . . they knew they were paying for it with their own blood." Thus, when news of the price increases spread, first at party meetings, "a woman stood up . . . and said that times had been less hard under Hitler, that she didn't know how she was going to manage, since she had three children and a fixed salary" (Walesa 1987, p. 60).

It would be a mistake, however, to assume that the protesting workers were motivated only by economic adversity. By the 1970s, workers had lost respect for the communist regime. People noted the favoritism given to Party members, who received aid in obtaining housing, land and financing. Many young workers who had been raised within the communist system and who should have been expected to be among its strongest supporters if the system really was operated for and by them (Malinowski 1984), did not feel that way about it. They clearly felt aggrieved by the arrogance of the authorities who were free to act without consultation with the rest of the society, and who safeguarded their own privileges. And in a socialist state, they resented the disproportionate benefits that flowed to the nomenclature: They wanted the equality that propaganda claimed to exist (Laba 1991, p. 40), particularly workers who earned less. Workers were becoming better educated, more sophisticated and self-confident and were "more interested in taking a share in running the country" (Blazynski 1979, p. 137). They resented the daily diet of lies they were fed from the media (Laba 1991, p. 27). In addition, with the widening income gap between managers and workers, and upward mobility constricted, workers felt that they were being pushed into the lowest social strata (Weydenthal 1981, p. 195).

Consequently, employees responded with work stoppages and demonstrations throughout the country; for example, in Katowice, Warsaw, Poznan, Slupsk, Elblag, Wroclaw and Cracow (Weydenthal 1981, p. 195). But, while every major city was affected by these activities, workers on the Baltic coast went much further and directly confronted the symbols of state power, in Gdansk and Szczecin attacking and burning and, in Gdynia and Elblag, stoning the Party headquarters. When the workers in the Gdansk Shipyard learned that tanks and armored cars were arrayed around the shipyards, they "went so far as to devise a method for blowing up a tank with the help of an acetylene bomb, while others constructed missile-launchers out of blocked pipes" (Walesa 1987, p. 71).

Meanwhile, the government deployed provocateurs who looted and vandalized, allowing the government spokesmen to claim that the protestors were vandals and German revanchists, seeking to return the city to German rule. Tadeusz Plawinski, who was one of the protestors, stated (1994, interview): "Some people used the occasion to steal from stores. I got hit while defending one. We put up temporary shields to cover the windows, but later all of them got looted completely. Generally, the police started the looting and took pictures." Given that the presence of looters was one of the justifications that was used to induce repression, Plawinski's hypothesis is plausible.

The crowds' behavior was used by the ruling regime as an excuse "to meet violence with violence." At the Lenin Shipyard in Gdansk, the police and army, equipped with heavy weaponry, shot, killed and arrested many workers. In prisons, the arrested were beaten and forced to run gauntlets between two lines of police armed with truncheons. The army also fired on people as they arrived for work at the train station in Gdynia, a city adjacent to Gdansk. Workers were shot without warning as they exited the commuter trains onto the platform. The shots kept coming even as more trains arrived, disgorging more workers. With nowhere to flee, possibly hundreds of workers were killed; many others injured. In the course of my interviews, I listened to an audio tape recording of the massacre and the shooting lasted longer than the duration of the tape.

Workers had come to the train station that morning after vice-prime minister and Politburo member Stanislaw Kociolek had appeared on television, calling on them to return to work. The tragic events likely could have been a set-up prepared by the regime. [Though some leading dissidents like Jacek Kuron contended that it was all a terrible mistake.] In Szczecin, the workers at Szczecin's shipyard stayed on strike, elected a leadership, organized a command quarter that kept order in the city, and drew up a list of demands which included the revolutionary idea of independent trade unions. The strike spread to other factories in the city. In a few days, ninety four companies were striking, which led to a general strike in the city. To protect city residents, food stores, food-delivery firms, bakeries, and clinics were not to strike. Workers' militia patrolled the streets. Newspaper and broadcast journalists were able to report a true account of the events because censorship was abolished in the city.

The strike in Szczecin spread to the surrounding provinces and to other cities in Poland. Workers and militia clashed in Cracow, Lodz, Slupsk, Elblag, Katowice, Poznan and Wroclaw. Overall, protests resulted in multiple injuries and deaths, especially on the coast. I am in possession of the records of hundreds of injuries brought to just one emergency room in one hospital in Szczecin. In Gdansk, Andrzej Jarmakowski, a high school student at that time, recalled, a priest in his parish made a record of what happened to his parishioners. Just from that one parish, there were more than 300 people wounded. According to my interview with Malgorzata Celejewska in the main hospital in Gdansk, "in the emergency room, they just pinned numbers on people. In just one hour they brought in 1300 wounded people! Nothing could be done for some of them" (Celejewska 1994, interview). Alicja Matuszewska added: "The police would arrive at night to the families of the dead; they would allow one person from a family to go with them to identify the body. They permitted both the mother and the father to go in only one case. His body was dirty from mud and sand. They did not allow it to be washed or dressed. They were just wrapped in sheets and taken to the cemetery, where they were buried in common graves. The newspapers said that 27 people were killed. His body was number 217. That says something about how many people were really killed" (Matuszewska 1994, interview).

Chilling as they are, these facts do not convey the impact of the events on individuals who lived through them. The next section presents eyewitness accounts of events in Gdansk, Gdynia and Szczecin. Each of the reports is particular, due to the unique experiences of the speaker. Malgorzata Celejewska and Alicja Matuszewska were observers of the protest actions in Gdansk and Gdynia; Aleksander Krystosiak was a member of the strike committee in Szczecin. Celejewska later served as treasurer of the Gdansk regional Solidarity union; Matuszewska as the Solidarity national treasurer. Krystosiak became the vice-chair of Solidarity in the Szczecin region. These are different people with different life histories and different sets of mind, discussing different aspects of the events. Their stories, however, present the trauma and despair of those who lived through that time. Invariably, when people started talking about what happened in December 1970 they cast a powerful emotional spell. Even on paper, their stories capture this feeling.

THE EVENTS IN GDANSK AS RECALLED BY MALGORZATA CELE-JEWSKA

In Decemebr 1970 Malgorzata Celejewska worked as an accountant in the North Shipyard in Gdansk. In 1980 she was the Gdansk regional treasurer of the Solidarity movement. She describes the December strikes of shipyard workers as follow:[2]

On the twelfth of December, Party members received a call to come to a meeting after work. We were threatened with punishment if we did not come. They collected us all in a big meeting room: engineers, workers, intelligentsia—everyone. A Secretary from the Gdansk Committee told us that there would be a fifty to sixty percent price hike on food and other products. People got really upset because everyone realized that they could not live with that price hike. She essentially screamed at people, and the meeting became a shouting match . . . On Monday, there was no real work done; people were just talking. Sometime around noon, a crowd of workers came from the Gdansk shipyard, calling us to go with them to the provincial Party Committee. They had sent a delegation of sixteen workers to talk to the First Secretary of the shipyard, and the delegates had not returned. A coworker and I decided to go see what was happening. We were told that the workers had changed their minds and had gone toward the radio station and seized a car that had loudspeakers. It became a public stump. Anyone who had something to say could speak his mind. They demanded that the radio announce that the Gdansk and the North Shipyards were on strike against the price rises. They called for a public meeting at 7:00 p.m. at the Gdansk Polytechnic University . . . I got there a little late. There were speeches, and a crowd of thousands of us headed for Party headquarters. As we went, we sang revolutionary songs, including the *Internationale*. We went towards the Blednik Bridge. As we came near, we smelled tear gas and heard shots. We came closer and it turned out that there was fighting going on in front of the Party headquarters: tear gas, bullets, stones and sticks. The Blednik Bridge is an overpass above the railroad station. Once you started, there was no way out because it is a high bridge, the crowd was very packed and you had to move with it.

That day, they used only tear gas. Still, the situation by the hotel was quite dangerous. I saw people tearing bricks and stones out of the street and catching tear gas grenades or picking them up off the ground and throwing them back at the police. A group of young men rode a tram loaded with stones and tear gas cans into the police and bombarded them. As I stood there, a policeman shot a tear gas canister into the crowd that flew just inches from my face. That was enough. I got out of there and went as far out of my way as possible to avoid any crowds, but there were crowds and tear gas everywhere—even in Brzesc, where I lived, about seven kilometers away, you could smell it.

On Tuesday morning, there was no work—just discussions about the workers' right to demonstrate and strike. They asked questions like, what kind of country is this if I cannot go on strike? If it's a free country, I should have a right to do so. People demanded explanations for the price rises, but there was no one to explain. Around noon, they sent us home. The Gdansk Shipyard workers and the North Shipyard workers once again went to the provincial Party headquarters, this time armed with sticks and such things to get their representatives who were never let out. That day, they set fire to the Party building.

In the afternoon, I went to visit the provincial self-help cooperative where I used to work and had very good friends. Everyone there was on the side of the strikers. I learned that a tank had crushed someone in front of the Party headquarters after the workers had attacked and burned the Party building . . . On Wednesday, when I came to work, it was just talk, talk, talk all the time. I was told by someone that a worker had been killed at the railroad station. The workers had soaked a handkerchief in his blood and taken an oath of revenge over his dead body. People were upset and terrified. The workers decided to continue the strike.

The Gdansk Shipyard already had a strike committee; so did we, and people were already working on demands to the Party Secretary and the shipyard management. So people were more peaceful, but more determined, concerning what should be done. By Wednesday evening, before people went home, we decided to have an occupation strike. People were told to stay by their work stations to protect them. My boss told me to go home because *it could be really dangerous.* But they just wanted to get rid of people. Then they could close departments in the shipyard and say there was no strike there. So to go home would have meant that I did not support the strike, and when you live in a community like that, that is impossible. And I did support the strike anyway. Staying there was the only way.

That night, police cars with loudspeakers called workers to come out of the shipyard, threatening them if they stayed. But, when you go on an occupation strike, you stay as long as the strike goes on. People talk; they open up, and that created new ties between us. There were also Party people—this evil, red spirit—floating around. Someone barged into our department, claiming that German army divers were coming to storm the shipyard from the sea. It was bullshit and people who were smart and politically educated understood what it was, but for some people, it was scary. And that was the whole idea: to create a feeling of panic among the workers. At night, we heard tanks coming; the police and the army surrounded the shipyard. Around 4 a.m., it was decided to leave the shipyard, though some of us felt very strongly that it was the wrong decision. Tanks and police were all around the shipyard and in front of the gates. Only later, we learned that they had used bullets against the workers at the Gdansk Shipyard gates. (Celejewska 1994, interview).

Walesa stated that the decision to leave the shipyards was difficult: "Most saw [it] as a betrayal, though they also understood that it would probably prevent the loss of more lives. Twenty thousand of us . . . left the yard through lines of soldiers and militiamen. It seemed to take hours for the immense regiment of workers to walk away from the yard " (Walesa 1987: 81)

Celejewska continues describing the results of the police action:

. . . that night there was there was a curfew imposed from 6 p.m. to 5 a.m. The military moved at night, going from Gdynia to Gdansk, and it was a scary picture: a company of tanks moving, so the buildings shook as they went by. There was no way you could sleep through it. I woke up Przemek, who was six at the time, and brought him to the window. I wanted him to see the military passing by at night, like thieves. There was an officer with a gun in his hand, sitting on a tank with a sharp light shining on the buildings, checking every window. As the light moved, this guy had his gun pointed at the windows. People moved away because you never knew what he would do—if he would shoot or not. Who knew what was in his mind?

From the train station, a man came, walking quickly, trying to get to the tram stop, which was right in front of our windows. Obviously, he was slightly drunk. He probably forgot the curfew. As he stood there waiting for the tram, a military car came by, and the military police got out and started talking with him. He momentarily stood up at attention. Then, the regular police came by and four guys got out of the car. Without warning, they pulled out their nightsticks and started beating him viciously all over, with no reason, no warning—nothing.

My neighbor was brave. She turned off the light, and we opened the window and started screaming at them: *What are you doing, you idiots! Why are you beating this guy who did nothing to you? He is innocent!* They momentarily quit and turned to look for us. We closed the window and jumped back. But the noise we made awoke the whole street. Windows all over opened up. There were too many witnesses, so they just put away their nightsticks and left. I saw another beating, and it was just as vicious. (Celejewska 1994, interview).

THE EVENTS IN GDYNIA AS RECALLED BY ALICJA MATUSZEWSKA

Alicja Matuszewska worked as a civilian accountant in the military shipyard in Gdynia. She is a heavy smoker, and during the afternoon she described what she saw in Gdynia in 1970, a lit cigarette never left her hands. Afterward, she remarked:[3]

It was like a film was playing in my head as I lived through that experience again. It was awful! We knew what was happening in Gdansk, even though the trains, buses and trams were stopped, because the ambulances carried the information. An ambulance from Gdansk would come to the city limits and meet with one from Sopot and exchange information. Immediately, it spread around. The distances were too small to prevent it. People just walked and carried the news. The day after the Gdansk strike started, the workers went to the mayor's office with a petition announcing that they were getting ready to strike. They said that they would come back for an answer the next day. I wanted to see it, so I told my boss that I wanted to take a few vacation days.

Tanks surrounded the whole city. They were everywhere. By my building, two tanks shone their headlights right into my windows, so it was like daylight. That was the sixteenth. The workers were really scared. They didn't know what to do. They knew what had happened in Gdansk.

Exactly at 6:00 in the morning, I was awakened by machine gun firing. My husband tore into the apartment and said: *Get up! They are shooting the workers by the Paris Commune Shipyard!* I had two kids at home. I woke them up and told them: *Your grandma is coming. Stay home and don't move.* And I left.

When people heard Kociolek's appeal to go back to work, it was late. There was no one to consult. So they just started coming to work at the train station by the Paris Commune Shipyard. There was a wooden overpass, which connected all the tracks and the living quarters of the city with the station. People who were arriving did not know what had happened by the gate to the shipyard. When the trains arrived, the workers disembarked and walked up to the overpass to get over to the shipyard. Very many people were killed there because the soldiers started shooting indiscriminately.

The first workers who arrived by the shipyard gates were shot with machine guns. That was the series that woke me up. Four workers were killed; others were wounded. From the other side of the overpass, the buses were coming, also bringing people to work. On one of the buses, there was a teacher who was in terrible shock because her student from the marine school had been killed.

The road to Gdansk was practically blocked by crowds in front of the mayor's office. The people surrounded that whole area, waiting for the shipyard workers. I stood across the street. A friend who lived upstairs recognized me and called us up. From there, I had a great view of what was going on. On one side, I could see the train station, and on the other, I could see what was going on in the mayor's office. We ran back and forth from room to room to see what was happening.

A tractor drove by the mayor's office. It could not get through because of the people standing there. The police waved at the driver to make a U-turn and go back. As he drove by, the police shot him. He fell out of the tractor and waved his hand to show that he was still alive. People ran to help him. Then they tore out bricks from the pavement and started throwing them at the police.

A horrible scream came from the other side, so we ran to that window. The shipyard workers were coming in an organized column to get their answer. They had the body of a murdered worker on a door from the train. I still remember it like today. He was young. He had light hair, thrown about. He was wearing a brown work jacket and pants and boots. Someone from a nearby flower shop came out and threw a bouquet of white and red flowers at his feet—the colors of the Polish flag. A military doctor came out of the building. He went over to the worker, checked the pulse on his hand and on his neck and waved that he was dead and they should take him away.

Then all hell broke loose. The people ran to the soldiers: *They are murderers! They are like the Gestapo! They are shooting us! Don't shoot us. Don't be like them.* The soldiers didn't know what to do. They did not shoot, but the police ran around and shot into the crowd for no reason. The hunting season had begun. Ambulances came. They put sheets over the faces and threw them into the ambulances, so we knew they were taking away dead bodies. The shooting lasted several hours.

A foreign journalist had set up a camera on our building. Having seen it, the police tore into the building and gassed the whole stairway. We started choking. The two women who lived there pulled out bandage tape and we started taping the windows and doors and putting wet rugs down by the doorways. Now, hundreds and hundreds of people ran to their windows, opened them and started screaming: *Murderers! Murderers!* The police looked up with glazed eyes.

They acted and behaved like wild savages! More police came and they used more tear gas. They shot, and people backed away. On the street, they would check the hands of young people—13, 14 years old—to see if they were dirty from handling stones. They caught a lot of them and put them in the mayor's office.

By 4:00, it seemed that the street was going back to normal, so we decided to go back home. We went back, scurrying from one building entrance to another. We were afraid to walk openly on the streets because shots could still be heard. There were thousands of people, and when they dispersed, the police chased them, looked for where they were hiding, and they would shoot them. When I finally got back home, it was after dark. The police announced a curfew.

They did horrible things. They would tear into the prison and get a shipyard worker, mess up his hair, put a piece of metal pipe in his hand and then take mug shots of him to prove that he was one of the hooligans. My mother's friend had a son who was a firefighter in the army. When the shooting began, there was a hospital close to the fire department that had a shortage of workers. So the army sent its firefighters to the hospital to work. Two days later, this man told me what he saw. He was 20 years old, pale and his hands were shaking. He could not collect himself. He said they just collected corpses! No one was alive.

Close to the train station, there was a big workers' hostel, where workers who came from other parts of Poland and worked in the shipyard, stayed. The building was surrounded by the police, so when they backed out of the train station, they had nowhere to go. They went into the forest, and stayed until midnight. Then they decided to go back home. When they finally got back to the hotel, the police arrived a few minutes later and massacred them in the building.

After a few days, I returned to work. I learned that my officers had no idea what had happened. During these events, they took all the officers to Oksywie, a military port. They have a huge bunker there. They collected all the officers and locked them up there!

For several months I could not stop thinking about it. I could not live with it. That year, people did not put up Christmas trees. There was nothing to celebrate. (Matuszewska 1994, interview).

THE EVENTS IN SZCZECIN AS RECALLED BY ALEKSANDER KRYSTOSIAK

Aleksander Krystosiak was a secondary leader of the 1970 strike and was one of the leaders of the strike committee during negotiations with the government in December 1970. In 1980, during the Solidarity movement he was vice-chair of Szczecin regional Solidarity. Krystosiak describes the 1970s strike in Szczecin as:[4]

Anger turned against the government at the very first moment of the strike. It wasn't said openly, but that was what it was really all about. When the strike began, the strike committee demanded that the government come talk to them. The government said nothing. It acted like it didn't hear; it tried to wait us out, hoping we would go away. People realized that the real power lay in the hands of the Party, so they went there. A few thousand workers went, joined by workers from a nearby factory. As they were walking toward the Party building, people on the streets joined the demonstration. The workers were very disciplined and well-organized. As the crowd walked down the street, if someone tried to break a shop window, or something like that, he was immediately kicked out by the workers themselves. They didn't need the police for that.

The crowd was attacked by the police with truncheons and batons. People felt that they had to defend themselves, so they broke apart benches and fences and tore up the pavement. There was hand-to-hand fighting. They pushed the police back, and reached the Party building. But Party Secretary Walaszek managed to get away through the basement to the military garrison.

When people entered, they saw the wealth: TV sets everywhere, incredible furniture, expensive carpets. They went to the cafeteria, where Party officials not only got fed, but could also buy things, and they saw what they had there. Some of it had not been on the market since before the war! There was smoked eye of tenderloin, salmon, smoked eel, caviar. This cafeteria was available to all the workers of the Party headquarters building and the officials in the provincial Committee. They were the privileged ones. Not only could they get those things, but the prices were so ridiculous that it was really free. The price was only symbolic. After people saw the cafeteria, there was one more demand: liquidation of the special stores available only to high Party officials and police and army officers, where they could buy things unavailable to anyone else. While in the Party headquarters they had only food, these stores had everything: furniture, carpets, food, foreign shoes, foreign pants, and foreign silk. These were luxuries unavailable to others.

People unloaded their anger on the building. There was no robbing; simply destroying. People dumped the TVs out the windows and burned the building down. The destruction began immediately because there was no Party leader to talk to. They also attacked the trade union leaders. It was simply their rage against people who worked for the government. People then stormed the police headquarters. The police started shooting to defend themselves. Even then, the workers distinguished between the secret police and the criminal police. The secret police were hated, and if they had been around, they would have been dead. But the criminal police had some respect. They protected society and individuals. So when they started shooting, people just backed off. There was no massacre; they shot above people's heads. But, there were a few victims. A 16-year-old girl, who stood on a balcony watching what was going on was hit by a stray bullet.

While everything was burning, the military came in. But there wasn't much to protect; everything had already burnt down. The soldiers didn't shoot; they just took position. The tanks moved in and were placed around the Party building. Young workers would climb on the tank and shove things into gun holes. (I remember one of the workers shouting to people to get off one of the tanks and not to burn it because his son was inside!) By the time the Party and trade union buildings were burnt, the workers had unloaded their rage and returned to the shipyard; some went back home. The crowd dispersed. People who had joined the workers from the streets went back to their homes, and the workers returned to their factories.

By the next day, all government buildings—police, administration, Party—were protected by tanks and heavy arms. My shipyard, Parnica, was also surrounded on land by the tanks. One tank stood there right by the fence, with its cannon stuck into the factory. We went to him and said: *Turn it around or we'll break it.* He turned it.

People got organized practically as soon as the strike began. When they decided to strike, each department immediately began choosing its strike committee. The department strike committees met and elected the factory strike committee. Then they returned to their departments. Why were they organized so quickly? The beginning of a strike is chaos. Once the strike committee was elected, it created order. Why these people and not others? The potential leaders were known to the workers. In every department, even before the strikes were conceived, there were always a few people who were known for being more active than others and more politically educated, who listened to foreign radio stations. These people knew how to read between the lines. They would say it quietly in your ear, but it spread around. There was a very small number of them, and they were in diapers in terms of organization, but they were known. Still, until they were elected, they kept quiet so they couldn't be picked as the organizers of the strike . . .

The demands of the strike also crystallized on the first day. Why? The strikes started spontaneously. Spontaneity doesn't last long. Emotions wear out, and then people are left with nothing. To make the strike last, the strike committee had to make sure that people understood what they were fighting for. So, in a few hours, there were demands. The day after the strike began, we published a strike newspaper. The strike committee immediately created a safety guard who organized people to watch over the factory. They announced to the directors, to management, to the Party officials that their rule had ended. The strike committee was taking over, and they had to comply with the committee's orders. On the first day, the strike committee ordered no alcohol in the shipyard. The workers themselves policed each other. If they found that someone had a beer or whatever, they would take it away and break it on the pavement. The strike committee also immediately demanded a ban on selling alcohol in the city.

There weren't any rules about how to conduct a sit-in strike. People were free to do whatever they wanted. At the beginning, some left; others stayed. Later, the strike committee gave special passes. Even though the factories were surrounded by tanks and soldiers, the people who went home got fed, slept and rested, and were allowed to reenter: the whole time, there were calls to go back to work.

The factory strike committee in Warski proclaimed itself to be an inter-factory strike committee. Each factory, which declared support and joined the strike sent two delegates to Warski. This was too large a body, but it elected a presidium. They made most of the decisions, but in some cases they had to go back to the plenum for a vote. The structure worked like a transmission belt: the inter-factory strike committee gave orders to the factory strike committees; which gave orders to department strike committees, which gave orders to the workers.

The strike committee demanded that phones be put in the cafeteria immediately—so the delegates could connect with their factories. They also demanded that these phones be connected directly to the city lines and not to a relay plant, so no one could listen to what was going on. Why were these phones so necessary? Because when the government representatives came to talk, the committee had to know what was happening in the other factories. As soon as a demand was negotiated, the representatives would run as fast as they could to the phone to tell their people.

There were no German natives to be found around Szczecin, so the propaganda they used in Gdansk would not work. Here, it [the strike] was organized by criminals, thieves, socially marginal people—and the CIA . . . The government's anger turned against the Warski Shipyard because those workers had initiated the march. It was surrounded by such heavy military equipment and so many armed servicemen that it seemed that they were gathered against the whole army of an enemy country. Those tanks and machine guns started the massacre in Warski. It was the government's revenge.

People were gathered in a crowd around the main gate to the Warski shipyard. The gate was open and some were outside, some inside. They were in a corner, with brick walls on two sides. I was 200-300 meters from the gate when it happened. The attack was completely unprovoked. All of a sudden, without even an order being given, the army fired. The fire was directed toward the crowd trapped in that corner.

People fell, dead and wounded. I really can't say how many people were killed or wounded because as soon as the crowd fell, the military moved in. Bodies and wounded were taken away. I cannot guarantee that they didn't shoot any wounded. No one knew who was wounded, what hospital they were in, what happened to them, nothing. These people disappeared. The funerals took place at night, and no family members were allowed to go. The victims were put in nameless graves, which were level with the ground. There was no trace of them. Some of the gravediggers and the people who did the funerals were brave enough to scribble the names of the victims somewhere. Later, we were able to get 17 names and to find their graves. But I have no guarantee that there weren't any more.

The rest of the people ran into the shipyard and closed the gate. I tried to see, but it was immediately surrounded. The people were fenced off and we were kept out. We couldn't see anything. I immediately went to my shipyard and told them what I had seen. (Krystosiak 1994, interview).

THE IMPACT OF DECEMBER 1970

Initially, people were terrorized and felt isolated. Walesa recalled "a complete lack of solidarity between the different sections of the population, in Gdansk itself and even in many workers' homes. There was a crushing sense of loneliness, fear, and uncertainty about the prospects of our movement . . . Nor was there any sign of international solidarity" (Walesa 1987:81). Bogdan Borusewicz[5] added: "I knew what had happened, and I saw how everyone was affected by it. I walked down the street, I saw tanks and patrols. I felt very helpless that there were no friends, no group, no organization in which we could meet together and assess everything. I was alone" (Borusewicz 1988, interview).

The regime appeared unmovable and willing to resort to any means to maintain its power.

There was incredible despair. People were really in deep mourning over those who were killed. Should we try to avenge our comrades? Should we demand something? Should we go after them? We didn't know what to do. After the massacre, many people considered giving up and going back to work. But others said, "No. We have to continue so these people won't have been killed in vain." The strike continued but there was a clear consciousness of defeat. (Krystosiak 1994, interview)

This was a crucial sentiment, as there would be no attempts at repeating the challenge to state power so long as the sense of the state's willingness to use deadly force remained. However, when that sense was removed by the actions of the state when once again confronted with a symbolic challenge in 1976, many people in the society began to feel that opposition activity was a viable possibility and opposition, both open and hidden, reemerged. (This statement is based upon several interviews I have conducted with oppositionists, some referred to here and some not.) These issues of conscious perceptions can be crucial in mass action (Kurzman 1996; Tocqueville 1955).

In addition, however, to confusion, loneliness and fear, people felt deep, abiding anger because justice had been mutilated. The agents of these tragic events, especially the police, became the targets for public retaliation. It was not simply revenge but a warning that police were responsible for the tragedy and would have to be accountable for it.

People hated the police so badly that in my area they would not show up at night for another half year. When the police would sit down in the inter-city trains, everyone would get up and leave the area. A number of police were killed. One was found with a paper that said "for my brother." It was standard practice that if a police patrol was on the street in the night, someone would shout something at them. They would run after him and there were ten guys waiting for them. Just across the street where I lived, some guys had a weight-lifting place in the basement of the apartment building. After the curfew, the police came there and tried to check on what was going on, and they got beaten and thrown out into the garbage. A lot of police quit at that time. They even moved their families from the area because they were afraid that there would be retaliation against them. (Plawinski 1994, interview)

Several police families left the seashore as a result. The impact of this public response was so powerful that in 1981, "when they arrested us, we said "Just remember what happened in 1970!"" (Matuszewska 1994, interview). These sentiments, and the disgust with the use of state power that they represent, served to inhibit the use of that power in the future: Not only were the agents of state repression less willing to repeat their actions later, but the government leadership was also inhibited from precipitating such actions. Gomulka's successor, Edward Gierek, stated on several occasions that he would never sanction the use of deadly force against the workers—and he did not.

The killing was isolated to the coastal cities and much of Poland was at first ignorant of it, or people learned from official sources that the troublemakers were Germans, hooligans or thieves. Information about what actually happened gradually seeped outward to other parts of the country. Some learned about it by listening to foreign radio broadcasts or, eventually, from the accounts of inhabitants of the Baltic cities in the form of rumors and anecdotes.

I worked in a restaurant in Swinoujscie. It was a small town, so among my clientele were policemen, and some of them I knew. Once, one of them, who was sort of friend with me, drank a little too much, and he became talkative. I asked him, "Where were you in 1970?" And he said, "I was in the tri-city area." So I said, "Tell me the truth. How many people were killed there?" He was drunk, but even so, when I asked him that, he looked at me more consciously, like being awakened. There was tragedy in his eyes, and he said, *"You tell me how many people can be killed after shooting a machine gun into a crowd for two hours."* (Gorecki 1994, interview)

Krzysztof Mlodzik was in the army during these events. He realized that what he was being told by the official sources did not accord with other information he acquired from friends and foreign radio broadcasts. For him, the events awakened the need to be educated on political issues that so far he had no interest in. In the interview with me he said "I felt that since my father and I were both workers, I would have a guilty conscience shooting at workers. Until then, I had only been interested in my work, but I started to buy books about politics and stopped believing what the government said on TV." (Mlodzik 1988, interview).

THE LESSONS OF DECEMBER 1970

The killings were deeply engraved into the consciousness of the people of the Baltic Coast, especially the young workers who, a decade later, became the Solidarity generation. What happened on the coast was a turning point and an experience they would never forget. Workers were able to draw conclusions from their experiences, which better prepared them for the future struggle with the communist regime and enabled them to prevail in 1980 (Goodwyn 1991; Laba 1991). Walesa recalled that: "It provided an incomparable experience, enabling us to understand what makes them behave the way they do in a crisis. And it convinced us that we would have to find other solutions" (Walesa 1987, p.75).

As a result of these events, the first lesson that workers learned was the understanding of the need to establish an independent trade union free from Party control. In December 1970, when workers demanded an independent union, the government encouraged them to elect their own people and put them in charge of the already established, regime-controlled unions. Initially, the workers followed government advice and elected their own people to the trade union bodies in Szczecin and nearby towns. Over time, they were able to see for themselves that this was not a viable road, as once the movement ceased to exist, the government simply repressed the newly elected leaders (Marx 1979). As a result of this experience, workers were unwilling to compromise on their demand for an independent union in 1980, although many of their intellectual advisers urged them to do so (Goodwyn 1991; Laba 1991).

"Gradually, management got rid of those who had been most active in the strike. I was always being given the worst work, and I was never allowed any kind of promotion" (Walesa 1987, p. 85). One of the strike leaders was found dead in his apartment from gas inhalation; another awoke in his apartment, after having been beaten, to find the gas turned on. He was arrested soon afterward, charged with rape and fired (Ost 1990, p. 56). Another independently elected trade union leader, Janusz Boryka, suddenly disappeared at the train station while returning from work. His coworkers learned that he had been pushed under a moving train and killed. The press claimed that it had been an accident caused by his being drunk. His friends, however, denied that he had been drinking and they contended that Janusz had been murdered. That accident scared many newly elected trade unions leaders and the prosecutions intensified. As Krystosiak described: "The leader of the regional trade union branch in Szczecin, Edmund Baluka, who attempted to create an independent, self-regulating, self-governing trade union, was offered a well-paid job that he had sought for years, as a sailor. As soon as the ship moored in the port of a Latin American country, a secret police agent came to Baluka, holding gun in his hand and ordered him to got off the ship in five minutes. Later, the Communist press announced that Baluka had betrayed the trust of the workers who had elected him and had taken the first chance to defect to the West." (Krystosiak 1994, interview).

The second lesson that the workers learned was to appreciate the value of occupation strikes. After the impulsive street demonstrations ended with mass killings and injuries and no gains, workers realized that the only way to protect themselves and to force the government to negotiate was to stay in the workplaces, as in Szczecin and Gdansk (Goodwyn, 1991; Laba, 1991). In doing so, the workers were not inventing new forms of struggle (Tarrow, 1993) but were recapturing old methods, as manifested in the workers' councils created during the Russian revolutions of 1905 and 1917. By staying inside the factories, workers were also protected from false accusations and the use of provocateurs (Goodwyn 1991, interview; Laba 1991, interview; Marx 1974). Occupational strikes became the new protest strategy (Bogacz 1992, interview; Celejewska 1994, interview; Tarrow 1993; Smithy & Kurtz 1999).

The third lesson the workers learned was that the strength of their protest was vastly increased with the creation of the inter-factory strike committees and worker unity. Workers came to understand the importance of supporting one another. "They came to realize that only in numbers was there strength. If they tried to deal with their demands factory-by-factory, they would have been crushed just like cockroaches, one-by-one. They understood that only if they gathered together could they win something." (Krystosiak 1994, interview). By 1980, this idea of common interests had become widely assimilated, and not only by the coastal workers. Indeed, many workers all over the country had come to understand that only their unity, their solidarity, could save them from the government's wrath (Bogacz 1992, interview; Frasyniuk 1988, interview). Thus, in 1980, protesting workers recognized that they must develop as widespread a movement as possible—both within the regions where the protest initiated, and as much as possible, throughout the country: "In 1980, the shipyard workers said, "Whoever goes on strike, even if it's a little place with five and

one half workers, we'll take it. Join us. You are all as important as we are".
(Krystosiak 1994, interview).

This idea of a common interest became widely accepted and was further enhanced by the strong understanding that only unity could save protestors from
government repression: Aleksander Krystosiak recalled that during the seventies, the shipyard workers in Szczecin made some effort to get to know their
counterparts in Gdansk, so that they could be better prepared and coordinated
should another opportunity arise. When it did, in 1980, the Szczecin inter-
factory strike committee demanded the right to have their representatives in
Gdansk in order to further cooperation between the two regions (Krystosiak
1993, interview). "We felt there was no hope of radical change if there were not
some kind of power among the workers. If we acted as a handful, we would lose
our jobs and the means of living, and we wouldn't be able to do anything. We
couldn't do anything. So we had to organize. People realized that they only had
power in the workplace. But they also knew that just one workplace going on
strike wasn't enough, that there had to be more and more, and the best would be
if all the regions would go on strike. People on the seashore asked, 'How will
(the heavily industrial region of) Silesia react?'" (Bogacz 1994, interview).
While some of these lessons have been considered in the literature, there has
been less discussion of the importance of workers beyond the coast considering
it important to come to the aid of other workers. Yet, this development was of
crucial significance in the 1980 strikes (Meyer 1999).

Finally, the fourth lesson was that December 1970 also produced a layer of
leadership who would play an important role in the 1980-1981 Solidarity
movement, and consequently, the Round Table negotiations in 1989 and Solidarity's victory in a democratic election in June 1989. While the leaders of that
time were persecuted and pursued with the end of discrediting them among their
followers, there was another layer of secondary leadership who survived. These
were people who had been active in the strike in 1970, who had helped to organize it and who had been trained by those above them. Walesa and Anna Walentynowicz in Gdansk and Krystosiak in Szczecin were among them. They were
to play a central role in leading the strike and in the negotiations with the government in 1980.

The line of blood these events drew between the workers and the communist regime changed things forever. Through the killings, the regime lost standing as a moral creature. Never again would the government attempt to appeal to
its population in moral or ideological terms (Blazynski 1979, p. 34). After December 1970, there was little sign that anyone really believed in Marxist ideology. Workers and students were alienated, and the nomenclature, many of
whom had newly attained their positions, were self-interested (Blazynski 1979,
p. 34, see chapter 1 on the turnover in the nomenclature after both 1968 and
1970).

Gomulka, who had come to power in 1956 on the hopes of so many people,
had lost his last base of support. Within a few days, he was replaced by Edward
Gierek, the Communist Party First Secretary from Silesia. Gierek's accession to
power did provide a breather for the regime, and it did create a wave of enthusi-

asm, though it was small in comparison to what Gomulka had enjoyed in 1956. To gain it, Gierek had to promise that he would improve the material basis of people's lives. He asked his countrymen to judge him only by his competence, specifically by the effect of his policies on their standard of living. It was what his administration would live or die by. When that failed a decade later, there was little to fall back on.

NOTES

1. This paper was originally presented at the 1996 meeting of the American Socio-logical Association in New York City.

2. The interview with Malgorzata Celejewska was conducted by the author in Po-land, in 1994. In December 1970 Ms. Celejewska worked as an accountant in the North Shipyard in Gdansk; In 1980 she was the Gdansk regional treasurer of Solidarity move-ment.

3. The interview with Alicja Matuszewska was conducted in Gdansk, Poland, in 1994. Alicja Matuszewska led the civilian workers who worked for the military and later became the Solidarity National Treasurer in 1980. She worked as a civilian accountant in the military shipyard in Gdynia at the time of the December 1970 strikes.

4. The interview with Aleksander Krystosiak was conducted by the author of this paper in Szczecin, Poland, in 1994. Aleksander Krystosiak was a secondary leader of the 1970 strike in a group that organized the 1980 strike in its shipyard and was one of the leaders of the strike committee during negotiations with the government in December 1970. In 1980, he was vice-chair of Szczecin regional Solidarity during the Solidarity movement.

5. The interview with Bogdan Borusewicz was conducted in Gdansk, Poland in 1988. Bogdan Borusewicz was a student activist in 1968, he spent three years in jail for that activity; he joined Komited Obrony Robotnikow (KOR) [a dissident organization] and worked with the opposition in Gdansk during the later 1970s; he was one of the or-ganizers of the strike in the Gdansk Shipyard that created the Solidarity movement. He continued in an active role during the sixteen months of legal Solidarity and later helped organize the underground.

INTERVIEWS CONDUCTED BY THE AUTHOR IN POLAND IN 1988-1994

Zbigniew Bogacz, interviewed in 1992 and 1994. He was active in Upper Silesia and served as secretary for the Jastrzebie inter-factory workers' committee, established after the 1980 strike, and as a member of the National Miner's Commission in Solidarity, a post that put him in the national leadership. After martial law was declared, he was one of the leaders of an underground strike for two weeks.

Bogdan Borusewicz, interview conducted in 1988. He was active in Gdansk as a student activist in 1968 and spent three years in jail for that activity. He joined KOR and worked with the opposition in Gdansk during the later 1970s and was one of the organizers of the strike in the Gdansk Shipyard that created Solidarity. He continued in an active role dur-ing the sixteen months of legal Solidarity and later helped organize the underground.

Malgorzata Celejewska, interview conducted in 1994. She worked as an accountant in the North Shipyard in Gdansk and was the Gdansk regional treasurer.

Wladyslaw Frasyniuk, interviewed in 1988. He was the leader of the regional Solidarity union in Wroclaw and a member of the Solidarity national committee.

Winicjusz Gorecki, interview conducted in 1994. He was active in Szczecin, where he served on the National Tourist Workers Commission

Krzysztof Kasprzyk, an interview conducted in 1988. He became the head of Journalist's Union in Cracow in October 1980.

Aleksander Krystosiak, interviewed in 1994. He was a secondary leader of the 1970 strike in a group that organized the 1980 strike in the Szczecin shipyard; he was one of the leaders of the strike committee during negotiations with the government. Later, he was vice-chair of Szczecin regional Solidarity.

Alicja Matuszewska, interview conducted in 1994. She was active in Gdansk, where she led the civilian workers who worked for the military; later she became the Solidarity National Treasurer.

Krzysztof Mlodzik, interviewed in 1988. He was active in Upper Silesia, where he played a leading role after martial law was declared in organizing an underground strike in his mine.

Tadeusz Plawinski, interview conducted in 1994. He was active in Gdynia, as the President of the Solidarity union in the Paris Commune Shipyard in Gdynia.

Adam Sucharski, interviewed in 1997. He was in the secret police from the late 1960s; he rose to be colonel and concentrated especially prosecuting people who were religious. His name is a pseudonym, which was the condition of his talking to me.

REFERENCES

Blazynski, George. 1979. *Flashpoint Poland.* New York: Pergamon Press.

Goodwyn, Lawrence. 1991. *Breaking the Barrier: The Rise of Solidarity in Poland.* New York, NY: Oxford University Press.

Green, Peter. 1977. The Third Round in Poland. *New Left Review, 101-2* (Feb-April), 69-108.

Kurzman, Charles. 1996. Structural Opportunity and Perceived Opportunity in Social-Movement Theory: The Iranian Revolution of 1979. *American Sociological Review* 61: 153-170.

Laba, Roman. 1991. *The Roots of Solidarity.* Princeton, NJ: Princeton University Press.

Majkowski, Wladyslaw. 1985. *People's Poland: Patterns of Social Inequality and Conflict.* Westport, CT: Greenwood Press.

Malinowski, Jan. 1984. Polish Workers. *International Journal of Sociology, 14* (Fall), 1-116.

Marx, Gary. 1974. Thoughts on a Neglected Category of Social Movement Participant: The Agent Provocateur and the Informant. *American Journal of Sociology, 80*, 2, 402-442.

Marx, Gary, 1979. External Efforts to Damage or Facilitate Social Movements: Some Patterns, Explanations, Outcomes and Complications. In M. Zald & J. D. McCarthy (Eds.), *The Dynamics of Social Movements: Resource Mobilization, Social Control And Tactic.* Cambridge, Mass: Winthrop Publishers.

Meyer, David S. 1999. Civil Disobedience and Protest Cycles. In J. Freeman & V. Johnson (Eds.), *Waves of Protest: Social Movements Since the Sixties*. New York: Rowan and Littlefield.

Ost, David. 1990. *Solidarity and Politics of Anti-Politics*. Philadelphia: Temple University Press.

Pelczynski, Z. A. 1980a. The Decline of Gomulka. In R. F. Leslie, *The History of Poland Since 1863*. New York: Cambridge University Press.

Rakowski, Mieczyslaw. 1973. December 1970: The Turning Point. In A. Bromke & J. W. Strong (Eds.), *Gierek's Poland*. New York: Praeger Press.

Singer, Daniel. 1989. *The Road to Gdansk: Poland and the USSR*. New York: Monthly Review Press.

Smithy, Lee & Lester R. Kurtz. 1999. We have Bare Hands: Nonviolent Social Movements in the Soviet Bloc. In K. Zunes & Asher, *Nonviolent Social Movements: A Geographical Perspective*. Malden, MA: Blackwell Publishers.

Tarrow, Sidney. 1993. Cycles of Collective Action: Between Moments of Madness and the Repertoire of Contention. *Social Science History, 17* (Summer), 281-308.

Tocqueviille, Alexis de. 1955. *The Old Regime and the French Revolution*. Translated by S. Gilbert. Garden City, NY: Doubleday Anchor.

Walesa, Lech. 1987. *A Way of Hope: An Autobiography*. New York: Henry Holt.

Weydenthal, Jan Bartel de. 1981. Poland: Workers and Politics. In J. F. Triska & C. Gati (Eds.), *Blue-Collar Workers in Eastern Europe*. London: George Allen & Unwin.

III

Impact on Economy

5

Transitional Economies and Income Inequality: The Case of Estonia

Nancy Brandon Tuma, Mikk Titma
and Rein Murakas

Transitional societies have substantially different economies. It has been argued that many of these differences will persist for some time and that western-type market economies will not quickly emerge in all post-socialist societies (Cornia 1996; Szelényi & Kostello 1996). An important economic and political issue in these countries is income differentiation, which was not only relatively low under state socialism but organized very differently than in market economies (Flakierski 1993; Titma & Tuma 1993). Previous analyses of income differentiation in post-Soviet countries (Burawoy 1997; Gerber & Hout 1998; Titma 1997) have found remarkable cross-country differences in patterns and determinants of income differentiation.

In this research,[1] we examine income differentiation in 1992 and 1997 in Estonia, the post-Soviet country that has arguably moved fastest toward a western-type market economy. We analyze data from *Paths of a Generation* (Titma & Tuma 1995), a longitudinal study of 1983-1985 graduates of secondary schools in fifteen regions of the Soviet Union. We focus here on the information collected in Estonia in the third and fourth waves (collections of data within a defined period) (PG:Waves 3 and 4), which obtained completed interviews from 2,128 and 2,141 respondents in Estonia in 1993 and 1997, respectively (Titma & Tuma 1995, 1997).

We address several aspects of income differentiation. As the market starts to function, is the overall level of income increasing as people living in socialist societies had hoped? Are income inequalities growing or shrinking? We ask these questions not only for the population as a whole but also for key subgroups. We also examine income mobility. Are those at the top and bottom of the income distribution the same in 1992 and 1997? Or has there been considerable income mobility? Finally, we examine various factors hypothesized to predict income of individuals, and we consider how their effects have changed between 1992 and 1997.

INCOME INEQUALITY IN TRANSITIONAL ECONOMIES

Two main phases are apparent in the development of transitional economies (Åslund 1995). First, in most countries, the initial development of a market economy starts from the top. The state adopts a certain concept of marketization and introduces the institutional and legal bases believed to be necessary for a market economy to develop and function (Vecernik 1991). In most instances, privatization of a socialist state's assets and shares in domestic enterprises occurres rapidly without genuine, open competition (Gottschalk 1997; Hassan and Peters 1996; Headey, Krause & Habich 1995; Szydlik 1994). Consequently, the entrepreneurs appearing in the first phase mainly obtain their economic advantages as a result of political decisions.

The second phase arises when market forces really begin to operate after private property exists. Then entrepreneurs must make their gains in tough competition with others. It is only in this second phase that the market really works and that the economy comes under the control of numerous economic actors competing and cooperating with one another. In this phase of the transition, political decisions do not directly drive economic processes though they have many indirect effects, for example, through policies affecting taxation and interest rates (Gottschalk 1997; Frick, Hauser, Muller & Wagner 1995).

As a market economy develops, income differentiation typical of that in western market societies can be expected to emerge. Capital (especially financial capital) lets people take risks, and some of them make profits—sometimes huge profits. The majority of the population in a country cannot afford such risks, however, and they sell their labor. A stable, historically-rooted labor market has institutionalized wage arrangements and a system of bargaining for adjustments in wages. In transitional societies, which formerly had guaranteed jobs and frozen, state-fixed, relatively equal wages, people have lacked even the belief that income differences are normal and depend on quality of work. Institutional arrangements about wage negotiations need to be developed and both employers and employees must learn to negotiate over wages. The establishment and acceptance of "normal" differences in income occurs even more slowly. Other new phenomena are unemployment (open and hidden) and the idea that individuals are responsible for finding their own jobs. In every transitional society, income differentiation depends on the phase of the transition and on the extent and nature of the development of the market as an institution (Szelényi & Kostello 1996).

Because Estonia has been in the vanguard of the post-communist transition among former Soviet republics, it is a useful country in which to study economic and political transitions, despite its small population of 1.4 million in 1997 (Titma, Silver, & Anderson 1997). Politically Estonia was at the forefront of *perestroika,* and since regaining independence, it has held two presidential and four parliamentary elections. Eight governments have been formed, and a multi-party system has developed. Though Estonia has few natural resources, its Nordic and Germanic heritage and its close proximity to Finland and Sweden have enabled it to move swiftly to a market economy, even though it was tightly linked to the

Soviet economy in the 1980s. Scandinavian firms and businessmen were quick to gain a foothold in Estonia, and their intervention radically shortened the learning process and provided resources that allowed a market economy to develop with surprising speed. The Estonian government's openness to foreign business and its decision in 1992 to peg the Estonian kroon to the German mark have facilitated Estonia's economic transition.

After abandoning a command economy, Estonia experienced an initial and entirely typical economic decline until 1995. In 1995, however, its economy began to turn toward positive growth in gross domestic product (GDP)—the first of the former Soviet republics to achieve this (UNDP 1995). GDP per capita was about $3,200 in 1997, based on data from the *Statistical Yearbook of Estonia* (1998, pp. 26, 53) and currency exchange rates reported by the Estonian (state) Bank (1999b). In 1996, only 16 percent of property was held by state and local governments, based on net turnover, and the share of property in private hands was 64 percent, including 20 percent in foreign hands (Estonian Bank 1999a). Although nominal wages remain low, they are increasing. Both inflation and unemployment are modest (below 20 percent) for a transitional society. With its openness to foreign investments, Estonia has become the only country of the former Soviet republics that conducts a majority of its trade with countries *not* formerly in the Soviet Union or in communist Eastern Europe (UNDP 1998). As a result, in 1998, Estonia began negotiations to join the European Union.

CONCEPTS AND HYPOTHESES

Income levels and income inequality are major political issues in post-communist societies because so many people are in poverty following the collapse of the command economy (Milanovic 1996). Many people think that the emerging market is pushing the majority of people into poverty while radically redistributing assets and income into the hands of a few. At the same time, the theory behind the whole was undertaken to provide people with a better life than they had under the economically inefficient command economy of socialist states. In at least some post-socialist countries (e.g., Poland or Hungary), the income of most people is higher now than during the socialist past (Vecernik 1996). Economically reasonable differentiation results from linking economic rewards to quality of results. For one thing, human capital starts to be rewarded in accordance with its value.

After the first phase in which assets are concentrated in the hands of a few and speculative capital is dominant (Burawoy 1997), the second phase of a normal market develops in most parts of the economy. Consequently, we focus our attention on income changes between 1992 (the start of marketization) and 1997 to see to what extent a market economy has begun to raise and redistribute income. In contrast to the cross-sectional data on Russia analyzed by Gerber and Hout (1998), we examine longitudinal data (Titma 1997).

We consider four aspects of income differentiation: overall levels, inequality, mobility, and attainment. By the *overall level of income*, we have in mind various measures of central tendency of income in the population or in some subgroup, such as the average or median income. By *income inequality*, we mean the extent of variation in income within a population or some subgroup. By *income mobility*, we mean the extent of change over time in real income of individuals, in an absolute and relative sense. *Income attainment* refers to the factors differentiating among individuals in their level of income at a point in time.

Overall Level of Income

For people in a transitional society to furnish political support for a market economy, the introduction of a market needs to improve the overall level of material well-being and, more particularly, the overall level of income. The facts that Estonia's GDP per capita reached $3,200 in 1997 and that growth in its GDP has been positive since 1995 suggest our first hypothesis:

Hypothesis 1: Overall income levels have risen between 1992 and 1997.

Income Inequality

Before the transition, people who lived in socialist societies, where material well-being was relatively low but also relatively equal, did not fully understand that the change to a market economy would bring greater inequality. Titma and Murakas (1997) found, for example, that in September 1992, a year after Estonia regained its independence, half of the total income of the PG cohort in Estonia was held by the richest 9 percent and the other half by the bottom 93 percent, indicating a very high level of inequality. Our second hypothesis (and hope) is:

Hypothesis 2: Income inequality is less in 1997 than in 1992.

Income Mobility

Greater levels of income inequality tend to be more politically acceptable to people if income mobility is high: People who are poor at one point in time can then hope and may expect that their material well-being will improve in the not too distant future. Such a hope and expectation may be realistic in a transitional economy where a market is developing, the private sector is expanding (though the state sector is shrinking), new enterprises are opening (though some are being closed), and, as a result, job mobility is high. We therefore hypothesize that:

Hypothesis 3: Mobility in real income has been high between 1992 and 1997.

Nevertheless, we do think that the elites are especially able to protect their positional advantages over time (Rònas-Tas 1994). Moreover, those at the bottom often either lack the resources to escape poverty or have certain enduring disabilities that confine them to the bottom. Consequently, we hypothesize that:

Hypothesis 4a: Those with the highest income levels in 1992 are more likely than others to have a high income in 1997.

Hypothesis 4b: Those with the lowest income levels in 1992 are more likely than others to have a low income in 1997.

Hypothesis 4c: Those whose income levels were in the middle in 1992 are likely to have experienced the most income mobility by 1997.

Income Attainment

The literature on socio-economic attainment (including income attainment) in the U.S. and in other western societies is voluminous. We do not attempt to review it here since key predictors of economic success are so well known (Topel 1997). One expects, first of all, that in a market economy, human capital (especially education) leads to higher income (as well as higher occupational attainment). We therefore hypothesize:

Hypothesis 5a: Income increases with educational level.

Hypothesis 5b: Income increases with educational level more in 1997 than in 1992.

In established market economies, there are institutionalized income differences among those in various occupations, net of the educational differences of occupational holders. Managers tend to earn a lot, even if they are not well educated, and unskilled workers tend to earn little, even if they have a university education. Thus, we hypothesize that:

Hypothesis 6a: Income depends on occupation.

Hypothesis 6b: Income depends on occupation more in 1997 than in 1992.

Allocation of rewards in socialist economies operate differently and was based on different principles. In socialist economies, branch of the economy (industry) and locality matter a lot (Titma & Tuma 1993). We expect that the dimensions important in differentiating people's well-being under socialism will have continuing but diminishing effects over time.

Hypothesis 7a: Income depends on branch of the economy (industry).

Hypothesis 7b: Income depends on branch of the economy (industry) less in 1997 than in 1992.

Hypothesis 8a: Income depends on locality (capital city, other large cities, towns, villages).

Hypothesis 8b: Income depends on locality less in 1997 than in 1992.

People in market economies sometimes move to improve their economic well-being, and the same was true in command economies, which had an institutionalized hierarchy of places and of rewards commensurate with position on that hierarchy. We therefore expect:

Hypothesis 9: Income depends on a person's migration history.

We have no a priori hypothesis about whether migration history would be more important in 1992 than in 1997.

In transitional economies, remnants of the old socialist system co-exist with the newly emerging market economy (Walder 1996). The two systems not only use different criteria in allocating income to people but also offer different levels of rewards (Titma & Tuma 1993). Enterprises in the private sector tend to be more profitable and to offer workers somewhat higher wages (Gerber & Hout 1998). Moreover, in a transitional economy, the state's direct control over society and the economy shrinks and state-owned enterprises are sold. Just as importantly, the sources of the state's revenue changes. After divesting itself of most of the socialist state's property, state revenues in a transitional society need to come largely from assorted taxes. In a state (such as Russia) where domestic tax revenues are paltry, employees in the state sector are poorly paid. In Estonia, however, the situation is quite different; government revenues have risen because of the profitability of the private sector. In our analyses we therefore distinguish work in the private sector, for state-owned enterprises and for organizations financed by the state budget (e.g., education, medicine, public security) and hypothesize that:

Hypothesis 10a: Income is higher in the private sector than in the state sector.

Hypothesis 10b: Differences in income in the private and state sectors are greater in 1997 than in 1992.

Although market societies are supposed to be meritocracies that reward people purely on the basis of their productivity and are not supposed to discriminate among them on the basis of ascriptive characteristics like gender and ethnicity, much empirical evidence on western societies challenges this claim. Although Estonia has a relatively strong historical tradition of gender equality, male labor was traditionally valued and rewarded more highly. As in East Germany (Sørensen & Trappe 1995) and Yugoslavia (Putnam 1990), Titma and Murakas (1997) found that income differentiation in Estonia in 1992 was based on gender more than on any other factor they examined (including education, occupation, industry, locality and nationality, among many others). We expect that gender equality in incomes has not yet been achieved by 1997.

Hypothesis 11a: Income is lower for women than for men.

Hypothesis 11b: Income differentiation is based on gender more than on any other factor.

During the Soviet period, nationality was a major dividing line, and it remains an important one (Laitin 1996; Chinn & Kaiser 1996; Titma, Tuma, & Silver 1998). The Soviet system sponsored a massive migration of ethnic Russians to Estonia, encouraged everyone to adopt the Russian language and, to a lesser extent, Russian culture, and used nationality to distinguish among Soviet citizens. ("Nationality" was the infamous "fifth line" on a Soviet internal passport.) Native Estonians resisted russification quietly during the Soviet period. After regaining independence, however, the Estonian state adopted a number of policies favoring Estonian nationals. Knowledge of the Estonian language was not only required for citizenship, but more to the present point, the Estonian language replaced Russian as the dominant language in commerce and in most workplaces, especially those in the private sector. Hence, we hypothesize that:

Hypothesis 12a: Income is lower among those whose nationality is not Estonian.

Hypothesis 12b: Income differences based on nationality are greater in 1997 than in 1992.

DATA AND METHODS

We use data for Estonia from the larger comparative longitudinal project Paths of a Generation (PG) (Titma 1985, Titma & Tuma 1995). The project, which was modeled on Coleman's study of American high school students—"High School and Beyond" (HS&B)—began as a study of the life careers of a cohort of 1983-1984 graduates from secondary schools in fifteen regions of the Soviet Union. In addition to the original base-year PG survey (Wave 1), there have been three follow-ups. The third follow-up (PG:Wave 4) is still in the field in some sites, but in Estonia, PG:Wave 4 began early in 1997 and was completed by the fall. The PG surveys have covered both factual items about people's lives (e.g., education, work, family history, political participation, income) and their opinions about education, work, life value, and political issues.

The sample for PG:Wave 1 used a two-stage stratified, clustered design (Tuma, Titma & Yakubovich 1995); the design was a modified version of the one used in HS&B. The stratification variables were the type of secondary school (general, specialized, vocation) and locality (regional capital, large city, town, village). Students in graduating classes of the selected schools were surveyed shortly before graduation. In Estonia 3,398 of the 15,636 individuals graduating from secondary schools in 1983 were surveyed in PG:Wave 1. Follow-up interviews of the respondents to PG:Wave 1 were conducted in Estonia, in 1987–1988 (PG:Wave 2), 1992–1993 (PG:Wave 3) and 1997 (PG:Wave 4).

Our analyses are based on PG:Waves 3 and 4, which used standardized, face-to-face interviews. In Estonia, 2,128 people were interviewed in PG:Wave 3 and 2,141 in PG:Wave 4. In both waves, the target samples were somewhat smaller than in the original survey because of funding limitations and some attrition, especially among Russian-speakers, many of whom emigrated from Estonia after 1991. Response rates among the target samples were 75 percent in PG:Wave 3 and 82 percent in PG:Wave 4. Refusal rates were very low among those who could be located. Aside from some reduction in the percentage of Russian-speakers, the composition of the respondents to PG:Waves 3 and 4 in terms of basic background variables resembles that of the original respondents to PG:Wave 1. We have done extensive checking of data from different waves to ascertain that the same person has actually been interviewed over time (Titma & Tuma 1997).

The sample is representative of the cohort that was enrolled in their last year of secondary school in Estonia in 1982-1983. This cohort obtained their education under the Soviet system, had their first work and political experiences during *perestroika* and Estonia's "Singing Revolution" in the late 1980s, and, being in the prime of adulthood, were well-positioned to build a market-based democratic society when Estonia regained its independence on August 21, 1991.

Table 5.1 gives basic information about the variables used in our analyses. In addition to the variables specifically mentioned in our hypotheses, in the multivariate analyses of income reported below, we also included as control variables the person's number of children and indicators of marital status, whether the person had had "odd jobs" in the relevant year and whether the person had received government benefits (e.g., unemployment benefits) in that year. In the multivariate analyses reported below, most polytomous variables were dummy-coded; however, occupation and branch of the economy (industry) were effect-coded because no natural reference category exists.

Table 5.1
Variables Used in the Analysis (reference categories indicated by *)

Variable	Source Variables		Description	Average	
	Wave 3	Wave 4		Wave 3	Wave 4
Respondent's total income in previous month (in USD) adjusted to March 1997 prices	Q265#1-Q265#3	J17$-J23$	Sum of income from misc. sources (e.g., salary, trading, state benefits, etc.) in previous month (Wave 4) or September 1992 (Wave 3). Adjusted to March 1997 using Estonian Bank's consumer price index; converted from Estonian kroons to USD using official exchange rates.	$260	$304
Log_e of respondent's total monthly income	same	Same	see above	4.84	5.21
Demographic Characteristics					
Female	Q5	A6		.59	.58
Not Estonian	Q4	B3		.20	.21
Unmarried	CHECK22, CHECK24-CHECK26	E3		.24	.20
Unmarried female				.14	.13
Number of children	Q252_1-Q266_6	G1		1.56	1.54
No children	Q251	G1		.23	.17
Education (years)	Q180	C7	Usual # of years to achieve current educational level	12.7	12.8
Settlement type	TYPE	B8.1			
Capital city				.28	.30
Other big city				.14	.21
Other towns*				.27	.18
Village				.31	.31
Migration experience	Q3, TYPE	B5.1, B8.1	Comparison of settlement types of birthplace and current residence		
Moved to bigger place				.22	.23
No change*				.57	.62
Moved to smaller place				.21	.15

Table 5.1 continued

Sector of economy	Q188_1- Q188_10	D9_1			
Private				.21	.62
State owned				.40	.16
Financed by state budget				.39	.22
Branch of economy	Q185_1- Q185_10	D11_1			
Agriculture				.19	.10
Industry, construction				.28	.31
Service, trade, finance				.18	.27
Education, medicine				.26	.22
State & social organizations				.03	.04
Other*				.05	.06
Occupation	Q189_1- Q189_10	D10_1	Standard groupings of ISCO codes		
Managers				.08	.14
Professionals				.21	.16
Semi-profess'ls				.18	.18
Clerks				.09	.09
Sales & Service workers				.09	.11
Skilled workers				.16	.15
Operators, drivers				.11	.10
Skilled workers in agriculture				.04	.03
Unskilled workers				.05	.05
Others*				.00	.00
Other variables:					
Odd jobs	Q1992_3- Q1992_6	D16_3 to D23_2	Various sources of income earned from irregular work	.40	.28
Got government payments	Q1992_12	J22$	J22$	.51	.51
Sample Size				1,643	1,916

Sources: PG Wave 4 and PG Wave 3 in Estonia.
Note: Reference categories USD= U.S. Dollars

In PG:Wave 3, respondents were asked their total income, as well as income from various sources, in September 1992. In PG:Wave 4, respondents were asked their total income in the previous year and in the previous month; they were also asked their income from eight different sources in the previous month. People's knowledge of their income is not very accurate or very reliable in any country, but the figures reported by respondents are at least highly correlated. For example, the correlation between the sum of income reported from the eight sources in the month before the interview in 1997 and their reported income for calendar year 1996 was .76.

Respondents reported their income in Estonian kroons, but we have converted them to U.S. dollars using the time series of currency exchange rates reported by the Estonian Bank (1999b). In addition, except where otherwise noted, income has been adjusted from the nominal to real value using the Estonian Bank's (1999b) time series on consumer prices for a standard basket of goods. We have chosen March 1997 as our base point in time since the bulk of interviews in PG:Wave 4 occurred around then.

Although we cannot comment at length on Table 5.1 because of space limitations, we do point out marked changes between 1992 and 1997. First, there are dramatic shifts among sectors of the economy, with the private sector sharply increasing and the two state sectors shrinking. There are also substantial shifts in industry, with the proportion in agriculture and in public-service institutions (e.g., education, medicine) declining and the proportion in service and trade increasing. Occupational composition has also changed significantly. In particular, the proportion of managers has grown while the proportion of professionals has diminished.

Most of our results involve fairly straightforward calculations of means, percentages and order statistics (e.g., medians and other percentiles). In analyzing income attainment, we regress the natural logarithm of the respondent's income in a particular month (plus one dollar because a few people reported zero income) on various hypothesized explanatory variables. Taking the logarithm of income is common in multivariate analyses of income to overcome the positive skewness of income. The standard assumption that the disturbance in the linear regression equation is normally distributed is more appropriate when this transformation of income is used.

RESULTS

Overall Income Levels

Data on the income of individuals and families in Estonia is nowadays relatively reliable because it is collected by the Estonian Statistical Office in accordance with internationally-accepted methods.[2]

Table 5.2 gives some information on income per household member in Estonia from these sources for January 1993 and December 1996 and from PG:Waves 3 and 4 for September 1992 and March 1997. For all Estonia, average *nominal* income has tripled, though in *real* (i.e., price-adjusted) terms, average income has increased only ten percent. We see a fairly similar pattern for the PG cohort: average *nominal* income tripled, whereas average *real* income grew by somewhat more than twenty percent.

Table 5.2
Income per Household Member in Estonia Compared with the PG Cohort

	All Estonia in January 1993	PG sample of 2,036 in September 1992	All Estonia in December 1996	PG sample of 1,864 in March 1997
Average income per household member (US $)	$38[a]	$47	$136	$176
Average income per household member in prices of September 1992	$38	$47	$42	$58
Ratio of income of 10th and 1st decile groups	9.6	29.4	12.6	18.7
Percentage of all income held by the poorest 40% of families	19.6%	12.3%	17.7%	14.8%
Percentage of all income held by the richest 20% of families	42.8%	58.9%	46.1%	52.1%
Gini index	.342	.535	.377[b]	.455
Average income per household member of the richest 10% of households (US $)	N.A.	$137	$426	$645

Notes: a. Information for this cell is available for September 1992 but not for January 1993.
   b. Based on monthly household expenditures per household member.
   c. USD=U.S. Dollars
Sources : Data for All Estonia:
   1. *Statistical Yearbook* 1993. Statistical Office of Estonia. Tallinn, 1993.
   2. *Statistical Yearbook* 1998. Statistical Office of Estonia. Tallinn, 1998.
   3. Estonian Statistics. *Statistical Office of Estonia Monthly* No. 5 (77) 1998.
   4. Statistical data from the WWW server of the Estonian Bank. http://www.ee/epbe
   5. Data from the Information Department of the Estonian Bank.

Table 5 .3
Percentile Values of Monthly Income (US \$) in September 1992 (adjusted to March 1997 Prices) by Respondent Group

		Percentiles					
Respondent Group	N	10	20	50	80	90	Mean
ALL in September 1992	2088	42	65	148	297	445	278
Gender							
Men	892	59	104	192	445	742	433
Women	1196	36	53	119	208	285	162
Nationality							
Estonians	1658	48	74	148	297	445	281
Non-Estonians	425	16	48	148	297	453	266
Settlement Type							
Capital city	571	18	53	175	356	594	333
Other major cities	277	48	76	148	273	570	414
Small towns	569	46	67	148	267	356	245
Villages	670	52	74	134	238	356	198

Table 5.3 continued

Completed Education   **Percentiles**

Vocational Education	459	30	65	134	282	445	297
Specialized Secondary	279	34	59	140	297	445	285
General Secondary	833	37	71	148	267	445	249
Higher Education	511	48	71	172	315	594	303
Sector of Economy							
Private	439	36	89	208	475	742	417
State budget financed	752	48	71	148	226	326	253
State-owned enterprise	828	36	62	134	267	416	221
Respondent Group	N	10	20	50	80	90	Mean
Occupational Group							
Managers	158	59	119	238	594	1215	520
Professionals	393	48	83	163	267	445	257
Semi-professionals	355	48	67	148	267	356	293
Clerks	169	36	54	122	208	342	243
Sales/service workers	165	23	53	119	208	297	158
Skilled workers	356	30	64	148	297	594	295
Operatives, drivers	236	32	89	148	297	445	286
Skilled workers in agriculture	85	33	59	119	222	297	166
Unskilled workers	92	47	59	107	184	318	172

Source: PG, Wave 3 in Estonia.

Table 5.4
Percentile Values of Monthly Income (US $) in March 1997 by Respondent Group

	N	Percentiles					Mean
		10	20	50	80	90	
ALL in 1996 (per month)	1679	48	93	208	388	554	285
ALL in prev. month 1997	2041	46	94	213	390	565	301
Gender							
Men	871	75	144	287	514	751	406
Women	1170	37	73	173	317	441	222
Nationality							
Estonians	1618	52	99	221	413	598	318
Non-Estonians	423	32	75	184	319	448	235
Settlement Type							
Capital city	586	35	97	270	540	790	392
Other major cities	434	58	113	215	388	489	310
Small towns	373	44	83	196	341	460	257
Villages	648	52	86	183	325	449˙	237
Completed Education							
Vocational Education	422	30	75	191	349	490	257
Specialized Secondary	260	33	71	173	323	406	215
General Secondary	817	49	88	184	359	494	260
Higher Education	542	62	165	301	539	859	438
Sector of Economy							
Private	1241	59	106	226	452	652	344
State budget financed	426	45	96	199	328	443	255
State-owned enterprise	325	34	81	177	322	443	222

Table 5. 4 continued

		Percentiles					
Respondent Group	N	10	20	50	80	90	Mean
Occupational Group							
Managers	282	109	213	395	738	1177	628
Professionals	314	50	152	265	467	649	334
Semi-professionals	358	61	115	199	369	471	262
Clerks	169	32	79	172	320	381	204
Sales/service workers	213	36	72	158	281	398	192
Skilled workers	299	36	95	203	339	467	253
Operatives, drivers	194	49	103	214	325	455	255
Skilled workers in agriculture	53	39	60	125	291	378	184
Unskilled workers	98	19	59	105	230	321	164

Source: PG, Wave 4 in Estonia.

Tables 5.3 and 5.4 give more detailed information on the real monthly income of individuals in the PG cohort in September 1992 and in March 1997. The monthly average for the PG cohort in March 1997 is $301, which is also about ten percent higher than the average in September 1992, $278. The ten percent increase is about half the increase for the PG cohort in table 5.2, presumably because Tables 3 and 4 given information about personal income whereas table 5.2 gives information about household income per household member. The general conclusion is, however, the same and supports our hypothesis H1: The PG cohort experienced real gains in average income between 1992 and 1997, but the size of the gains was modest.

A comparison of median personal income in 1992 and 1997 for the PG cohort (see Tables 5.3 and 5.4) gives a more encouraging picture of economic improvement. The median monthly income in 1997 was $213 versus $148 in 1992, a 44 percent increase. It may seem odd that the mean has increased modestly when the median has increased so much. The explanation stems from the fact that the median is a highly robust statistic whereas the mean is very sensitive to outliers—in this instance, one PG respondent reported an unusually high income in 1992 that raised the average well above what it would otherwise have been. It should not be concluded that outliers are troublesome only when analyzing sample survey data: A handful of millionaires and billionaires in a population can raise average income enormously without the general populace noticing any improvement in their economic well-being.

Income Inequality

It is important scientifically, as well as for policy reasons, to understand income inequality. As Table 5.2 reports, official statistics for all of Estonia reveal small increases in inequality between 1992 and 1997. For example, the Gini coefficient (Alker 1965; Schwartz & Winship 1979) increased from .342 in January 1993 to .377 in March 1997, only slightly below what Kuznets (1963) reported for the United States in the 1960s (.393). In the same period, the ratio of the income of the top decile to the bottom decile rose from 9.6 to 12.6, the share of income of the poorest 40 percent of families fell from 19.6 percent to 17.7 percent, and the share of income of the richest 20 percent increased from 42.8 percent to 46.1 percent. Income inequality in Estonia has not yet lessened, though the 1997 figures do not seem very high when viewed from the perspective of the U.S. It should be noted that roughly one fourth of Estonia's population consists of retired individuals, a hard-hit group in every transitional society.

Table 5.2 gives a quite different picture of both the degree of inequality and changes in inequality over time for the PG cohort. For these young adults, the Gini coefficient for household income per household member was quite high (.535) in September 1992; it is still high in March 1997 (.455) but substantially lower. In the same period, the ratio of the income of the top decile of the PG cohort to the bottom decile fell from 29.4 to 18.7, the share of income of the poorest 40 percent of families rose from 12.3 percent to 14.8 percent, and the share of income of the richest 20 percent decreased from 58.9 percent to 52.1 percent.

An increasing fraction of the PG cohort of young adults (who have at least a secondary school education) have been able to take advantage of the new opportunities offered by the developing market economy, and inequality among them has fallen. Those who were at the bottom of the income hierarchy in 1992 have gained more by 1997 than those who were at the top.

The picture of income inequality is somewhat rosier when based on information about the PG cohort, a group of relatively well-educated young adults who are among those most likely to be able to benefit from the transition to a market economy. Although the ratio of income at the ninetieth percentile to income at the tenth percentile rose from 10.6 ($445/$42) in September 1992, to 12.3 ($565/$46) in March 1997, the ratio of income at the eightieth percentile to income at the twentieth percentiles fell from 4.5 ($297/$65) to 4.1 ($390/$94) over this same period. This means that between 1992 and 1997, not only the income associated with each decile rose, but inequality declined somewhat within the middle 60 percent of the PG cohort (i.e., those falling between the twentieth and eightieth percentiles). It is also worth noting that the ratio of the income of the ninetieth percentile to the median fell from 3.0 ($445/$148) to 2.65 ($565/$213) over this period. The PG cohort apparently has an expanding "middle income group" that has become better off and less differentiated in terms of income by 1997.

Note, however, that the income at the tenth percentile rose from $42 in September 1992 to $46 in March 1997, a small increase in a very small income. The main source of income for people in this bottom group is government benefits, which are small and have not risen much.

It is also interesting to examine changes in the distribution of income within various subgroups. Tables 5.3 and 5.4 also report various percentiles of monthly income in 1992 and 1997 within subgroups defined on the basis of gender, nationality, settlement type, education, economic sector and occupation.

Gender differences in income declined between 1992 and 1997, even though income was clearly lower for women than for men in both 1992 and 1997. Average income rose for women (from $162 to $222) but dropped for men (from $433 to $406). Women above the median had higher gains than those below the median. Among men, the opposite is apparent. Men above the median gained much less, and those below the median gained more. In other words, women in the top half gained substantially and their income became closer to men's.

Between 1992 and 1997, income differences pertaining to nationality became sharper. In 1992, the distribution of income for Estonians and non-Estonians (mainly ethnic Russians) in the PG cohort was fairly similar, but in 1997, Estonian nationals clearly appear to have higher income. Among Estonian nationals, the upper half gained more than the bottom half. In contrast, income of non-Estonians increased more among the bottom half than among the top half. In other words, income equality among non-Estonians seems to have decreased.

Between 1992 and 1997, the income at most percentiles rose more for those living in the capital city than for those living in villages. Structural differences in the labor market lie behind this trend. The existence of a functioning market economy in Estonia's capital (Tallinn) leads naturally to higher incomes there than in villages, where a market economy is still a future promise. However, income at the tenth percentile is highest in the countryside and lowest in the capital. In the countryside, ways to earn money can almost always be found (mainly by raising and selling farm products) whereas very poor people in a very large city have few means to earn money and tend to depend on government hand-outs. Locality-based differences in 1997 median income are considerable; the median is $183 in the countryside but $270 in the capital. Average income in 1997 also varies a lot, $237 in the countryside and $392 in the capital.

Changes in the income distribution during this five-year period varied dramatically for different educational groups. The average income of university graduates rose substantially, from $303 in 1992 to $438 in 1997. In contrast, average income was fairly flat for those with a general secondary education and actually declined for those with a vocational education (from $297 in 1992 to $257 in 1997) and for those who attended a specialized secondary school or "tekhnikum" (from $287 in 1992 to $215 in 1997).

Comparing economic sectors, we see that in both 1992 and 1997 income is higher within the private sector than in enterprises financed by the state budget and also in those owned by the state. But over this five-year period, there are noticeable signs of greater equalization of incomes across the sectors. It is noteworthy that median income rose considerably in all three sectors.

Income also varies noticeably among occupational groups (defined on the basis of standard ISCO codes); in particular, average income is markedly higher for managers than for others in both 1992 and 1997. Differences in income among other occupations exist in 1992 but are more surprising for being rather small, at least when viewed from the perspective of "normal" income differences in the United States. By 1997 there are relative gains in income for professionals and relative losses for unskilled workers and for skilled workers in agriculture. (The latter probably reflects the massive infusion into Estonia of agricultural products from abroad.)

Income Mobility

In addition to changes between 1992 and 1997 in the overall level of income and in income inequality, income mobility has been very high. In the PG cohort, the correlation between respondents' monthly income in September 1996 and in the month before the interview in 1997 is .33. Stated differently, variation in 1992 income explains only 11 percent (100x.33x.33) of the variation in 1997 income. We have not yet located comparable figures for established market economies, but to us, this figure seems astonishingly low.

Table 5.5 gives information about income mobility in terms of subgroups based on the quintile in which a respondent's income fell in 1992 and in 1997. Panel A shows outflows from the 1992 quintile groups; panel B shows the inflows into (i.e., the 1992 origins of) the 1997 quintile groups.

Table 5.5
Quintile of Respondent's Monthly Income in 1997 by Quintile of Respondent's Monthly Income in 1992

Panel A. 1997 Destination of Those in 1992 Quintiles (and those not interviewed in 1992)

1997 Quintile	No 1992 Interview	1992 Quintile					% (N)
		0-20.0%	20.1-40%	40.1-60%	60.1-80%	80.1-100%	
0-20.0%	19	28	30	19	14	9	20% (405)
20.1-40%	26	24	24	24	13	8	20% (402)
40.1-60%	17	19	21	23	26	13	20% (402)
60.1-80%	19	16	13	22	24	28	20% (402)
80.1-100%	19	13	12	12	22	42	20% (405)
% (N)	100% (381)	100% (324)	100% (376)	100% (282)	100% (332)	100% (323)	100% (2,018)

Panel B. 1992 Origins of Those in 1997 Quintiles (for those interviewed in 1992)

1997 Quintile	1992 Quintile					% (N)
	0-20%	20.1-40%	40.1-60%	60.1-80%	80.1-100%	
0-20%	27	34	16	14	9	100% (334)
20.1-40%	26	30	23	14	8	100% (302)
40.1-60%	19	23	19	26	13	100% (337)
60.1-80%	15	15	18	24	27	100% (332)
80.1-100%	13	13	10	22	41	100% (332)

Sources: PG, Waves 3 and 4 in Estonia.

There is indeed persistence in the top quintile over time. Forty-two percent of those in the top quintile in 1992 are also in the top quintile in 1997, and 41 percent of those in the top quintile in 1997 were in the top quintile in 1992. But is the glass half full or half empty?

Framed differently, 58 percent of those in the top quintile in 1992 were *not* in the top quintile in 1997, and 59 percent of those in the top quintile in 1997 were in a lower quintile in 1992. Other cells of the bivariate tables given in panels A and B suggest remarkably high levels of mobility. And, while 28 percent of those in the bottom quintile in 1992 remained there in 1997, 9 percent moved into the top quintile and another 14 percent ended up in the second highest quintile. Only 27 percent of those in the bottom quintile in 1997 were in this bottom group in 1992.

Both the low correlation between 1992 and 1997 incomes and the cross-tabulations in Table 5.5 provide support for our hypothesis (H3) that real income mobility between 1992 and 1997 has been high. The figures in table 5.5 also offer support for hypotheses H4a, H4b, and H4c concerning which segments of the income distribution have experienced the greatest income mobility.

Income Attainment

Table 5.6 presents ordinary least squares estimates of the regression of the naturallogarithm of the respondent's monthly income in 1992 and in 1997 on the various independent variables mentioned in our hypotheses, plus a few control variables: number of children and (0-1) indicators for unmarried men, for unmarried women, for having income from "odd jobs" and for receiving income from the government (e.g., unemployment benefits). The models reported in Table 5.6 improve significantly on a null model of "no effects" in both years, as indicated by the F-statistics listed near the bottom of the table.

Although the sample sizes (after listwise deletion of missing cases) are fairly similar (1,643 in 1992, 1,916 in 1997), the adjusted R-square value is much higher in 1997 (.21) than in 1992 (.08), meaning that income is more predictable in 1997 than in 1992. There are various possible reasons why income was less predictable in 1992. One is simply that allocation of rewards in 1992 was truly more random. As the market begins to function, it begins to reward people differentially on the basis of their education, occupation and so forth. We next consider evidence concerning hypotheses about the effects of various independent variables on income and about how these effects have changed between 1992 and 1997.[3]

Education. As we hypothesized (H5a), income significantly rises with years of education in 1997; however, the effect of education on 1992 income is tiny and statistically insignificant. We did not expect that the effect of education would be so small in 1992, but clearly its effect is sizable by 1997, supporting our hypothesis (H5b) that education would become a more important determinant of income as the market began to function.

Table 5. 6
Linear Regression of Natural Logarithm of Previous Month's Income (in US $ adjusted to March 1997 prices)

Independent Variables	Coefficients for 1992	Coefficient for 1997
Demographic Characteristics		
Female	-.652**	-.368**
Not Married	-.050	-.287**
Unmarried female	.343*	.591**
Nontitular nationality	-.210*	-.368**
N of children	.065+	.090**
Education (years)	.002	.083**
Settlement type[a]		
Capital city (Tallinn)	-.048	.016
Small towns	-.148	-.177*
Villages	-.161	-.270**
Migration history[a]		
Moved to bigger place	.018	.036
Moved to smaller place	.060	.126+
Branch of economy[b]		
Agriculture	-.121	-.463**
Manufacturing, Construction	.085	-.022
Services, trade	-.002	-.107+
Education, health	-.102	-.066
Government	.049	.508**
Sector[a]		
Private	.207*	.274*
State-budget financed	.150	-.006

Table 5.6 continued

Independent Variables	Coefficients for 1992	Coefficients for 1997
Occupation[b]		
Managers	.500**	.464**
Professionals	.225	.028
Semiprofessionals	.156	.126
Clerks	.110	-.084
Service & sales workers	-.148	-.175+
Skilled workers	-.154	-.126
Operatives, drivers	-.136	-.117
Skilled workers in agric.	-.214	.075
Unskilled workers	-.081	-.290*
Other		
Had odd jobs in current year	.175*	.256**
Got government benefits in current year	.029	-.194*
Intercept	4.959	4.263
Adjusted R-square	.075	.206
F statistic (29 d.f.)	5.6**	18.2**
Sample size	1,643	1,916

Notes: + = $p < .10$; * = $p < .05$; ** = $p < .01$. [a]Omitted (reference) category for (0-1) indicators of polytomous variables are "other big cities" (i.e., large cities other than Tallinn) for settlement type, "no change" for migration history, and "state-owned enterprise" for sector. [b]Omitted categories for effect-coded variables are "others" for branch of economy and occupation.
Sources: PG, Waves 3 and 4 in Estonia.

Occupation. We hypothesized (H6a) that income depends on occupation, other things being equal, and the estimates in Table 5.6 provide support for this in both 1992 and 1997. However, the results are not exactly what we had expected in several respects. First, in 1992, managers are the only group whose income significantly differs from that of the other occupational groups. Second, the coefficient for managers is roughly the same in 1992 and 1997; there is certainly no apparent gain for this occupation. Third, support for our hypothesis (H6b) that the effect of occupation would be greater in 1997 than in 1992 is weak, appearing in the form only of a significant negative effect for unskilled workers, who are clearly "losers" in Estonia's new market economy.

Branch of the Economy (Industry). We hypothesized that the branch of the economy would influence income in both 1992 and 1997 (H7a), though less so in 1997 than in 1992 (H7b). Results in Table 5.6 support H7a only partly and H7b not at all. Income does *not* depend on industry in 1992 when the old socialist economy was collapsing, but it *does* depend on it in 1997. Not surprisingly, 1997 income is significantly lower for those working in agriculture; this is typical in established market economies. Surprisingly (except to those more cynical than we), income is significantly higher for those working for the government, *ceteris paribus*.

Locality. We hypothesized that locality would influence income in both 1992 and 1997 (H8a) but less so in 1997 than in 1992. Findings in Table 5.6 for locality parallel those for branch of the economy. Namely, locality does affect income significantly in 1997 (small towns and villages are notable "losers" in the competition for income) but the effects are statistically insignificant in 1992, though the signs and magnitudes of coefficients for small towns and villages in 1992 are similar to those in 1997.

Migration History. In both command and market economies, some people change their place of residence in order to try to improve their material well-being. Although migration to the "suburbs" is often associated with upward economic mobility in post-industrial western societies, we expected that gains in income would result from moves to larger places in an emerging market economy such as Estonia's (H9). Results in Table 5.6 do not support this hypothesis. Migration history does not significantly affect income in 1992, and its effect in 1997 borders on statistical significance. Moreover, contrary to our expectation, it is moving to a smaller place, if any move at all, that seems to lead to higher income in 1997.

Sector. We were confident in our hypotheses that income would be higher in the private sector than in the state sector (H10a) and that the income advantages of working in the private sector would increase between 1992 and 1997 (H10b). The estimates in table 5.6 clearly support hypothesis H10a in both years. The advantage from working in the private sector indeed seems to have increased between 1992 and 1997, supporting hypothesis H10b. In 1992, those working in the private sector had incomes 23 percent higher than those in state-owned enterprises; in 1997, those in the private sector had incomes 32 percent higher, a sizable increase in percentage points.

Gender. Gender inequality in income has been found around the world, leading to a clear expectation that income in Estonia would be lower for women than for men (H11a) in both 1992 and 1997. Indeed, Titma and Murakas (1997) had analyzed PG:Wave 3 data for Estonia (using different explanatory variables for a somewhat different set of individuals) so our results for 1992 only confirm their earlier finding that income is significantly lower for women than for men in 1992. Income is also significantly lower for women than for men in 1997 according to the estimates in Table 5.6, supporting our hypothesis H11a.

Our specification differs from that of Titma and Murakas (1997) in an important way that leads to a somewhat different interpretation, however. Namely, in the analyses reported in Table 5.6, we include the interaction between gender and marital status, in the form of a (0-1) indicator of unmarried women, as well as (0-1) indicators of gender and marital status. Results in Table 5.6 imply that income is significantly lower for married women than for married men in both 1992 and in 1997; income is also significantly lower for married women than for unmarried women in both years. However, in 1997 income to unmarried women does not significantly differ from that of married men; rather, it is unmarried men whose incomes are significantly lower than those of married men. We are not yet prepared to speculate on the reason for this change in patterns of income for married and unmarried men and women, but we plan to investigate this finding more deeply in the near future.

Nationality. Finally, like many post-socialist societies, Estonia has experienced considerable tension over issues pertaining to nationality – issues that may have been latent in the socialist past but that a transitional society has brought to the fore of public attention. Using different explanatory variables and analyzing data on a somewhat different set of individuals, Titma and Murakas (1997) found that income differentiation in Estonia in 1992 was not significantly influenced by nationality. Nevertheless, we re-examined the hypothesis that nationality affected income in 1992 as well as in 1997 (H12a) since we analyzed additional cases and had different explanatory variables. We thought that even if nationality was not a significant predictor of income in 1992, nationality would have a larger impact in 1997 than in 1992 (H12b).

Results in Table 5.6 offer some support to both hypotheses. The estimates in table 5.6 imply that income was roughly 20 percent lower for non-Estonians than for otherwise comparable Estonian nationals in 1992, and roughly 30 percent lower in 1997. Controlling for the other variables in the model, nationality affected income significantly in 1992, and even more in 1997. These findings are of potential political as well as scientific interest since many electoral campaigns and legislative battles over policies have focused on the "nationality issue."

Control Variables. In addition to controlling marital status, which we implicitly discussed in our results pertaining to gender, we controlled for number of children, whether the individual had had odd jobs and whether he or she had received government benefits. All three variables have statistically significant effects in 1997; odd jobs also has a significant positive effect on income in 1992. Number of children has a positive effect in 1992 that is somewhat smaller in magnitude in 1992 than in 1997; it would be just significant at the .05 level if we had hypothesized that its effect would be positive. The effect of government benefits is significantly negative in 1997, which is what one would expect, since such benefits are small and mainly given to people who are not working either because they are unemployed, disabled or on maternity leave.

CONCLUSION

The transition from a socialist command economy to a market economy radically changes the way a society works, and thereby reshapes individuals' lives. A market economy distributes almost all goods and services through the medium of money. For those with money, life can be very good; for those without, it tends to be bad. Individuals in a transitional society need to learn both that money is important and how to obtain it. Since few people have the capital, energy and wits to start and run a successful business, most adults have no option except to earn money by selling their labor.

Being an employee was not new in transitional societies, but people who lived in socialist societies expected to be given some sort of job and living. Taking responsibility for your own life and for finding a well-paying job *is* new. People must learn that the labor market evaluates skills and capabilities and then rewards people very differently on the basis of their output. Learning this lesson is hard. Even countries must learn how to be productive and are making the whole transition through trial and error. This adds to the volatility of the environment of a transitional society. So it is hard to overestimate the role of money in people's lives in transitional societies.

After abandoning a command economy, most transitional societies had an early phase in which speculative capital and noncompetitive privatization schemes created a high degree of inequality that left most people with a minimal standard of living. A decent life came first to countries that had access to foreign aid and to individuals in a position to benefit from privatization—these were relatively few in number. This was the situation in Estonia in 1992.

But, after five years, the market has begun to work as economists predict. There is *visible improvement in the real income* of many people in Estonia, especially among the young adults whom we have studied (the *Paths of a Generation* cohort of graduates of secondary schools in 1983). Between September 1992 and March 1997, average real personal income in the PG cohort rose from $278 to $301, and the median grew even more impressively, from $148 to $213. Moreover, *gains were broadly distributed*: Most major subgroups of the PG cohort experienced positive growth in both their average and median real income. The gains in median income are especially indicative of the successful working of the market in Estonia.

Further, although official data for all Estonians (of whom about a quarter are retired) exhibit modest increases in income inequality over this five-year period, *income inequality within the PG cohort decreased* substantially, both overall and within most major subgroups. This is an important finding, but it is especially surprising that a working market was developed and managed to achieve this change in so few years.

Even more amazing was the *high level of income mobility* during this brief interval. Real income in 1992 is a poor predictor of real income in 1997, explaining only 11 percent of the variation in the latter. While roughly 40 percent in the top quintile of the income hierarchy in 1992 were also in the top quintile in 1997, we found extensive mobility into the top quintile in 1997 from lower in the income hierarchy, as well as much mobility out of the top quintile in 1992. It means that the market distributes opportunities widely, even in a transitional society. In responding to these new opportunities, people started from positions of relative equality. It reveals that the PG cohort in Estonia lives in a society where previous positions and social ties have not greatly influenced income mobility. This may be a general feature of a transitional economy or a specific result of Estonia's path to a market economy.

Both market and command economies allocate income differentially to various subgroups of the population. We compared the overall real income of key subgroups of the PG cohort and also examined the effects of individual characteristics on real income in multivariate analyses.

Gender differences in income are almost universal, with women having lower income than men. This was true in Estonia in the Soviet era, and still holds, even though women's average education exceed men's. Women in Estonia were (and are) more likely than men to be professionals, semiprofessionals, clerks and services workers, and less likely to be operatives or unskilled laborers. But women were (and are) less likely to be managers, the main occupational group whose income has shot up in Estonia's emerging market economy.

Our multivariate analyses found some reduction of gender differences in real income, at least within the PG cohort. Interestingly, when education and occupation are controlled, real income for unmarried young women is about the same as for married men and higher than for young unmarried men. Thus, in terms of income, the net disadvantage of being female appears to be concentrated among married women, who may be living off their husbands' earnings. Since young women have markedly lower real incomes *overall* than young men, this finding suggests that occupational segregation based on gender is at the root of women's income deficit (cf. Petersen & Morgan 1995).

An important finding is that income is linked with *nationality*, with non-Estonians (the vast majority of whom are Russian-speakers) having lower real incomes than Estonian nationals. This is contrary to the popular view in Estonia that Russians and Estonian nationals are equally represented among the rich. Moreover, our analyses indicate that nationality is a stronger predictor of income in 1997 than in 1992. This finding is not surprising because the change in the official language in Estonia (from Russian to Estonian) has denied Russian-speakers access to many of the better-paying jobs. But it suggests that more attention should be paid to ethnically split labor markets within Estonia.

In most countries, and certainly in the Soviet Union, residents of the capital cities are better off than those who live in the rest of country. In Estonia, *urban-rural differences* in income are even more apparent than during the Soviet period since those living in the Estonian countryside lived relatively well during the Soviet period. Income differences between the capital and large cities on the one hand, and small towns and villages on the other, widened in the five years between 1992 and 1997. This is a deep-seated problem (though not surprising) because the infrastructure supporting life in the countryside in Estonia is deteriorating rapidly, and the government cannot afford to pay for maintaining this infrastructure. Multivariate analyses suggest, however, that for individuals in the PG cohort, the urban-rural divide in income operates through the structure of occupations and branches of the economy and that it is not large when these and other individual characteristics are controlled.

We found a clear change in income differences associated with *education*. Between 1992 and 1997, the real income of university graduates has risen substantially. In multivariate analyses of real income, education is an important predictor of real income in 1997, whereas it had a tiny net effect on real income in 1992. This is a sign that the market has started to reward people differentially on the basis of their qualifications.

Another noteworthy finding is that income differentiation based on the *occupational structure* is substantial. We found that some of the biggest net differences in income are between occupational groups. In a functioning market economy, income is highest for managers and entrepreneurs, and this holds in Estonia, too. Compared to other occupations, unskilled manual laborers were overpaid and professionals underpaid in 1992. Both groups experienced income mobility by 1997: Real income of professionals rose, while real income of unskilled workers dropped. Some branches of the economy (in particular, agriculture) were overpaid (relative to their productivity) in 1992, and those still working in them in 1997 had lost economic ground. These findings suggest that income mobility partly resulted from a change in real income associated with the same job.

Social stratification in post-communist countries may turn out to be based on classes in the traditional European manner or on the occupational structure, as in the United States. Our findings of very high levels of income mobility and substantial labor movement suggest that class cleavages are not re-emerging in Estonia. Rather, Estonia appears to be moving toward an American-type system of social stratification based on the occupational structure.

A final important finding is that *real income is much more predictable in 1997 than in 1992*, and that the effects of most of the typical predictors of income in western market societies are larger in 1997 than in 1992. This signals that Estonia's new market economy is working: rewarding people who have better qualifications and who contribute more to its economic productivity. Many social as well as scientific problems remain to be solved, but these preliminary results offers signs of hope for transitional societies that are truly engaged in building market economies.

NOTES

1. We gratefully acknowledge the support of the M. Jacobs Foundation, which provided funds for the PG:Wave 3 surveys, and the National Council for Soviet and East European Research, which provided the funds for the PG:Wave 4 survey in Estonia under contract 812-10. We thank Ellu Saar, Juri Saarnit, Henri Soova and others in Estonia who helped with data collection in PG:Wave 3. The research reported below was supported by

National Science Foundation Grant SBR 9710399 and by Spencer Foundation Grant 199800085.

2. Data on family budgets and income come from household surveys conducted by the Estonian Market Opinion and Research Center by order of the Estonian Statistical Office for the period 1992 through June 1995 and from Household Income and Expenditures Survey conducted by the Estonian Statistical Office starting in July 1995 (Statistical Yearbook of Estonia 1996).

3. We have not yet conducted formal tests of differences in effects over time but plan to do this in the next draft of this paper. Here we simply note apparent differences that "appear large"to the eye.

REFERENCES

Alker, Hayward R. 1965. *Mathematics and Politics.* New York: Macmillan Company.

Åslund, Anders. 1995. *How Russia Became a Market Economy.* Washington, DC: Brookings Institution.

Burawoy, Michael. 1997. The Soviet Descent into Capitalism. *American Journal of Sociology, 102*, 1430-1044.

Chinn, Jeff, and Robert Kaiser. 1996. *Russians as the New Minority.* Boulder: Westview.

Cornia, Giovanni Andrea. 1996. *Transition and Income Distribution: Theory, Evidence and Initial Interpretation.* New York: The United Nations University, World Institute for Development and Economics Research.

Estonian Bank. 1999a. *Estonian Bank Datasets.* Information Department of Estonian Bank. Unpublished.

_____. 1999b. *Estonian Bank World Wide Web Homepage.* http://www.ee/epbe/

Estonian Statistical Office. 1998. *Statistical Office of Estonia Monthly, 77*, 5.

_____. *World Wide Web Homepage.* http://www.stat.ee/

Financial Statistics of Enterprises 1997 I. 1999. Tallinn: Estonian Statistical Office.

Flakierski, Henryk. 1993. *Income Inequalities in the Former Soviet Union and Its Republics.* Armonk, NY: M.E. Sharpe.

Frick, Joachim R., Richard Hauser, Klaus Muller, & Gert G. Wagner. 1995. Income Distribution in East Germany in the First Five Years after the Fall of the Wall. *MOCT-MOST, 5*, 4, 79-108.

Gerber, Theodore P., & Michael Hout. 1998. More Shock than Therapy: Market Transition in Russia. *American Journal of Sociology, 104*, 1, 1-50.

Gittleman, Maury & Mary Joice. 1996. Earnings Mobility and Long-Run Inequality: An Analysis Using Matched CPS Data. *Industrial Relations, 35*, 2, 180-196.

Gottschalk, Peter. 1997. Inequality, Income Growth, and Mobility: The Basic Facts. *Journal of Economic Perspectives, 11*, 2, 21-40.

Hassan, Fareed M. A. & R. Kyle Peters. 1996. The Structures of Income and Social Protection during the Transition: The Case of Bulgaria." *Europe-Asia Studies, 48*, 4, 629-646.

Headey, Bruce, Peter Krause & Roland Habich. 1995. East Germany: Rising Incomes, Unchanged Inequality and the Impact of Redistributive Government 1990-92. *British Journal of Sociology, 46*, 2, 225-243.

Kuznets, Simon. 1963. Quantitative Aspects of Economic Growth of Nations. *Economic Development and Cultural Changes* (January), 1-80.

Laitin, David D. 1996. Language and Nationalism in the Post-Soviet Republics. *Post-Soviet Affairs, 12* (Jan.-March), 25-39.

Milanovic, Branko. 1996. Income, Inequality and Poverty during the Transition: A Survey of the Evidence. *MOCT-MOST, 6,* 1, 131-147.

Petersen, Trond & Laurie A. Morgan. 1995. Separate and Unequal: Occupation-Establishment Sex Segregation and the Gender Wage Gap. *American Journal of Sociology, 101,* 329-365.

Putnam, George W. 1990. Occupational Sex Segregation and Economic Inequality under Socialism: Earnings Attainment and Earnings Decomposition in Yugoslavia. *Sociological Quarterly, 31,* 1, 59-75.

Rònas-Tas, Akos. 1994. The First Shall Be the Last? Entrepreneurship and Communist Cadres in the Transition from Socialism. *American Journal of Sociology, 100,* 40-69.

Rosenfeld, Rachel A. & Arne L. Kalleberg. 1990. A Cross-National Comparison of the Gender Gap in Income. *American Journal of Sociology, 96* , 1, 69-106.

Rukavishnikov, V. O. 1994. Sotsiologiya perekhodnogo perioda (The Sociology of the Transition Period). *Sotsiologicheskie Issledovaniya, 21,* 6: 25-32.

Schwartz, Joseph & Christopher Winship. 1979. The Welfare Approach to Measuring Inequality. In Karl F. Schuessler (Ed.), *Sociological Methodology 1980* (Pp. 1-36). San Francisco: Jossey-Bass.

Sørensen, Annemette & Heike Trappe. 1995. The Persistence of Gender Inequality in Earnings in the German Democratic Republic. *American Sociological Review, 60,* 3, 398-406.

Statistical Yearbook of Estonia. 1993. Tallinn: Statistical Office of Estonia.

_____. 1998. Tallinn: Statistical Office of Estonia.

Szelényi, Ivan, & Eric Kostello. 1996. The Market Transition Debate: Toward a Synthesis. *American Journal of Sociology, 101,* 1082-1096.

Szydlik, Marc. 1994. Incomes in a Planned and a Market Economy: The Case of the German Democratic Republic and the "Former" Federal Republic of Germany. *European Sociological Review, 10,* 3, 199-217.

Titma, Mikk (Ed.). 1985. *Zhiznennyi put pokoleniya: ego vybor i utverzhdenie* (*Life Path of a Generation: Its Choice and Outcome*). Tallinn: Eesti Raamat.

_____. 1997. *Sotsial'noje rasslojenie vosrastnoi kogorty* (*Social Differentiation of the Age Cohort*). Moscow: Institute of Sociology of Russian Academy of Science.

Titma, Mikk, & Rein Murakas. 1997. Vlijanije rynotshnykh preobrashovanii na voshniknovenije neravenstva v dokhodah (The Influence of Market Reforms to the Formation of Income Inequality) (pp. 146-185). In Mikk Titma (Ed.) *Sotsial'noje rasslojenie vosrastnoi kogorty* (*Social Differentiation of the Age Cohort*). Moscow: Institute of Sociology of Russian Academy of Science.

Titma, Mikk, Brian D. Silver & Barbara A. Anderson (Eds.). 1996. 1997. Estonia's Transition from State Socialism: Nationalities and Society on the Eve of Independence. *International Journal of Sociology, 26,* 1-3.

Titma, Mikk & Olga Tereshchenko. 1997. Sub'jektivnije i ob'jektivnije faktory rassloenija pokolenija po dokhodam (The Subjective and Objective Factors of the Income Differentiation inside Generation). In Mikk Titma (Ed.) *Sotshial'noje rasslojenie vosrastnoi kogorty* (*Social Differentiation of the Age Cohort*) (pp. 146-185). Moscow: Institute of Sociology of Russian Academy of Science.

Titma, Mikk & Nancy Brandon Tuma. 1993. Stratification Research in a Changing World. In J. Szmatka, Z. Mach, J. Mucha (Eds.), *Eastern European Societies at the Threshold of Change* (pp. 225-254). Lewiston, NY: Mellen Press.

_____. 1997. *Field Work for Wave 4 of "Paths of a Generation" in Estonia.* Unpublished report to the National Council for Soviet and East European Research on Contract #812-10.

_____. 1995. *Paths of a Generation: A Comparative Longitudinal Study of Young Adults in the Former Soviet Union.* Technical Report, Department of Sociology, Stanford University.

Titma, Mikk, Nancy Brandon Tuma & Brian D. Silver. 1997. Winners and Losers in the Post-Communist Transition: New Evidence from Estonia. *Post-Soviet Affairs, 14,* 2, 114-136.

Topel, Robert H. 1997. Factor Proportions and Relative Wages: The Supply-Side Determinants of Wage Inequality. Inequality, Income Growth, and Mobility: The Basic Facts. *Journal of Economic Perspectives, 11,* 2, 21-40.

Tuma, Nancy Brandon, Mikk Titma & Valery B. Yakubovich. 1995. *Sampling Design and Realization for Paths of a Generation.* Technical Report, Department of Sociology, Stanford University.

Vecernik, Jiri. 1991. Earnings Distribution in Czechoslovakia: Inter-temporal Changes and International Comparison. *European Sociological Review, 7,* 3, 237-252.

_____. 1996. Earnings Disparities in the Czech Republic: The History of Equalisation. *Czech Sociological Review, 4 ,* 2, 211-222.

United Nations Development Program (UNDP). 1995. *Estonian Human Development Report 1995.* Tallinn.

_____. 1996. *Estonian Human Development Report 1996.* Tallinn.

_____. 1997. *Estonian Human Development Report 1997.* Tallinn.

_____. 1998. *Estonian Human Development Report 1998.* Tallinn.

Walder, Andrew. 1996. Markets and Inequality in Transitional Economies: Toward Testable Theories. *American Journal of Sociology, 101,* 4, 1061-1073.

6

Fiscal Policy and Capital Formation in Transition Economies

Grzegorz W. Kolodko

In the 1990s the transition economies of Eastern Europe and the former Soviet Union suffered significant recession and persistent imbalances. Over ten years of vast changes the gross domestic product (GDP) has contracted significantly and income inequality has increased. In several countries post-socialist depression still continues. The best example, Poland, the GDP in 1999 was at about 120 percent of the pre-transition level of 1989, for countries such as Russia and Ukraine which have been involved in a decade of economic depression, it is around a meager 30 to 40 percent.

During transition fiscal reforms and policies have been aimed mainly at structural adjustment, liberalization and stabilization. The issues of raising the propensity to save and enhancing capital formation have been somewhat overlooked. A primary concern of fiscal policy was an overhaul of the public finance system and tax regime in a way that would facilitate the needs of emerging market economies. A number of new taxes have been introduced, including personal income tax and value added tax (VAT). Owing to shrinking output and despite attempts to widen the tax base, the revenues have not been sufficient to cover even downward adjusted expenditure. The government budget deficits remain.

More recently, especially in the countries that are well along in transition and already on the path of growth, capital formation is gaining momentum, based on growing domestic savings. The increase in savings is a function of growing real income, however, fiscal measures (i.e., the structure of taxes and accompanying system of deductions and other intensive measures), are helping to raise the marginal propensity to save and therefore the investment in fixed capital.

The nondebt flow of foreign capital plays an important role, too. Whereas in emerging post-socialist markets the strategy for sustainable development must rely essentially on domestic savings, the foreign savings—specially long-term capital flowing as direct foreign investments—are also of significant importance. Fiscal policy should therefore encourage such a flow of capital.

Policies facilitating sustainable growth ought to target a shift from direct to indirect taxation, thereby gradually reducing the corporate tax burden, narrowing the personal tax brackets and widening the tax base. In the countries that are following such direction and sequence of fiscal reforms, the recovery has come earlier and the growth is stronger. This process calls for sound institutional building, since for transition to succeed the new institutional arrangements are as important as liberalization and privatization.

During the ongoing process of catching-up in the areas of development and growth, fiscal policy must play a more active than so far role in capital formation. Following the initial period of transition and approximately ten years of creating a new economic framework, it is essential to use more aggressive fiscal measures as the means for capital formation and sustainable development, including higher investments in human capital.

OUTCOMES OF THE FIRST DECADE OF TRANSITION TO A MARKET ECONOMY

The first decade of the post-socialist transition to a market economy has been rather disappointing endeavor. *The expectations of durable growth and improvement of the standard of living have not been met.* Only a few countries have been able to overcome the pre-transition level of output. If measured in terms of GDP, after ten years of the transition process (1999), one finds that the level of national income since 1989 has been exceeded only in 3 out of 27 countries (Table 6.1). Yet it must be noticed that the composition of the output has changed significantly and in the meantime the quality of the products, together with the removal of the shortage phenomenon, has improved remarkably. In some countries, for example, the Czech Republic or Slovenia, as much as two thirds of foreign trade is now with the European Union and up to 80 percent is with the Organization for Economic Cooperation and Development (OECD) countries (IMF 1998; OECD 1998).

Moreover, transition is a complex, historical process of change from a centrally planned economy, based on state-owned property, to the market economy, based on private property. This endeavor consists of three simultaneous processes: (1) liberalization and stabilization; (2) institutional building and (3) Microeconomic restructuring of the industrial capacities.

Considering the great range of administered prices and large price distortions, on the one hand, and severe financial imbalances, on the other hand, initial liberalization caused an acceleration of price and wage inflation. Thus a main target of policies that followed was financial stabilization. The fiscal policy, therefore, was firstly subordinated to this end, without too much concern about other aims of economic and social policy, especially the need to shift the economy toward the path of sustainable growth and contain growing income inequity.

Table 6.1
Growth in Real GDP in Transition Economies, 1990-98

	1990	1991	1992	1993	1994	1995	1996	1997	1998	1997 (1989=100)	1998 (1989=100)
Albania	-10.0	-27.7	-7.2	9.6	9.4	8.9	9.1	-8.0	10.2	79.1	87.2
Armenia	-7.4	-10.8	-52.6	-14.8	5.4	6.9	5.8	3.3	5.7	41.1	43.0
Azerbaijan	-11.7	-0.7	-22.6	-23.1	-18.1	-11.0	1.3	5.0	7.9	40.5	43.6
Belarus	-3.0	-1.2	-9.6	-7.6	-12.6	-10.4	2.6	10.0	4.2	70.8	71.2
Bulgaria	-9.1	-11.7	-7.3	-1.5	1.8	2.1	-10.9	-7.4	3.5	62.8	65.0
Croatia	-6.9	-20.0	-11.7	-0.9	0.6	1.6	4.3	5.5	5.5	73.3	77.3
Czech Republic	-0.4	-14.2	-3.3	0.6	3.2	6.4	3.9	1.0	1.4	95.8	97.1
Estonia	-8.1	-7.9	-14.2	-8.5	-1.8	4.3	4.0	10.0	6.4	77.9	82.8
Georgia	-12.4	-13.8	-44.8	-25.4	-11.4	2.4	10.5	10.0	7.2	34.3	36.3
Hungary	-3.5	-11.9	-3.1	-0.6	2.9	1.5	1.3	4.3	5.4	90.4	95.2
Kazakhstan	-0.4	-13.0	-2.9	-10.4	-17.8	-8.9	1.1	1.8	1.4	58.1	59.0
Kyrgyzstan	3.0	-5.0	-19.0	-16.0	-20.0	-5.4	5.6	10.4	3.0	58.7	60.2
Latvia	2.9	-8.3	-34.9	-14.9	0.6	-0.8	2.8	6.0	6.0	56.8	60.3
Lithuania	-5.0	-13.4	-37.7	-17.1	-11.3	2.3	5.1	5.7	5.0	42.8	45.0
FYR Macedonia	-9.9	-12.1	-21.1	-8.4	-4.0	-1.4	1.1	1.0	2.8	55.3	56.9
Moldova	-2.4	-17.5	-29.1	-1.2	-31.2	-3.0	-8.0	1.3	-2.2	35.1	34.3
Poland	-11.6	-7.0	2.6	3.8	5.2	7.0	6.1	6.9	4.8	111.8	117.2
Romania	-5.6	-12.9	-8.7	1.5	3.9	7.1	4.1	-6.6	-2.1	82.4	80.7
Russia	-4.0	-13.0	-14.5	-8.7	-12.6	-4.0	-4.9	0.4	-4.8	52.2	49.7
Slovakia	-2.5	-14.6	-6.5	-3.7	4.9	6.8	6.9	6.5	4.0	95.6	99.5
Slovenia	-4.7	-8.1	-5.5	2.8	5.3	4.1	3.1	3.3	4.1	99.3	103.4
Tajikistan	-1.6	-7.1	-29.0	-11.0	-18.9	-12.5	-4.4	2.2	4.3	40.0	41.8
Turkmenistan	2.0	-4.7	-5.3	-10.0	-18.8	-8.2	-8.0	-15.0	4.7	48.3	50.6
Ukraine	-3.4	-9.0	-13.7	-14.2	-23.0	-12.2	-10.0	-3.2	-2.3	38.3	37.4
Uzbekistan	1.6	-0.5	-11.1	-2.3	-4.2	-0.9	1.6	2.4	4.5	86.7	90.6
25 countries of EBRD*	-5.0	-11.5	-10.5	-5.5	-7.1	-1.1	-1.3	1.6	2.0	71	72
East/Central Europe	-6.8	-11.0	-4.1	0.7	3.5	5.3	4.2	3.5	3.2	95	98
CIS	-3.7	-12.0	-14.3	-9.3	-13.5	-4.9	-4.6	0.5	-0.8	56	55

Note: *GDP-weighted average The weights used are EBRD estimates of nominal dollar-GDP for 1996.
Sources: EBRD 1998a. Estimations for 1998 from Plan Econ 1998 a and 1998 b, and author's own primary evaluation.

Table 6.2
Inflation, 1991-98 (percentages)

	1991	1992	1993	1994	1995	1996	1997	1998
Albania	104.0	236.6	30.9	15.8	6.0	17.4	42.0	14.0
Armenia	25.0	1,341.0	10,896.0	1,885.0	32.0	5.8	21.9	13.0
Azerbaijan	126.0	1,395.0	1,293.8	1,788.0	84.5	6.7	0.5	4.5
Belarus	93.0	1,159.0	1,996.0	1,960.0	244.0	39.2	63.1	84.0
Bulgaria	339.0	79.4	63.8	121.9	32.8	310.8	578.6	17.0
Croatia	250.0	938.2	1,149.0	-3.0	3.8	3.4	3.8	5.0
Czech Republic	52.0	12.7	18.2	9.7	7.9	8.6	10.0	6.8
Estonia	304.0	953.5	35.6	42.0	29.0	15.0	12.0	11.0
Georgia	131.0	1,177.0	7,488.0	6,474.4	57.4	13.8	8.1	8.0
Hungary	32.0	21.6	21.1	21.2	28.3	19.8	18.4	10.4
Kazakhstan	137.0	2,984.1	2,169.0	1,160.0	60.4	28.6	11.3	8.5
Kyrgyzstan	170.0	1,259.0	1,363.0	95.7	31.9	35.0	14.8	12.1
Latvia	262.0	959.0	35.0	26.0	23.0	13.1	7.0	5.0
Lithuania	345.0	1,161.1	188.8	45.0	35.5	13.1	8.5	6.8
FYR Macedonia	230.0	1,925.2	229.6	55.4	9.3	0.2	4.6	5.0
Moldova	151.0	2,198.0	837.0	116.0	23.8	15.1	11.2	10.0
Poland	60.0	44.3	37.6	29.4	21.6	18.5	13.2	8.6
Romania	223.0	199.2	295.5	61.7	27.8	56.9	151.6	47.0
Russia	144.0	2,508.8	840.1	204.7	131.3	21.8	11.1	84.5
Slovakia	58.0	9.1	25.1	11.7	7.2	5.4	6.4	7.0
Slovenia	247.0	92.9	22.9	18.3	8.6	8.8	9.4	8.0
Tajikistan	204.0	1,364.0	7,344.0	1.1	2,133.0	40.5	165.0	19.3
Turkmenistan	155.0	644.0	9,750.0	1,328.0	1,262.0	446.0	21.5	50.0
Ukraine	161.0	2,730.0	10,155.0	401.0	182.0	39.7	10.1	19.0
Uzbekistan	169.0	910.0	885.0	1,281.0	117.0	64.0	28.0	35.0

Note: Change in the year-end retail and consumer price level.
Sources: EBRD 1998a. Data for 1998 are EBRD early projections and for Poland, Russia Hungary and Czech Republic. Plan Econ 1999.

Despite the sound commitment to fight inflation for the sake of stabilization and improvement of efficiency, the inflation has remained rampant and, in each case, was higher and more difficult to be conquered than envisaged earlier (Table 6.2).

In all transition economies through the 1990s *income inequity was on the rise*. The emerging pattern of income distribution and equity issues were not at the top of the policy agenda at the time—not of the national governments, nor the international financial organizations. The fiscal policy, at large, does not prevent the natural tendency accompanying liberalization and privatization toward increasing inequity. In several countries the pattern of distribution has changed significantly, causing growing poverty and mounting social tensions. The social tensions in some countries with sluggish progress in the real sphere of the economy, that is, where the recovery is still to be accomplished, will continue to grow even further in the foreseeable future.

Table 6.3
Changes in Inequality During Transition. Gini Coefficient (income per capita)

Gini Coefficient: Income per capita	1987-88	1993-95
Krygyzstan	26	55†
Russia	24	48†
Ukraine	23	47‡
Lithuania	23	37
Moldova	24	36
Turkmenistan	26	36
Estonia	23	35†
Bulgaria	23#	34
Kazakhstan	26	33
Uzbekistan	28#	33
Latvia	23	31
Romania	23#	29‡
Poland	26	28§
Belarus	23	28†
Czech Republic	19	27‡
Slovenia	22	25
Hungary	21	23
Slovak	20	19

Note: For most countries the income concept in 1993-95 is disposable income. In 1987-88 it is gross income, since at that time personal income taxes were small, and so was the difference between net income and gross income. Income includes consumption in kind, except for Hungary and Lithuania in 1993-95. †Quarterly. ‡Monthly. #1989. §Semi-annually.
Sources: UNDP 1996; Milanovic 1998.

Poverty is an even bigger problem to be tackled. Growing inequality has occurred during transitional contraction, thus a great number of people have been driven into poverty, especially in Russia and Ukraine, two of the biggest post-socialist countries (with the populations of about 200 million), where between 1988/99 and 1995/96 the income disparity, measured by the Gini coefficient, has at least doubled (Table 6.3). There is not yet available comprehensive data illustrating the developments *vis-à-vis* the income dispersion pattern in recent years, but the anecdotal evidence clearly suggests that the inequity was continuing to rise in 1996-99. Moreover, based on implemented policies, and ongoing economic tendencies, it is safe to assume that such a trend willnot be reversed in the early twenty-first century.

So far the most successful case of transition has been, Poland, which was able to raise its GDP in 1998 to over 117 percent of the pre-transition levels of 1989. The overall situation is far better than the average in transition economies (EBOR 1998; PlanEcon 1998b, 1999), due, *inter alia*, to fiscal and income policies that slowed the increases in inequity by 1994-96. These policies set the country on the path of a high rate of growth which resulted in savings starting to grow again.

Yet the economy recently seems to be losing momentum, owing to unfavorable external shocks, but mainly because of recently implemented policies. The attempt to cool the economy, following the mistaken assertion that it had been overheated, has brought the average rate of growth from 6 to 7 percent in 1994-97 down to about 2 to 3 percent in 1998 (Figure 6.1). Consequently, industrial output and employment after several years of growth have started to decline again and the rate of unemployment has increased from about 9.5 percent in mid-1998 to as much as 12 percent in the spring of 1999 (Figure 6.2).

After ten years of transition, the output of the overwhelming majority of post-socialist countries is well below where it was a decade ago. Several of them are still on the decline and some others are affected by the overall recession regadless of preceeding short term recoveries. In 1998-99, six or seven countries in Eastern Europe (EE) and the Commonwealth of the Independent States (CIS) were involved in contraction, yet until recently there were optimistic expectations that, with a few exceptions, the whole region should have been on the upswing by 2000 (Table 6.4).

However, in the aftermath of the global financial crisis and especially owing to the Russian contagion and its negative impact on CIS economies, these predictions have been recently corrected downward, and in some cases, like Russia or Poland, quite significantly. For example, in Poland, owing mainly to unnecessary overcooling of the economy, the expected rate of growth of 6.9 and 5.8 in 1998 and 1999, respectively, was adjusted down to 4.8 percent in 1998 (*ex post* data) and to a still unrealistic 5.1 percent in 1999. The latter index, being also a foundation for the 1999 budget and agreed with the International Monetary Funds (IMF) as late as in March 1999, was recently predicted by J.P. Morgan for a mere 1.5 percent (J.P. Morgan 1999). Most probably, it will be slightly over 3 percent.

Table 6.4
Forecast of Economic Growth in Transition Economies, 1998-2002

	GDP index, 1989 = 100	Rate of Growth					Average	Ranking*	GDP index, 2002	
	1997	1998	1999	2000	2001	2002	1998-2002		1997 = 100	1989=100
Poland	111.8	6.5	5.9	5.8	5.8	6.1	6.0	7	133.9	149.8
Slovenia	99.3	4.1	4.1	4.8	4.2	4.9	4.4	20	124.1	123.3
Albania	79.1	10.2	9.7	10.6	8.6	3.7	8.6	4	150.6	119.1
Slovakia	95.6	4.0	2.3	2.5	5.0	5.0	3.8	22	120.2	114.9
Czech Republic	95.8	1.4	3.3	4.3	4.5	4.7	3.6	24	119.5	114.5
Hungary	90.4	5.4	4.6	4.5	4.8	4.5	4.8	19	126.2	114.1
Uzbekistan	86.7	5.8	4.3	4.9	4.5	4.5	4.8	16	126.4	109.6
Estonia	77.9	6.4	5.5	5.9	5.6	5.9	5.9	8	132.9	103.6
Romania	82.4	-2.1	3.3	5.8	5.5	4.9	4.9	21	118.4	97.6
Croatia	73.3	5.5	3.4	5.4	5.4	4.9	4.9	15	127.1	93.2
Kyrgyzstan	58.7	6.5	6.8	6.0	5.5	5.6	6.1	6	134.3	78.8
Bulgaria	62.8	3.5	5.4	5.7	4.4	4.0	4.6	18	125.2	78.6
Yugoslavia	62.7	3.7	2.3	3.9	5.0	6.0	4.2	9	122.7	76.9
Kazakhstan	58.1	4.4	3.8	4.9	7.0	7.0	5.4	11	130.1	75.6
Latvia	56.8	6.0	3.9	4.6	5.8	5.7	5.2	12	128.8	73.2
Belarus	70.8	-7.1	-1.5	2.7	3.7	5.5	0.7	26	102.8	72.8
Turkmenistan	48.3	4.7	12.1	16.0	3.5	4.2	8.1	3	14o.8	70.9
FYR Macedonia	55.3	2.8	3.4	3.4	4.9	5.0	3.9	17	121.1	66.9
Azerbaijan	40.5	7.1	9.0	10.7	11.2	10.7	9.7	1	159.1	64.4
Armenia	41.1	6.6	6.5	6.7	7.8	6.9	6.9	5	139.6	57.4
Lithuania	42.8	5.0	5.0	5.7	5.1	4.9	5.1	13	128.5	55.0
Georgia	34.3	10.2	10.1	9.3	9.1	7.6	9.3	2	155.7	53.4
Tajikistan	40.0	4.5	5.1	5.7	6.0	6.1	5.5	10	130.6	52.2
Russia	52.2	-3.8	-4.7	-1.8	1.4	3.1	-1.2	25	94.1	49.1
Ukraine	38.3	1.2	3.0	4.8	5.2	6.0	4.0	23	121.8	46.7
Moldova	35.1	1.2	6.6	5.0	6.3	5.8	5.0	14	127.4	44.7

Note: *Ranking is according to the 2002 GDP index (1997 = 100) and 1998-2002 average rate of growth.
Sources: Plan Econ 1998a and 1998b.

Figure 6.1
Poland: Selected Economic Indicators, 1991-1998

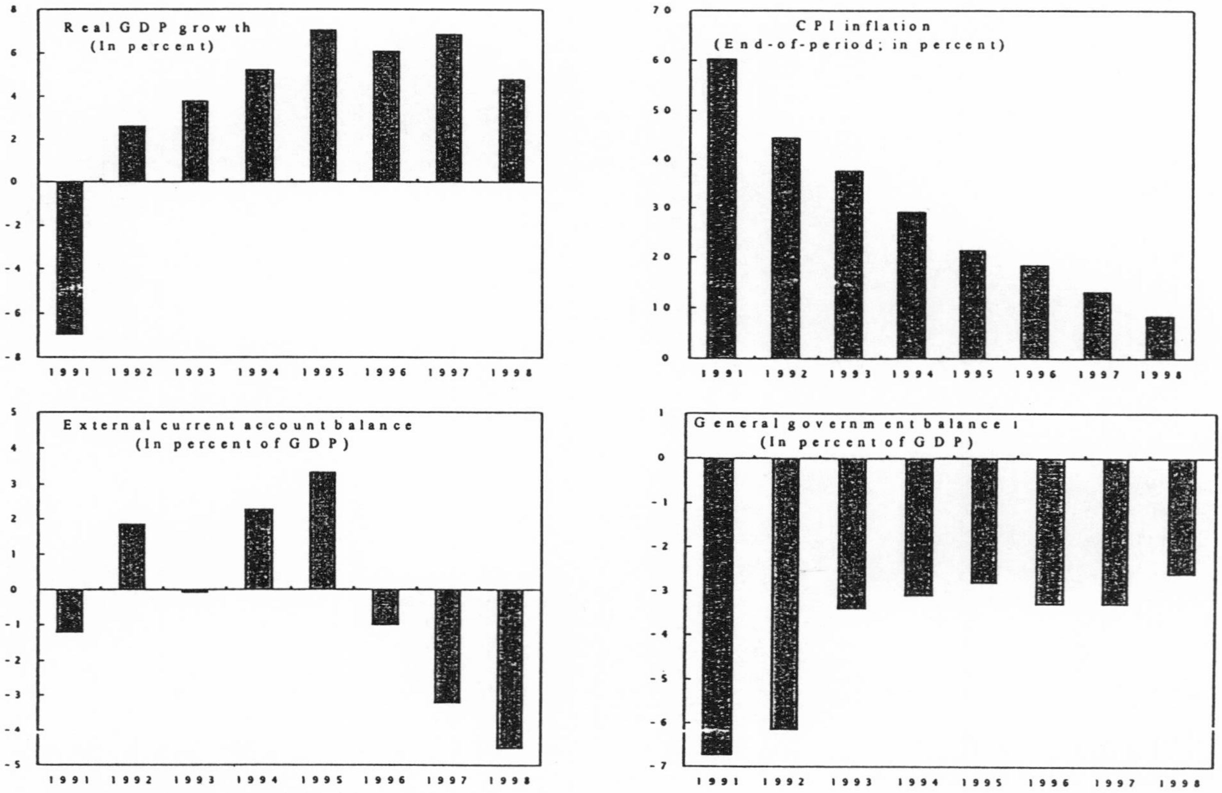

Real GDP growth
(In percent)

1991 1992 1993 1994 1995 1996 1997 1998

CPI inflation
(End-of-period; in percent)

1991 1992 1993 1994 1995 1996 1997 1998

External current account balance
(In percent of GDP)

1991 1992 1993 1994 1995 1996 1997 1998

General government balance 1
(In percent of GDP)

1991 1992 1993 1994 1995 1996 1997 1998

Notes: 1 general government balance on a cash back.
Source: Polish government and governmental staff estimates.

Figure 6.2
Poland: Industrial Output and Unemployment 1993-99

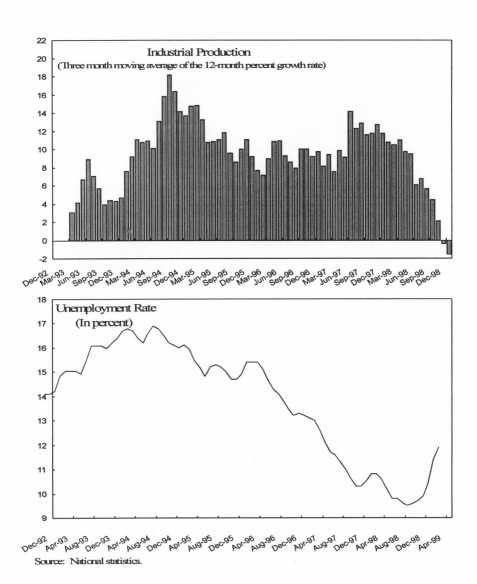

Source: National statistics.

FISCAL POLICY DURING TRANSITION

The main purpose of fiscal policy is the redistribution of income. The same is true for transition economies, yet—due to long-lasting depression—the redistributive policy becomes much more difficult. *Whereas the needs for financial resources are growing, the ability to satisfy them is weakening, because of the shrinking income.* Resulting fiscal policy, therefore, is likely to lead to social tensions and political conflicts.

It was assumed by many that liberalization-cum-stabilization, supported by fast privatization—the shift of assets from the state sector (presumed to be inefficient and thus a burden for the budget) to the private sector (seen as efficient, thus contributing to the improvement of the fiscal stance)—would soon improve the overall fiscal position of an economy. Yet for a number of reasons it didn't happen. Owing to the systemic vacuum created in an aftermath of negligence for institution building—indispensable for the success of the early stage of transition—one type of inefficiency has been replaced by another. *Inefficiency typical for the outgoing system of central planning and bureaucratic interference has been exchanged for the specific inefficiencies of post-socialist emerging markets with weak institutions.* The pace of liberalization and privatization turned out to be too rapid for transition economies to establish new, sound institutional arrangements; the latter must underlie the former. Hence, the fiscal problems remain serious.

In several cases, due to the so-called perverse effect of fiscal adjustment (Kolodko 1992), the fiscal deficit is even larger than it was under the previous systemic arrangements, prior to transition. After initial improvements mainly due to the reduction of unproductive transfers, the drop in revenue was even larger, thus the deficits reappeared (if they were contained in the first place, as for instance in Poland in 1990) after a short period of time. To close such deficit is now more difficult, since the removal of subsidies can be executed only once.

There were three main concerns of fiscal policy at the early stages of transition. First, there was an effort to make a quick improvement of the budget situation by balancing it with a downward adjustment of expenditure and, later—when the recovery had occurred and the taxation base has started to widen—through growing revenue. The aim of these policies was to provide the resources to finance indispensable expenditures that had to be covered by the government, either central or local ones.

Second, it was necessary to stabilize inflation, mainly by containing the fiscal deficit and financing the budget, in a noninflationary way. Third, an overhaul of the tax system and administration to facilitate the needs of the emerging market economy was imperative. In the short run there were contradictions and trade-offs but in the long run all these concerns were supposed to be compatible and positively support each other.

The outcomes of these fiscal policies have been mixed. In several countries there continues to be large budget deficits and in many cases budgets can hardly be financed without at least a partial monetization of the occurring deficits (Table 6.5). As a consequence, the inflationary pressure lingers. Many countries struggle to contain the existing deficits by further cuts of the expenditure, since their policies to raise the revenue are not working properly, owing to continuing contraction, or a narrow taxation base, or both—as, for instance, is the most spectacular instance of Russia.

Table 6. 5
General Government Balance, 1990-98 (In percent of GDP)

YEARS	1990	1991	1992	1993	1994	1995	1996	1997	1998
Albania	-15.0	-31.0	-20.3	-14.4	-12.4	-10.4	-11.4	-17.0	-14.8
Armenia	--	-1.8	-8.1	-56.1	-10.1	-12.0	-9.3	-6.7	-5.6
Azerbaijan	--	--	2.8	-12.7	-11.4	-4.2	-2.6	-2.8	-3.0
Belarus	--	--	0.0	-1.9	-2.5	-1.9	-1.6	-2.7	-3.3
Bulgaria	--	--	-5.2	-10.9	-5.8	-6.4	-13.4	-2.7	-1.6
Croatia	--	--	-4.0	-0.8	1.7	-0.9	-0.5	1.4	2.1
Czech Republic	--	--	-3.1	0.5	-1.2	-1.8	-1.2	-2.1	-0.9
Estonia	--	5.2	-0.3	-0.7	1.3	-1.2	-1.5	2.3	1.7
Georgia	--	-3.0	-25.4	-26.2	-7.4	-4.5	-4.4	-3.8	-3.0
Hungary	0.4	-2.2	-6.8	-5.5	-8.4	-6.7	-3.5	-4.6	-4.9
Kazakhstan	1.4	-7.9	-7.3	-1.3	-7.2	-2.0	-2.5	-3.4	-4.5
Kyrgyzstan	0.3	4.6	-17.4	-14.2	-11.6	-17.2	-9.6	-9.2	9.0
Moldova	--	0.0	-26.2	-7.4	-8.7	-5.7	-6.7	-7.5	-7.5
Latvia	--	--	-0.8	0.6	-4.1	-3.5	-1.4	1.3	-0.4
Lithuania	5.4	2.7	0.5	-4.3	-5.4	-4.5	-4.0	-2.4	-3.0
FYR Macedonia	--	--	-9.6	-13.6	-3.2	-1.3	-0.4	-0.6	-0.8
Poland	3.1	-6.7	-6.6	-3.4	-2.8	-3.6	-3.1	-3.0	-3.0
Romania	1.0	3.3	-4.6	-0.4	-1.9	-2.6	-3.9	-4.5	-5.0
Russia	--	--	-21.6	-7.4	-10.4	-5.7	-8.2	-7.5	-6.0
Slovakia	--	--	--	-7.0	-1.3	0.2	-1.9	-3.4	-2.1
Slovenia	-0.3	2.6	0.2	0.3	-0.2	0.0	0.3	-1.5	-1.0
Tajikistan	--	-16.4	-28.4	-23.6	-10.2	-11.2	-5.8	-3.5	3.0
Turkmenistan	1.2	2.5	13.2	-0.5	-1.4	-1.6	-0.2	-0.5	-5.0
Ukraine	--	--	-25.4	-16.2	-7.8	-4.8	-3.2	-5.8	-4.0
Uzbekistan	-1.1	-3.6	-18.4	-10.4	-6.1	-4.1	-7.3	-2.3	3.0

Note: General government includes the state, municipalities, and extra budgetary funds. Balances are reported on a cash basis except for Albania and Poland. Data for Armenia refer to the consolidated state government, for Croatia to the consolidated central government, and for Uzbekistan to state and extra budgetary funds.
Sources: EBRD 1998a.

Against such a background, the financing of social sphere and human capital has deteriorated. And budget transfers are falling further, owing to the conviction of the mainstream neo-liberal economic thought (and also at the insistence of the IMF) that the so- called small government is always the better government. The absolute level of government investment into human capital has declined in all transition economies—including the leaders that were able to return to the path of growth several years ago. These unfavorable events will affect negatively the ability to grow in the long run. Thus it may be claimed that throughtout 1990s fiscal policies contributed to a worsening of the situation *vis-à-vis* human capital formation, accompanied with all the negative implications for sustainable development.

As for the systemic changes, the aims of the fiscal policies have been accomplished to quite an extent. The fiscal system, if not yet overhauled entirely, has been changed substantially (Ebrill, Escolano & Stotsky 1998; Tanzi 1991) and is well advanced to serve the purpose of the emerging post-socialist market economies. It was especially difficult to create a new system of opublic finance in the countries that didn't reform their centrally planned economies before transition, especially in the former Soviet Union (FSU). Not only were legal foundations for a new fiscal system necessary, but changes in behavior and a new fiscal culture were needed. To create such systemic changes requires the permanent attention of governments and legislatures as well as an involvement of nongovernmental organizations (NGOs) supporting transition to a market economy and civic society, on the one hand, and continuing technical assistance and monitoring by the international organizations, mainly the IMF, on the other hand.

Another important aspect of fiscal policy, which somehow has been overlooked during the initial stages of post-socialist transition, the capital formation. The fiscal policies just discussed were not enough involved in the process of capital formation that is necessary for durable growth financing. Fiscal policies focused on short-term stabilization measures and the systemic changes did not fully take into account the impact of these changes and policy decisions on savings, investment and long-term capital accumulation. It was assumed that capital formation would be automatically boosted if stabilization and critical structural reforms were accomplished. So far, this has not been the case accomplished on the sustainable basis.

Moreover, a significant proportion of accumulated capital ahs been wasted because of the lack of government policy assisting its allocation at the infant stage of market economy. In the extreme cases, for example, in Albania or Russia, there was vast *capital flight*. Weak institutional arrangements and inconsistent policies allowed for the development and later collapse of disastrous financial pyramids. Among the results of such ill-advised endeavors was a meaningful capital outflow, which was not vigorously counteracted by the international financial community (together with the international financial organizations, that have reacted too late). What had been saved and accumulated through unregulated financial intermediaries, has left the country.[1]

FISCAL POLICY AND CAPITAL FORMATION

Under the centrally planned allocation, the rate of savings was relatively high. Actually, it was higher at the time than it is recently in any country of the region. Yet such a propensity to save was basically stemming from the mechanism of forced savings and the shortage phenomenon or—if accompanied by open, price and wage inflation—so-called shortageflation (Kolodko & McMahon 1987). Nevertheless, the price distortions and financial disequilibria led to growing allocative inefficiencies and thus the centrally planned economies had been losing momentum and their earlier ability to grow. Consequently, the rate of growth declined and the system came to an end. So, despite high rate of investment (the ratio of investment over GDP), the late centrally planned economies were less and less able to expand. The inefficiency of capital allocation was eating out the high, although forced, rate of savings and investment.

$$I/GDP\ (\%) \tag{1}$$

It was expected that liberalization and privatization would soon bring an acceleration of growth by quickly eliminating wasteful allocation of capital. It was presupposed as well, that even if the rate of investment was not as high as it used to be under the socialist regimes (i.e., within the range of 25-35 percent of GDP), the investment efficiency would to be raised fast and by a large margin. A rationale for such expectations was based on the assumption that market allocation should, at least to some extent, compensate for a decline in the rate of savings and investment. This, however, has not occurred, because of new kinds of inefficiencies that have emerged together with the beginning of transition. They are linked to poor institutionalization of the new economic mechanisms and to weak policies. Fiscal policy must take care of capital formation, whereas other policies and the self-performing market forces ought to look after its most efficient allocation.

Capital formation is a function of: the level of income and the propensity to save. That is:

$$cf\ (t) = f\ (i_0, ps(t)) \tag{2}$$

where: i_0 =absolute disposable income in the starting year,
$ps(t)$=propensity to save of the interval t.

Hence *the fiscal policy, either by direct or indirect means, can influence the process of capital formation by affecting the amount of net disposable income, or through the change of the marginal propensity to save.*

Fiscal policy, as the means of income redistribution, can be either neutral from the viewpoint of capital formation, or can influence the structure of final absorption of GDP. If the GDP's absorption consists of:

$$GDP = C_t + I_t + G_t \tag{3}$$

where: C_t=individual consumption over the interval t,
I_t=investment,
G_t=government consumption,

than the fiscal policy can influence capital formation either through raising the share of investment in the GDP's absorption (i.e., I_t), or the invested part of the government outlays (i.e., invested fraction of G_t). The common feature of the market economy, gradually gaining momentum during transition period, is that whereas the role of private accumulation is ascending, the role of the public sector is descending. However, before emerging private sector and, to some extent, NGOs are able to substitute the services so far provided by the state (quite often under socialism free of charge, for example, a number of education or culture services), the government cannot abandon furnishing such services.

As for capital formation and investment from the point of view of direct contribution by the state, it depends on the *composition of government consumption*. It is widely believed—and thus has a strong impact on the actual policies carried forward along the line of the so-called Washington consensus (Alesina 1998; Williamson 1990, 1993)—that the smaller the government, the faster the pace of growth. Yet this common wisdom has been challenged recently by both strong theoretical arguments (Kolodko 1999c; Stiglitz 1998; Tanzi 1997) and a convincing set of evidence from different economies, including the countries in transition (World Bank 1997). In fact, the size of the government can affect the process of capital formation and thus, *ceteris paribus*, the rate of growth in either way. If a larger government, has relatively higher taxation and spending is aimed at the larger outlays for human capital (education, healthcare, R&D, culture, etc.) and the hard infrastructure (roads, telecommunication, transport facilities, etc.), than the larger government enhances the ability to grow. If, on the contrary, the bulk of government expenditure goes for unproductive targets (government and local bureaucracy, defense, transfers to support uncompetitive industries, etc.), it will hamper the ability to expand. This has obvious implications for fiscal policy and structuring the budget outlays.

Amid various growth formulas, some authors rightly emphasize the implications of human capital formation and the size of the government. Undoubtedly, in the long run these are the decisive factors sustaining high quality growth and socio-economic development. One of the predictions for growth in the transition economies (Fischer, Sahay & Vegh 1998) is based on the following equation:

$$g(t) = f(Y_0, PS_0, SS_0; INV(t), GOV(t), POP(t)), \qquad (4)$$

where: $g(t$=per capita growth during the time interval t,
Y_0 =per capita income in the starting year,
PS_0 =primary school enrollment rate (in percent of total primary school- aged population,
SS_0 =secondary school enrollment rate (in percent of total secondary school-aged population),
$INV(t)$ =gross capital formation (in percent of GDP) during the time t,
$GOV(t)$=government consumption expenditure (in percent of GDP) during the time interval t,
$POP(t)$ =growth rate of the population during the time interval t.

In this approach how the direction of government expenditure influences growth is discussed, since such influence is much more ensuing from the composition of these outlays than from their absolute level. Hence, development policies should not insist unconditionally for the expansion of the size of the government or for its limitations, but on the shift of government expenditures toward investment in both human capital and hard infrastructure, because both in the long run do facilitate growth.

It seems to be agreed that more than the overall propensity to save (and thus the rate of capital formation) is influencing the conduits through which the accumulation of capital occurs. If incentives are targeted at increasing savings through bank deposits rather than by investing in shares on the capital market, then the capital gains on securities can be taxed and the revenue from interest-bearing banking deposits should remain tax free. If the governments are keen to raise the savings of households—and at the same time to finance their budget deficit through selling government bonds and treasury bills on the open market—they may even introduce a tax deduction scheme that makes a specific portion of personal income spent on the purchase of government papers tax free. Yet under such fiscal preferences the structure rather than the general level of savings is changing. If the preferences are, for instance, aimed at accelerated privatization, then capital gains accrued throught stock exchange should remain untaxed. If the priority of economic policy is to finance in a noninflationary way (yet debt-creating) the existing fiscal deficit, then the purchase of government papers must be accompanied by some additional tax preferences, especially encouraging the savings of the households.

IMPACT OF FISCAL POLICY ON CAPITAL ACCUMULATION

In transition economies, where various means of fiscal policy have been introduced for the first time—for example, the general taxation of personal income or a value added tax (VAT), covering if not all, then a vast range of goods and services—the level of disposable income is rather lower than it might be under alternative arrangements, that is without or with less of taxation. At least in the short and medium term, the *new measures of direct and indirect taxation, particularly vis-à-vis the households, have not raised the overall propensity to save.*[2]

Part of the income that was collected by the state for the sake of redistribution was basically channeled into government consumption (i.e., G_t), especially for social-related expenditures. Due to the accelerated process of retiring of the governments from direct economic activities it was not invested in the real assets. Hence, at least at the initial stages of transition, the new tax measures have contained net disposable incomes of the household sector, including that which could be otherwise saved if only the taxation were lower. At the other end, the social groups that benefited from redistribution by the government, were still receiving a rather modest real income and thus their propensity to save was low, too.

As for the propensity to save, this becomes the earnest concern of fiscal policy only when the financial stabilization is generally accomplished, the economy is relatively stable and the output is already on the rise. As long as there is financial instability and production is falling, fiscal measures cannot change meaningfully the proportions of income being consumed and saved (i.e., invested, on the behalf of the latter).[3]

Because of their ability to consolidate stabilization and their capacity to run a growth-oriented policy, in the countries more advanced in transition it has become possible to expand the output as well as increase the propensity to save. Consequently, the *marginal propensity to save cannot increase as long as real income is decreasing.* When real income is falling over a number of years—and its contraction is occurring by a large margin—then even an aggressive fiscal policy, favoring higher rate of savings, is not able to work. Tax incentives are incapable of raising the absolute or even the relative level of savings because of the significant lose of the real income.

Notwithstanding fiscal policy shouldn't be blamed exclusively for real income falling, although it has contributed to this process. Instead of enhancing the propensity to save, fiscal policies and reforms through their negative impact on net real income have lowered the propensity to save. Fiscal policy is aimed primarily at financial stabilization, and not only at the onset of transition. To this end, most efforts have been to restrain overall demand through budget expenditure cuts as well as with the control of the net wages [4] and the pensions [5] through direct and indirect taxation. Consequently, for a long time (longer than the GDP contraction that lasted three years in Poland and ten years in Ukraine) disposable income was declining together with shrinking output. Therefore, the fiscal squeeze, did contribute to falling real income. At the lower level of real income the savings—and, consequently, the capital formation—became lower, too.

Like elsewhere, in transition economies there are two contradictory expectations. On the one hand, there is a strong pressure to *raise* taxes for the purpose of meeting the needs of prudent financing of mounting government expenditures. On the other hand, there is a pressure to cut taxes, for the purpose of raising disposable income and thus higher savings and capital formation. The former usually is the strong request of the trade unions and supported in business circles. The government is always cruising in between, inclined to go toward one or the other end depending on its political agenda.

The outcome of the confrontation of these two options depends not as much on the accuracy (or inaccuracy) of theoretical arguments with the respect to the optimal design of a fiscal system, as it does on the political situation (Alesina 1997). However, moving too fast or too far toward either of these ends may ultimately harm the capital formation. A shift toward the opposite end will not offset the damage, since the losses have already occurred either because the hypothetical savings and investments didn't take place or because the inflationary pressure deteriorated allocative efficiency.

Transition to a market economy means also that the *changes of the composition of general government revenue* must take place. Whereas the ratio of total revenue over GDP is declining, the share of the corporate taxes in GDP is falling much faster than the share of individual taxes (Table 6.6).

Table 6. 6
General Government Revenue by Category (In percent of GDP)

	Total revenue	Total tax revenue	Corporate taxes	Individual taxes
EE ECONOMIES Pre-transition	49.5	39.0	9.9	6.6
Currently	39.6	35.5	2.7	6.2
Difference (in percentage points)	9.9	3.5	7.2	0.4
CIS**				
Pre-transition	34.0	26.4	7.0	3.3
Currently	21.8	17.9	3.4	1.7
Difference (in percentage points)	12.2	8.5	4.6	1.6

Source: EBRD 1998b. *Note:* 'Pre-transition' refers to 1989, but for Hungary to 1990 and for Armenia, Azerbaijan, Estonia, FYR Macedonia, Georgia, Latvia, Moldova, Slovenia and Ukraine to 1991. 'Currently' is either 1996 or 1997 data. * –excluding Albania and Bosnia-Herzegovina, but including the Baltics, ** –excluding Belarus and Uzbekistan.

If prior to transition always the revenue from corporate taxes were larger than those accruing from the individual taxes, that is:

$$Tc > Tp \qquad (5)$$

in the aftermath of the fiscal reforms the sequence has been reversed, that is, currently it is:

$$Tc < Tp \qquad (6)$$

where: T_C=corporate taxes,
Tp=individual (personal) taxes.

Therefore, the governments must now rely more on individual than on business sector for taxation revenue. The reasoning for such a significant shift is industry's concern for capital formation and investment. Since businessed pay relatively less taxes than they used to do under the centrally planned regime, they are left with relatively higher net income, which can be invested either directly, or through the financial intermediaries (i. e., the banking sector and the emerging capital markets). Nonetheless, there must be concern for the limits of such dramatic change in the structure of revenues. Neither the shift from corporate taxes to individual ones, nor from direct to indirect taxes paid by the household sector should go too far, for this kind of disequilibrium is unsustainable.

Execution of a tax cut for the sake of enhancing the propensity to save and hence capital formation is difficult to accomplish since at the beginning of post-socialist transition there is a very weak pro-growth lobby and a strong consensus in favor of a tax-and-spending policy, regardless of the political appearance of the ruling parties .[6] Policy aimed at high-speed growth requires the formation of a specific growth lobby. Yet such a lobby, oriented at investment and expansion and increasing productivity and competitiveness, must not rely too much on its insistence on tax cuts, because tax reductions that are too radical can lead to financial imbalances and rising social tensions. Eventually, these occurrences—together with increasing income inequality—may turn against the ability to expand and thus also against the autonomous interests of the emerging growth lobby.

The best way to manage gradually the growing propensity to save is by reforming the tax system by *shifting the major tax burden from direct to indirect taxation.* A policy better facilitating savings and capital formation is one containing the ratio of direct income taxes over the gross income, and raising the ratio of indirect taxes (e.g., VAT, excise taxes) over that income. Such a policy must take care with a gradual introduction of VAT and widening the range of its application. [7] This process will last several years and is still not completed even among the countries most advanced in transition.[8]

The shift from direct (income) toward indirect (consumption-related) taxes also changes the priorities of households toward the treatment of their personal income and time horizon for preferences *vis-à-vis* its spending. If the growing share of income is taxed not at the end of the earnings, but at the end of spending, than it is better to earn as much as possible and to save as much as possible, instead of spending the income at the time of, or immediately after, it has been earned.

So far, the time series and evidence from transition economies are too scanty to support a claim that in the countries that have tried to exercise fiscal policy along such lines, the overall propensity to save has become relatively higher. Yet the anecdotal facts from countries such as Croatia, the Czech Republic, Estonia, Kyrgyzstan, Hungary, Poland and Slovenia seem to suggest that the fiscal reforms aimed at raising the relative burden of indirect taxation, while ceasing the burden of the direct one, have contributed to growing savings and, therefore, toward improvements of capital accumulation.

Of great importance for capital formation are *the rules regulating the pace and scope of asset depreciation.* As elsewhere, the accelerated depreciation of assets used by firms facilitates the process of capital reproduction and its formation in the longer run. Although exercising a scheme of accelerated asset depreciation may influence the process of current inflation by pushing relatively higher the costs of production (hence the cost-push inflation mechanism is set in force), in the long term the increases in productivity and growing competitiveness, owing to technological progress based on the accelerated replacement of old assets, should offset the negative consequences of such approach. Nevertheless, particular solutions must be based on specific cases and analyses, because, under some conditions, an additional cost-push inflation can strengthen an already running inflationary spiral that may hurt the whole process of capital formation.

Although domestic savings and capital formation are crucial for sustainable growth an inflow of foreign savings is also necessary. Of major significance are foreign direct investments (FDI), which—on the top of domestic savings—are contributing to the accumulation of capital financing for growth in the long run. Unlike short-term portfolio investments (often of a speculative nature), FDI are long-term endeavors and usually facilitate competitiveness, and thus ability of export-led growth. In transition economies the flow of FDI is a function of several features, yet the most important are: the pace of structural reforms; progress toward stabilization, both from political and economic perspectives; and the extent of the market.

For these reasons, the economies more advanced in systemic transformation,[9] as well as countries that despite their meager institutional progress are rich in natural recourses (e.g., Azerbaijan or Turkmenistan), attract the core of FDI. In 1990-98, the flow of FDI per capita to countries considered as "advanced reformers" (EBRD 1998b; IMF 1998) was fourfold larger than to countries seen as "intermediate reformers" and almost eight times larger than to countries seen as the "slow reformers" (Table 6.7).

Additionally, larger countries, for example, Ukraine or Kazakhstan, for the obvious reason of the attractiveness of the scope of their markets, gain more attention than do smaller economies, for example, Moldova or Tajikistan. Post-socialist economies, even more than other emerging markets, may be very vulnerable to the swings of the short-term capital flow (EBRD 1998b). Unlike long-term capital flowing from FDI—which is essentially nondebt-creating capital flow—the short-term investment, though it contributes to the growth of the savings rate, is a debt-creating capital flow.[10] Thus, from the viewpoint of capital formation and growth sustainability, develop- ment strategies should focus on attracting nondebt creating capital flow. Yet in transition economies— especially with still unstable financial situations and poor fiscal stance—this is not the foremost case.

As an indispensable part of transition, the liberalization of the current accounthas been put forward. Only recently has the IMF been keen to admit that such liberalization should be done with great care, and only when stabilization has been already accomplished on the sustainable basis. Over the years of the first decade of transition there was an insistence, if not at least a clear expectation, to liberalize the current account still further. What followed, was an inflow of short-term capital. This capital was still more robust, since a number of countries had been running twin deficits, that is, both the government budget (see Table 6.5) and the current account (Table 6.8).

Table 6.7
Foreign Direct Investment, 1991-97

	1991	1992	1993[1]	1994	1995	1996	1997 [2]	Cumulative FDI inflows 1991-97 Total	Per capita, $	FDI inflows 1997 Per capita, $
Albania	--	32	45	65	89	97	33	369	115	10
Bulgaria	56	42	40	105	82	100	575	1,000	121	69
Croatia	--	13	72	95	83	509	500	1,276	267	105
Czech Republic	511	983	517	749	2,526	1,388	1,275	7,473	726	124
Estonia	--	58	160	212	199	111	131	809	557	90
Hungary	1,459	1,471	2,339	1,097	4,453	1,986	2,100	15,403	1,519	207
Latvia	--	43	51	155	244	379	415	1,287	515	166
Lithuania [3]	--	--	30	31	72	152	327	612	165	88
FYR Macedonia	--	--	--	24	13	12	16	65	31	8
Poland [4]	117	284	580	542	1,134	2,741	3,044	8,442	218	79
	305	**662**	**1,775**	**1,846**	**3,617**	**4,445**	**6,600**	**19,250**	**497**	**171**
Romania	37	77	94	347	404	415	998	2,389	106	44
Slovakia	--	100	156	203	183	177	150	912	912	169
Slovenia	41	113	112	128	176	186	321	1,074	538	161
Eastern Europe	**2,184**	**3,216**	**4,196**	**3,753**	**9,657**	**8,252**	**9,885**	**41,111**	**357**	**86**
Armenia	--	--	--	3	19	22	26	70	19	7
Azerbaijan	--	--	20	22	284	661	1,006	1,993	262	132
Belarus	50	7	18	10	7	75	100	267	26	132
Georgia	--	--	--	8	6	25	65	104	19	12
Kazakhstan	--	--	473	635	859	1,100	1,200	4,267	272	76
Kyrgystan	--	--	10	45	96	46	50	247	54	11
Moldova	--	--	14	18	73	56	71	249	58	17
Russia	--	700	400	584	2,021	2,040	3,900	9,743	66	26
Tajikistan	--	8	9	12	17	20	20	86	14	3
Turkmenistan	--	11	104	103	233	129	108	652	139	23
Ukraine	--	170	200	100	400	526	700	2,096	41	14
Uzbekistan	--	9	73	73	-24	50	60	216	9	3
CIS	50	905	1,321	1,613	3,991	4,750	7,306	19,900	70	26
Total	**2,234**	**4,121**	**5,517**	**5,366**	**13,648**	**13,002**	**17,191**	**61,100**	**153**	**43**

Notes: 1/ Net inflows recorded in the balance of payments. In million s of dollars unless otherwise
    indicated. 2/ Estimated. 3/ FDI figures for Lithuania are only available from 1993. For 1993-
    94, figures cover only investment in equity capital. For 1995-96, equity and reinvested earn-
    ings are covered, but inter-enterprise debt is excluded. 4/ The second series for Poland (in
    bold) supplements the data with information from a survey of foreign enterprises that was pro-
    vided by the State Agency for Foreign Investments. The differences arise, in part, from in-
    vestments in kind and reinvested earnings.
Source: EBRD 1998a.

Table 6.8
Current Account and Trade Balance, 1996-97

Current Account and Trade Balance, 1996-97	Current account balance 1997	Merchandise trade balance, 1997	Current account balance, 1997	Merchandise trade balance, 1997	Change in current account balance, 1996-97	Change in merchandise trade balance, 1996-97
	($ millions)		(percent of GDP)		(change in GDP share, percent)	
Albania	-195	-415	-8.5	-18.0	0.8	-7.8
Armenia	-428	-559	-23.4	-13.8	-0.4	-6.1
Azerbaijan	-961	-569	-23.6	-8.0	0.2	-5.8
Belarus	-995	-1,497	-7.5	-11.2	-0.7	-1.3
Bulgaria	184	311	1.8	3.0	0.5	0.8
Croatia	-1,900	-4,800	-10.3	-26.1	-5.6	-6.7
Czech Republic	-3,156	-4,600	-6.1	-8.8	1.5	1.7
Estonia	-610	-1,188	-13.1	-25.6	-3.4	-1.6
Georgia	-318	-366	-6.2	-7.1	-1.3	0.8
Hungary	-987	-1,700	-2.2	-3.8	1.6	2.2
Kazakhstan	-1,000	-500	-4.8	-2.4	-1.4	-0.9
Kyrgyzstan	-187	-134	-11.5	-8.2	12.5	12.6
Moldova	-310	-275	-14.9	-13.2	-1.4	0.2
Latvia	-350	-887	-6.4	-16.3	-0.5	-0.4
FYR Macedonia	-254	-343	-8.1	-10.9	-0.8	-2.3
Lithuania	-945	-1,115	-10.3	-12.2	-1.0	-0.6
Poland	-4,300	-11,300	-3.2	-8.4	-2.2	-2.4
Romania	-1,900	1,414	-5.5	4.1	1.8	8.8
Slovakia	-1,500	-1,500	-7.9	-7.9	3.2	4.3
Slovenia	70	-770	0.4	-4.3	0.2	0.4
Russia	3,900	16,600	0.8	3.5	0.3	-0.4
Tajikistan	-15	-5	-1.3	-0.4	5.8	3.2
Turkmenistan	-596	-245	-26.1	-10.7	-28.0	-17.5
Ukraine	-1,500	-4,800	-3.1	-9.9	0.3	0.2
Uzbekistan	-754	-254	-5.2	-1.8	2.7	5.1

*Notes:*Changes in the current account and merchandise trade balances in 1996-97 represent the difference between the ratios of the current account and merchandise trade balances to GDP in respective years. The current account balance for Armenia excludes transfers.
Sources: EBRD 1998a.

Policies in a number of transition economies—being not able to close the fiscal gap owing to persisting contraction (see Table 6.1) and a weak flow of revenue—were tempted to accept the inflow of short-term capital, seeing it as helpful for financing their short-term needs.[11] Under both domestic and external pressure for more gradual and restricted liberalization, the capital had been flowing in. Yet because its very nature it is a speculative flow, aiming for quick profits gained from short-lasting portfolio investments, not necessarily linked to investments in the real economy and hence not necessarily contributing to the growth of efficiency, once it has found better opportunities elsewhere and when the situation has turned to look less stable in post-socialist economies, such inflow may be converted into an outflow. Then the particular economy is not absorbing the savings from the outside; instead, its savings are invested in foreign countries.

Later, if there is still a positive balance of such swings of short-term capital flow, its alternating rampant inflow and outflow does contribute to an increase in financial instability. Consequently, it harms the overall propensity to save and the ability to enhance the capital formation on a sustained foundation. Aside from the direct effects of these kind of ups and downs, there is also a contagion effect, stemming from both the aftermath of the East Asian crisis (to a lesser degree) and from the Russian crisis (to a larger, though most often exaggerated degree) (Krzak 1998).

Capital formation under institutional arrangements of the centrally planned economy was relatively high (in international standards), though it was a result of forced savings rather than voluntary accumulation of capital. Therefore, the slowdown of economic growth in the late 1980s in the EE and FSU economies was due more to misallocation of capital than an overall shortfall of it (Kolodko 1986, 1999c; Poznanski 1996). It was not the lack of capital, but the increasing allocative inefficiency that was the main cause of sluggish growth.[12]

The gross capital formation plummeted rapidly in the transition economies, much more than the GDP contracted at the time. This was the outcome of a systemic vacuum following the collapse of the previous system, while a new one had only begun to emerge. The scope of the fall of investment in fixed capital served as a specific caution against otherwise still deeper decreases of consumption and the fall of the standard of living. As a result, not only the absolute level of capital formation and investment decreased significantly, but so did the rate of investment, that is, in its relation to the falling GDP. Moreover, the fluctuation of the rate of growth of gross investment in fixed capital is by large margin bigger than the fluctuation of the GDP rate of growth (Table 6.9; see also Table 6.1).

Table 6.9
Gross Investment in Fixed Capital, 1993-98 (Annual Percent Change)

YEARS	1993	1994	1995	1996	1997	1998
Eastern Europe						
Albania	30.0	15.0	12.5	23.9	-31.2	5.0
Bulgaria	-17.5	1.1	16.1	-21.2	-22.1	8.9
Croatia	--	--	--	--	--	--
Czech Republic	8.0	17.0	14.8	8.7	-4.9	-8.8
Hungary	2.0	12.5	-4.3	6.7	8.8	9.0
Macedonia	-21.7	-15.1	-5.0	-5.0	2.7	5.8
Poland	2.9	9.2	18.5	20.6	20.6	19.0
Romania	8.4	26.4	10.7	3.1	-15.9	-2.9
Slovakia	13.1	2.1	7.0	40.6	11.7	5.0
Slovenia	11.2	21.1	11.4	6.9	8.7	10.0
Yugoslavia	-37.3	4.4	-16.0	4.8	36.9	4.9
Former Soviet Union						
Armenia	-8.7	44.8	10.0	11.1	22.7	7.2
Azerbaijan	-39.0	89.0	-18.0	110.0	67.0	15.1
Belarus	-14.7	-11.0	-31.0	-5.0	20.0	-8.6
Estonia	22.4	11.3	-2.8	-14.7	9.2	11.0
Kazakhstan	-39.0	-15.1	-43.0	-35.0	-8.0	9.9
Kyrgyzstan	-31.0	-45.0	82.0	19.0	-35.0	-30.8
Latvia	-40.8	7.1	-4.3	5.0	9.2	15.0
Lithuania	-28.7	18.8	9.7	-0.3	10.4	10.8
Moldova	-44.0	-51.0	-17.0	-8.0	-6.0	-0.5
Russia	-11.5	-24.3	-13.0	-18.0	-5.0	-9.0
Tajikistan	0.1	-43.0	-25.0	-22.9	15.5	6.6
Turkmenistan	45.0	-38.2	6.7	-15.2	-13.2	-8.3
Ukraine	-10.3	-22.5	-28.6	-20.0	-7.5	-3.3
Uzbekistan	-5.0	-22.0	4.0	6.9	17.0	4.3

Source: PlanEcon 1998b.

Such was the point of departure toward market transition and the following sequence of changes that led to the situation that gross capital formation in the mid-1990s stood at around 22 percent of GDP, on average. In the second half of the decade it had started to increase gradually and by the end of 1990s it could be estimated at close to 25 percent. It is stressed that, "While this average figure is comparable to the one prevailing in the industrial countries during the period 1950-73, it is low compared to the average of 30 percent for the fast growing economies during 1985-94" (Fischer, Sahay & Vegh 1998: 27).[13]

It should be expected that as the recovery goes on and the growth is being recouped together with further consolidation of stabilization into stability, that *the gross investment in fixed capital will increase both in absolute and relative terms*. This process, recently gaining momentum in several countries, is opposite to the one observed at the beginning of transition.

It is predicted (PlanEcon 1998a, 1998b) that until 2000 the only exceptions from this rule are going to be Russia, Ukraine, Belarus and Yugoslavia, and afterward all transition economies should maintain accelerated rates of growth of investment in fixed capital[14] (Table 6.10). Taking into consideration the differences between the rates of GDP growth (measured in various ways) and the rates of growth in the absorption of GDP through private consumption and gross investments in fixed capital, one might develop various hypotheses.

First, as a result of ongoing economic liberalization and openness, this time in a context of growth, the gap between GDP counted in constant prices in the domestic currency (see Table 6.4) and the estimates of GDP on a purchasing power parity basis will tend to decrease. This is a strong tendency, as shown by the A indexes, which measure the ratio of the average annual rate of per capita GDP growth at market exchange rates over the average rate of per capita GDP growth at purchasing power parity during the period 1999-2002, that is:

$$A = \frac{\text{per capita GDP}_{NER}}{\text{per capita GDP}_{PPP}} \qquad (7)$$

where: GDP_{NER} = forecast of rate of growth of the gross national
product at nominal exchange rate;
GDP_{PPP} = forecast of the rate of growth of the gross national
product at purchasing power parity.

In each case (Table 6.11)—with the exception of Russia, for which any forecast must be taken with great reservation—the index is greater than unity, and the difference is meaningful. If this trend occurs, then *the market exchange rate and the purchasing power parity exchange rate will move closer*, and the current gap between these rates, usually between 1.5 and 2, will steadily diminish.

Second, the B indexes, which measure the ratio of the average real GDP growth rate (in domestic currency, at fixed prices) over the average GDP growth rate at PPP, reveal two likely tendencies in shifts in relative exchange rates.

$$B = \frac{\text{GDP}_{NER}}{\text{GDP}_{PPP}} \qquad (8)$$

where: GDP_{NER} = forecast of the rate of growth of real gross national
product,
GDP_{PPP} = forecast of the rate of growth of gross national
product at purchasing power parity.

Table 6.10
Gross Investment in Fixed Capital, 1999-2003 (Annual percent change)

	1999	2000	2001	2002	2003
Eastern Europe					
Albania	10.0	22.4	13.0	11.6	8.4
Bulgaria	10.6	12.2	12.6	7.8	5.5
Croatia	--	--	--	--	--
Czech Republic	-1.8	1.6	2.0	5.7	6.1
Hungary	6.4	5.0	5.8	5.8	5.6
Macedonia	8.3	8.1	7.1	7.0	8.9
Poland	11.3	8.7	7.2	5.7	5.4
Romania	1.3	5.9	6.2	6.9	4.8
Slovakia	-9.4	0.5	3.2	4.2	3.6
Slovenia	6.4	6.6	5.9	6.3	4.3
Yugoslavia	-2.5	-4.1	10.1	10.7	8.6
Former Soviet Union					
Armenia	1.1	4.6	10.3	10.5	--
Azerbaijan	13.1	11.6	11.1	10.7	--
Belarus	-10.2	-4.3	5.8	7.5	--
Estonia	6.1	6.1	6.4	5.4	--
Kazakhstan	10.9	13.4	15.1	23.1	--
Kyrgyzstan	7.5	21.7	26.3	43.0	--
Latvia	6.1	3.8	4.0	6.0	--
Lithuania	10.5	2.0	3.7	6.5	--
Moldova	-6.2	11.2	10.2	19.9	--
Russia	-13.0	-3.9	12.5	10.5	--
Tajikistan	3.5	7.1	5.6	7.1	--
Turkmenistan	-6.7	10.8	2.1	3.2	--
Ukraine	-10.2	-3.8	9.9	13.1	--
Uzbekistan	3.8	6.6	2.3	4.8	--

Source: PlanEcon 1998a.

Table 6.11
Indexes of Structural Change, 1999-2002

	A	B	C	D	E
Albania	1.134	1.020	1.496	0.931	0.982
Armenia	1.388	1.016	1.156	0.887	1.057
Azerbaijan	1.386	1.047	1.503	0.817	0.964
Belarus	1.581	1.016	1.127	0.934	1.005
Bulgaria	1.411	1.011	1.181	1.009	1.000
Croatia	1.166	0.995	1.112	0.946	0.929
Czech Republic	1.508	1.006	0.979	1.030	0.962
Estonia	1.391	1.009	1.020	0.958	0.975
Georgia	1.346	1.022	1.367	0.839	0.897
Hungary	1.177	1.005	1.087	0.977	0.984
Kazakhstan	1.188	0.998	1.236	0.998	0.963
Kyrgyzstan	1.124	1.057	1.379	0.931	0.981
Latvia	1.149	0.981	1.288	0.942	0.963
Lithuania	1.195	1.003	1.067	0.965	1.000
FYR Macedonia	1.092	1.027	1.138	0.955	0.981
Moldova	1.118	1.008	1.744	0.977	0.990
Poland	1.240	1.004	1.021	0.977	0.904
Romania	1.237	0.991	1.157	0.970	0.981
Russia	0.798	0.985	1.129	1.045	0.958
Slovakia	1.110	1.003	0.939	0.990	1.002
Slovenia	1.074	0.994	1.094	0.960	0.981
Tajikistan	1.460	1.083	1.155	1.057	0.963
Turkmenistan	1.533	1.054	0.849	1.201	0.964
Ukraine	1.269	0.998	1.139	0.972	0.973
Uzbekistan	1.508	1.113	0.956	0.994	0.981
Yugoslavia	1.224	1.016	1.362	0.939	0.962

Notes: A = Ratio of the per capita GDP growth rate at market exchange rates to the per capita GDP
       growth rate at purchasing power parities. B = Ratio of the real per capita GDP rate to the per
       capita GDP growth rate at PPP. C = Ratio of the growth rate of gross fixed investments to the
       real GDP growth rate. D = Ratio of the growth rate of private consumption to the real GDP
       growth rate. E= Ratio of the growth rate of average real wages to the real GDP growth rate.
Source: Author's computation based on data from PlanEcon 1998a and 1998b.

In a number of countries the process of the real appreciation of national currencies will continue, contributing to the closing gap between the value of national income as expressed on a PPP basis and its value as expressed in constant
prices in the national currency. If this index is higher than unity, then the relative efficiency of the economy is growing, and therefore the competitiveness of
the economy is improving, too. If it is less than unity, the relative efficiency and
competitiveness are declining.

The index of only about one-third of the transition economies is anticipated
to be (slightly) below 1, indicating that there may be a limited depreciation in
the national currencies. With an index significantly lower, only 0.985, the Russian economy, which was forecast before the financial crisis of the summer of

1998 to grow at a rate of 4.1 percent over 1999-2002 (in terms of real GDP at constant prices in 1998 rubles), should still grow, but due more to extensive than to intensive factors. In any case, both tendencies mean that the integration of these countries with the world economy should continue.

Third, the C, D, and E indexes indicate a growth tendency in all but a few of these nations. The C Indexes, which measure the ratio of the average rate of growth of gross fixed investments over the real GDP growth rate, that is:

$$C = \frac{I_R}{GDP_R} \tag{9}$$

where: I_R = forecast of the rate of growth of investment in fixed capital;

GDP_R = forecast of the rate of growth of gross national product,

show that the process of capital formation should gather speed. This will result from an increasing propensity to save and thus a declining marginal propensity to consume, both of which are apparent in the D and E indexes, that is:

$$D = \frac{C_P}{GDP_R} \tag{10}$$

where: C_P = forecast of rate of growth of private consumption, and

$$E = \frac{W_R}{GDP_R} \tag{11}$$

where: W_R = forecast of rate of growth of real wages.

If these indexes are below 1, then capital formation should rise more quickly than consumption and GDP, and this should create a strong foundation for more growth. For rapid and sustained expansion, domestic capital formation is always more decisive than the inflow of foreign savings. Only for the Czech Republic, Slovakia, Turkmenistan and Uzbekistan are the C indexes forecast to remain below 1, which means that consumption is going to increase more quickly than investment. If this does happen, then eating the fruits of the future may take place, and the rate of growth may slow after 2002.

POLICY CONCLUSIONS

Over the first decade of post-socialist transition to a market economy (1990-99) the expectations for growth and improvement of standard of living have not been met. While the GDP has contracted much more than foreseen both by the governments and the international organizations, the income inequality has been on the rise over the whole period. The challenge to shift transition economies from financial destabilization and economic slowdown of the late centrally planned period toward stabilization and growth has turned out to be paramount, well beyond expectations. It is also true that the policies advised and implemented with the support of the Bretton Woods organizations were not able to deliver what had been earlier foreseen.

Relatively more successful have been the countries more advanced in institutional building, which implemented stabilization policies in rather gradual yet comprehensive and determined ways, without any unnecessary and harmful shocks. Stabilization, ongoing within the framework of liberalization, is more fruitful if supported by sound attempts at new, market institutional arrangements, and if enhanced by the government structural policies. However, even among the countries leading in transition, stabilization still must be consolidated into stability.

So far, in transition economies the main concern of fiscal policy has been financial stabilization and reforms of the system of the public finance. The matter of raising the propensity to save and capital formation were rather auxiliary concerns. However, in countries that have tried to use the fiscal system and its adjustment as a means for savings enhancement, through, for example, lenient or nonexistent taxation of capital gains, decreasing taxation brackets, or narrowing the tax brackets, domestic savings have been growing faster than at the initial stage of transition. These policies should be continued.

The shift of the fiscal burden from direct to indirect taxation ought to be considered as one of the main elements of fiscal policy aimed at savings facilitation and capital formation. In the long run, an accent on taxing the expenses (through VAT and excise taxes) will encourage savings—and thus capital formation—while relatively lenient taxation of income should raise labor incentive and hence its productivity. In consequence, such attempts stimulate competitiveness and growth.

While new institutional arrangements are being established and when new capital is most needed, the capital gains (especially from interest rates on bank savings of the household sector [15] and gains earned on the emerging stock exchange) should not be taxed. In transition economies the policy instruments can be composed in such a way that even if the absence of taxation does contribute to growing inequity,[16] it may also contribute to growing income and hence overall poverty reduction. It must be, however, supported by other means of structural reforms and policies, especially as far as income and labor policies are concerned. Introduction of taxation of capital gains must be introduced only when the economy is on the path of fast and sustainable growth. It may be on the agenda early in the twenty-first century, at the earliest.

Considering the current stage of transition to a market economy—that is, the scope of liberalization and privatization as well as the openness of the EE and FSU countries, on the one hand, and the advancement (or delay) of new institutional arrangements, on the other hand—there are many policy options. The whole region of post-socialist countries at the end of the 1990s is even more diversified than it was at its beginning. Fiscal polices cannot be uniformed. In countries still lagging behind in systemic transformation and working development strategies, the fiscal policy must firstly take care of the matter of stabilization, yet the issue of capital formation must not to be overlooked. In the countries more advanced in institutional changes and relatively more stable, fiscal policy must focus much more on the issue of capital formation. This means that fiscal policy should encourage savings, since in the longe run a growing propensity to save serves the purpose of financial stability. The policy conclusion is that it should be routine—including via IMF missions and technical assistance— to monitor the fiscal policy and reforms from an angle of their influence on the long-term capital formation.

Although the considerations presented here have emphasized the formation of physical capital, fiscal policy must also aim at the improvement of the human capital. Despite the multiplying and complex tax deductions and other fiscal incentives that tend to spoil the fiscal system (especially under the circumstances of a weak tax administration, which is a rather typical feature of transition economies), it is worth a serious attempt to use such means for the purpose of increasing investment in human capital. Of crucial importance here are the investments in education. Tax deductions encouraging a higher share of household expenditures on education should be advised and implemented. In the long term it improves, not deteriorates, the fiscal situation, since it contributes to durable and balanced growth. Thus, it serves well the purpose of sustainable development, that is the ultimate aim of economic policy.

NOTES

Material for this article was presented at the IMF as a working paper of the international monetary fund and was authorized for distribution by Vito Tanzi.

1. There is not a reliable evaluation of how much capital may have left Albania prior to the collapse of fraudulent financial schemes, but some estimates put it as much as two-thirds of the annual GDP. In the case of Russia the estimates vary between US$40 billion and US$400 billion, likely being somewhere close to US$100 billion (which is more than the overall capital inflow to this economy during the 1990s).

2. Of course, there were many other, simultaneously occurring developments enhancing the propensity to save. In the aftermath of the shortage removal effect—the greatest achievement of the post-socialist transformation—the market has become well supplied in durable consumer goods, and so a desire to posses them has become a driving force behind growing savings, particularly for a relatively better remunerated strata of the society.

3. And this, unfortunately, is still the prevailing situation amid almost thirty countries going through the process of post-socialist transition to a market economy.

4. The usual means of such control is wage-based taxation, often used as an additional anchor in stabilization programs advised and supported by the IMF. In Poland, the famous popiwek, program which lasted from January 1990 until June 1994, was abandoned on behalf of a system of partnerships between the government, trade unions and employers. The latter is much more auspicious for labor productivity growth (Kolodko (1999c).

5. Growth of pensions—as long as there is a pay-as-you-go social security system, which indeed is the case in all transition economies—is directly controlled by the gov-

ernment. Considering the ongoing inflation, usually a system of indexation is used as the instrument of such control. The rate of indexation is a function of the anti-inflationary policy and the ability to accomplish sensible political compromise in each subsequent budget, heavily subsidizing the social security system, because of the latter's inability to finance itself from the flow of current contributions (Andrews & Rashid 1996; Hausner 1998).

6. With increasing long-term propensity to save such a scheme of tax reduction, proposed by the minister of finance, has been implemented in Poland under the program "Package 2000" within the "Strategy for Poland." Whereas personal income tax was cut, in two steps executed in 1997 and 1998, from 21, 33 and 45 percent to 19, 30 and 40 percent, respectively, the corporate tax has been subsequently reduced from 40 percent by two percentage points yearly since 1997. So, in 1999, it had declined to 34 percent and in 2000 fell to 32 percent. Such schemes should also contribute to higher economi competitiveness on an international scale (Kolodko & Nuti 1997).

7. It must be gradual, considering the point of departure, when many basic goods, for example, food or construction materials, were not taxed at all. Prior to transition, indirect taxes often were not imposed on many consumer goods considered as basic, or substantial for cost of living and for house constructing.

8. From this angle, the recent decision taken by the Russian parliament (the Duma)—contrary to IMF advice—to decrease significantly the rate of VAT has been a severe mistake. Such a move should be not only postponed, as already agreed, but abandoned. Particularly in Russia—a country with vast tax evasion, and a weak and corrupted tax administration—the best way to improve tax collection is to shift faster and further toward indirect taxation, and not the other way around.

9. Especially the group of five countries invited to negotiate the accession to the EU, that is, the Czech Republic, Estonia, Hungary, Poland and Slovenia.

10. FDI is usually seen—and rightly so—as nondebt creating financing. Nevertheless, in the end it is also repaid as either direct repatriation of profits, or through dividends. It is stressed, however, that "In the most favorable case, the current account gap can be viewed as being fully financed up to the amount of net FDI inflow" (J.P. Morgan 1999: 10). A good example of such a case is Poland, where the current account deficit, though exceeding 4.5 percent of GDP in 1998 (see Table 6.8), was up to 93 percent financed by the inflow of record high FDI (see Table 6.7).

11. It has been observed "All advanced reformers have managed to keep their external debt burden roughly constant at an annual average of less than 10 percent of GDP during 1992-97, while attracting progressively rising flows on nondebt capital, especially foreign direct investment, to support their rising deficits" (Valdivieso, 1998: 11).

12. Yet the growth was still taking place, which is what must be remembered and what matters, particularly in the countries suffering most from the long-lasting depression over the course of the 1990s.

13. These fast growing economies were, *inter alia*, Chile, Hong Kong, Korea (South), Malaysia, Singapore, Taiwan Province of China and Thailand.

14. Of course, as the result of the NATO strike against Yugoslavia one may expect that the situation will deteriorate also in neighboring countries, especially in Albania, Bosnia-Herzegovina and Macedonia (less in Croatia). The chance for fast growing investments has probably evaporated in the real-term, even if there was such a possibility prior to the escalation of the military conflict in the region.

15. Hence the proposal presented by the IMF mission to Poland (Ebrill, Escolano & Stotsky 1998) to introduce within the next stage of fiscal reform that taxation of income received from interest-bearing bank deposits must be seen as inappropriate. It may im-

prove the clarity of the system, though such a reform should then call for the taxation of all capital gains. At the current stage of development it would change not only the structure of savings (by shifting a part of money from banks accounts toward stock exchange), but could also harm the propensity to save.

16. Indeed, most often this is a fact both in developed market economies as well as in transition economies. Nevertheless, in the latter case, if there is a sound strategy for development and the economy is on the path of growth, inequality can be to some extent contained (Kolodko 1999a).

REFERENCES

Alesina, Alberto. 1997. The Political Economy of High and Low Growth. In Boris Pleskovic & Joseph E. Stiglitz (Eds), *Annual Bank Conference on Development Economics*. Washington, D. C.: World Bank.

_____. 1998. *Too Large and Too Small Governments*. Paper presented at the conference on Economic Policy and Equity, International Monetary Fund. Washington, D. C., 8-9 June.

Andrews, Emily & Mansoora Rashid, 1996. The Financing of Pension Systems in Central and Eastern Europe, *World Bank Technical Papers, 339* (October).

Ebrill, Liam P., Julio Escolano & Janet Stotsky. 1998. *Poland: The Next Stage of Tax Reform*. Washington D. C. : International Monetary Fund (October).

European Bank for Reconstruction and Development (EBRD). 1997. *Transition Report 1997*. London: Enterprise Performance and Growth.

_____. 1998a. *Transition Report Update*. London: Enterprise Performance and Growth.

_____. 1998b. *Transition Report 1998, Financial Sector in Transition*. London: Enterprise Performance and Growth.

Fischer, Stanley, Ratna Sahay & Carlos A. Vegh. 1998. *From Transition to Market: Evidence and Growth Prospects*. IMF Working Paper, WP/98/52. Washington D.C.: IMF.

Hausner, Jerzy. 1998. *Security through Diversity: Conditions for Successful Reform of the Pension System in Poland*. Paper presented at the Focus Group on the Interaction of Politics and Economic Policy in the Post-Socialist Transition, Budapest.

International Monetary Fund (IMF). 1998. *World Economic Outlook*. Washington D.C.: IMF.

J.P. Morgan. 1999. *Poland: Losing it!*. Economic Research Note, London: Morgan Guaranty Trust Company.

Kolodko, Grzegorz W. 1986. *Economic Growth Cycles in the Centrally Planned Economies: A Hypothesis of the "Long Cycle."* Faculty Working Papers, no. 1280. Champaign-Urbana: College of Commerce and Business Administration, Bureau of Economic and Business Research, University of Illinois.

_____. 1992. *From Output Collapse to Sustainable Growth in Transition Economies: The Fiscal Implications*. Washington, D.C.: IMF.

_____. 1996. *Poland 2000: The New Economic Strategy*. Warsaw: Poltext.

_____. 1999a. Equity Issues in Policymaking in Transition Economies. In Vito Tanzi, Ke-young Chu & Sanjeev Gupta (Eds.), *Economic Policy and Equity*. Washington, D.C.: IMF.

_____. 1999b. *Ten Years of Post-socialist Transition: The Lessons for Policy Reforms*. Policy Research Working, Paper Series, no. 2095. Washington, D.C.: The World Bank .

_____. 1999c. *From Shock to Therapy: The Political Economy of Postsocialist Transformation.* Oxford, UK: Oxford University Press.

Kolodko, Grzegorz W. & Walter W. McMahon. 1987. Stagflation and Shortageflation: A Comparative Approach. *Kyklos, 40,* 2, 176-97.

Kolodko, Grzegorz W. & D. Mario Nuti. 1997. The Polish Alternative: Old Myths, Hard Facts, and New Strategies in the Successful Transformation of the Polish Economy. *Research for Action, 33.* Helsinki: WIDER, United Nations University, World Institute for Development Economics Research.

Krzak, Maciej. 1998. Contagion Effects of the Russian Financial Crisis on Central and Eastern Europe: The Case of Poland. *Focus on Transition, 2,* 22-37. Vienna: Austrian Central Bank.

Milanovic, Branko. 1998. *Income, Inequality, and Poverty during the Transition from Planned to Market Economy.* Washington, D. C. : The World Bank.

Organization for Economic Cooperation and Development (OECD). 1998. *OECD Economic Outlook.* Paris: OECD.

PlanEcon. 1998a. *Review and Outlook for the Former Soviet Union.* Washington, D .C. : PlanEcon.

_____. 1998b. *Review and Outlook for Eastern Europe.* Washington, D.C.: PlanEcon, Inc. (December).

_____. 1999. *Monthly Report, Russia, Poland, Czech Republic, Hungary.* Washington, D. C.: PlanEcon.

Poznanski, Kazimierz. 1996. *Poland's Protracted Transition: Institutional Change and Economic Growth.* Cambridge, UK: Cambridge University Press.

Stiglitz, Joseph E. 1998. More Instruments and Broader Goals: Moving toward the Post-Washington Consensus. *WIDER Annual Lectures,* no. 2, Helsinki: UNU/WIDER.

Tanzi, Vito. 1991. Tax Reform and the Move to a Market Economy: Overview of the Issues. In *The Role of TaxReform in Central and Eastern European Economies.* Paris: OECD.

_____. 1997. Reconsidering the Fiscal Role of Government: The International Perspective. *American Economic Review, 87,* 2 (May), 164-168.

Tanzi, Vito & Howell H. Zee. 1996. *Fiscal Policy and Long Run Growth.* IMF Working Paper, no. 96/119. Washington D. C. : IMF.

United Nations Development Program (UNDP). 1996. *Human Development Report 1996.* New York: Oxford University Press.

Valdivieso, Luis M. 1998. *Macroeconomic Developments in the Baltics, Russia, and Other Countries of the Former Soviet Union, 1992-97.* Occasional Paper, no. 175. Washington D. C.: IMF.

Williamson, John. 1990. What Washington Means by Policy Reform. In John Williamson (Ed.), *Latin American Adjustment: How Much Has Happened?* Washington, D.C.: Institute for International Economics.

_____. 1993. Democracy and the "Washington Consensus." *World Development, 21,* 8, 1329-36.

World Bank. 1997. *World Development Report 1997: The State in a Changing World.* New York: Oxford University Press.

7

Privatization Politics in Russia: Success or Failure? Privatization and the Development of Corporate Governance Structure

Alexei Makeshin

In the past several years, interest in privatization has been growing in both developed and developing countries. Among the many reasons for this interest is the mounting evidence that the competitive discipline of private markets increases efficiency and produces greater quality goods at a lower price. In highly developed industrial countries (such as the United Kingdom under the Thatcher government), privatization has been most readily accepted and has been successful, but in the former communist countries, the policy encounters many obstacles.

A major obstacle has been the change in economic organization and technology. The so-called communist countries totally failed to create an effective economy, competitive with the West. Private business essentially ceased to exist (among the few exceptions were family-run businesses and private farms in Poland) and prices set by the government were left unchanged for extended periods, making them virtually unrelated to costs and useless as a way of rationing scarce goods. A system of detailed central planning and extensive vertical information flow was instituted to replace market processes of decentralized decision-making, horizontal communications and price-guided coordination. Especially harmful was the initial intent of the communist system to replace economic incentives with political and moral appeals to the workers' patriotism and communist consciousness. These problems, belonging to the sphere of mass consciousness and politics, are the focus of this chapter.

Many groups, including the military, labor, government bureaucrats and intellectuals, have their own attitudes toward privatization. Some are suspicious of plans to allow ownership of the economy to pass to "powerful elites" or foreign investors. Others try to reach their political interests through the revision of postcommunist power and ownership. Today, in Russia, the most challenging question of privatization is what will fill the gap created by the withdrawal of the state from the position of control over production and ownership?

In the West these functions are carried out by the capital market and the rational structure of corporate governance, in which the economic and political interests intersect with the mass consciousness of the population. Corporate governance structure in the West is not only the product of economic relations, but is also deeply rooted in mass consciousness as an important component of the economic culture. In Russia, however, political goals have been suppressed over economic reasoning and there is no cultural environment to support the mechanisms of corporate governance. The inertia of the masses and the lack of a mass entrepreneurial consciousness are the main factors that need to be taken into consideration when designing and implementing different projects in post-privatization Russia. Therefore, what is needed is a careful sociological monitoring of the current situation. The communist consciousness of the population must be transformed into corporate consciousness, hospitable to the market environment being created. Hence, I will here discuss the issues of privatization politics in Russia which so far are more of a political than economic process.

THE CONCEPT OF PRIVATIZATION

It was Mikhail Gorbachev who developed the concept of "reforms, undertaken by supreme power" in late 1980. However, this method was unsuccessful in overcoming the resistance of the communist party and the administrative bureaucracy. It was clear that new approaches had to be implemented to remove these political obstacles. Unable to resolve these problems, Gorbachev left the political scene together with his doctrine of *perestroika*. Boris Yeltsin then introduced a new course of reforms "according to the Western recipe." Launched in August 1991, Yeltsin's system reflected the interests of: (1) radical democratic political forces wanting power; (2) former communist party bosses ready for reforms and willing to accept a new type of power without Communist party dominance; and (3) Western countries interested in downfall of the USSR as a united political, economic and military power, competitor and permanent military threat (Popov 1994: 44). The core of this new political and economic course was shock therapy, which was highly recommended by Western experts. The basic features of this policy were to convert the ruble to hard currency, to introduce a rational pricing system and free up prices, to allow uncompetitive companies to go bankrupt and to privatize.

This last recommendation, privatization, was the center of severe political battles and academic discussions. It was evident that privatization would be the decisive factor in the outcome of future economic reforms. Much of the privatization discourse was generated by two diverse approaches: (1) implementation of privatization through the simple transfer of ownership rights from the state to private parties (free of charge), and (2) implementation through the introduction of a buy-out option. According to Organization for Economic Cooperation and Development (OECD) experts the "free" privatization was not a wise decision because it would significantly dilute ownership and, thus, inhibit control over managers. This outcome would not be a problem if there were well-functioning capital markets with transaction costs through which people could sell their shares, but such markets did not exist. Moreover, it was difficult to estimate the value of a share because of the inadequate accounting system inherited from the communist economy. All these factors made unreasonable the expectation that the markets would be very efficient if they were created according to free privatization principles.

However, political motives assumed higher priority than economic reasoning and a voucher privatization scheme was adopted, generously transferring state-owned companies to the whole population for free. This course, paying so little attention to economic considerations, addressed one main goal: it made the political reforms irreversible by dismantling the communist and soviet bureaucracy that had existed based on the state-owned monopoly over property. At this stage, then, privatization was guided by political goals. It was implemented under the guidance of Anatoliy Chubaise, the chairman of GKI (Goskomimushestvo, or State Committee for Property of the Russian Federation) since November 1992. This period was characterized by:

1. The obligatory character of privatization and its forced tempo
2. Simplistic economic design, and a very limited array of privatization options
3. Lack of structural priorities for privatization
4. A poor legislative and organizational basis for privatization (Pravitelstvennyi Vestnik 1991: 10).

Both miscalculations and accomplishments characterized the first stage of privatization, which ended in July 1994. Among them were: a dismissal of previous mechanisms of the centralized, planned economy and the powerful political forces supporting it; and the dissemination of major stock of the privatized companies among the company's employees and replacement of the old power structure by millions of new proprietors—the shareholders/employees. It was thought that having a share of the company would make one more responsible for the final output of his /her company and for the efficiency of his/her labor. In reality, however, the share was understood as a right to dividends, not as a right to manage the company, and the general population was not ready to fulfill their new social function as proprietors.

Consequently, the reality of privatization was different than anticipated by the State Program for Privatization. A good illustration of this situation were small-scale private businesses in Russia. According to Western economists, small businesses play an important role in limiting monopolism, promoting structural economic change and creating new job opportunities. What is more important, these businesses create the economic and social basis for an emergence of a middle-class. For example, in the United States small business contributes nearly 40 percent of the gross national product (GNP) and half of the working population is involved in this sector. In Russia, small-scale businesses contribute to only 8 percent of GNP and only 1 out of 77 million employees work in this sector. In addition, in Russia, instead of expecting small-scale privatization to introduce a positive role model in the businessman as a key figure of the new order, it developed a negative stereotype of business people as a mendacious mafia, with dirty money earned by shady businesses (Shamhalov 1993: 155).

Moreover, the initial dissemination of shares created a situation in which shareholder/employees and managers were free from government control yet, at the same time, they lacked the understanding and skills of management and corporate governance. In addition, former Communist party officials opposed the evolution of privatization because it gave potential power to employees, and hence, was against the vital interests of ministry bureaucrats and directors of the enterprises.

The situation led to a worsening of economic conditions and inhibited fast economic improvement. The end of the first stage of Russian privatization left citizens with standards of living comparable to those in the Soviet Union in the 1970s. One third of the population was living below the poverty line with another 30 percent close to this level. All consumer spending was allocated to food (46 percent of total spending), housing and clothing while culture, health care and education expenditures were minimized to 7 percent of the total spending in an average household. The social disparities rapidly grew. Accordingly, in 1994, the income of the richest 10 percent of the population was eleven times higher than that of the poorest 10 percent. At the same time the income of only 3 to 4 percent of the population, those called "the new Russians," could be compared with that of a middle class in Western Europe (Dostoinstvo 1994: 133-134).

Thus, the elections in December 1993 demonstrated that the vast majority of the population did not support tough economic measures and the politics of market reform. Economic efficiency and functionality of enterprises whose shares were disseminated among the population were the main concerns. Consequently, the most important task in the second stage of privatization was a change of political rationale from that creation of *mass proprietors* to the creation of *effective proprietors*. July 1994 was the watershed dividing the first stage of privatization, which was more politically oriented, from the second stage, which could be described as privatization formed on economic principles.

One of the major methods of the second stage was cash privatization, which required buying a property with real money instead of receiving it "for free." Accordingly, cash privatization facilitated purchasing a company by wealthy investors, who could collect large blocks of shares, and thus, have a greater impact on the company activity. This was realized through cash auctions of two types: (1) selling big blocks of shares to big investors, and (2) selling single shares to everybody interested, mainly to private persons. The second type was an important addition to the classical auction where only big blocks of shares could be purchased. Big investors, unable to acquire controlling blocks of shares during the classical auction, could collect the rest of the shares during the second type of auction. Thus the controlling shares were accessible to investors and this led to a considerable shift in the mechanisms of management. The second stage of privatization allowed for a transition to a new type of property and new methods of governing this property. This privatization goal was to establish corporate property and corporate governance mechanisms creating a great challenge for Russian economy.

This new initiative, however, is evolving very slowly. According to GKI data, only half of the privatized companies questioned were willing to produce the second sell-off of shares. Furthermore, out of 20,000 privatized companies, only 400 have held special investment competitions to stimulate the activity of big investors (Kotelnikova 1994).

AMO-ZIL: A PRIVATIZATION STORY

I present the case of ZIL Company as an illustration of the complexity of the privatization process. ZIL used to be one of the biggest truck producers in Russia with more than 80,000 employees. This company was privatized in 1993 according to the first privatization option when 50 percent of the total stocks were given to the company employees (including management). After privatization, the ownership structure of ZIL was as follows: the company managers owned 20 percent, 26 percent belonged to the private trading firm Micron, 23 percent remained owned by the state, and the rest of shares were disseminated among 180,000 private shareholders/employees. Before privatization ZIL produced more than 200,000 trucks per year. This company was among the most prestigious enterprises in Russia, characterized by high salaries, good social benefits and promising career opportunities. The major customers of ZIL products were the agricultural sector and the military. There were no problems with the market, since production was supported by the state budget. ZIL owned its own higher school of engineering and a number of kindergartens and vocational health centers all over the Soviet Union. ZIL also owned the housing where employees lived. This company seemed to be a successful and well-established enterprise. However, after privatization, production fell to 80 percent and more than 14,000 employees were dismissed. In 1994 ZIL produced only 34,000 trucks with further plans to dismiss another 20,000 workers. The company seemed to be set on a course for liquidation. How it did happen? Eugeniy Brakov, president of the shareholder company AMO-ZIL explained the situation in terms of irrational government policies. He insisted that the regular state donations of 100 thousand million rubles annually (more than $50 million) should be paid to the company until the year 1999. Otherwise, Brakov threatened to stir up the workers against the government (Brakov 1994). As a response, the government established a special commission led by the vice-premier, Oleg Siskovets, to discuss this issue. Evidently if a deal was made with ZIL management, the mass pressure on the government budget from the side of other big companies that were suffering from the loss of their markets and economic hardships would be expected (Ostapov 1994).

The Russian government proposed an assessment of ZIL to learn whether the company suffered from market transition or whether its bad luck originated from the way it was managed. This assessment was provided by the French experts from Renault, who had audited ZIL in 1992. The cost of this inspection, covered by the Russian government, was 1 million US dollars. The Renault experts concluded that the quality of assembling equipment at ZIL surpassed that at Renault plants and that the qualification of the engineering personnel met international standards. In addition, they noted that the labor productivity of this Russian company was only 20 percent lower than at Renault in France. What looked different was the final quality of the production and the market demand for ZIL's products. Hence the logical conclusion of the French team was that the major problem of ZIL was not economics, but unprofessionalism, the incompetence of strategic management and the lack of any marketing policy. For instance, there was market demand for two types of trucks: a powerful trailer carrier of 30-ton capacity and a small 1.5 ton city van. Both models needed to be equipped with diesel engines. These trucks were not produced at ZIL. ZIL introduced only one 6-ton modification to produced trucks and it had a gasoline engine of low adaptability for special requirements of particular customers. In addition, ZIL was selling its trucks only by batches of 100 units or more. This outdated strategy at a time when the agricultural sector and military were lacking financial support from the state and therefore were not reliable customers anymore did not work. As the result, there were more than 1500 trucks at the factory yard awaiting buyers and the factory even stopped production for two weeks in April 1994. Amazingly, all this happened when the market demand for trucks of the city class and trailer carriers was very high in Russia. Business people were buying trucks in the West. According to the French estimate, ZIL could restructure its production in less than a year. Engineers at ZIL were capable of developing new models and workers were capable of assembling them. Taking into consideration the low cost of labor in Russia, such trucks would be considerably cheaper than their Western counterparts. In order for this strategy to be implemented, however, a radical change and replacements in management were inevitable. Managers at ZIL, however, fought desperately to keep and to secure their position and wages, which were excessively high (over 100 times higher then the wages of the average ZIL worker). They had a strong motivation to oppose any change, which is why change in production or management did not occur.

The experts' opinion was shared by the GKI, which understood that ZIL's problems should be solved not with huge state subsidies but through radical improvement of the management cadre. GKI experts recommended the introduction of external management, an increase in turnover capital by selling some administrative buildings and the establishment of a dealer network (Kotelnikova 1994:3). Such a program was difficult to implement for two reasons: opposition of managers as just described, and opposition of workers. A majority of the employees trusted their old bosses and did not want to undertake a new role as proprietors of the company. Frightened to explore new opportunities, they demanded support from the state instead of demanding changes in management. For example, at the first ZIL shareholder meeting held on 29 April 1994, workers supported the development plan of the company introduced by the old administration (Ostapov 1994: 8).

MONITORING OF PRIVATIZATION

The example of with ZIL is not exceptional but a typical example of what was happening with the corporate mechanisms of the privatized companies in Russia. This was confirmed by a research program on new tendencies in Russian business that investigated the obstacles to development of private business (Roshina 1994). During that study, 350 top managers of private companies in the Moscow region were questioned. One of the surprising results was that, according to the managers' opinion, special skills and knowledge about management, advertisement and marketing did not play a significant role in the efficient management of their companies. These skills were evaluated much lower than factors such as good personal relations with state bodies, personal business contacts and holding capital. More than half of the managers said that they had no need for any type of consultants. Many of them preferred to solve unfamiliar problems by themselves or to ask their friends or relatives for help, instead of inviting qualified professionals from outside the "family clan." Lack of managerial culture and experience obviously hindered the successful development of the enterprise, yet this problem ranked fourteenth in the managers' own list of obstacles—after bureaucratization of the state bodies, the bad political climate in the country and corruption. The most important obstacle to the effective functioning of a private business was, in the managers' opinion, political instability and the worsening macro-economic situation in Russia (inflation, debts and taxes). Contrary to expectations, the appraisal of obstacles did not differ according to the managers' age, sex or education. Corporate governance problems were always found as the lowest priority on managers' lists (Roshina 1994: 94-107). This did not mean that corporate governance was something alien to economic reform in Russia but that the notion of "corporate governance" was very new to Russian consciousness and mentality.

The joint research of the World Bank and Central European University (World Bank & Central European University 1994) that took place simultaneously with the above survey depicted a number of problems of corporate governance in privatized companies. During the pilot study, in January 1994, twenty interviews with top management of privatized companies with the number of employees ranging from 250 to 1,200 were held in five cities in Central Russia (Moscow, Vologda, Voronez, Petrozavodsk and Rostov-on-Don). These enterprises were selected according to their property structure (with 30 percent or more of the shares belonging to private parties, not to the state) and the study was not interested whether this was a "success story" or whether the company was close to bankruptcy. The research was addressed to companies that had privatized according to all options allowed by the privatization legislation and all the companies had similar corporate structures. Two primary results were depicted. First, at the vast majority of the companies the "new" management was the old administration that had led the company for quite a long time in the past. Only a few new figures were noticed, and they functioned mainly as consultants. Second, the workers were passive proprietary owners who did not intend to acquire more shares than offered by the minimal norms of voucher privatization. This was contrary to the behavior of the managers, who wanted to hold as many shares as possible. The resulting situation was the worse-case scenario for privatization: the title of managers had changed, but not the mechanisms or motives of management. It was often difficult to distinguish between the council of directors and the management board of a company. A typical case was when a general director or president of a company was at the same time the chairman of the management board. This situation could be changed by the introduction of the corporate control mechanism but, unfortunately, as of 2001 such a mechanism does not exist.

The negative tendencies discovered by the World Bank study were in accord with the GKI statistical data. According to GKI, 74.4 percent of the companies privatized chose the second privatization option, where 51 percent of shares were sold to the workers and the former workers of the company. In turn, this situation led to two negative ways of managing the shareholder companies (Radigin 1994: 21). Either the old managers dictated their decisions to the shareholders because the shares of shareholders were so dissipated that the collective of workers could not negotiate a united policy against the managers, or the workers' collective negotiated its policy against the management. In the latter case the workers often turned into an "aggressive consumer majority" acting against the strategic interests of the management and the company. Both outcomes discourage large investors from potential investment. Investors usually prefer a company with a well-defined corporate majority mechanism, a number of blocks of shares and a real possibility of negotiating policies with these large shareholders, which is the classical, but very uncommon in Russia, model of the shareholder company. Another difference between classical and Russian shareholder companies is lack of the rational principles of corporate organization and control. According to the World Bank study, the most difficult problems in Russia were control over the blocks of shares belonging to the state, the transfer of voting rights of these blocks of shares, trust operations and the general design of the voting system at large corporations (World Bank & Central European University 1994).

CONCLUDING REMARKS

To be able to evaluate the privatization politics of the Russian government and to assess it as a success or a failure, one need to understand that privatization has won in terms of quantity and lost in terms of quality. Despite the difficulties mentioned above, the tempo of privatization increases. Among companies being privatized one finds a noticeable number of big and medium-sized enterprises. By April 1994 more than 20,000 Russian companies were in different stages of transition to private corporations. A similar tendency among near 10,000 medium-sized companies established special commissions for privatization as an act of good will, that is, without being on the compulsory privatization list of the government. One of the major goals of privatization is to create a mass group of proprietors to guarantee the irreversible character of the economic reforms. Russia established such a guarantee but not through the creation of a mass proprietorship but through the creation of fewer but more socially powerful groups of directors of companies. The director corps of the former state-owned enterprises and the people who represent finance and trade capital actively oppose any attempt to return to a communist-type economy. This new political force is incapable, though, of solving the economic problems of privatization politics. Thus, in Russia in 2001, one can easily find many large shareholder industrial companies that are not "corporations" comparable to Western enterprises. As to ownership structure and corporate control mechanisms, the

Russian companies still lag behind their foreign counterparts. Russian-based shareholder companies lack any form of efficient control both from banks and capital markets. The economic side of privatization politics has failed to create an efficient proprietor and mechanisms for providing industrial investments, which is the failure of the economic politics and strategy of the government. In an economic situation where inflation reaches 10 percent per month and an average investment into industry makes a profit of about 30 to 50 percent a year, it is difficult to wait for an investment boom in the industrial sector. For instance, in 1994 one could find better investment opportunities in trade, yielding 500 to 700 percent of interest per year, or in finance and hard currency operations, where the profits are calculated at up to 1,500 percent per year.

Moreover, we cannot assess the success or failure of the privatization politics separately from the government's doctrines. All parts of economic and political reforms have to come together and fit reasonably well. Basic determinants of privatization are factors that could secure the course of reforms for a long time, such as stable political power. Although there are signs of stabilization of political power and ownership has been established, the prognosis of Russian economic development is unclear. I propose two scenarios of potential development.

The first scenario could be characterized by state support to uncompetitive companies, centralized economic management by state-owned enterprises and by protectionism. Such a scenario is the choice of the managers and those commercial, banking and financial circuses making money on the inflation processes. Regrettably, this option is the most likely scenario of economic policy in Russia, so long as the division of power remains.

Successive liberalization of economic life, tough measures in the financial sphere and accomplishment of the privatization process can best characterize *the second scenario*. This course suggests the withdrawal of the state from its direct presence in economic relations, the regulation of structural change by market measures, the stabilization of the financial sphere and control of inflation. This would be the best option for economic development in respect to the general well-being of the Russian population. The withdrawal of the state from the position of control, however, remains the main problem in considering this option.

Inevitably the Russian economy needs a free market that will introduce a rational pricing system which will force companies to sink or swim, to survive or be liquidated and restructured in bankruptcy proceedings. In this context, privatization is often understood as the state's withdrawal from the running of firms, thereby subjecting companies to a genuine discipline of the market (Frydman & Rapaczynski 1994: 48-49). But markets function well (by providing an effective external coordination of economic agents) if they are embedded in a system of institutional control in which the managers are in charge of coordination of production but they are controlled by workers and outside institutions. The external control imposes on managers the actions that serve the best interests of shareholders. It is this control structure that the state enterprises in all post-communist countries are lacking. Without this system of control, the deregulation and decentralization of means of production will not produce a well-functioning market economy. It seems that, in early 2000s the main task of privatization needs to be an introduction of such a control system.

NOTE

This chapter is a result of my work at the World Bank and Central European University as a consultant on the research projects *Corporate Governance in Central Europe.* I greatly acknowledge the help and support I received from the World Bank and Central European University while working on this paper. Currently I am working on similar research regarding Organization Development and Management Change in Russia with the support of ECA/USIA Alumni Small Grants Program of year 2000.

REFERENCES

Dostoinstvo. 1994. *Moscow daily*, no. 4 (27 April), 5.

Frydman, R. & Rapaczynski A. 1994. *Privatization in Eastern Europe: Is the State Withering Away?* Budapest: Central European University Press, 48-49.

Hanke, Steve H. (Ed.). 1988. *Privatization & Development.* Washington, D. C.: Institute for Contemporary Studies.

Kotelnikova E. Brakov. 1994. Stavit ultimatum vlastyam. *Kommersant-Daily*, no. 78 (29 April), 3.

Ostapov E. 1994. Aktsionernoye obshestvo reshilo zatyanut poyas potuze. *Kommersant - Daily*, no.79 (30 April): 8.

Panorama Privatizatsii. 1993. *Moscow Daily*, no. 23, 40.

Popov G. 1994. Problemi puti stabilizatsii. *Voprosi Economiki, 2*, 44.

Privatisatsia: kak eto delayetsa. 1991. *Pravitelstvennyi Vestnik*, no. 25, 10.

Radigin A.D. 1994. Rossyiskaya privatizatsya v 1993 gody; itogi i problemi. *Problemi Prognosirovanya, 2*, 21.

Roshina J.M. 1994. Chastniy sector: predprinimately o problemah hozyastvovanya. *ECO, 1*, 94-107.

Shamhalov F. 1993. Maloye predprinimatelstvo v sisteme rinochnih reform: problemi rosta ili vizivanya. *Voprosi Economiki, 10*, 155.

Sotsialno-economitcheskay situatsia v Rossii. 1994. *Voprosi Economiki, 2*, 133-134.

IV

Social Problems and Policy Issues

8

Nouveaux Riches Versus *Nouveaux Pauvres*: Policymaking in Transition Economies

Grzegorz W. Kolodko

The biggest challenge an economist can face is not answering a difficult theoretical question but introducing reforms and making the day-to-day policy decisions that will prove that theory works. However, often that theory does not work. The next challenge, then, is to modify the theory or to keep trying to change the reality to follow that theory.

In the real world, far from the ivory tower of academia and elegant models, political life is brutal. What matters is political power, not the logical arguments and statistical evidence. In a classroom or at a conference it may be enough to be right and to be able to prove it in a scholarly way; policymakers, however, need a majority in the parliament and, more important, social and political support for reforms. Policymakers need to be wise and effective, but these attributes do not always go together.

Equity issues in policymaking are difficult to resolve because they are linked not only to economic matters but also to social constraints and political conflicts. What is fair and what is not, seems to be more a matter for ideological or philosophical dispute, not mathematical models. Equity is always a concern of the policymaker, especially in transition economies' early years of systemic change and severe contraction.

This chapter discusses the changes taking place during transition to a market economy. Expectations for income patterns and wealth distribution are examined as is the issue of increasing inequality. I then review policy options and evaluate the transition's impact on inequity and inequality, and conclude that although inequality inevitably rises during transition, policymakers must link income distribution and growth to sustainable development. The recent successful implementation of Poland's transition strategy suggests that it is feasible.

EXPECTATIONS

There is no doubt that one of the main causes of the post-socialist revolution in Central and Eastern European countries stemmed from the peoples' conviction that income distribution was unfair and unequal, contrary to political claims and the system's ideological foundations. It is difficult to say whether the people were more concerned about the level of their income or the way it was distributed, however, it is likely that the latter played a greater role in sparking the transition. The desire for fair and equal income distribution was very strong, and social dissatisfaction and political tensions were rising due to the growing disparity in real income.

Of course, there were other factors that helped push these countries toward a market-oriented economy. The people played, in fact, three roles simultaneously: as producers, they were disappointed that some of their efforts were wasted by mismanagement, stagnating output, and the lack of ability to compete; as consumers, they were irritated by the growing inefficiencies of the distribution system and the time they had to spend for shopping; and as citizens, they were dissatisfied by their inability to influence economic, social, and political changes. Only the combination of these three motives was strong enough to ignite the push out from a centrally planned economy toward a market system.

However, not only at the onset of the transition but still today, some do not want to move from relatively egalitarian socialism to less egalitarian capitalism.[1] There is still considerable naïveté that the market regime will bring higher and more equitably distributed income.

Ongoing political debates and the role modeling on industrialized countries have fueled unrealistic expectations. The excessive optimism among the new political class does not take into account these industrialized countries' histories. The common people are even more unrealistic. They have been told by the new elite that as soon as they get rid of the old system, the distribution of income (of course, higher) will be more favorable. The best example of this is the populist Solidarity movement in Poland.

Hence, at the beginning of the transition, there was the widespread conviction that this process would quickly bring both higher income and more fair distribution of the fruits of a better-performing economy. As naïve as this attitude is, it is still present, even among some professionals and leading politicians familiar with the economic and social realities. Optimism increased when five of the transition countries began accession negotiations with the European Union in March 1998, leading some to believe that the development gap between the transition countries and those in Western Europe would be closed within 10 years or so.[2] Unfortunately, it will take longer.

The gap is too large to close in one generation.[3] Closing the institutional gap will take a long time, closing the development gap even longer. This can be accomplished only when the rate of growth in Eastern Europe is much faster than in Western Europe. Due to the severe collapse in output during the first eight years of the transition, the gap between these two parts of the continent has widened. To increase the gross domestic product (GDP) by $300, a country with a GDP of $15,000 needs 2 percent growth, a country with $6,000 needs 5 percent growth, and one with $3,000 needs 10 percent.

Unrealistic expectations for quick transition results and world economic integration can be explained more by political, ideological and psychological factors than economic ones. In addition, these countries were relatively backward and did not expect such high costs of structural adjustment and recession, which caused an additional increase in social and political tensions. However, in the observed social process something different has occurred. On the one side, the strong component of ideological and political struggles raised expectations beyond anyone's capability to satisfy them in the foreseeable future. On the other side, the irrational temptations to get to a "better world" faster than feasible, enhanced by the spread of the demonstration effect and intentional, although ill-advised, postcommunist propaganda have strengthened the social and political tensions that have stemmed from the inability to meet unrealistic hopes.

Political leaders assumed that price liberalization and the elimination of shortages would lead to more equal income distribution. In some countries, such as the Czech Republic and Russia, these leaders thought that privatization through free asset distribution would improve income distribution. Vast circles of professionals and politicians believed that the reforms of the transfer system, especially of pensions, should not raise income inequality, but rather the opposite. Nevertheless, for a number of reasons, this has not been the case.

Short-term results did contribute to more equal income distribution, for instance, price liberalization improved access to goods that had been in short supply. Politicians and policymakers took advantage of this to improve their constituents' standards of living. Soon after, however, other transition events, such as the severe contraction of real salaries and the rapid increase in unemployment, worsened income inequality and increased the number of poor.

Thus, the policy was, in a sense, to walk from one point-of-no-return to the next. The clearest example of this is still seen in Russia, where the gap between expectations and achievements has grown since the transition began. In Poland, this gap existed in the early stage of transition only, because the accompanying costs were too high; thereafter, policy design was more realistic (Kolodko & Nuti 1997; Poznanski 1996). In the early 1990s in Poland, there was indeed shock, but not much therapy. It was assumed that output (in terms of real GDP) would contract by as little as 3.1 percent; in fact, it collapsed by about 12 percent in 1990 and by an additional 7.2 percent in 1991. During the same period, industrial output shrank by 40 percent (in real terms), leading to a steep drop in household income and to mass unemployment. Although the government promised that unemployment would not exceed 5 percent, by the end of 1993 it had reached 16 percent and was growing. Using as a stabilization target inflation (in terms of CPI) of less than 1 percent per month, the year-end inflation was about 250 percent in 1990 and over 70 percent in 1991.

The greatest disappointment among populists in political parties of the left and right was in privatization. The higher the expectation for an egalitarian mass privatization, the greater the disappointment. As in many other transition countries, the populist anticipation that post-socialism would evolve into a "people's capitalism"—due to the wide, free distribution of denationalized assets—led to frustration.

Although many people did receive free stock shares, they got rid of them quickly.[4] Due to ongoing redistribution, the shares are now accumulated by fewer individuals, and they are oriented more toward entrepreneurship and accumulation of wealth than consumption. There is nothing wrong with this type of redistribution as long as the people are not misled by their leaders, the emerging market rules are transparent, public interest is taken into account and redistribution patterns contribute to sound development. [5] Unfortunately, this has not been the case in all transition countries.

These countries also expected that the transition would bring a lessening of regional differences and tensions. In the former centrally planned economies, income levels and living standards differed significantly by region. The largest differences were seen in the former Soviet Union and former Yugoslavia. The dismantling of those countries did ease the regional tensions between the richest and the poorest former republics after they became independent; for example, between Estonia and Tajikistan in the former Soviet Union, and between Slovenia and Macedonia in the former Yugoslavia. Other countries experienced contradictory expectations, which has had significant policy implications. People living in the more backward regions expected a quick improvement in their standard of living; those living in the richer regions assumed they would be forced to transfer part of their income to the poorer regions, and they have been quite reluctant to do so. Such contradictory expectations have had significant policy implications. The larger the income gap at the outset of transition, the stronger the current tensions. [6]

REALITY

Although income distribution varies among countries, all transition economies have some common features. Income inequality is rising in all these countries, as expected. The fluctuations in people's income—first it fell, then it grew—and in its distribution have led to higher than ever in their lifetime income inequality. The greatest changes occurred during the early stages of transition, when real income contracted significantly but at a different pace by income group. Hence, in a matter of couple of years, the income proportions have changed significantly.

From this perspective, Milanovic (1998) has divided the transition economies into three groups. In the first, consisting of Hungary, the Slovak Republic, and Slovenia (with a combined population of 18 million), income distribution, measured by the quintile relations, has not changed. No quintile group gained or lost more than 1 percentage point, so the income shift did not occur between those groups but within them. The changes were rather minor: in Hungary, the Gini coefficient went up by 2 percentage points (from 21 to 23); in Slovenia, by 3 points (from 22 to 25). In the Slovak Republic even more equal distribution was observed in 1993–95 than in 1987–88, since the Gini coefficient fell from 20 to 19 points (see Table 8.1).

In the second group, which consists of Belarus, the Czech Republic, Latvia, Poland and Romania (with a combined population of 84 million), moderate regressive transfers were noticed. Maximum losses were within the range of 1 to 2 percentage points and occurred only toward the three lower quintiles. At the same time, the gains of the top quintile varied from about 6 points (for the Czech Republic and Latvia) to below 2 points (for Poland). Thus, only the highest quintile benefited, and only in terms of the share of income. Due to the severe contraction, the absolute level of real income declined in all quintiles although the higher the quintile, the lower the decrease. In this second group of countries, the Gini coefficient rose by only 2 points in Poland (from 26 to 28) but by a significant 8 points in the Czech Republic (from 19 to 27).

Table 8.1
Changes in Income Inequality During Transition

Country	Gini Coefficient (Income per capita)	
	1987–88	1993–95
Kyrgyz Republic	26	55 [3]
Russia	24	48 [3]
Ukraine	23	47 [2]
Lithuania	23	37
Moldova	24	36
Turkmenistan	26	36
Estonia	23	35 [3]
Bulgaria	23 [1]	34
Kazakhstan	26	33
Uzbekistan	28 [1]	33
Latvia	23	31
Romania	23 [1]	29 [2]
Poland	26	28 [4]
Belarus	23	28 [3]
Czech Republic	19	27 [2]
Slovenia	22	25
Hungary	21	23
Slovak Republic	20	19

Notes: For most countries, the income concept for 1993–95 is disposable income. In 1987–88, it is gross income, since, at that time, personal income taxes were small, as was the difference between net and gross income. Income includes consumption in-kind, except for Hungary and Lithuania in 1993–95. [1] 1989; [2] Monthly; [3] Quarterly; [4] Semiannual.
Sources: Data from Milanovic (1998); UNDP (1996).

In the third group, which consists of Bulgaria, Estonia, Lithuania, Moldova, Russia and Ukraine (with a combined population of more than 220 million), the changes were much greater. Income decline of the bottom quintile was 4 to 5 percentage points, and the second and third quintiles lost similar margins of their earlier share. In Russia, Ukraine and Lithuania, the fifth quintile gained as much as 20, 14 and 11 points, respectively. The greatest shift occurred in Russia, where the bottom quintile share of income was halved—from 10 percent to 5 percent—while the top quintile jumped from the relative high of 34 percent to as much as 54 percent. The Gini coefficient increased by 11 points in Bulgaria, and doubled in Russia and Ukraine, jumping from 24 and 23 to 48 and 47 points, respectively (See Figure 8.1).

Figure 8.1

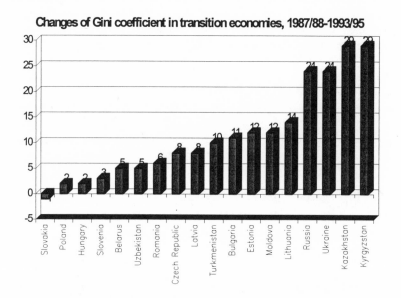

Changes of Gini coefficient in transition economies, 1987/88-1993/95

Sources: Data from UNDP (1996); Milanovic (1998).

At the end of the first five years of transition, income distribution in the first and second groups of countries was, on average, still more equal than in the market economies. In the third group, however, especially in the former Soviet Union countries, income distribution continued to be less equal than in OECD member countries.

Lately, the process had taken another route. Although in most of these countries income inequality has continued to grow, albeit at a much slower pace than before, in a few, it has stabilized. In recent years, this inequality has hovered around the dispersion structure that resulted from the changes that followed the earlier shocks. Of course, the income of some households and professional groups still fluctuates, but the changes are not as remarkable as they were in the first half of the 1990s, that is, they no longer fluctuate between quintiles and deciles.

However, these observations must be made with proper caution. Although the transition economies are going through a vast, intensive process of liberalization, they still lack sophisticated market institutional arrangements. Thus, their common feature is an extensive shadow economy, consisting of unregistered economic activities, the income from which is significant but impossible to estimate. The shadow economy, estimated to contribute from 15 to 50 percent of GDP in these countries, does affect inequality. [7]

Because there are many types of unregistered activities, the real challenge is to find the most appropriate way to institutionalize the shadow economy. Whereas some activities should be blocked and eliminated, others should be made official in a controlled way. The parallel economy encompasses organized crime, which has to be toughly fought, but primarily it is composed of a lot of small-scale businesses in many sectors—sectors that produce the goods and provide the services, jobs and income.

In transition societies, the people being offered the opportunity to take their fate into their own hands are quite keen to do so; however, they are not that eager to register their activities and pay taxes and social security contributions on these activities. Changing such attitudes will take time. For now, however, this type of emerging entrepreneurship, which creates a reasonable source of income, should be tolerated and gradually incorporated into the official economy by various means of the "stick and carrot." Before this task is accomplished a significant amount of income will be made in the shadow economy and simultaneously, a significant part of the total income will be redistributed through the parallel sector. The size of the former and the range of the latter is again, anyone's guess. These corrections in the dispersion pattern definitely complicate the picture drawn from the analysis of official income distribution alone.

At one end of the spectrum, many households engaged in the shadow economy, particularly in the trade, housing construction, maintenance and some traditional service sectors, have higher income than is recorded formally in the household budget survey (HBS). Although most—if not all—of the unemployed are officially counted in the bottom quintile, some should instead be counted in the second, at least. Given the substance of the shadow economy and the methodological problems in accurately measuring unemployment, it is obvious that an important fraction of this group makes money outside the registered economy. Therefore, their true earnings are higher than the state statistics, or even the more comprehensive HBSs, show.

At that other end of the spectrum, many activities of the new entrepreneurial class are not recorded at all, and hence, the official picture of this class may be biased as well. Using various means, they are often able to conceal from tax officials a significant part of their actual income. Both tax evasion and tax avoidance are widespread in transition economies, primarily due to poor tax administration and low moral standards of emerging capitalists. Whereas the creation of effective fiscal order and an efficient tax collection system is a long-lasting process, taxation is often treated as a sort of punishment. It is often believed that taxation limits the business sector's ability to expand and is rarely seen as a fair and rational instrument of income redistribution.

The range of the informal sector, with all its merits and drawbacks for income dispersion, depends on maturity of institutional arrangements and the developments in the real economy. In economies with relatively more advanced market institutions and a higher market culture—for example, in the countries invited to begin their accession negotiations with the EU—the scope of tax evasion is much smaller than in the countries lagging behind. Although it is difficult to measure and impossible to quantify, it seems to be feasible to claim that the shadow economy is larger in Ukraine than in Poland, larger in Armenia than in Latvia, larger in Romania than in Hungary, and larger in Croatia than in Slovenia.

As for real developments, the tendencies are mixed. In the fast-growing countries, at least part of the expansion is due to vigorous activities in the parallel economy, thus its impact on income levels and its structure is greater. As output rises, more people considered jobless make ends meet by working in the shadow economy than by collecting the dole from the safety net. The business communities are also able to take greater advantage of soaring shadow markets. At the same time, weak regulations allow them to hide at least part of their actual revenue. In the countries with continuing recession, an increasing number of people are looking for an opportunity to earn money wherever they can, including in the shadow economy, but they have fewer opportunities than in a growing economy.

The outcome of what has happened thus far is a puzzle and can only be roughly estimated. It is recognized that the shadow economy contributes to the higher income of all social strata, but it is impossible to estimate precisely how it influences the final proportions of disposable real income. Although the informal sector contributes to higher production and welfare as a whole, it also transfers part of the income from some households to others. Because one cannot map these income flows, one can only draw general conclusions. Income redistribution conducted within the borders of the parallel economy—as well as between the parallel and the official economy—can enhance overall growth. Thus, in the long run, it can contribute to a higher standard of living for the whole society. It seems, therefore, that the parallel economy, through its contribution to actual national income, and its impact on its redistribution, raises inequality. Moreover, it may be claimed that in the transition economies, as in the less-developed market economies, the difference between the official and the true picture of income distribution—if one takes into account the shadow economy—is much greater than in the more developed market economies.

MECHANISM

The income distribution pattern has changed qualitatively during transition. Some events and processes of vital importance have resulted from the elimination of a number of fundamental features and rules exercised under the centrally planned regime. In spite of considerable confusion as to what the outcome of these political, institutional and structural changes would be for equity versus inequity and equality versus inequality, the mechanism of change has been set in motion in an irreversible way.

Particularly important is that a majority of the subsidies and allowances previously provided by the state to some groups to support their consumption in kindhave been radically reduced or eliminated completely. Since the beginning of the transition, the removal of the subsidies has been seen as absolutely necessary by various international organizations, especially by the International Monetary Funds (IMF). The IMF was willing to back only structural adjustment polices that led to the liquidation of all subsidies. This external pressure was mixed with domestic tugs-of-war between the countries' political extremes, that is, between the old left and the new right populists on one side, and the free-market zealots on the other.

Depending on the social and political situation as well as on the chosen path of price liberalization and adjustment, the way the subsidies were removed influenced income dispersion. The more radical the subsidy cuts, the deeper the shift in income inequality. Whereas some shortages did indeed disappear rather quickly (the shops were full of goods), the real income and money balances of households shrank even faster (because consumers' pockets were almost empty). Consequently, the ultimate effect of slashing subsidies and price liberalization did contribute to an improvement of the fiscal stance and the introduction of a market-clearing mechanism, but it was achieved at the cost of growing inequality.

Setting aside the way the subsidy-removal policies have been executed in some countries, this approach should pay off in the longer run. [8] The transparency of free-market rules, the efficiency of market-clearing pricing and its influence on the allocation of resources, as well as the liquidation of distribution pathologies related to the shortageflation syndrome have contributed to improving economic performance and increasing competitiveness. If not now, then in the foreseeable future, these reforms will be fruitful for all people in the transition countries and make these countries more competitive internationally.

In the meantime, however, the unavoidable part of transition—price liberalization together with far-reaching subsidy reductions—has been causing high inflation. This was the case in Poland in 1989–93, it was still an issue in Bulgaria and Romania in 1997–99, and will continue to be a serious challenge in Belarus and Ukraine in 1999–2001. Whether such inflation is corrective or not does not matter for additional income redistribution, due to the very diversified price adjustments on products and services. Often, what rises first and the most is the basic cost of living—the prices of food, housing, utilities and public transport. Later, partial commercialization (i.e., the marketization) of other basic services, including health care, leads to further increases in living costs.

Inflationary income redistribution—executed through the downward adjustment of real income by different rates per household group—significantly increased income inequality in the early 1990s. This process is far from over in countries less advanced in liberalization and stabilization (Belarus, Bulgaria, Macedonia, Romania and Ukraine, and especially in Kazakhstan, Turkmenistan and Uzbekistan).

With extremely high inflation, real income distribution depended on the indexation procedures used at the time of the stabilization policy. Although the desire to stabilize the economy called for much faster growth of prices than wages or other income, such as pensions and hence a larger drop in the real income, social expectations and political pressure pushed the governments toward more lenient downward adjustments. Against this background, the actual indexation was always a function of political compromise, not necessarily a logical consequence of strictly economic arguments. Some social and professional groups bargained harder for compensation than others. For instance, it was easier for workers, especially in the large industrial centers, to get relatively more compensation for the growing costs of living than for teachers or paramedics.

Because of this unequal indexation, inequality continues to fuel social tensions (Gregory 1997). Since that problem is far from solved in any transition economy, the leading countries notwithstanding, the continuing change in relative wages will continue to cause political friction. As a result, the shifts of income among certain groups will also continue, regardless of the change of these groups' contributions to the national welfare. However, in terms of inequity, these changes will not cause significant alterations in the existing pattern of income distribution, only in the relative position of some professional groups vis-à-vis others.

Another aspect of inflationary redistribution that affects equity and equality deals with household savings. Because of the shortages under the centrally planned system, there was always some disposable net income that could not be spent on desired goods and services. This set in motion forced substitution and boosted the parallel, often semi-legal, black markets. However, households were left with some residual "disposable" income that was not "real" since it was not possible to spend it. So, it was involuntarily saved. When eventually the time for structural adjustment arrived—together with the post-socialist revolution—the prices were freed and raised to the market clearing level. However, the purchasing power of money balances, including those held in banks, was protected only partially. They were indexed, but only to some extent. [9]

The extent of the indexing depended on the stabilization programs and, of course, took into account the situation within the banking sector. Indexation was rather awkward, and when considered with the even worse standing of the public finance system and the state budget, did not allow for full compensation. So people's savings depreciated significantly. Only the most flexible, well-informed and entrepreneurial households were able to protect the real value of their savings. In some of the most successful cases, these savings became the seed capital for future businesses. This course of events has deepened income inequality in the post-socialist societies (Kolodko 1992a); in a direct way, it has impacted solely on the savings accumulated in the past, but indirectly it influences current income and savings as well.

Economic reforms liberalized wage setting in the state sectors.[10] Regardless of the initial pace of denationalization, by the mid-1990s, in most transition economies, more than half the labor force earned their salaries in the state sector. Whereas under the socialist system, due to ideological and political constraints, the dispersion of wages was quite limited, a much wider dispersion has been accepted during the transition. Thus, income has become more tightly linked to qualifications, experience, occupation and performance. The transition has meant a closer relation between an individual's past investment in human capital and its current remuneration, which has led to greater wage dispersion (Cornia 1996a). Because the quality of human capital varied more than did salaries under central planning, the later realignment of wages with levels of human capital has increased income inequality. It may, however, be claimed that income equity increased. That is true for both blue-collar and white-collar workers. [11]

Even more significant for rising income inequality is the shift of labor from the state to the private sector. Not only is the dispersion of wages in the latter larger than in the former, but the average income earned is higher. This is due mainly to the higher labor productivity in the private sector as the state is in control of a number of obsolete, noncompetitive industries and poorly managed, relatively low-paid services, such as education, health care and central and local administrations. Because of the meager budgetary situation, these sectors have not been able to compete with remuneration provided by other industries performing profitably on a commercial basis. Therefore, the rising share of labor engaged in the rapidly growing private sector has raised income inequality. This is merely a reflection of the accommodation of the market to the higher quality of labor engaged in these activities. Nevertheless, in transition economies, to the extent that the labor market is still quite rigid and far from perfect, the salary ratio remains somewhat distorted.

When an economy moves from the centrally planned to the free-market system, the most revolutionary and fundamental changes take place in asset ownership. The basic features of the beginning of capitalism after socialism are denationalization, privatization, property restitution, participation of foreign direct and portfolio capital and the development of financial intermediaries to accompany private sector's expansion. These events have a major impact on changes in income distribution.

During transition, the share of wages in total income decreases, while that of capital gains—for example, profits, dividends, interest and rents—increases. This process itself contributes significantly to growing inequity as well as inequality. Market reforms inevitably result in some unjustified redistribution, as it is an unavoidable byproduct of the transition process. Whereas limiting the range of the post-socialist redistribution is a matter of sound policies, containing and regulating it entirely is simply impossible.

The fundamental shift of assets from state to private hands has been followed by a shift in the income earned on these assets. Obviously, these changes have also increased the inequity and inequality. Therefore, one must decide how the property rights transformation is to be designed and by what means it will be managed. The two options would be, at one extreme, to sell state property to any investor, especially a strategic one, at the market-clearing price; [12] and, at the other extreme, the utopian option of freely distributing all assets among eligible citizens.[13] Of course, in the real world, some combination of the two is needed. Hungary chose a path closer to the first option; the Czech Republic, closer to the latter; and Poland, between the two.

The implications for corporate governance and microeconomic efficiency differ by option, but so ·do the consequences for income inequality. The choice between the two options is not simple. More unequal privatization, by selling to strategic investors, favors competitiveness and income level, whereas a more egalitarian distribution of assets favors income equity but does not necessarily improve efficiency.

The populist mainstream in both economics and politics has suggested that mass privatization through the free distribution of shares can offset the hardship caused by structural adjustment, especially growing unemployment and falling real earnings and pensions. This may be true, but only to some extent and only as temporary compensation for lost income. In fact, in several countries, workers have gone on strike—not against privatization but in favor of it. These strikers were not zealots of capitalism and a free market; they just wanted quasi-money—the shares or the vouchers, certificates, and coupons entitling them to shares'—which they felt was rightly theirs. However, it is bizarre that a poor person could have no access to an adequate social safety net yet own one or two shares of a privatized enterprise. This poverty and lack of social protection did not accord with the vision of market economy under "people's capitalism;" furthermore, it barely reduced the inequality and resulting tension. [14]

The problem of equity and equality versus inequity and inequality is even more serious. The basic problem is not the change in the income distribution pattern in, say, 1990–99—although for some 15 percent of the population these are their last years—but the irreversible foundation that has been laid for income distribution in the future. This change is the result of the stormy and indeed badly regulated and controlled process of asset distribution linked to the privatization process. In other words, when some were fighting for fairer indexation of their modest income (i.e., the current flow), the more cautious were trying to acquire as much property as possible (i.e., stock or future income).

In conclusion, taking only the flow of income into account, one cannot accurately answer the question about the scope, direction or pace of inequality.

Those that are, in fact, rich (owning many assets) may report very little income, whereas somebody else—a relatively poorer person—may pay the highest possible taxes. To properly measure inequality, one must analyze not how the flow of income is dispersed, but how it is distributed and how the stocks of denationalized assets are divided. Otherwise, one will get a distorted if not false, picture. Unfortunately, there is not even a rough statistical basis for such considerations. Most income flows are registered, but asset transfers are not.

The introduction of comprehensive taxation systems has changed the income distribution mechanism and its final outcome. Fiscal order in transition countries is not yet the same as in the mature market economies. The personal income tax—for some countries, entirely new—is always progressive, although the brackets and scales vary by country and can change in either direction. Because higher income is taxed at a higher margin, taxation decreases the net disposable income gap between better- and worse-remunerated people and, subsequently, narrows the scope of inequality.

In transition economies, the fiscal regimes and policies are not stable and neither is the equalizing effect of fiscal policy. There are continuous debates and political battles between the parties on raising and lowering the taxes. The resulting system is never a masterpiece of public finance theory and policy, but always a political compromise.

In spite of these reservations, it should be noted that redistribution does, at least to some degree, contribute to an impartial correction of the primary income distribution. As the market is in the process of being born, it cannot, of course, distribute national income in a way that guarantees both the fair participation of specific groups in the flow of current wealth and its future growth. What makes transition countries truly different from advanced market economies is that, in most cases, capital gains are not taxed at all. As they are not taxed, they are not recorded. Or is it the other way around? This approach has serious policy implications, but regarding the fiscal system's impact on equity and equality, the lack of capital gains taxation definitely increases inequity and inequality.

POLICY

The heart of the transition matter is to change a stagnant, centrally planned economy to a market economy that can expand and compete internationally. Issues, such as income and wealth distribution are often seen as secondary goals of economic and social policies, or simply as by products of the systemic changes. The redistribution of income can be treated simply as a means of superior policy for the overhaul of the system, that is, the radical alteration of the distribution pattern serves only as an instrument for the further accumulation of wealth. Such accumulation, in turn, should create a foundation for the new middle and upper classes, without whom the market system cannot exist. In fact, in transition economies one can observe the frantic process of wealth accumulation, which can be called post-socialist primary capital accumulation. If not immediately, then soon thereafter, people get the message that capitalism cannot

be restored or created without capital and capitalists—and the inherent consequences for inequity and inequality. The conclusion is obvious. During transition inequality must rise, and policymakers should try to shape such inequality
in a way that facilitates the transition's goals. Thus, the challenge is, first, to
define and design this line of policy, and, second, to implement it in the best
possible fashion. This is not easy; it may be even more difficult than it was in
the past during periods of primary accumulation, because now it must take place
during a severe transitional recession.

Whatever the explanation for the great post-socialist slump,[15] the fact remains that the officially registered GDP of twenty-five countries in Eastern
Europe and the CIS has contracted by almost 30 percent (weighted average) in
the first seven years of transition. Only in the eighth year (1997) was a modest
recovery recorded, albeit not in all countries involved (see Table 8.2).[16]

From social and political points of view, it is a challenge—and rather risky,
politically—to allow for any meaningful shift of income from the bottom to the
top quintile, even at the time of robust growth. Certainly, it is much more difficult to do so during a period of collapse in output. For the transition, the latter
has been the case for a number of years. Therefore, in considering the issue of
inequality, one has to distinguish between the stages of contraction and growth.

Contraction has lasted from a relatively short period of three years in Poland to eight years in Ukraine. [17] In some countries—and not only those experiencing regional conflicts—it may continue for some years. While the average
income is on the decline and policy favors promotion to the new middle class,
poverty must also be increasing. During the period of contraction, the redistribution mechanisms transfer additional portions of already falling income from the
poorer parts of society to the richer. This is the picture as seen from a macroeconomic perspective.

On the micro level, however, the changing pattern of income flow reflects
mostly the shift in certain population groups' contributions to GDP. The poor
are getting poorer because their contribution to declining national income is
falling faster that the contributions of other groups. The shorter this extremely
difficult period, and the smaller the fall in output, the better. It may be argued
that both the scope and the length of the transitional recession, which is, to some
extent, unavoidable could be reduced (Kolodko 1992b). Hence, *the first general
conclusion* is that in addressing the issue of inequality in transition countries,
one must try to limit the scope and length of the recession as much as possible.
Avoiding a recession is not possible, but counteracting it is necessary. Sooner or
later, transition economies will grow. After all, the whole exercise is motivated
by a commitment to bring them into the global economy as open markets that
can expand much faster than before. The World Bank (1997) estimated that the
transition economies could grow in a quarter of a century (1996–2020), by as
much as 5.8 percent annually.

Table 8.2
Recession and Growth in Transition Economies: 1990-97

Countries	Number of years of GDP decline	Did GDP fall again after recovery?	1990-93	1994-97	1990-97	1997	Rank-ing
			Average annual rate of GDP growth)			GDP index (1989 = 100)	
Poland	2	no	-3.1	6.3	1.6	111.8	1
Slovenia	3	No	-3.9	4.0	0.0	99.3	2
Czech Republic	3	No	-4.3	3.6	-0.4	95.8	3
Slovakia	4	no	-6.8	6.3	-0.3	95.6	4
Hungary	4	no	-4.8	2.5	-1.1	90.4	5
Uzbekistan	5	no	-3.1	-0.3	-1.7	86.7	6
Romania	4	yes	-6.4	2.1	-2.2	82.4	7
Albania	4	yes	-8.8	4.9	-2.0	79.1	8
Estonia	5	no	-9.7	4.1	-2.8	77.9	9
Croatia	4	no	-9.9	3.0	-3.4	73.3	10
Belarus	6	no	-5.4	-2.6	-4.0	70.8	11
Bulgaria	6	yes	-7.4	-3.6	-5.5	62.8	12
Kyrgyzstan	5	no	-9.3	-2.4	-5.8	58.7	13
Kazakhstan	6	no	-6.7	-6.0	-6.3	58.1	14
Latvia	4	yes	-13.8	2.2	-5.8	56.8	15
Macedonia	6	no	-12.9	-0.8	-6.9	55.3	16
Russia	7	no	-10.1	-5.3	-7.7	52.2	17
Lithuania	5	no	-18.3	0.5	-8.9	42.8	18
Turkmenistan	7	no	-4.5	-15.0	-9.8	42.6	19
Armenia	4	no	-21.4	5.4	-8.0	41.1	20
Azerbaijan	6	no	-14.5	-5.7	-10.1	40.5	21
Tajikistan	7	no	-12.2	-8.4	-10.3	40.0	22
Ukraine	8	no recovery	-10.1	-12.1	-11.1	38.3	23
Moldova	7	no	-12.6	-10.2	-11.4	35.1	24
Georgia	5	no	-24.1	2.9	-10.6	34.3	25

Source: National statistics, international organizations and author's own calculations.

Although that may seem impossible—especially in light of the weak performance of 1996–97, which showed almost no growth at all—some countries may achieve even more; it depends on the quality of the policies. With sound fundamentals, proper institutional arrangements, active involvement of the redefined state and some luck it may happen.

Recently the leader in the transition, Poland, has enjoyed a remarkable rate of growth. Under a properly fashioned program known as the Strategy for Poland, [18] which covers both transition and development, the economy has moved from early "shock without therapy" to "therapy without shock." Not surprisingly, in 1994–97, Poland recorded a GDP growth of about 29 percent, or 6.4 percent on average. This growth was accompanied by further progress in institutional advancement, which brought Poland to OECD membership in the summer of 1996 and, together with five other Eastern European nations, to EU accession negotiations in March 1998. At the same time, further progress toward the consolidation of stabilization into stability has been accomplished. Inflation has fallen threefold, from 37.7 percent at the end of 1993 to 13.2 percent at the end of 1997; the unemployment rate has declined by more than one-third, from 16.4 percent to 10.5 percent; and the fiscal-deficit-to-GDP ratio was halved from 2.8 percent to only 1.4 percent.

When an economy is on the rise, the issues of inequity and inequality can be addressed in a different way. During a recession, the question is, How can the loss of income be shared? or, How can particular social groups participate in its decline? Under an expansion, the questions can be modified to, How should growing income be distributed? How should the increment in national income be divided between population groups? Even in the most advanced market economies policy affects how income is shared, as it cannot be left exclusively to spontaneous market forces. This is true even more so in transition countries, where the market forces are, by definition, in their infancy. The best policy guideline for the government is to intervene only to the extent that guarantees a compromise between the interests of particular income groups and provides sufficient incentives for capital formation to facilitate development and hence the growth in the standard of living for all (Tanzi & Chu 1998).

A group that is definitely gaining from recovery and growth are those who have found jobs. In Poland's case, unemployment peaked in the summer of 1994 at close to 17 percent, or almost 3 million people. By the end of 1997, due to an active employment policy that took advantage of both directed subsidized credit and fiscal instruments, joblessness fell by 1 million. These 1 million people and their families have improved their absolute and relative income positions and thus the previous income inequality has been mitigated. Hence, the *second general conclusion* is that only a policy that lowers unemployment can reduce inequality.

The income policy as well as the asset redistribution policy must facilitate the accumulation of capital, which is mainly the domain of richer people. During a period of strong growth, it seems to be easier to accomplish this target because the two policies benefit each other—although only in the medium and long term. Growth facilitates capital formation and, vice versa, capital formation favors growth. If these interrelations are set in motion by the policy instruments and events in the production and financial sectors, then it is easier to get society's approval for such policies.

If some are getting richer while some are getting poorer—which is unavoidable during periods of contraction and thus increasing inequality—there is no way to convince the latter that they are better off. [19] If one is poor, but a little less so than before because someone else who is now richer is contributing to overall growth one accepts the situation. It may and will happen that on such a path, the income dispersion will increase even more. Nevertheless, if the increase in the wealth of some does not occur at a cost to others, these changes are likely to be accepted by most of society.

This attitude can be seen in the public's reaction to changes in the standard of living and income distribution in two distinct transition economies. One seems to be a success story; the other one is, so far, a failure. In Poland, the percent of households that assess their situation as "good or very good" is slowly but steadily growing. It rose from a single digit in the early 1990s to 12.2 percent in 1995 and to 13.1 percent in 1997.[20] This change in public opinion reflects both the growth of absolute income as well as greater acceptance of changes in the income distribution pattern. Not only does the reality change, but the public's perception of it changes as well.

In Russia, the public is convinced—and not without a cause—that transition has brought a plague of corruption and "crony capitalism" which are related to the continuing recession, growing inequality and spreading poverty. Even the country's leading politicians and international organizations have admitted on several occasions that this is indeed the case.[21] Consequently, the Gini coefficient doubled in the first five or six years of transition and will likely rise further. The growing arrears on unpaid salaries and pensions, as well as, the accumulation of wealth from insider privatization, lucrative financial market deals and especially pervasive organized crime, have contributed to the increasing income inequality. Both reality and beliefs are reflected in the very discouraging public opinion. When between 80 percent and 90 percent of society is convinced that wealth accumulation depends on connections or dishonesty and that poverty is a result of the economic system, then the future does not look bright (see Table 8.3).

In contrast, in Poland, due to the robust growth initiated by the Strategy for Poland and an income policy aimed at achieving more fair distribution, the Gini coefficient has stabilized in recent years. According to an OECD study, it grew from about 25 percent in 1989 to about 30 percent in 1994, then declined slightly to 29.4 percent in 1995 (OECD 1996). Estimates show that the Gini coefficient has remained around this level since or has increased only slightly in terms of wage dispersion, but that it has increased rather substantially in terms of income per capita (see Figure 8. 2).

Likewise, the deciles ratio increased to 3.03 in 1993 and 3.36 in 1994; since then it has stabilized or risen by only a small margin. More meaningful changes have occurred within the top decile due to wealth accumulation by the richest, but the actual income for the top ventile is unknown (World Bank, 1995). One must be careful in drawing conclusions from these observations. Particularly at the top of the top decile, the picture can be seriously distorted and the difference between the decile (or ventile) ratio for wages and for overall income seems to be indeed significant (see Figure 8.2).

Table 8.3
Russia: Placing the Blame —What are the causes of poverty?

Causes	Poverty (In percent) [1]
Economic system	82.0
Laziness and drinking	77.0
Unequal opportunities	65.0
Discrimination	47.0
Lack of effort	44.0
Lack of talent	33.0
Bad luck	31.0
	Wealth (In percent) [1]
Connections	88.0
Economic system	78.0
Dishonesty	76.0
Opportunities	62.0
Talent	50.0
Luck	42.0
Hard work	39.0

Note: [1]Percentage of respondents agreeing to each cause.
Source: Survey by Interfax-AIF of 1,585 respondents (Moscow, November 1997).

Has this recent drive toward more equitable income distribution in Poland been just a coincidence or the result of a deliberately chosen policy? Both. On the one hand, the market forces set in motion by the transition changed the distribution mechanism (Cornia & Popov 1997). Developing economies with fast-expanding private sectors and the simultaneous restructuring of state industries have been able to provide growing income for all social strata. As far as the decile groups are concerned, since 1995, their gains have been rather proportional.[22]

Figure 8.2

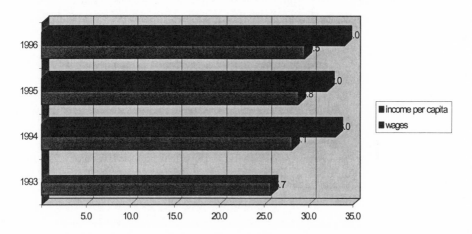

Gini coefficients during implementation of *Strategy for Poland*

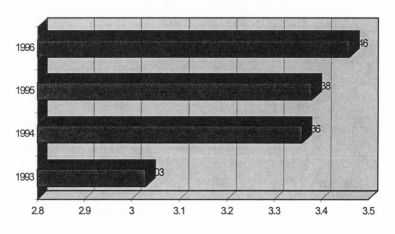

Decile ratio for wages in Poland, 1993-96

Source: Data from Polish National Satistics, 1993-1996 (Warsaw: GUS).

On the other hand, a decision was made and became a fundamental part of the Strategy for Poland that more fair income distribution should be not only the autonomous policy target but also an instrument to facilitate further growth.[23]

At the beginning of the transition, the shift of labor from the state to the private sector quickly caused an increase in wage inequality. This worsened when discriminatory measures were used against the state sector. Tough, if not too restrictive, wage-based taxation was used to contain nominal salaries; this was an essential instrument of anti-inflation policy at this stage. Later, especially in 1991–93, the famous Polish *popiwek* (the wage-based punitive tax), was used exclusively as leverage on state companies to push them toward privatization. Although the *popiwek* served this purpose, it also facilitated increasing income disparity and hampered the motivation for labor productivity growth in the public sector.

When the *popiwek* was finally abandoned at the beginning of 1995, state sector output soared. As a result, the growth in the income of the workers employed in this sector was on a par with the growth of remuneration in the private sector. Thus, the *third general conclusion* is that it is unwise to use a punitive measure that favors one sector at a cost to another even if it accelerates privatization, because it may slow the rate of growth and stifle competitiveness not only in the state sector but throughout the economy. If such a measure is used, inequality will rise and growth will slow in the medium term.[24]

Another important policy challenge was related to income policy at the initial stage of structural adjustment within inflationary surroundings. In 1990, at the beginning of stabilization, attempts were made to contain aggregate demand by cutting the civil servants' wages by a larger margin than the fall in the remuneration of the industrial workers. Later, the objective was to increase more quickly the average compensation to civil servants. This move was based not only on the conviction that such compensation was more fair but also that this type of investment in human capital would contribute to higher growth in the long term, and strengthen the relationship between investment in human capital and earning levels, which was rather weak prior to and at the beginning of the transition.

Therefore, the *fourth general conclusion* is that although the regulation of commercial sector wages should be left basically to market forces, the state should keep civil servants remuneration at an optimal ratio to the average industrial wage, and this proportion must be at a socially acceptable level, and facilitate the development of human capital in the long term. Fiscal policy should serve this purpose as well.

A further shift in policy was linked with difficult issues of indexation of pensions and benefits for the disabled. At the beginning of stabilization, instead of indexing pensions to the cost of living, they were indexed to nominal wages. This was another serious policy mistake, since the solution was short-lived (Kolodko 1991). This indexation was based on the assumption that real pensions should follow the path of wage adjustment—there should be a steep fall in real wages and a simultaneous deep contraction of real pensions. However, as soon as wages began to increase, due to growing labor productivity, so did pensions, despite the lack of financial sources to pay for such increases. Because the government was forced to borrow to finance the expanding fiscal gap, the commercial sector was crowded out of the credit market. This, in turn, acted against potential growth. It would have been much more reasonable to first decrease real pensions by less than the drop in wages, then allow them a smaller growth in real terms. Afterward, it turned out to be extremely difficult to adapt the indexation rules to the new circumstances, which has serious consequences for the public finance stance and delayed the social security system reform.[25]

In 1996, modification of the indexation rules allowed for real pensions to be adjusted upward yet kept within the limits of noninflationary financing; this has led to only a moderate increase in the ratio between average salaries and pensions. Considering the very high dependency ratio, these reforms did not significantly change the income dispersion.[26] Contrary to popular belief in Poland, only about 15 percent of retired people are poor or worse-off than the working class.[27] Therefore, most pensioners are actually in the second or third quintile, a fact sustained by the new indexation rules, which allow for a modest growth in purchasing power.

Crucial to the success of transition and development is a capital formation policy. It is assumed that a market economy, unlike a centrally planned economy, will be characterized by a greater ability to save and a more efficient allocation of capital. In the past, however, the severe output collapse caused a substantial decline in the propensity to save and the emerging post-socialist markets were caught in the trap of serious capital deficit. Although the inflow of foreign savings is important, especially long-term capital and preferably as direct investments, domestic savings are even more so.

During transition, income policy must deal with many contradictions. Although the drive to encourage saving suggests more lenient taxation of some types and sources of income, growing inequality suggests the opposite. How to solve this alternative, that is precisely a matter of policy options. If the economy is expected to recover quickly and expand, then some fiscal preferences for capital gains have to be introduced. This option is politically difficult not only because of quite strong populist temptations in the post-socialist societies as well as among influential politicians, but also because it is strange to tax unemployment benefits or minimal pensions yet not capital gains on speculation (e.g., on the stock exchange).

Often in transition economies, in fact, such policies are exercised for the sake of raising the propensity to save. The capital gains from the appreciation of stocks, interest on bank deposits and dividends on shares are mostly free of taxation or taxed only modestly, with the rationale of promoting capital formation and increasing national saving.[28] Of course, this approach increases inequality but also, through savings and investment, facilitates growth and the future standard of living of the entire nation.

At the beginning of transition, especially during a contraction, the above-mentioned capital formation policy worked for only the more affluent, namely, those who have disposable income from which a fraction can be saved and invested. Later, when the economy is on the rise and more social strata are enjoying growing real income, the expanding capital markets and better performing financial intermediaries, together with a preferential fiscal policy, encourage further saving. Consequently, the size of the emerging middle class increases and the poorer parts of society are able to save a growing percentage of their earnings.

As expected, this policy was quite controversial in Poland. In late 1992 through 1993, the lack of taxation on gains from stock speculation and a general euphoria led to an expanding bubble in the capital market. This situation—typical for emerging markets—was fueled by the frantic mass media. The rate of return, although not sustainable, was extremely high, thus demands for the taxation of extraordinary profits earned during a period not that favorable to the overall economy seemed to be justified. Unfortunately, no corrective steps were taken until it was too late—the bubble burst at the beginning of 1994. The stock exchange index declined by some two-thirds, at which point there was no reason to tax this type of capital gain, if there was any. For a couple of months, a rather neutral turnover tax was imposed on short-term stock exchange transactions, but it was soon eliminated.

In 1996, the Polish government adopted Package 2000, a program aimed at sustaining growth. Under this program, capital gains remain tax free at least until the end of 2000. Between 1993 and 1997, national savings increased by about 4 percent of GDP, mostly from higher domestic savings. If such actions had not been taken, perhaps inequality would be slightly less, but growth would not be as robust. Thus, the *fifth general conclusion* is that, if the policy alternative is less inequality and a lower rate of growth, or greater inequality and a higher rate of growth, then the choice should be higher growth and acceptance of a relatively higher income disparity. In the end, everyone will be better-off if this policy is chosen.

Package 2000 reduced corporate and personal income tax for all income groups. Prior to 1996, the corporate income tax was a flat 40 percent. Since 1997, it has been cut by 2 percentage points per year, to 32 percent in the year 2000 and afterward. These rate changes should enhance corporations' ability to invest and, in the longer run, increase international competitiveness.

Package 2000 reduced the personal income tax in two steps.[29] First, after a parliamentary compromise, each of the three brackets was lowered in 1997 by 1 percentage point—to 20, 32 and 44; in 1998, they have been cut to 19, 30 and 40 percent. Once again, there was a hot political debate on making these tax cuts. Strong opposition to the proposed cuts emerged in both the ruling coalition and among their political opponents.[30] For the corporate tax, in government circles it was argued that it would be better to widen the existing system of tax deductions, which was aimed at promoting investment, than to lower the tax burden for all enterprises. Opponents argued that it would be better to give up the entire system of investment allowances and lower the tax rate even further.

As for the personal income tax, the leading argument of the parties supporting the government was that the proposal favored the richer part of society, providing them a nominal tax reduction of as much as 5 points, whereas for the overwhelming majority of the population it would be only 1 point. But it must be remembered that personal income taxes had been raised previously by these very margins.

The attitude of the opposition liberal party was a bit strange. Although they declared their strong probusiness orientation, they simply did not want the tax reduction plan to be *realized* by a government led by the leftist party, which—according to their rhetoric motivated by ideology and politics—was supposed to be in favor of taxing and spending. Eventually, the reduction of the lowest bracket was raised to 2 percentage points and some minor changes were made in deductions linked to investment in human capital, particularly in higher education. This scheme was accepted.

As for income distribution, these changes in the tax code may raise inequality slightly, especially the ratio between the tenth and the other deciles. Although all taxpayers will gain from the reduction of the fiscal burden, the top decile will gain more than the other nine. Income dispersion and the personal taxation system in Poland work in such a way that only those in the top decile for at least a few months pay taxes in either of the two upper brackets (30 and 40 percent). Hence, their net income increases more than that of the remaining 90 percent of society. The final results of these changes will not be known until after 2001, when the first year's gross personal income and tax records are available.

In spite of the drawbacks, a capital gains preference policy does encourage savings. It also enhances one's capacity to invest more in one's human capital. Due to robust growth, real income is increasing; given this improvement in the fiscal situation, a tax reduction was feasible. From the macroeconomic angle, it is much less costly in terms of alternative budgetary revenue to cut the upper tax bracket than the lower. From a political viewpoint, it was more difficult, because a lot got a little and a few got a lot. Inevitably, as a result of growing gross income and lower taxes, the propensity to save is rising, which eventually should finance additional investments and facilitate further growth.

NOUVEAUX RICHES VERSUS *NOUVEAUX PAUVRES*

Under central planning, there were poor and rich people. Determining the number of each depends on how they are counted. Whatever method is used, it is undeniable that the market transition has increased the number of both rich and poor. Because inequality has been increasing, so has the number of people at each end of the spectrum. Poverty and affluence can be measured in relative and absolute terms. Although some studies have focused on the former group, we still do not know much. For example, we do not know what proportion of the population should be counted as relatively, or even absolutely, rich. But, no doubt, they exist.

The range of poverty in the transition countries, due to the decline in output and the long-lasting crisis, has increased significantly in the 1990s. As long as this decline in output is directly linked to the way the transition to a market is managed, growing poverty will be associated with transition. Only a few who were already poor prior to the post-socialist revolution, have been able to take fate into their own hands in such manner that they were lucky enough to escape poverty. Unfortunately, the poor segment of society is growing. Although circumstances vary among countries, it is possible to group these countries into one of four categories, which range from "very high poverty" (a country where more than half the total population is counted as poor) to "low poverty" (where less than 5 percent is poor) [31] (See Figure 8.3).

Figure 8.3
The Range of Poverty in the Transition Countries

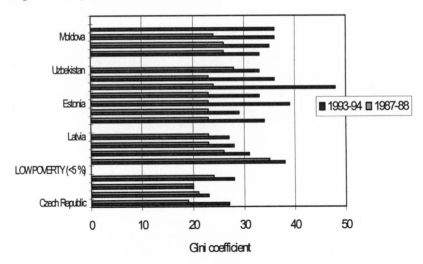

Source: Honkkila 1997; Milanovic 1998; Pomfret and Anderson 1997; UNICEF, 1995.

An important issue related to this increase in poverty is the impact of increasing inequality on destitution. Several studies (Honkkila 1997; Milanovic 1998; Pomfret & Anderson 1997; UNICEF 1995) have noticed that in some countries (e.g., Bulgaria, Estonia, Poland, Romania, and Uzbekistan), the rise in poverty is more a result of the decline in income equality than of falling income itself. This phenomenon should be considered a very negative by product of transition (see Table 8.4).

Table 8.4
Increase in Poverty and GDP Decline During Transition, 1987–94

Country	Poverty Relative to the Country (21–27 percent of average income)			Poverty Relative to the World (Income less than $120 PPP)			1995 GDP Index (1989=100)
	1989–90	1993–94	Increase	1987–88	1993–94	Increase	
	(Percentage change)			(Percentage change)			
Azerbaijan	11.1	65.2	54.1	...	...	...	34
Belarus	...	...	...	1	23	22	54
Bulgaria	2.0	32.7	30.7	2	33	31	73
Czech Republic	0.2	1.4	1.2	0	<1	0–1	87
Estonia	1.0	27.0	26.0	1	40	39	66
Hungary	1.1	4.0	2.9	<1	3	2–3	85
Kazakhstan	...	...	...	5	50	45	46
Kyrgyz Republic	...	...	...	12	84	72	42
Latvia	1.3	33.5	32.2	1	25	24	54
Lithuania	1.5	39.1	37.6	1	46	45	41
Moldova	2.4	40.6	38.2	4	65	61	40
Poland	5.8	10.9	5.1	6	19	13	99
Romania	7.0	25.3	18.3	6	39	33	84
Russia	...	...	...	2	45	43	54
Slovak Republic	0.1	5.1	5.0	0	<1	0–1	86
Slovenia	4.5	6.1	1.6	0	<1	0–1	93
Turkmenistan	...	...	...	12	57	45	63
Ukraine	...	...	...	2	41	39	40
Uzbekistan	...	...	...	24	47	23	83

Sources: UNICEF (1995). Poverty lines: 21 percent of average income for the Czech Republic and Slovenia; 24 percent of average income for Estonia, Hungary, Latvia, Lithuania, Poland; and Slovak Republic; and 27 percent of average income for Azerbaijan, Moldova, and Romania (Máhovic (1996); EBRD (1996)).

Although it has been simply impossible to contain poverty at the time of contraction of GDP—from 20 percent in Poland between mid-1989 and mid-1992 to as much as 65 percent in Georgia, Moldova and Tajikistan between 1990 and 1997—there are other significant factors that contribute to the poverty.

First, the above-mentioned decline of production ignores the regional aspect of crises. Even when the economy is on the rise, the situation continues to deteriorate in the backward regions, so poverty grows.

Second, transition creates a labor market, so it brings unemployment, which is then worsened by the ongoing recession. The unemployed are provided with modest (if any) benefits. Many remain jobless for a long period and become more impoverished (Rutkowski 1997). The transition countries were unprepared to tackle unemployment, especially a long-lasting one. Whereas in some advanced market economies, such as the United States, less than 5 percent of the unemployed remain jobless for more than one year, in a country like Poland, the figure is over 40 percent.

Third, most of the population, including the retired and those receiving relatively low pensions, had their savings eroded by rampant inflation and the lack of appropriate indexation mechanisms. In extreme cases, such as Russia's MMM schemes or Albania's disastrous, fraudulent pyramid schemes, weak and inefficient financial intermediaries as well as political negligence destroyed the savings of many households.

Fourth, the ill-advised drive toward illusory fiscal prudence pushed some governments—again, Russia's case is the most spectacular—into postponing the payment of pensions and civil servants' salaries. The growing arrears, which are merely hidden budget deficits and disguised public debt, reflect the nominal equivalent of unpaid income, which further lowers the standard of living.

Fifth, the agricultural sector is still quite large. In Poland, which is already an OECD member, as much as 24 percent of the labor force is still engaged in farming. The rapid trade liberalization and inflow of imported food products from more competitive markets have ruined many small farms and left those farmers in poverty.

These five crucial factors led to *nouveaux pauvres* in the transition economies. While, the *nouveaux pauvres* are a consequence of the series of unavoidable events; they emerged because of policy mistakes. If it could not be better then it was under the former centrally planned economy, at least it should not be as bad as it has turned out to be. The collapse in output and growing inquality have caused widening poverty, which, in turn, has caused a series of misfortunes: homeless people have appeared on the streets, crime rates are rising, economically motivated emigration has expanded, black markets have mushroomed, life expectancy has fallen (significantly in some countries) and mortality due to social stress has increased (Cornia 1996b, Paniccià 1997). Life expectancy in Russia and some other former Soviet Union countries (e.g., Latvia, Ukraine) has fallen by several years between 1989and 1995, it dropped for men by a staggering six years. It is claimed that, due to this kind of demographic crisis, as many as two million people who were expected to live longer, have passed away (Cornia, Honkkila, Paniccia & Popov 1996; UNICEF 1995). These authors claim that this excessive mortality has stemmed from the extraordinary hardships imposed by the way transition has been implemented and by the negative, accompanying factors, such as crime and violence.[32]

Poverty has widened in all transition economies, including those leading in both systemic change and growth, because of the time lag between recovery and growth and the improvement in the living standard for society's poorest. First, real output recovers, then employment grows, and finally the budget allows for better financing of the social needs of the poorest. Thus, an economy may be on the rise, but poverty will not decline for several years.

This sequence of events was seen in Poland, where until at least 1995, despite the resurgence of growth that began in the second half of 1992, the scope of poverty did not decline. Unemployment rose until the summer of 1994, and salaries in many sectors did not grow until 1995. If the poor are counted as those living below the relative poverty line, defined as the equivalent of half of average monthly household expenditures, then the poor in Poland increased from 12 percent in 1993, to 13.5 percent in 1995, and to 14.0 percent in 1996 (GUS 1996, 1997a). Of course, this is a relative measure and does not mean that more people were driven at that time into absolute poverty; in fact, the opposite is true. The portion of the population that benefits from the ongoing economic expansion has been on the rise for a few years. This fact is confirmed by the households' own evaluation of the standard of living changes. Whereas more than 50 percent of Poland's households declared their economic position to be "bad" or "very bad" at the time of contraction (early 1990s), this figure fell to 32.5 percent in 1995 and to 30.3 percent in 1997 (GUS 1997b).

Although it is true that the phenomenon of growing poverty has ended, it is also true that poverty still presents a tremendous challenge for the future. The next few years will determine what income distribution pattern will prevail in the transition economies. Not all countries will follow the same distribution model. It will not be that easy to correct the mistakes that have been made thus far; since inequality has increased, it will be extremely difficult, maybe impossible, to decrease it significantly in the coming years.

Transition has created a class of *nouveaux riches* as well. Most are well-educated, hard-working people, and capable not only of taking care of their own wealth but of doing so by establishing new opportunities for other citizens to improve their standards of living. Of course, as frequently happens—again, because of weak institutional arrangements and market experience—there are the thieves, swindlers and crooks. These and other pathologies must be combated. However, in most transition countries, the majority of the nouveaux riches are members of the new entrepreneurial class.

Some distribution mechanisms help the rich first and only later help the rest of society. After a crisis and the following recession, it takes far longer for the real economy to recover output and profits for the financial markets to soar.

Thus, the living standard of the poor, lowered by the contraction, tends to last longer than that of the rich.[33] In extreme cases, when the real economy continued to shrink and therefore the poor became poorer, the financial markets were flourishing, so at least some of the *nouveau riches* became even richer.

Every market economy has its entrepreneurial class. They are keen to risk their income in the new ventures on which overall expansion depends. However, how a society distributes its income and wealth depends on historical processes and current policies, which have caused a much more unequal distribution in Latin American countries than in South East Asia. The way the post-socialist transformation has been managed so far and how it will deal with income distribution in the future will determine the distribution pattern. We can already see that some of them remind us of Latin American countries, others of South East Asia. Despite these similarities they create their own patterns with both the *nouveaux riches* and the *nouveaux pauvres* at the same time. These are just two sides of the same coin.

CONCLUSION

Thus far, transition has brought mixed results. Although inequality has increased in all transition countries—from Albania to Estonia and from the Czech Republic to Mongolia—in some, it has doubled (e.g., Russia and Ukraine); in some, it has grown by only a couple of points (e.g., Poland and Slovenia); and in yet others, it has stabilized.

Nonetheless, not all changes reflecting income dispersion are going in the same direction. Inequality can be measured by different methods often with conflicting results. For instance, in Poland between 1994 and 1995, the Gini coefficient (in terms of wages) increased from 28.1 to 28.8; however, the decile ratio for wages was virtually unchanged, hovering around 3.4. This difference is significant, as people usually pay more attention to the latter, that is, to the ratio of rich to poor and how it has changed.

The biggest challenge for policymakers is how to deal with growing inequality and widening poverty. This challenge is made more difficult by the interrelationship between the two as well as a severe, long-lasting recession. Hence, growing inequality is not only a political issue that will provoke tensions and conflicts, but one that creates an economic obstacle to durable growth.

One should not confuse the means with the ends of economic policy (Stiglitz 1998). Income distribution and a socially acceptable distribution of wealth are just some of the important long-term policy targets. From this perspective, the goal of transition is not only systemic change, but, more important, greater efficiency, increased competitiveness, faster growth and more sustainable development. Thus, transition is expected to improve the standard of living for all, or at least for the overwhelming majority. Otherwise, the exercise would not make much sense.

Considering the equity and equality issues in policymaking, one has to have a vision not a delusion. Although inequality must rise during transition, changes

in inequity should be controlled and managed by sound policies. The scope and the pace of these changes cannot be left entirely to the just-released market forces.

In the real world, accomplishing these tasks and getting political support for the implementation of necessary measures is quite difficult. Politics and policy-making are nothing more than the ability to tackle, time and again, conflicts of interest. This is especially true during a transition, when the policies must lead the shift from stabilization to growth, and consolidate the stabilization process into lasting stability.

When a policymaker trying to catch up with a more advanced world faces a trade-off between faster growth with higher inequality (but less poverty) and slower growth with lower inequality (but widening poverty), he or she can be happy because the choice is clear: *Policy should facilitate sustainable development, and income policy should support that goal.* That way, in the long run, everyone's standard of living may improve. After the initial surge of inequality, and when the economy is on the rise, it may be even possible to reduce disparity without harming the ability to expand. This seems to be even more true for in-equity. Therefore, the more the transition advances and the stronger the founda-tions for fast and durable growth, the weaker is the trade-off between equity and efficiency.

NOTES

1. The results of recent elections in some transition countries (e.g., in March 1998 in Armenia and Ukraine) support this observation.

2. These five countries (the Czech Republic, Estonia, Hungary, Poland and Slove-nia) have been EU associate members since 1994. Five other countries (Bulgaria, Latvia, Lithuania, the Slovak Republic and Romania) are associated with the EU, but have not yet been invited to begin accession negotiations.

3. According to EU Commission and Eurostat estimates, the GDP per capita on a PPP basis is $ 3,900 in Estonia, 5,300 in Poland, 6,300 in Hungary, 9,100 in the Czech Republic, and 10,100 in Slovenia. Thus, the average income is between 35 and 65 per-cent of the average income in Western Europe. This is indeed a very large gap.

4. Paradoxically, Russia has, in relative terms, more stock owners than the United States; Poland has more than Germany; and the Czech Republic more than Austria, but that does not mean there is more capitalism. In Poland, a special program of so-called mass privatization, together with many denationalization measures, has been imple-mented. Over 500 state companies with book value of about 10 percent of total state assets pending privatization, were transferred through fifteen specially established Na-tional Investment Funds (NFI) to the population for a nominal fee (equivalent of US$7, or 2 percent of the average monthly salary at the time). As many as 97 percent of eligible citizens participated in the program. Among the remaining 3 percent were the president of Poland, and the first deputy premier and the finance minister, but they did not collect their certificates exclusively because of the lack of time. After trading at the secondary market, it is estimated that, at most, one-third of participating citizens had retained their acquired shares, while two-thirds sold their certificates to other entities for prices five to seven times higher than at the primary market. Most shares so distributed were concen-trated by some institutional investors, including banks and other financial intermediaries.

5. If one wants to take care of the long-run public interest, one should exercise a policy of simultaneously reducing both the public property and public debt. Hence, it is unwise to give up assets through any type of free distribution, without "giving" up at the same time at least a proportional part of the public debt—domestic and foreign alike. From this angle, debt-to-equity swaps should be used more widely than occurred in transition countries. The main obstacle here was again political. Under the Strategy for Poland program, the ratio of public debt to GDP fell from about 86 percent in 1993 to less than 50 percent in 1997.

6. In Poland, the most difficult problem stemmed from allegations made by the industrial center (coal mines and steel mills) in Upper Silesia. Regional claims for a national income redistribution were addressed in the program, A Contract for Silesia, adopted in 1995. The program focused not on more favorable transfers but on enhancing local activities and entrepreneurship, raising investment potential, increasing the ability to absorb FDI and better coordinating regional development policy. As a result, tensions have been eased.

7. For the advanced market economies, the scope of the shadow economy is estimated at about 15 percent of GDP for the European Union countries and below 10 percent for the United States. For Poland, estimates differ, although Herer and Sadowski (1996) believe that it stands at about 25 percent of the official GDP, the author estimates that it is more in the range of 15 to 20 percent of GDP. What it is in the other post-socialist countries is anyone's guess. "Russian tax police First Deputy Director Vasily Volkovsky told *Nezavisimaya Gazeta* that one-third of Russian businesses are not paying any taxes, and a further 50% pay tax only occasionally. Volkovsky said in the next few years the authorities intended to aggressively scale down the gray economy to a level at which it ceased to pose a threat to Russia's economic security. He said the gray economy accounted for 45% of GDP in 1996" . (Agence France Presse, as quoted in "Russia, IMF agree on 1998 Economic Program," *Morning Press*, 13 April, 1998 [Washington: International Monetary Fund]).

8. There is a long way to go in countries still at the early stage of transition, such as Turkmenistan. In the most extreme case, Belarus, shortages reappeared in the spring of 1998 due to the government's attempts at direct price control and the scope of subsidies. They by no means will be sustainable considering the overall state of the economy and, especially, the fiscal position of the government.

9. Dealing with the aftermath of the severe depreciation of accumulated savings is still on the policy agenda in some countries, for example, in Lithuania.

10. In some countries, such as the former Czechoslovakia and Romania, which initiated market reforms at the onset of 1990s, economic reforms have caused more fundamental changes. In others, such as Hungary and Poland, which started reforms and wage deregulation much earlier, this process was only (yet significantly) accelerated.

11. Although during the socialist era it was accepted that the ratio of state-determined wages between unskilled workers and university professors should not exceed, approximately, 5:1, during the transition—if the market so determines—this ratio may exceed, approximately, 15:1.

12. That is fine if the assets are sold at market clearing prices, but often they are not. And, if not, who is eligible to acquire the assets pending denationalization? When the author asked in 1993 the then deputy minister of finance in charge of the privatization of Poland's financial institutions why they were selling the shares of Bank Slaski at many times below the market-clearing price, he was told that the reason was simple: to provide the new owners with enough capital gains that they will soon be able to acquire the next

bank. And they were. The Bank Slaski shares, a couple of months later on the floor of Warsaw's stock exchange, were traded at more than 13 times the asking price by the Ministry of Finance on the primary market! The budget had lost a lot, but a few had gained a lot as well. And the Minister of Finance was fired.

13. The point is that assets distributed on the primary market, for free or for a nominal, symbolic fee, are sooner or later redistributed on the secondary market. Again, people are free to do so, but in the end it leads to the accumulation of these assets by only a few.

14. Juha Honkkila (1997: 6) rightly claims that "for individuals brought up in a communist society, the loss of safe employment or other social benefits provided by the state sector cannot be offset by minor opportunities to enjoy the personal ownership of assets."

15. For different views on this subject see Blanchard (1997); Bruno (1992); Gomulka (1996); Kolodko and Nuti (1997); Kornai (1993) and Lavigne (1995).

16. According to IMF estimates, in 1997 GDP for the whole region increased by a modest 1.7 percent and was predicted to grow by 2.9 percent in 1998. In 1997, for the first time since the transition began, none of these countries is to undergo a decline in output. The overall expansion is expected to increase further in the medium term (IMF 1998). It is worth noting that, in the past, the IMF, in its annual *World Economic Outlook*, wrongly predicted a turnaround.

17. During these eight years (1990-97), the official GDP decreased by as much as 58 percent, which is much more than in any other country during peacetime.

18. See Kolodko (1996) and OECD (1996).

19. In 1991, an advisor to the Polish government was asked to name the greatest achievement of the stabilization program. His answer was that kiwis can be bought on Warsaw's streets. In 1997, another advisor said that in Russia there was already a market economy (which, of course, is supposed to serve society better than the previous system), but that people were not yet able to understand it. The problem is that a market economy consists not only of private property and liberal market rules, but must also have sound institutional arrangements, a market culture, and appropriate behavior by the people. Thus, as long as people do not understand what a market economy is, they do not have a market economy.

20. Data from the HBS provided by the Polish Central Statistical Office (see GUS 1997a: 6).

21. In 1997, the then first deputy prime minister, Boris Nemtsov, during his first days in the office made a point that Russia must choose between "bandit-capitalism" and "capitalism with a human face". The Managing Director of the European Bank for Reconstruction and Development, Jacques de Larosiere, claimed at the EBRD 1997 annual meeting that with respect to Russia and other former Soviet Union republics, in 1996 alone the outflow of capital from the region probably exceeded the total invested by the EBRD since its creation (Financial Times, 1997). Most of this outflow is believed to be linked to illegal economic activities, organized crime and money laundering.

22. Of course, this hypothesis should be carefully re-examined when more data on income dispersion for 1996-98 becomes available.

23. Some claim that too great an income inequality acts against growth (Alesina 1997; Alesina & Perotti 1996). Transition economies are no exception in this respect.

24. It has to be stressed that in the Polish success story, the acceleration of growth in 1994-97 was mainly due to gradual privatization, the fast-growing new private sector

and the commercialization of state enterprises (Kolodko & Nuti 1997; OECD 1996; Pozanski 1996).

25. Nevertheless, the comprehensive social security system reform was prepared and launched within the framework of the Strategy for Poland, but not until 1997.

26. A relatively high dependency ratio is common to all transition economies. Although in Poland, due to another miscalculation of the early stabilization policy, many older people were given early retirement. Hence, at the onset of the transition (1990–91), the size of the retired population jumped significantly, despite the natural demographic tendencies that would suggest otherwise. Since that period, the average retirement age has fallen to as low as 59 years for men and 55 years for women.

27. This is more the result of the assets accumulated in a lifetime than the effect of the current income flow.

28. In Poland, dividends are taxed, but at the relatively low rate of 20 percent, which matches the lowest personal income tax bracket; the corporate income tax rate is currently 36 percent.

29. Earlier, at the beginning of 1994, the personal income tax had been raised from 20, 30, and 40 percent to 21, 33, and 45 percent, respectively.

30. About 91 percent of the population are in the lowest bracket. About 7 percent of taxpayers are in the middle bracket, and only 2 percent in the highest.

31. Regarding the poverty classification for the transition countries, see Milanovic (1995). The poverty group consists of those with an annual income of less than US$120 (on a PPP basis). Regarding the concept of poverty in China and Vietnam, see UNDP (1994).

32. In Russia, in 1996, deaths exceeded live births by 60 percent due to the deterioration of health standards. This deterioration was caused by poor diet, the breakdown of water quality control, the worsening of workplace safety and the growing mortality due to violence, suicide, cardiovascular diseases and stress. The maternal mortality rate continues to be 5 to 10 times higher in Russia than in Western Europe, and infant mortality 2 to 4 times higher. Deaths from tuberculosis in 1992–96 rose by as much as 90 percent.

33. Vice President of the World Bank, Mark Malloch Brown, in addressing the issue vis-à-vis the recent East Asian crisis, stressed that, "Although imbalance in distribution of income declined with growth, the pace of correcting this disparity has slowed down. . . . Government-driven growth policies have focused on export industries, and no sufficient commitment was made for improving living standards." Quoted in *Development News—Daily Summary*, The World Bank, Washington D. C., 12 March, 1998, after *Asahi Shimbun*, 11 March, 1998, p. 12.

REFERENCES

Alesina, Alberto. 1997. *The Political Economy of High and Low Growth*. Paper prepared for the Annual World Bank. Conference on Development Economics, Washington, 30 April–1 May.

Alesina, Alberto & Roberto Perotti. 1996. Income Distribution, Political Instability, and Investment. *European Economic Review*, 40 (June), 1203–1228.

Atkinson, Anthony B. & John Micklewright. 1992. *Economic Transformation in Eastern Europe and the Distribution of Income*. Cambridge, UK: Cambridge University Press.

Atkinson, Anthony B., Lee Rainwater & Timothy M. Smeeding. 1995. *Income Distribution in Advanced Economies: Evidence from the Luxembourg Income Study*. Work-

ing Paper 120, Luxembourg Income Study (LIS). Syracuse University, Maxwell School of Citizenship and Public Affairs.

Blanchard, Olivier. 1997. *The Economics of Post-Communist Transition.* New York: Clarendon Press.

Bruno, Michael. 1992. *Stabilization and Reform in Eastern Europe: A Preliminary Evaluation.* IMF Working Paper 92/30. Washington, D.C.: IMF.

Cornia, Giovanni Andrea. 1996a. Transition and Income Distribution: Theory, Evidence and Initial Interpretation. *Research in Progress, 1* (March). Helsinki: United Nations University, World Institute for Development Economics Research.

_____. 1996b. Labour Market Shocks, Psychological Stress and the Transition's Mortality Crisis. *Research in Progress, 4* (October). Helsinki: United Nations University, World Institute for Development Economics Research.

Cornia, Giovanni Andrea & Vladimir Popov. 1997. *Transition Strategies, Growth and Poverty.* Unpublished. Helsinki: United Nations University, World Institute for Development Economics Research.

Cornia, Giovanni Andrea, Juha Honkkila, Renato Paniccia & Vladimir Popov. 1996. *Long-Term Growth and Welfare in Transition Economies: The Impact of Demographic, Investment and Social Policy Changes.* United Nations University /WIDER Working Paper 122. Helsinki: United Nations University, World Institute for De velopment Economics Research.

Deininger, Klaus & Lyn Squire. 1996. A New Data Set Measuring Income Inequality. *World Bank Economic Review, 10* (September), 565–591.

Done, Kevin. 1997. Investors Give Eastern Europe a Miss. *Financial Times* (London), 15 April.

European Bank for Reconstruction and Development (EBRD). 1996. *Transition Report 1996.* London: EBRD.

Glowny Urzad Statystayczny (GUS). [Poland, Central Statistical Office]. 1996. *Ubostwo w swietle badan budzetow gospodarstw domowych (Poverty, Based on Household Budget Surveys).* Warsaw: GUS.

_____.1997a. *Monitoring warunkow zycia ludnosci (Monitoring the Population's Living Conditions).* 15 September. Warsaw: GUS.

_____. 1997b. *Wskazniki ubostwa (Poverty Indicators, Based on Household Budget Surveys).* Warsaw: GUS.

Gomulka, Stanislaw. 1996. *Causes of Output Decline, Sources of Recovery and Prospects for Growth in TransitionEconomics.* Unpublished. London: London School of Economics.

Gregory, Paul R. 1997. *Transition Economies: Social Consequences of Transition.* Paper prepared for United Nations Development Programme. Houston: University of Houston.

Herer, Wiktor & Wieslaw Sadowski. 1996. *Szara gospodarka w Polsce—rozmiary, przyczyny, konsekwencje* (The Gray Economy in Poland—Range, Sources, and Outcomes). Warsaw: Zespol Badan Statystyczno-Ekonomicznych, GUS.

Honkkila, Juha. 1997. *Privatization, Asset Distribution and Equity in Transitional Economies.* Working Paper 125. Helsinki: United Nations University, World Institute for Development Economics Research.

International Monetary Fund (IMF). 1998. *World Economic Outlook, May 1998: Financial Crisis—Causes and Indicators.* World Economic Financial Surveys. Washington, D. C.: IMF.

Kolodko, Grzegorz. W. 1986. *Repressed Inflation and Inflationary Overhang Under Socialism.* BEBR Faculty Working Paper No. 1228. Urbana-Champaign, Ill.: University of Illinois.

_____.1991. Inflation Stabilization in Poland: A Year After. *Rivista di Politica Economica, 81* (June), 289–330.

_____.1992a. Economics of Transition. From Shortageflation to Stagflation: The Case of Poland. In A. Clesse & R. Tokes (Eds.), *Preventing a New East–West Divide: The Economic and Social Imperatives of the Future Europe* (pp. 172–81). Baden-Baden: Nomos Verlagsgesellschaft,.

_____1992b. *From Output Collapse to Sustainable Growth in Transition Economies: The Fiscal Implications.* Washington: IMF.

_____. 1996. *Poland 2000: The New Economic Strategy.* Warsaw: Poltext.

Kolodko, Grzegorz W. & Walter W. McMahon. 1987. Stagflation and Shortageflation: A Comparative Approach. *Kyklos, 40,* 2, 176–97.

Kolodko, Grzegorz W. & D. Mario Nuti. 1997. *The Polish Alternative: Old Myths, Hard Facts and New Strategies in the Successful Transformation of the Polish Economy.* United Nations University/WIDER Research for Action 33. Helsinki: United Nations University, World Institute for Development Economics Research .

Kornai, János. 1980. *Economics of Shortage.* Amsterdam: North-Holland Publishing Co.

_____ . 1993. Transformational Recession: A General Phenomenon Examined Through the Example of Hungary's Development. *Economie Appliqué, 46,* 2 (July), 181–227.

Lavigne, Marie. 1995. *The Economics of Transition: From Socialist Economy to Market Economy.* New York: St. Martin's Press.

Milanovic, Branko. 1995. *Poverty, Inequality, and Social Policy in Transition Economies.* Policy Research Working Paper 1995-11. Washington,D.C.: World Bank.

_____. 1998. Income, Inequality, and Poverty During the Transition from Planned to Market Economy. *World Bank Regional and Sectoral Study, 2.* Washington, D.C.: World Bank.

Nuti, D. Mari. 1989. Hidden and Repressed Inflation in Soviet-type Economies: Definitions, Measurements and Stabilization. In C. Davis & W. Charemza (Eds.) *Models of Disequilibrium and Shortage in Centrally Planned Economies* (pp. 101–46). London : Chapman and Hall.

Organization for Economics Cooperation and Development. 1996. *OECD Economic Surveys: Poland.* Paris: OECD.

Paniccià, Renato. 1997. Short- and Long-term Determinants of Cardiovascular Mortality: An Econometric Assessment of the Working Age Population in Russia, 1965–95. *Research in Progress 14* (June). Helsinki: United Nations University, World Institute for Development Economics Research.

Pomfret, Richard & Kathryn H. Anderson. 1997. *Uzbekistan: Welfare Impact of Slow Transition.* Working Paper 135. Helsinki: United Nations University, World Institute for Development Economics Research.

Poznanski, Kazimierz. 1996. *Poland's Protracted Transition: Institutional Change and Economic Growth.* Cam bridge: Cambridge University Press.

Rutkowski, Jan. 1997. *Labor Markets, Welfare and Social Policy During Economic Transition in Poland.* Warsaw: World Bank Field Office.

Stiglitz, Joseph E. 1998. More Instruments and Broader Goals: Moving Toward the Post-Washington Consensus. *WIDER Annual Lectures* No. 2 (January). Helsinki: United Nations University, World Institute for Development Economics Research.

Tanzi, Vito & Ke-young Chu. (Eds.) 1998. *Income Distribution and High-Quality Growth*. Cambridge, MA: MIT Press.

United Nations Development Programme. 1994. *Human Development Report 1994*. New York: Oxford University Press.

_____.1996. *Human Development Report 1996* . New York: Oxford University Press.

United Nations International Children's Emergency Fund (UNICEF). 1995. Poverty, Children and Policy: Responses for a Brighter Future. Regional Monitoring Report No. 3, *Economies in Transition Studies*. Florence: UNICEF Centre.

World Bank. 1995. Understanding Poverty in Poland. *A World Bank Country Study*. Washington, D.C.: World Bank.

_____.1996. *World Development Report 1996: From Plan to Market*. New York: Oxford University Press for the World Bank.

_____.1997. *World Development Report 1997: The State in a Changing World*. New York: Oxford University Press for the World Bank.

9

Vision of the Polish Working Class: A Well-Ordered Economy

Juliusz Gardawski

What does the working class[1] regard as a desirable economic system? This was the central research question that was to be answered by empirical studies conducted in 1986-98, which was based on the assumption that the vision of the desired economic order is an important component of economic consciousness.

The notion of "economic consciousness" is understood in the broad sense. In keeping with the definition proposed by Jerzy J. Wiatr, it includes "the entirety of views and appraisals relating to economic relations between people and their technological determinants occurring in a given society" (1987:33).[2] Wiatr reached the conclusion that "with regard to individual societies, one might try to determine the dominant pattern of economic consciousness, and it is also possible to try to establish a model of economic consciousness of individual classes"(p.33). I also accepted Marek Ziółkowski's suggestion that normative visions of a well-ordered economy may be the central element of the pattern of economic consciousness (1987).

INDICATOR OF DESIRABLE ECONOMIC ORDER

Polish workers' economic preferences were studied in relation to many detailed matters, crucial from the point of view of the economy and its changes. The questions in many research concerned the desirable economic order (monocentrism or market and autonomy of enterprises); the attitude toward state ownership, private capital (both Polish and foreign) and to privatisation, industrial democracy (participation in management); the role of trade unions in economic life, egalitarianism and other issues. Research questions were formulated as opinions which a respondent could accept, reject or refuse to take a stand on. The choice and formulation of the principles were subjected to verification in the course of unstandardized interviews with the workers.

The incentive to work with the complex indicator of economic consciousness was the desire to bypass certain limitations characteristic of other analyses of this area of social consciousness. In the 1980s and early 1990s, Polish social sciences saw the wide acceptance of a paradigm dichotomising and simplifying social consciousness, labelled as "transition to democracy." In his criticism of this paradigm, Andrzej Rychard wrote that its central assumption was the illusion that "communism was but an artificial coat of armour constraining the natural forces and inclinations of the society and after its removal, . . . the natural forces will come to the fore, meaning the forces seeking to introduce modern Western economic rules (Rychard 1994: 6). Rychard argued, "the real direction [of the society's adaptation reactions] is often quite distant from that normative pattern understood as 'transition to the market and democracy'" (p.7). Similarly, Mirosława Marody pointed out that sociologists' great involvement in the transformation processes distorted their studies to some extent because with such an attitude, "one tends to focus on the processes that take you closer or further away from the desired future state, ignoring many other aspects" (1994: 171).

In the studies of social consciousness, the "transition to democracy" paradigm could be seen in the tendency to construct bipolar theoretical models, in which one pole contained a set of modern, market-economy and democratic principles while the opposite pole was composed of communist, obsolete principles, characteristic of a monocentric, etatist order. Analysis consisted of measuring the extent to which the respondents' declarations in questionnaire studies were removed from the principles making up these theoretical polar models and of recording the degree of modernity (or conservatism) of the mentality of selected categories of respondents.

As I wrote earlier (Gardawski 1992a: 39), it was legitimate to classify the content of social consciousness in terms of dichotomous models separating "progress" from "obsolescence," and the use of such divisions genuinely enriched our knowledge, but it also had one drawback. Namely, all the views that could not be classified as either one of the two extremes of a polarized model were lost from sight and rarely became the subject of separate inquiry. The few exceptions include analyses made by Morawski (1991), Kolarska-Bobińska (1986), or Ziółkowski and Koralewicz (1990). As Rychard critically observed, as a result of the adoption of the "transition to democracy" paradigm, views that did not match the dichotomous theoretical models were treated as "interim chaos," separating the socialist past from the democratic, market-economy future.

As I embarked on studies of workers' economic consciousness in 1991, I made the assumption based on several years of empirical studies of that milieu that the use of the theoretical dichotomy might not take me closer to true differences in worker attitudes but in fact it might take me away from that goal. I decided that while searching for the prototype that would be helpful for describing the working class's ideas about a well-ordered economy, I must not limit my approach to the dichotomous models on which there was plenty of literature: the "pluralist," "market-oriented" and "market-and-efficiency oriented" ones at one end and the "monocentric," "egalitarian" or "egalitarian/etatist" ones at the opposite end.

Therefore, I approached the study of the extent to which workers accept individual economic principles as a prelude to the search for the logic of their thinking, the inner organization governing the preferences. The key goal of the long analyses of normative visions of the economy was to reconstruct the syndromes into which the respondents arranged their visions. The range of replies obtained in the study clearly indicated that the widely used method of constructing theoretical dichotomous models is not the best method of identifying the structure of the workers' thinking about a well-ordered economy.

ECONOMIC PREFERENCES AND THEIR CHANGES IN THE YEARS 1991-1998

The years 1991-98 were characterized by the considerable pace and depth of transformations of the socio-economic system; the transition from the economy of shortages, crises and recession to shops full of merchandises, the suppressing of inflation, and the development of private enterprise. Also of particular note were disproportionately low pay compared with deregulated wages as well as unemployment and an uncertain future.[3] How did these processes affect the workers' thinking about a well-ordered economy?

In 1991, surveys revealed relatively high support for efficiency/market principles and a certain dislike of state interference in the economy (Gardawski 1992a). The questionnaire interviews conducted at the same time and numerous informal exchanges made it possible to reconstruct the nature of workers' expectations. As in the case of Frank Parkin's analyses (1971), it turned out that most workers idealized and mythologized elementary macroeconomic institutions. Competition was perceived not as a tool guaranteeing a just reward for honest work but rather as the flip side of the sick system of distributing the rewards for work under authoritarian socialism. The support for efficiency, involving the closing down of loss-making plants, laying off redundant workers, and so forth, was not associated with unemployment but with a war on waste. Inevitably, the attitude toward unemployment was one of reluctance but at the same time the workers believed, paradoxically, that for the time being unemployment was not possible because there was always so much left to do in Poland. In 1991, workers often escaped stress by not believing that the threat of unemployment was not real. On the whole, the respondents were expecting a friendly market economy, that is, one that would be characterized by market relations and a capitalist system but at the same time guarantee decent living and working conditions.

An important research question appeared in this context: How are workers' preferences going to change in step with the development of the market and financial market institutions and with the expected growth of unemployment along with other hardships? Will workers reject market economy and privatisation and will they want a return to the welfare-state economy known from authoritarian socialism? The studies from the years 1992-98 showed that this did not occur, although characteristic shifts took place on the map of preferences (Table 9.1). Changes going in two directions took place during those seven years; on the one hand, they attested to the growing support for some lines of transformations, while on the other hand, they pointed to a growing willingness to go back to some principles of the centrally managed economy and the welfare state.

It is worth noting the very high level of acceptance of Polish capital, especially the proposal regarding the construction of new factories by that capital. With regard to this principle, support increased by as much as 23 percent, which resulted in a move from the fifth place on the list of determinants in my questionnaire in 1991 to first place in 1998. In the autumn of 1998, 89 percent of workers agreed to the establishment of large enterprises by Polish capital. More and more workers wanted the existing state enterprises to be sold to private owners (a growth from 65 per cent in 1991 to 86 per cent in 1998, with a move from the seventh to the third place on the list of determinants in my questionnaire).

Some workers liked the idea of the state owning large industrial establishments, but few liked the idea of state ownership of all enterprises, big or small. In the three surveys (encompassed by Table 9.1) acceptance of a full monopoly of state ownership in the economy never exceeded 24 percent.

There were expectations those institutions representing employees (particularly trade unions) would intervene in economic affairs.[4] In the case of the trade union Solidarity members, support grew by 2 percentage points (from 28 in 1991 to 30 percent in 1998) while support for the All-Poland Trade Union Federation (OPZZ) grew by 8 percentage points (from 18 to 26 percent). The proportion of those who wanted both Solidarity and the OPZZ to interfere in the economy rose from 12 percent in 1991 to 19 percent in 1998. This means that in 1998 one worker out of every five expected that both labor unions would simultaneously provide him with a safety net protecting him from unfavorable economic phenomena, so it is possible to speak of a certain growth of support for solutions of a corporatist nature. It should be remembered, however, that this backing is too small to speak of workers' *expectations* of a corporatist system. Workers might perhaps support paternalistic corporatism that would protect the weakest groups (Tatur 1994: 126), but they would not like corporatism of an authoritarian nature, the forms of which were described by Jerzy Hausner (1995). Workers' scepticism toward such formations was mainly due to the low level of confidence in trade unions.

In the years 1991-98, there was a substantial decrease in support for efficiency-oriented principles and for moves to rationalize management, especially for the idea layoffs of redundant personnel. In 1991, this principle was widely supported (71 percent backing and fourth place on the list of determinants in my questionnaire) but seven years later it was accepted by less than half the workers (44 percent and ninth place on the list). Also, the backing of the second

Table 9.1

The Frequency of Choice of Principles Making up the Indicator of Economic Consciousness in Successive Years of the 1991-98 Period (Percentages)

Content of a principle [1]	1991	1994	1998	1998 /91
1. Creation of possibility of setting up small crafts businesses by anyone.	85	91	51	-34
2. Full autonomy of enterprises and fierce competition between them.	84	80	88	+4
3. Bankruptcies of loss-making enterprises.	72	66	63	-9
4. Layoffs of non-essential employees by enterprises.	71	48	44	-27
5. Facilitations for Polish capital in setting up large enterprises.	66	87	89	+23
6. Selling of state enterprises to Polish capital.	65	78	86	+21
7. Making it possible for employees to become owners of the enterprises they work for.	65	76	64	-1
8. Facilitations for foreign capital in setting up big enterprises.	55	52	37	-18
9. Increasing the influence of the president on the economy.	52	40	X*	---
10. Bigger influence of the Sejm and the Senate on economy.	50	56	X*	---
11. Striving to equalise the incomes of all people.	50	48	35	-15
12. Introduction of an upper limit on pay, binding on all people in Poland.	47	48	45	-2
13. Permitting the operation of enterprises managed solely by employee self-management body.	46	61	X*	---
14. Exclusive state ownership of large industrial enterprises.	45	57	46	+1
15. Depriving trade unions of influence on the economy.	39	25	X*	---
16. Abandonment of state ownership of all or most enterprises.	35	30	31	-4
17. Increasing the influence of Solidarity on the economy.	28	33	30	+2
18. Permitting unemployment and paying minimum benefits to the unemployed (shortened to "permitting unemployment" in 1993 and 1994)	26	22	10	-16
19. Exclusive state ownership of enterprises, regardless of size.	22	24	22	0
20. Government control over the operations of enterprises, e.g. by assigning production targets for them, defining the level of pay, supervision of the performance of the management.	19	29	20	+1
21. Increasing the influence of OPZZ-affiliated unions on the economy.	18	27	26	+8
22. Sale of state enterprises to foreign interests.	16	16	21	+5
23. Growth of influence of political parties on the economy.	11	20	X*	---
24. Growth of the influence of the Church on the economy.	5	6	3	-2

Note: [1] In order of decreasing frequency of choices in 1991. *The variable was omitted in the questionnaire. Number of workers responding were: 1991, N=2817; 1994, N=997; 1998, N=1225
Source: "Workers '91" N=2817, "Workers '94" N=997, "Industrial Relations '98", N= 1225.

efficiency principle, that of closing down loss-making enterprises, decreased (from 72 to 63 percent, and a slide from third to fifth place). There was also much less acceptance of unemployment: down from 26 to 10 percent.

I should emphasize the decrease in support for the proposal that foreign investors should be able to set up large enterprises in Poland without any complications. Over the seven years, the backing for this principle fell by just 18 points (from 55 to 37).

The last group of economic principles are those for which the level of support changed little during the seven years. Between the spring of 1991 and the autumn of 1998, support for the principle of competition grew from 84 percent to 88 percent. The principle that enjoyed quite stable acceptance was one that proclaimed social "moderate egalitarianism"—idea of introducing an upper limit on pay. It should be noted that a relatively high proportion of workers supported this solution: in 1991, 47 percent, in 1998, 45 percent. Furthermore, I also noted a decrease of support for "definite egalitarianism"—idea of equal incomes. The information about changes in support for individual principles presented above indicates that on the macro scale, workers did not turn out to be enemies of the development of capitalist ownership or the introduction of foreign capital to Poland. They supported the elementary rules of market economy: the autonomy of enterprises and competition between them. However, those general pro-capitalist declarations were accompanied by a growth of support for demands leading to the softening up of the economic regime. The workers wanted the consolidation of the role of the state in the economy, more say for trade unions and a greater level of social security. These expectations can be understood; after all, it is obvious that most workers, when asked about what they consider to be the desirable economic model, will choose a variant that guarantees greater security rather than one which, in their opinion, threatens to lead to higher unemployment.

LONG-TERM ANALYSIS OF WORKERS' VISIONS OF A WELL-ORDERED ECONOMY

Already in the years 1986-90, the purpose of my research was to identify the syndromes formed by workers' economic views. The studies conducted in those years suggested that three rather than two orientations were present among workers. The restriction of attention to "pro-reform" and "anti-reform" attitudes alone leads to ignoring a certain important current that is clearly present in worker mentality. At that time, however, these doubts could not lead to definitive conclusions because the studies were not representative: While the empirical material was quite abundant (the average sample was about 500 respondents), in each case it was collected in just several industrial enterprises.

When the replies to a question about a preferred economic order were examined in 1990 with the use of exploratory factor analysis, it was discovered that next to the two extreme orientations, labelled as the " liberal model" and the "*homo sovieticus* model," there was also a third group, which was designated "petty bourgeois socialism."[5]

The liberal model signified the acceptance of foreign capital and consent to unemployment and bankruptcies. The second pattern corresponded to the communist vision, namely, support for full authority of the state in the economic field, and was associated with dislike of all economic changes (the development of private ownership, bankruptcies of loss-making enterprises, handing over of control over enterprises to worker self-management bodies, etc.).

Factor analysis applied to the 1990 data revealed the existence of a third syndrome of principles whose inner cohesion was confirmed by the correlation matrix. This syndrome signified a specific selection of economic principles. It was characterized by the combination of a preference for the participation of employees in management and self-management with support for the development of small retail and crafts firms and also with objections both to monopoly state ownership in the economy and to the introduction of big foreign capital to Poland (Gardawski 1992b). This was the syndrome that was called "petty bourgeois socialism."

On the basis of data from that period it was not possible to determine whether this petty bourgeois socialism was widespread among Poland's industrial workers or whether it was going to last. In order to answer those questions, it was necessary to meet at least two conditions: (1) devise a possibly comprehensive indicator of economic consciousness and (2) conduct repetitive studies on a sample that would be representative of all industrial workers. It was possible to meet those conditions during the surveys taken in the spring of 1991 and in subsequent years.

The findings of the "Workers '91" survey made it possible to identify the general scope of differences of views and to demonstrate that there were indeed three types of working-class thinking about a well ordered economic system. This typology was subsequently verified in successive representative nationwide surveys of industrial workers called "Workers '92", "Workers '93", "Workers '94" and "Industrial Relations '98."

WORKERS' VISIONS OF A WELL-ORDERED ECONOMY IN THE SECOND YEAR OF TRANSFORMATION (1991)

The aforementioned studies from early 1990 were conducted when the reforms were just getting off the ground. There was already much talk about the new rules of engaging in business activities, but in practice they only materialised in trading: next to state-owned warehouses and state-owned shops there appeared private imports, and private wholesale operations, private vendors, initially selling their wares off camping beds and later from folding steel sheet stalls that became a veritable symbol of the transition from socialism to market economics. The approaching capitalism was seen as a system whose central feature was the abundance of all sorts of goods. Meanwhile nothing was changing in the enterprises employing our respondents and the threat of restrictive policies against the state sector was not yet reflected in government actions.

When the 1991 survey was taken in the spring, the economic reform was in place and the government already taken action directed against state enterprises. However, massive unemployment had not got appeared although there was already much talk about the instances of foreign capital buying out enterprises (or parts thereof), layoffs and conversion of industrial facilities into warehouses for the distribution of imported goods. The 1991 survey therefore made it possible to grasp the views at the moment when real transformations directly affecting workers' lives were beginning to take effect. The study was planned as a useful point of reference for subsequent analyses of the dynamics of economic orientations.

Syndromes of Workers Economic Consciousness

In 1991, factor analysis made it possible to identify six sets of principles, which are referred to as syndromes (Table 9. 2).

A characterization of each of them follows:

1. Egalitarianism and etatism is a traditional vision, with emphasis on the economic principles of state socialism. This syndrome includes the demand for equal incomes in two variants: the moderate one (an imposition of an upper ceiling on wages) and a categorical one (striving for identical incomes). The state was expected to own all the enterprises and manage them directly, carrying out the demand for "manual control." During interviews with workers in 1991, those who supported such solutions said that only the state could be "the whip directors fear" and a potentially good defender of workers' interests.

2. Privatisation and subjectivity embraced a vision of a market economy but with peculiar limitations. Namely, the respondents falling in this category accepted the development of private capital only so long as it was of Polish origin and placed emphasis on small-scale ownership, on a scale that was within the reach of workers (employee stock ownership, small crafts and trading companies). The implementation of this syndrome would give workers a chance of becoming co-owners of their enterprises (state enterprises could be transformed into employee-owned companies) or a chance to start one's own business. It was therefore a concept of petty bourgeois "home-bred" capitalism. With some reservations, this pattern could be regarded as a modified version of the aforementioned petty bourgeois socialism.

The appearance of Polish (but not foreign) capital in this syndrome is not necessarily a sign of xenophobia. Most of the workers that were interviewed believed that all the capital that comes to Poland are of a speculative, not "genuine" or "honest" nature. According to the respondents, speculative capital does not guarantee lasting jobs, speculators will be dishonest employers and will pursue a cut-and-run policy, all profits will be exported, and so on.

It is noteworthy that this syndrome is accompanied by anti-etatism. The correlation between appropriate variables showed that this syndrome was not only associated with a disapproval of state monopoly of ownership in the economy but also of exclusive state ownership of large industrial plants and other forms of pervasive presence of the state in the economy. The dislike of state institutions displayed in 1991 by the supporters of petty bourgeois capitalism is significant because in subsequent years they showed renewed support for state intervention. The situation recorded in 1991 indicates that the development of capitalist relations led to a negative reaction to authoritarian state socialism.

3. Liberalism. In 1991, this syndrome included principles that were rarely accepted by workers (allowing unemployment to occur, sale of state enterprises to foreign investors). This position was embraced mainly by those respondents who worked abroad in the past and were aware of the costs of the transformation that had to be borne by Poland. As for permitting the occurrence of unemployment, they admitted it was a bad thing but in Poland's current situation it was inevitable. Liberalism also signified the rejection of the idea of state ownership of large industrial plants, which was an element of the set of values that met with universal public approval in the times of authoritarian socialist rule.

Respondents who approved of the liberal pattern also supported other modernization principles included in the "privatisation and subjectivity" and "efficiency and competition" syndromes. The liberal principles were a kind of filter dividing the large group of supporters of the modernization of the economy into consistent advocates of reforms (liberals) and less consistent, ambivalent supporters of change (moderate modernizers).

4 & 5. The authorities control the economy and *associations control the economy* contained the demands for a greater influence over the economy, exercised by all the organizations and associations that workers thought would be more inclined to listen to "labour" than to "capital." It can be said that they illustrate the aforementioned inclination of some of the worker milieu to support elements of a corporatist system.

6. Efficiency and competition. This syndrome encompassed demands that were popular in the last decade of authoritarian socialist rule and in the early 1990s. Workers were very much exhausted by the "socialist mess," the waste and the dismal working practices. To some extent, they were exploiting the loopholes that emerged as a result of this disorderliness (mass moonlighting) but the physical and psychological cost of the mess was not offset by the advantages. Therefore they expected that the new system would give them the comfort of doing well-organized work. Besides, authoritarian socialism destroyed the link between work and pay: a lazy and negligent worker earned as much as a good worker. The system of wages was seen as being grossly unjust. The respondents hoped that a market economy would restore just relations—they expected order that may be termed as "justice-oriented capitalism" and "justice-oriented competition." By that version of capitalism and competition they understood the kind of order in which an honest worker would always be appreciated and duly rewarded while the only losers would be the lazy loafer.

Table 9. 2
Preferences and Syndromes of Workers'' Economic Consciousness in 1991

	Preferences and their syndromes (54.2% of overall variance was explained)	Factor Loading
I.	**Egalitarianism and etatism**	
	1. Equal pay	.701
	2. Introduction of upper ceiling on incomes	.611
	3. The state runs enterprises (monocentrism)	.368
	4. The state owns all enterprises	.363
	5. Establishment of enterprises managed by employees	.226
II.	**Privatisation and subjectivity**	
	1. Polish capital buys state enterprises	.598
	2. Polish capital sets up large enterprises	.554
	3. Enfranchisement of employees (employee stock ownership)	.454
	4. Development of private crafts	.317
	5. Elimination of state ownership in the economy	.267
III.	**Liberalism**	
	1. Foreign capital buys state enterprises	.582
	2. Foreign capital sets up large enterprises	454
	3. The state as owner of big industrial establishments	-.275
	4. Permitting unemployment	.207
IV.	**The authorities control the economy**	
	1. Increased parliamentary control over the economy	.932
	2. Increased presidential control over the economy	.529
V.	**Associations' control the economy**	
	1. Growth of Solidarity's influence on the economy	.689
	2. Growth of OPZZ unions' influence on the economy	.630
	3. Growth of Church influence on the economy	.392
	4. Growth of influence of political parties on the economy	.369
	5. Depriving trade unions of influence on the economy	-.387
VI.	**Efficiency and competition**	
	1. Laying off of redundant employees	.495
	2. Bankruptcies of loss-making enterprises	.372
	3. Competition and autonomy of enterprises	.190

Source: "Workers '91" N=2817.

Remarkably, the respondents at that time did not notice the relationship between dismissing redundant employees and unemployment. The former was seen as nothing more than the elimination of wastefulness and poor working practices (it was believed that the laying off of redundant employees would not lead to the emergence of unemployment).

Economic Orientation

Second-degree factor analysis, that is, one in which the units were the six syndromes presented above, demonstrated a clear structure composed of three economic consciousness orientations: the moderate modernisation liberal (Table 9.3).

Table 9.3
Three Economic Orientations Among Workers in 1991, Second-Degree Factor Analysis

	Syndromes and orientations (60.8% of total variance was explained)	Factor Load-ing
I.	Moderate modernisation	
	1. Privatisation and subjectivity	.513
	2. Efficiency and competition	.434
II.	Traditionalism	
	1. Associations control the economy	.624
	2. Egalitarianism and etatism	.251
	3. Authorities control the economy	.232
III.	Liberalism	
	1. Liberalism	.640

Source: "Workers '91" N=2,817.

1. Moderate modernization encompasses two syndromes: "privatisation and subjectivity" and "efficiency and competition." It was the vision that was the most popular among the workers, the modal one for that milieu. It was also referred to as the vision of a "friendly market economy." It assumed the acceptance of a market economy but to the exclusion of those principles that were seen by workers as (actual or potential) sources of unemployment. It was, in a nutshell, an economy that was friendly from the workers' point of view and free from the threat of unemployment; this view prevailed as the most characteristic one throughout the period encompassed by the study, that is, until the autumn of 1994. However, during that period the workers changed their mind about the potential causes of unemployment. In 1991 the rationalization of management at the enterprise level (laying off of redundant employees, bankruptcies of loss-making firms) was not associated by workers with unemployment whereas the sale of state enterprises to foreign investors was seen as a prelude to the dismissal of most of the current staff and a source of unemployment.

2. *Traditionalist* encompasses three syndromes: "associations control the economy," "egalitarianism and etatism" and the "authorities control the economy." This orientation was an articulation of the fear of a market economy and a longing for a paternalist state guaranteeing full security to the employees. Traditionalism rejected all new economic institutions connected with ownership transformations. The only exception was competition, whose tie to traditionalism was weak but nevertheless positive.

This happened to be one of the more pronounced contradictions in the workers' thinking. The traditionalists expected enterprises to remain state property and to be centrally managed by state bodies but at the same time they wanted competition between such enterprises (naturally, there could be no question of redundancies or bankruptcies in the traditionalists' vision). This attitude was a manifestation of the mythologization of the notion of competition, which was already described in the mid-1980s. Within the "Poles" project, Kolarska-Bobińska (1986) reconstructed the social myth of competition free from any social costs.

3. *Liberal* only encompassed the "liberal" syndrome. In 1991, it turned out that this orientation was marginal in the pattern of working class mentality; it was, however, predominant among engineers and managers rather than manual workers.

The correlations between the orientations were basically consistent with the expectations: there was a positive correlation (0.18) between moderate modernization and liberalism and a negative one (-0.15) between liberalism and traditionalism. The moderate modernisation and traditionalist orientations were neutral toward one another (0.02)

WORKERS' VISIONS OF WELL-ORDERED ECONOMY AFTER NINE YEARS OF TRANSFORMATIONS (1998)

The important finding of the subsequent studies (1992, 1993, 1994 and 1998) was the confirmation of the lasting character of the three orientations identified in 1991. The visions of a well-ordered economy did undergo some changes, and the sets of principles associated with individual orientations differed but the changes were relatively small (Tables 9.4 and 9.5). When the findings of the factor analysis from 1991 (Table 9.2) are compared with those from 1998 (Table 9.5), it is obvious that the record of syndromes from 1998 is practically the same as that of 1991. During the nine intervening years, the content of the three orientations, did not change, they still included the same preferences that were known from the 1991 study.

Table 9.4
Preferences of Workers' Economic Consciousness in 1998, Factor Analysis

	Preferences and their syndromes (50.6 % of overall variance was explained)	Factor Load-ing
I.	**Egalitarianism and etatism**	
	1. Equal pay	.706
	2. Introduction of upper ceiling on incomes	.523
	3. The state owns all enterprises	.498
	4. The state runs enterprises (monocentrism)	.223
II.	**Labour organizations control the economy**	
	1. Growth of Solidarity's influence on the economy	.878
	2. Growth of OPZZ unions' influence on the economy	.691
III.	**Liberalism**	
	1. Foreign capital buys state enterprises	.802
	2. Foreign capital sets up large enterprises	556
	3. Permitting unemployment	.319
IV.	**State ownership of big industry**	
	1. The state as owner of big industrial establishments	.782
	2. Elimination of state ownership in the economy	-.207
V.	**Efficiency**	
	1. Bankruptcies of loss-making enterprises	.645
	2. Laying off of redundant employees	.478
VI.	**Polish privatisation vs. influence of the Church on the economy**	
	1. Polish capital buys state enterprises	.664
	2. Polish capital sets up large enterprises	.431
	3. Growth of Church influence on the economy	-.294
VII.	**Employee stock ownership and competition**	
	1. Development of private crafts	.394
	2. Enfranchisement of employees (employee stock ownership)	.299
	3. Competition and autonomy of enterprises	.297

Source: "Industrial Relations '98", N=1029

Table 9.5
Economic Orientations Among Workers in 1998, Second-Degree Factor Analysis

	Syndromes and orientations (60.8% of total variance was explained)	Factor Load- ing
I.	Moderate modernization	
	1. Employee stock ownership and competition	.613
	2. Efficiency	.312
	3. Polish privatisation vs. influence of the Church on the economy	.295
II.	Traditionalism	
	1. Egalitarianism and etatism	.652
	2. State ownership of big industry	.261
	3. Labour organizations control the economy	.133
III.	Liberalism	
	1. Liberalism	.447

Source: "Industrial Relations '98". N=1,225.

ATTITUDE TOWARD PRIVATISATION

Earlier studies and analyses (Gardawski, Gilejko & Żukowski 1994) indicated that there were no integrated patterns of thinking about privatisation, but that the preferences underwent fragmentation and a peculiar autonomization: a fair part of the respondents proclaimed different views when asked about the rules that should be in force in the economy as a whole versus when they spoke about their own enterprises and livelihood.

The respondents' attitude to the basic institutions connected with the restitution of capitalism and with privatisation (e.g., the sale of enterprises to private investors, the establishment of new large enterprises by such investors, etc.) does not exhaust the list of problems related to socio-political transformations. It is still necessary to explain the views on various aspects of private property, starting with questions of an ideological and political nature and ending with the attitude to privatisation in the respondents' social milieu.

One of the important peculiarities of the economic consciousness of industrial workers, especially those subscribing to the moderate modernisation orientation, was the deepening inconsistency of their convictions, the ambivalence of views about privatisation on the macro and micro scales. The discrepancy was evident in that over the course of seven years (1991-98), the level of acceptance of privatisation plans on the national scale increased while the level of consent to the privatisation of state enterprises employing the respondents decreased. Simultaneously, the respondents' readiness to take employment with a private entrepreneur also decreased. The process is partly described in Table 9.1 line 6. It contains the aforementioned information about the growing acceptance of the idea of selling state enterprises to Polish capital (from 65 percent in 1991 to 86 percent in 1998) and for facilitating in the establishment of large enterprises by Polish capital (from 66 to 89 percent). Asked about general economic solutions, the respondents showed growing acceptance of privatisation, especially if Polish capital was involved. But foreign capital in the form of an investor setting up new enterprises lost workers' support (55 percent in 1991 and 37 percent in 1998).

A different pattern of the respondents' views is obtained at the micro level, that is, in relation to their own enterprises and plans. In 1991, as well as in 1998, only 18 percent of the respondents were ready to accept privatisation of their enterprises by Polish capital. Another inconsistency turned up in their personal preferences: in 1991, 25 percent of them were ready to move to a privately owned enterprises but seven years later only 14 percent said so.

Origins and Consequences of Privatisation Dissonance

The privatisation dissonance has been getting deeper: on the one hand, social legitimacy of important institutions of the capitalist economy is rising but at the same time the fears of the hardships that that economy may hold in store for the respondent himself are also growing. This, in turn, elicits dual reactions: the desire that the enterprise in which the respondent is employed remain in state hands and that it remains a "friendly social niche" (without layoffs, the risk of bankruptcy, and the like). This peculiar yes-no conflict is a fact whose significance can hardly be overestimated. Let us now attempt to identify the sources of this dissonance.

The discord in the attitude toward Polish capital is highly unequivocal and impossible to interpret with the use of simple patterns. Questionnaire studies and qualitative analyses, however, produce a fairly clear pattern of the dissonance. What are the factors behind a positive attitude toward privatisation?

First of all, a new atmosphere began to surround the notion of "private capital." The change was connected with a phenomenon that might be described as the "'wearing thin of socialist values." In a nutshell, among the symbols referring to a general economic order, there was a growth of support for some capitalist institutions while the social scope of acceptance of some—but not all—crucial socialist ideals and values declined. The monocentric idea of manual control over enterprises by the state was losing ground and the distrust of private capital was waning. The idea of social (state) ownership in industry lost its former supremacy over the idea of private ownership. Even so, this change of climate was not a categorical one: most respondents were in favour of economic pluralism, rejecting both the complete elimination of state ownership and monopolistic state ownership. Most workers also remained moderately egalitarian, expecting guarantees of justice from social institutions, and so forth.[6]

The "wearing thin of socialist values" is connected with two very important effects of the change of the socio-political system. First, sociological analyses indicate that market economy freed the society from the nightmare of perennial shortages of goods and made people satisfied with the role of consumers (Rychard 1995). Gone are the night queues outside shops, meat rationing and the importance of having friends in the right shops. Second, many working-class households were able to adapt to the new situation and maintain, albeit with difficulty, the ability to satisfy their elementary needs. It is important that the unemployed members of households have a chance of finding work in the "grey sector" economy, that is, temporary, not taxed earning, such as "tax free" small trading on the open-markets or street bazaars.

However, the conviction about the victory of capitalism, which reduces the possibility of return to an etatist, monocentric and extreme egalitarian traditionalism, clashes with the fear of changes and with some stereotypes and with the early, not very encouraging experience with new capitalism, both Polish and foreign (Gardawski, Gilejko & Żukowski 1994). It should also be noted that employees had and still have a certain inclination to idealize "real" capitalism: they expect from it the stability they got accustomed to under authoritarian socialist rule, good human relations in enterprises.

The privatisation dissonance is the outcome of a peculiar way of thinking, of associations connected with Polish and foreign capital. The strong growth of support for Polish capital stems from the attitude toward foreign capital. The view has often been voiced that if capitalism is to develop (which is taken for granted), then let it be chiefly our own, domestic capital because "at least it will not export profits," because it will curb "the sell-out of national assets." The support for Polish capital and the positive emotional attitude that accompanied this notion stemmed from automatically juxtaposing with the unacceptable and dishonest foreign capital. Let me add that the dislike of foreign capital was not so much an outcome of xenophobia as of the conviction that foreign capital coming to Poland was not "honest" or "genuine" foreign capital but merely speculators in search of a quick buck. However, when the notion "Polish capitalist" appeared in the interviews with the workers, the pattern of associations changed instantly. The comparison was then made not to a foreign capitalist but to a Polish state employer. The homebred capitalist was suspected of dishonesty (because how else would he make a fortune?), and a dishonest businessman cannot be a good employer, according to the workers, because "a crook will always be a crook." By contrast, a state enterprise, for all the reservations about it, was perceived as a welfare institution. This produced an important consciousness effect in workers, one that was absent in the managers and engineers' thinking and consisted in legitimising Polish capital but refusing to legitimise Polish capitalists.

The most important consequence of this dissonance was the dual picture of the economy. The workers thought about the economy as a whole from a different perspective than about their own enterprise. The simplest explanation of this approach is this: most respondents supported the privatisation of many branches of the economy and of many large enterprises, agreeing that this was a current economic imperative. However, they also wanted to preserve some enclaves of state ownership (they most often mentioned the raw materials industries, power generation and defence industries in this context), and they wanted their enterprise to be included in that enclave. As a result, something that was a great strength of the working-class in the times of the first Solidarity movement had disappeared; that is, the conviction that there is only one truth, one way of improving the situation, and that the interest of all Poles is identical and that it is worthwhile to unite to fight in its defence (Kowalski 1990).

MODERATE MODERNISATION AND PRIVATISATION DISSO-NANCE AS MANIFESTATIONS OF AMBIVALENT MENTALITY

The inconsistency in workers' views on economic matters can be interpreted at least to some extent by referring to some generalizations and sociological concepts developed in the course of the observation of workers in developed market economies. These include the theses about the ambivalence of workers' thinking (related in particular to Frank Parkin's [1971] concepts) and the Polish concept, developed by Włodzimierz Wesołowski, which differentiated between "transgressive" and "existential" interests.

For Parkin, the basic type of working-class mentality was characterized by an ineradicably inner incoherence, due to the fact that workers were simultaneously under the influence of two different axiological currents: the system of values of the dominant class, which was moulding the world precisely in the interest of that class, and the values, expectations and aspirations evolving from their own experience and reflecting the situation of workers. According to Parkin, whose concept of worker ambivalence can be particularly useful for interpreting the views of Polish workers, the inconsistencies stem from the fact that some representatives of the subordinate classes may perceive social reality from the angle of "meaning systems" provided by the dominant class. These systems and their component values assume one of two forms after they are internalised by the workers: the "official" or "idealized" form or the negotiated form. Therefore, there may be cases of idealization of some important institutions; in the Polish case these could be the market and competition, for example. At the same time, many existential questions are not perceived by workers from the angle of dominant values but of values shaped in a local working-class milieu. What occurs here is a peculiar compromise between value systems and there can be a specific continuity, whose borders are determined, on the one hand, by the dominant values in the pure, idealized form, and on the other, by the subordinate class's own values. In between the two boundaries there is room for many compromise configurations, with varying degrees of saturation by the dominant values. This is the area of ambivalence and inconsistency.

This interpretational pattern provides a good language for describing the moderate modernisation orientation and especially the phenomenon referred to as privatisation dissonance.

Apart from the notions of the system of dominant and subordinate values and of the negotiated system of values, another important reference system is the pattern proposed by Wesołowski (1993), who distinguished between existential and transgressive interests. For the present situation in Poland, the patterns borrowed from English sociology of the working class have one shortcoming: Poland lacks a clearly dominant class and a system of dominant values such a class should produce. The dominant values are not articulated and disseminated by a narrow modernisation elite indoctrinating the subordinate class; instead, these values are taken from the world market economy and its social legitimacy rests on the collapse of authoritarian socialist rule and the fall of the world communist system. The Polish working class accept the market and capitalist values mainly for pragmatic reasons and not because of a prolonged socialization of the subordinate class by the dominant class. For these reasons, the notions proposed by Wesołowski appear more useful, especially with regard to the moderate modernisation vision.

Let us then assume that a specific ambivalence effect appears in the consciousness of Polish industrial workers, especially the moderate modernisation ones, consisting of the fact that they are aware of the transgressive interest of the national economy in privatisation and in attracting investors, especially foreign ones. These transgressive values assume an idealistic nature in their mentality and the proposals they formulate are sometimes of an extreme nature (competition, for example, is sometimes seen as a tool of justice). As a result, the degree of support for some market-economy or capitalist institutions was higher among workers (especially the upper strata of workers) than among managers and chairmen of supervisory councils. Using a spatial metaphor, one could say that the sphere of negotiated values was placed below this idealized sphere of transgressive values in workers' consciousness. Both were of a compromise nature, which means that restrictions were imposed on some solutions that were consistent with transgressive interests. For example, workers accepted competition and some inconveniences ensuing from it but they said no to the most drastic inconvenience, namely unemployment, and were beginning to withdraw their acceptance of dismissing redundant employees. They consented to the privatisation of other enterprises but defended the status of their own state enterprise and were not ready to take up employment with private firms.

As for the view of a desirable general economic order and the idea of a good employer, the workers' consciousness turned out to have many dimensions: It was not oriented to existential values alone but also contained some specific internalised transgressive values.

It is almost certain that it is precisely the ambivalence of social consciousness of the industrial working class that makes the relatively fast reconstruction of the economic system of Poland possible. It appears that if the workers thought in the traditionalist or existentialist vein, they would rally round some populist and anti-capitalist ideology articulated by the unions which could effectively slow down the process of reforms.

NOTES

1. The notion of "workers" or "working class" used in this chapter is composed of two categories of industrial workers employed in large and medium plants (with a workforce of at least 500 persons). The first one includes skilled manual workers with basic vocational education and unskilled workers with primary and incomplete primary education. The second one includes skilled workers with secondary technical education and foremen, heads of small plant departments and their deputies with technical college degrees (engineers). Our concept of working class excluded top management and administrative workers of plants.

2. J. J. Wiatr (1987: 33) wrote that there were no theoretical obstacles to using the notion of economic consciousness, even though it is not in widespread use.

3. This work examines the findings of surveys taken in the years 1991 — 1998. These were nation-wide representative surveys of industrial workers employed in large and medium size plants. The samples of the surveys were prepared by the prestigious Centrala Badania Opini Spolecznej [Centre of Public Opinion Research] (CBOS) opinion research agency. CBOS also carried out the field studies.

4. There are two main trade union organizations in Poland. The first one is Solidarity, organized in 1980, de-legalised by communist authority in 1981 and re-legalised in 1989. In 1980-1981 Solidarity (so-called first Solidarity) institutionalised the division of Poles into social camps, "us" versus "them" (communist authorities). First "Solidarity" was the largest mass organization that has ever been in Poland (about 9 million members). Numerous studies have demonstrated that Solidarity membership of these years was not related to any characteristic pattern of demographic, social or professional features. Solidarity was not a classic trade union but a broad anti-communist social movement. Re-legalised, or "second" Solidarity, particularly in industry become a real workers' labour union. Solidarity now includes more skilled workers with vocational educations. The OPZZ (All-Poland Trade Union Federation) was organized by communist government in 1983. There were many reports of pressure being exerted on workers (especially foremen) to join the OPZZ union. In 1980s the OPZZ embraced two groups of employees: foremen, professionals, workers of higher status, Communist party members; and low-status workers who found social protection in this organization. Some researchers assumed that the OPZZ would disintegrate in 1989, after the collapse of communism, expecting ranking-and-file members to move to Solidarity. However, these expectations proved wrong. OPZZ unions have survived and its membership now includes more workers in lower supervisory posts and more elderly people.

5. At that time, I was using relatively condensed indicators of economic consciousness, containing not more than 12 variables (Gardawski 1992b).

6. It is also important to remember about the existence of numerous additional factors that complicated the process of change in attitudes. Such factors included the growth of support for state intervention in the economy and for the proposal for keeping the biggest, strategic industrial enterprises in state hands.

BIBLIOGRAPHY

Gardawski, J. 1992a. Robotnicy 1991. *Świadomość ekonomiczna w czasach przełomu [Workers 1991. Economic Consciousness in Turning Points in History]* Warsaw: Friedrich Ebert Foundation.

Gardawski, J. 1992b. Arbeiter im Zeitraum des Umschwungs. Eine Vergleichsanalyse 1987-1990. In H.Weber (Ed.), Ökonomie und Ökologie im Widerspruch? Düsseldorf: Manuskripte 56.

Gardawski J., Gilejko L. & Żukowski T. (1994). *Związki zawodowe w przedsiębiorstwach przemysłowych [Trade Unions in Industrial Enterprises]*. Warsaw: Friedrich Ebert Foundation.

Hausner, J. 1995. Modele systemu reprezentacji interesów w społeczeństwach postsocjalistycznych [The Models of the System of Representation of Interests in Post-Socialist Societies]. In J. Hausner (Ed.). *Narodziny demokratycznych instytucji*. Krakow: Economic University in Krakow— Fundacja "Polska Praca".

Kolarska-Bobińska, L. 1986. Pożądany ład społeczny i polityczny w gospodarce [The Desirable Social and Political Order in the Economy]. In W. Adamski, K. Jasiewicz & A. Rychard (Eds.). *Polacy '84. Dynamika konfliktu i konsensusu*. Warsaw: Warsaw University.

Kowalski S. 1990. *Krytyka solidarnościowego rozumu [Critique of the Solidarity Mind]*. Warsaw: PEN.

Marody, M. 1994. Społeczeństwo w centryfudze [The Society in a Centrifuge]. *Krytyka*, *44/45*.

Morawski, W. 1991. Społeczna wizja gospodarki rynkowej w Polsce [Social Vision of a Market Economy in Poland]. In W. Kozek & W. Morawski (Eds.). *Społeczeństwo wobec wyzwań gospodarki rynkowej*. Warsaw, Poland: Warsaw University Press.

Parkin, F. 1971. *Class Inequality and Political Order*. London: MacGibbon & Kee.

Rychard, A. 1993. Społeczeństwo w transformacji: koncepcja i próby syntezy [The Society in Transformations: A Concept and Attempt at Synthesis]. In A. Rychard & M. Federowicz (Eds.). *Społeczeństwo w transformacji*. Warsaw: IFiS PAN.

Tatur, M. 1994. "Corporatism" as a Paradigm of Transformation. In J. Staniszkis (Ed.). *W poszukiwaniu paradygmatu transformacji*. Warsaw: Instytut Studiów Politycznych PAN.

Wesołowski, Włodzimierz. 1993. Transformacja Charakteru i Struktury Interesow: Aktualne procesy, szanse i zagrozenia. [Transformation of Character and Structure of Interests: Current Processes, Chances and Risks]. In A. Rychard & M. Federowicz (Eds.). *Spoleczenstwo w Transformacji*. Warsaw, Poland: IFiS PAN.

Wiatr, J. J. 1987. Świadomość ekonomiczna jako kategoria teorii rozwoju społecznego [Economic Consciousness as a Category in Social Development Theory]. In *Świadomość ekonomiczna jako czynnik postępu gospodarczego. Materiały konferencyjne*. Warsaw: Akademia Nauk Społecznych.

Ziółkowski, M. 1987. Wartości wielkoprzemysłowego środowiska robotniczego na podstawie badań empirycznych w czterech przedsiębiorstwach przemysłowych [The Values of Big Industry Working Class Milieu on the Basis of Empirical Studies in Four Industrial Enterprises]. In L. Gilejko & P. Wójcik (Eds.). *Potrzeby i aspiracje robotników*. Warsaw, Poland: Akademia Nauk Społecznych. Instytut Badań Klasy Robotniczej.

Ziółkowski, M. & J. Koralewicz J. 1990. *Mentalność Polaków. Sposoby myślenia o polityce, gospodarce i życiu społecznym w końcu lat osiemdziesiątych*. [The Poles' Mentality. Ways of Thinking About Politics, Economy and Social Life in the Late 1980s]. Poznań: Nakom.

10

A Country in Transition: Health Crisis in Ukraine, with a Focus on Tobacco and Alcohol

Lara A. Romaniuk

With the collapse of the communist block of Eastern Europe and of the Soviet Union, a new term has gained currency in public discourse: the *country in transition,* as a distinct entity from the now conventional dichotomy of the *developed* and *developing* country. It describes countries in transition from a totalitarian state—politically highly centralized with a command economy and limited individual choice—to a democratic state with a market economy and a more individualistic, self-reliant citizenry. Some people speak of societies in search of an identity, others of a profound and protracted crisis. What is certain is that these are societies in a state of flux, in which old values, though being eroded, cohabit with nascent ones. Whereas the old institutions have disintegrated or are being swept away, the new ones are in their infancy and, more often than not, are far from being fully functional. Welfare, poorly managed under the communist regime, has fallen into disarray. Production output has dropped dramatically resulting in mass pauperization. The demographic situation has not escaped the prevailing social and economic malaise. Ukrainian demographers (Steshenko et al. 1999) speak of a general demographic crisis: the collapse of fertility and the sharp rise in mortality and morbidity, aging and depopulation are some of its essential features. Ukraine's population dropped from 52.2 million in 1993 to 50.1 million in 1999—a loss of 2.1 million people in six years—due primarily to excess mortality over fertility. The proportion of elderly (over 65) at 14 percent is among the highest in Europe. Many of Ukraine's elderly bear the debilitating consequences of World War II, the Afghan war and the Chernobyl disaster. Ukraine has the highest proportion of pensioners of all CIS countries—284 per 1,000 inhabitants in 1996 (United Nations Development Program [UNDP] 1996).

Against this background of pervasive socio-economic and demographic crises, the health crisis emerges as acutely troublesome as it affects the vital substance of the nation. The general state of Ukrainian's health has deteriorated irrespective of age, sex, education, habitat or ethnicity (Piskunov 1996). The most affected, however, are adult men of working age. Mortality has increased and, by corollary, longevity has decreased. This unfolding crisis has its antecedents; a number of ills predate the collapse of the communist order. Stagnation in health was already manifested during the Brezhnev regime.

The leading causes of death suggest that Ukraine has completed its epidemiological transition from pre-modern mortality/morbidity patterns, characterized by the dominance of infectious and parasitic diseases, to modern patterns, marked by degenerative diseases and traumatic accidents as the main causes of death. The state of medical technology in Ukraine is, however, unable to cope with the modern, age-associated degenerative diseases. This situation is not new, having been evident under the Soviet regime, though worsening in recent years. The current situation has been further complicated by the re-emergence of old infectious diseases such as tuberculosis and the emergence of new ones, the most troublesome of which is AIDS.

The causes underlying the general health malaise in Ukraine, virtual in the pre-collapse years and real in the post-collapse years, are many, and evade easy explanation. Researches are looking into at least three major health-related problem areas. The first is the deterioration of medical services. The second is Ukraine's ecological state, characterized by a high degree of pollution from radiation, chemical contamination, industrial fall-out and air pollution. The third relates to lifestyle. Much of this chapter will be devoted to the latter. In view of the limited space and my particular interests this analysis is confined to the smoking of tobacco and the drinking of alcohol.

Whereas a great deal of my analysis is descriptive—that is, the measurement of the incidence and intensity of smoking and drinking, as well as the possible impact, direct and indirect, on health and mortality—I also focus on the cultural dimensions of smoking and drinking, particularly in relation to gender differences. As Ukrainian society evolves toward greater personal freedom and modernity, people's behavior is shaped by advertisement and new, more attractive varieties of tobacco and alcohol products. Moreover, the spread of smoking and alcohol consumption takes place in the midst of a population whose health is already impaired due to the deterioration of health services and living standards, and the increase in levels of stress. Hence, we can expect a compounded effect of excess smoking and drinking on the overall health of Ukrainians.

Before dealing in greater detail with the core issue of the paper—smoking and alcohol consumption—a general examination of recent and current trends in the basic indicators of mortality and morbidity is in order.

LONGEVITY, MORTALITY AND MORBIDITY INDICATORS

Life Expectancy at Birth

As a longevity indicator, life expectancy at birth is all-age encompassing, yet remains unaffected by age variations; therefore, comparison can be made in time and space between various populations. Table 10.1 examines the trends in the life expectancy at birth for the past thirty years in Ukraine; Table 10.2 positions Ukraine in regard to neighboring countries experiencing similar socio-economic situations, as well as in regard to a few selected countries with advanced Medicare. What strikes most immediately in terms of longevity is the number of years by which Ukraine and other countries in transition lag behind their Western counterparts and other countries at the forefront of medical progress. Ukraine lags behind Western Europe by seven years and Japan by as much as eleven years. Unlike western countries, and other wealthy countries, which are steadily making gains in longevity, the life expectancy in Ukraine is shortening. For example, the life expectancy at birth in Canada has increased by 3.4 years for females and 5.2 years for males between 1975 and 1995. During the same period, the life expectancy of women in Ukraine has decreased by over 2 years and that of men by as much as 4 years. The losses in life occurred primarily, but not exclusively, in the first half of 1990s.

Table 10.1
Life Expectancy at Birth in Ukraine, By Sex

	1969	1975	1980	1985	1990	1991	1992	1993	1994	1995	1996	1997	1998
Male	66.7	65.1	64.9	65.2	65.7	64.7	63.9	63.2	62.4	61.3	61.6	62.3	63.3
Female	74.5	74.3	74.1	74.2	75.0	74.4	74.1	73.4	73.1	72.6	72.8	73.2	73.7

Source: Courtesy of the Center of Demography and Human Resource Development, Institute of Economics, National Academy of Sciences of Ukraine.

Table 10. 2
Life Expectancy at Birth for Selected Countries, By Sex

	Life expectancy at birth (years)					
	1970-75			1990-95		
Country	Male	Female	Difference	Male	Female	Difference
Turkmenistan	..	..	..	62	69	7
Russian Fed.	..	..	..	62	74	12
Ukraine	**67**	**74**	**7**	**64**	**74**	**10**
Romania	67	71	4	67	73	6
Belarus	68	76	8	66	76	10
Poland	67	74	7	67	76	9
Western Europe	69	75	6	74	81	7
France	69	76	8	73	81	8
Canada	70	77	7	74	81	7
Sweden	72	78	5	75	81	6
Japan	71	76	6	76	82	6

Source: Data from *The World's Women*. 1995. New York: United Nations.

There is a wide gap between the sexes in terms of longevity. Ukrainian women outlive their male counterparts by 10 years: the life expectancy at birth was 73 and 63 years in 1998, respectively. In comparison, the life expectancy in Canada for women and men stood at 81 and 74 years, respectively. The Canadian woman outlives her Ukrainian counterpart by 8 years; Canadian men survive Ukrainian men by as much as 11 years. In general, in the most advanced countries, we are witnessing a narrowing of the gap between females and males; in Ukraine, the gap is widening.

Leading Causes of Death

Deaths from infectious diseases in 1994 (see Table 10.3) represented an insignificant 1 percent of total deaths, whereas in earlier historical time they were the leading cause of death. (Some of the infectious diseases may have been included under "other"; nevertheless, the picture of cause-specific death distribution remains essentially the same.) By contrast, the percentage of total deaths from degenerative diseases is increasing. Close to 60 percent of deaths are imputed to circulatory ailments (strokes); neoplasm (cancer) is a distant second with 13 percent; accidents of all kinds claim 10 percent of deaths; and respiratory complications account for 6 percent of all deaths. By 1960, Ukraine completed the process of health transition from a pre-modern pattern, characterized by the dominance of infectious and parasitic diseases, to a modern pattern dominated by degenerative diseases and accidents—the so-called civilization diseases. Degenerative diseases are to a significant extent age-associated diseases, implying that as the population age degenerative diseases, such as those due to the complications of the circulatory and respiratory systems, as well as cancer, increase in frequency.

Table 10.3
Leading Causes of Death, Ukraine, 1994

Cardiovascular (stroke)	432,300	57
Respiratory	44,500	6
Cancer	102,300	13
Accidents/poisoning/violence	74,900	10
Infectious diseases	8,200	1
Other	102,000	13
Total deaths	764,700	100

Source: Courtesy of the Center of Demography and Human Resource Development, Institute of Economics, National Academy of Sciences of Ukraine.

In order to make the analysis of trends over time and the differences between males and females more meaningful, age standardized death rates by cause of death have been calculated in Table 10.4. Deaths from strokes and cancers among both men and women have increased over time. However, the greatest increase can be seen in mortality from accidents, intoxication and injuries.

Table 10.4
Standardized Death Rate (using 1994 age distribution) per 100,000 Population by Main Causes of Death, for Males and Females, Ukraine, in Specified Years

Type of morbidity	1970		1980		1985		1990		1994		1997	
	M	F	M	F	M	F	M	F	M	F	M	F
All cases	1449	867	1636	923	1655	950	1559	879	1866	1022	1866	997
Including:												
Diseases of the circulatory system	722	531	913	628.7	939.5	657.6	741.9	499.1	942.1	625.0	978.6	637.8
Diseases of the respiratory organs	221.3	114.5	168.5	72.1	154.1	59.9	121.0	38.8	146.9	41.0	138.7	36.8
Cancers	199.0	114.7	219.9	115.4	246.7	121.1	276.2	130.4	275.5	130.5	255.3	124.2
Accidents, homicides, suicides, and other external factors	155.2	34.8	196.0	43.8	170.9	42.2	183.6	43.2	250.8	55.4	254.8	56.5
Infectious and parasitic diseases	48.7	14.1	29.0	8.0	26.7	7.0	20.9	4.8	28.8	6.4	39.6	7.0

Source: Courtesy of the Center of Demography and Human Resource Development, Institute of Economics, National Academy of Sciences of Ukraine.

There are significant differences between the sexes in mortality by causes of death. The ratio of female to male is about 1 to 5 for accidents, 1 to 3 for respiratory diseases, and 1 to 2 for cancer. Much of the difference is attributable to male/female differences in smoking and alcohol consumption.

Smoking and Alcohol Consumption: Harmful Effects

Smoking and alcohol consumption are serious public health problems. In Ukraine, among men of working age 27 percent of all deaths are estimated to be related to alcohol consumption and 20 percent to smoking (Table 10.5, Table 10.6). By contrast, only 4 percent and 1 percent of deaths among women of working age are attributed to tobacco and alcohol, respectively. This in itself suggests the deleterious effects of smoking and alcohol consumption, as men are much more exposed than women to either of these two harmful substances. The increase in mortality in Ukraine and the relapse in longevity are particularly severe among adult males; smoking and excessive alcohol consumption are important contributing factors.

Table 10. 5
Deaths Related to Smoking and Alcohol Consumption Among Population of Working Age, in Percent of Total Deaths, Ukraine, 1995

Cause related deaths	Percent
Alcohol (men)	27
Alcohol (women)	4
Smoking (men)	20
Smoking (women)	1
Other causes (men)	26
Other causes (women)	12

Source: Data courtesy of Alcohol and Drug Information Center, Kiev.

Smoking kills mainly through bronchitis and emphysema, cardiovascular diseases and lung cancer. Smoking, along with high blood pressure, elevated blood cholesterol and a sedentary lifestyle are the four major risk factors of heart disease. Studies in various western countries have conclusively proven that smoking is a significant independent contributor to incidence of stroke among both sexes and every age group. The risk of stroke is approximately 50 percent higher among smokers than among non-smokers and rises substantially with the number of cigarettes smoked per day, according to a study done in Canada (Statistics Canada 1997: 50)

Smoking is the main cause of lung cancer, responsible for the highest death rate among all cancer sites for men. Canadian data reveal that as smoking increased over the years so did the incidence of cancer and related deaths. In the mid-eighties, as smoking diminished among men, so did, with some lag, the incidence of lung cancer. No such regression in cancer is apparent among women; however, smoking has not significantly diminished among women. One would expect a similar correlation to hold for Ukraine as well.

Table 10. 6
Mortality Rates: Alcohol Poisoning, Alcoholism, Alcohol Psychosis, And Liver Cirrhosis, Ukraine

	1980	1981	1982	1983	1984	1985	1986	1987	1988	1989	1990	1991	1992	1993	1994
Alcohol poisoning	6615	6643	6842	6320	6771	5621	3753	3785	3654	4381	5412	6393	8119	8371	8436
Per 10,000 inhabitants	13.2	13.2	13.6	12.5	13.3	11.1	7.4	7.4	7.1	8.5	10.4	12.3	15.6	16.0	16.2
Alcoholism	862	1114	1055	1092	1111	965	525	518	470	532	684	784	933	1177	1209
Per 10,000 inhabitants	1.7	2.2	2.1	2.1	2.1	1.9	1.0	1.0	0.9	1.0	1.3	1.5	1.8	2.3	2.3
Alcohol psychosis	334	413	320	289	312	180	82	87	59	82	146	218	232	233	327
Per 10,000 inhabitants	0.66	0.82	0.64	0.58	0.61	0.35	0.16	0.17	0.11	0.16	0.28	0.42	0.44	0.45	0.63
Liver cirrhosis	7349	7501	7699	7947	8011	7888	6379	6114	5966	6244	7030	8218	8658	9260	9632
Per 10,000 inhabitants	14.7	15.0	15.4	15.7	15.8	15.5	12.5	11.9	11.6	12.0	13.5	15.8	16.6	17.7	18.5
Alcohol liver cirrhosis						654	345	322	250	278	321	417	371	537	582
Per 10,000 inhabitants						1.3	0.7	0.6	0.5	0.5	0.6	0.8	0.7	1.0	1.1

Source: Data courtesy of Alcohol and Drug Information Center, Kiev.

It is well known that smoking presents specific hazards to pregnant women. The life-threatening effect of second hand smoke is now also well recognized. As with tobacco, the immoderate consumption of alcohol may produce debilitating effects. It is a significant independent factor of ischemic strokes. Heavy alcohol intake aggravates hypertension, and the relationship between alcohol, traffic accidents, violence and family disruption is well known (Kurylo & Rudnitsky 1996).

Smoking and alcohol consumption exact both a personal and economic toll. Again Canadian data are illuminating: In 1991 substance abuse (tobacco, alcohol and illicit drugs) is estimated to have cost more than $18.4 billion (Canadian dollars), or $649 per capita. Alcohol accounted for $7.5 billion, or $265 per capita. Tobacco accounted for more than $9.5 billion, or approximately $340 per capita. The economic costs of illicit drugs were estimated at $1.4 billion, or $48 per person. Lost productivity due to morbidity and premature mortality, direct health costs and law enforcement are the main economic costs of substance abuse (Canadian Center on Substance Abuse 1997: 231).

FACTORS RESPONSIBLE FOR DETERIORATION OF HEALTH: AN OVERVIEW

Deterioration of health services, along with the general impoverishment of the population, environmental degradation, lifestyle, smoking and alcohol abuse in particular are the major health-threatening factors responsible for Ukraine's relatively poor status of health. While this may be deemed acceptable as a broad analytical and explanatory framework, to more fully comprehend the health problems in Ukraine one needs to look to the *systemic* weaknesses and inefficiencies thereof. This includes a combination of obsolete medical technology, the resistance to reform and the inability to adopt innovative Medicare methods. These conditions were prevalent in the former Soviet Union, and they still are in today's post-communist Ukraine. Thus, there is the added difficulty of overcoming historical legacy.

When measuring certain medical endowments, such as the ratio of inhabitants to medical doctors and hospital beds, Ukraine outranks even the most advanced Medicare countries. In 1995, while deep in economic crisis, there were 222 inhabitants to one physician in Ukraine, as compared to 428 in the U.S., 464 in Canada, 729 in England and 656 in Germany. Ukraine's relatively high medical endowment, as measured quantitatively by the latter ratios, and the rather low status of its population's health is in itself one of the paradoxes of Soviet life; it has to do with systemic inefficiency and backwardness as well as the low productivity typical of medical services in the former Soviet Union. The lack of modern medical equipment for diagnostic and curative applications was notorious, as was the absence of up-to-date medication that was available on Western markets; moreover, medical science cross-fertilization suffered from the isolation of the country. Excessive centralization and bureaucratization hampered personal initiative and inventiveness. Access to medical services was neither democratic nor egalitarian.

As early as the 1980s, the highly extensive Soviet medical system showed signs of deterioration, due to insufficient funding and heavy reliance on central control and procurement (UNDP 1995: 22). By the early 1990s—the time of the independence of Ukraine and the disintegration of the Soviet Union—the systemic problems inherent to the Soviet era were exacerbated, and new problems typical of a country in transition emerged. The UN report mentions:

[The] long-standing problems have been deeply aggravated by adverse circumstances of transition. Funding problems have been exacerbated but no formal means have been developed for local cost recovery. Local initiative takes the form of doctors receiving private payments from hospital patients. Some sources estimated that, even in 1987, three quarters of all hospital patients in the Soviet Union were making such "donations." (UNDP 1995: 22).

The disintegration of the Soviet Union also disrupted the centrally run supply of medical equipment and supplies. According to the UN report, it is estimated that only 10 percent of the raw materials needed for production are available domestically. Domestic manufacturing practically collapsed and only very recently domestic production of certain types of medication and appliances has resumed. At the same time, the country's rapidly reduced pharmaceutical and medical production comes at the time when the economic situation does not permit large spending on and purchases of imported medical supplies.

Moreover, the retrogression of medical services is taking place simultaneously with severe economic hardship and deep, mass impoverishment of the Ukrainian population. People's income and living standards have drastically declined. By the end of 1994 real wages were barely one-third of the average level for 1990 (UNDP 1995: 9). The official income for over three-quarters of the population is estimated to be below the subsistence level. Both the quantity and quality of food consumed has also significantly deteriorated. Since 1989, the consumption of higher-value protein-rich foods, such as meat, milk, eggs and fish, has decreased. According to official statistics, the average daily caloric intake has declined from 3,517 kcal per capita in 1989, to 3,151 and 2,860 in 1992 and 1993, respectively, falling to a low 2,765 kcal per capita in 1994. More that half of the protein consumed is provided by vegetable sources, rather than animal sources (UNDP 1995: 21). As a consequence of declining nutrition, bodily resistance to sickness has diminished.

The pollution of the environment, which in the experts' opinion has reached the crisis level, is in the limelight of public perception. A great deal has been written about the Chernobyl catastrophe and its dreadful effects on the health of those living in the regions of the radiation fall-out. But pervasive pollution is also due to industrial waste, sewage, automobile dioxide release, and so forth. Though ecological deterioration in Ukraine predates its independence and the current slowdown in industrial activity is expected to cause pollution to subside, the health sector is unable to cope with the cumulative and long-term effects of diseases caused by the radiation and pollution of past years. One study (Riabov 1999) suggests a close correlation between geographic distribution of

Transition to Democracy in Eastern Europe and Russia

the incidence of industrial pollutants and mortality due to cancer. However, the cause-effect linkage is obscured by the interference of many other health-threatening elements and the poor quality of data on pollution.

As illustrated earlier, tobacco and alcohol are of particular significance to Ukraine's relatively low status of health. In the remainder of this paper I explore in greater detail the incidence and intensity of these ills.

LIFESTYLE: TOBACCO AND ALCOHOL

Lifestyle, neglected in the past as a health factor, is now very much in the fore-front of public and expert debate. Substance abuse, particularly among youth, has reached proportions in all modern societies, but the consumption of tobacco and alcohol are the two primary direct and indirect causes of premature death in Ukrainian society.

Smoking Incidence

The Russian Federation, with 67 percent of its male population over the age of 15 smoking, is one of the highest ranked countries in terms of smoking preva-lence among males. Compared to Russia, Ukraine exhibits a significantly lower rate of male smokers, but it ranks well ahead of western European countries and Canada, as shown in Table 10.7. Note, however, that the figure for Ukraine stands for the population between the ages of 20 and 59—ages more prone to smoking. Generally there is an almost inverse correlation between male smoking incidence and the wealth of a country. Sweden, *par excellence* a wealthy and welfare state, has the lowest percentage of male smokers, with 22 percent.

Table 10.7
Estimated Smoking Prevalence Among Men and Women of 15 Years of Age for Selected Countries

Country	Percentage of smoking	
	Men	Women
Russian Federation (1993)	67	30
Poland (1993)	51	29
France (1993)	40	27
Germany (1992)	37	22
Sweden (1994)	22	24
Canada (1994)	31	29
Ukraine (for 20 to 59 ages only)(1995)	49	21

Sources: World Health Organization, *The Tobacco Epidemics: Global Public Health Emergency*, Special Issue, 1996. The data for Ukraine were obtained from the Alcohol and Drug Information Center, Kiev.

A different picture emerges for female smokers. Ukraine with 21 percent of females between the ages of 20 and 59 smoking, scores relatively low as compared to the other countries, particularly Russia and Poland. Again one should note that the Ukraine rate is calculated for the age group with the highest proportion of smokers, and as such overstates the incidence of smoking among the population over age 15 applied to the other countries in Table 10.7. In wealthy countries the gender differences in regard to smoking have almost disappeared. In some cases, as in Sweden, women have actually overtaken their male counterparts in terms smoking prevalence.

Smoking habits in Ukraine analyzed by sex and age categories reveal a slight downward tendency in smoking among younger men (20 to 29 years) (Table 10.8), but no such tendency among all other age groups (Tables 10.9 and 10.10). If anything there has been an upward trend since 1990, precisely during the years of harsh economic conditions and increased poverty associated with higher health risks. The percentage of women smokers in their twenties and thirties doubled and in some cases tripled in the years 1994-1995 as compared to 1987-1988. The increase in smoking among women partly results from the trend to modernity and rapid urbanization; the incidence of smoking is insignificant among rural women irrespective of age (see Table 10.11).

Table 10.8
Intensity of Smoking, by Number of Cigarettes (in Percent of Total Cigarettes Smoked), in Urban Male and Female Population, Ukraine

Year	Men			
	<10	10-12	>20	Average
1977/1978	13.3	58.2	28.5	17.2
1994/1995	23.3	54.8	21.9	13.4
	Women			
1977/1978	71.8	28.1	0.1	6.2
1994/1995	65.0	34.3	0.7	8.5

Source: Data courtesy of Alcohol and Drug Information Center, Kiev.

Table 10.9
Smoking Incidence by Age, Male Population, Ukraine (Percentage)

Year	Age				
	20-59	20-29	30-39	40-49	50-59
1977-1978	51.1	65.1	51.1	50.8	37.2
1982-1983	50.6	62.4	52.0	50.0	38.0
1987-1988	49.9	63.1	49.7	49.5	37.6
1994-1995	48.5	60.5	50.9	49.7	38.4

Source: Data courtesy of Alcohol and Drug Information Center, Kiev.

Table 10. 10
Smoking Incidence by Age, Female Population, Ukraine (Percentage)

Year	Age				
	20-59	20-29	30-39	40-49	50-59
1977-1978	5.2	7.9	7.3	3.2	2.6
1982-1983	5.0	7.5	7.0	3.4	5.0
1987-1988	8.3	12.8	10.6	6.5	8.3
1994-1995	20.3	31.9	23.6	19.1	20.5

Source: Data courtesy of Alcohol and Drug Information Center, Kiev.

Table 10.11
Smoking Incidence Among Women in Specified Age, For Urban and Rural Population, in 1996 (Percentage)

Age	Urban	Rural
20-29	31.9	0.4
30-39	23.6	0.5
40-49	19.1	0.6
50-59	7.5	0.4

Source: Data courtesy of Alcohol and Drug Information Center, Kiev.

Comparative, cross-country data on smoking show that smoking habits stand in inverse correlation with the level of education and income but directly correlate with poverty. For example, in Canada, *proportionally* to its number of smokers, there are more smokers among blue collar than among managerial and professional groups, more among people with an elementary education than with a university education, and more among people in low-income than in upper income categories. This seems to corroborate the general thesis that poor societies, with comparable lifestyles and customs, are more prone to smoking than wealthier societies. Ukraine's data show the distribution of smokers according to their degree of education (Table 10.12), and as such do not lend themselves to an analysis similar to the one done for Canada. For that, one would need to have smoker rates calculated for population of a given level of education. However, even so, the data in Table 10.12 tell volumes about trends in smoking in the post-communist society of Ukraine. Women most likely to smoke are not the least educated but the most educated: of those women who smoke, 60 percent have a post-secondary education, whereas only 1 percent of women who smoke have an incomplete secondary education.

Table 10.12
Distribution of Smokers According to the Level of Education, Ukraine

Level of education	Men	Women
Post secondary	20.2	62.3
Secondary	51.4	36.7
Primary and incomplete secondary	28.4	1.0

Source: Data courtesy of Alcohol and Drug Information Center, Kiev.

Alcohol

Measuring the real incidence of alcohol consumption in Ukraine is not straightforward, and the easiest way to do so it is to use the sale of alcohol per capita as a proxy for alcohol consumption. However, anyone knowing anything about the situation in Ukraine is all too aware of the widespread unlicensed production, consumption and sale of domestic alcohol. *Samohon* (or, more affectionately, *samohonka*) is on the table of every village-home and not infrequently in the city-home.

Table 10. 13 show both the recorded sale and estimated unrecorded consumption of pure alcohol per capita of population. The unrecorded consumption, depending on the year, is two or three times higher than the recorded consumption. Over time, except in the years 1985 to 1989 during Gorbachev's anti-alcohol campaign, the combined recorded and unrecorded alcohol consumption was around 11 liters per capita a year. For comparison, the average per capita consumption in recent years was around 12 liters in France, 11 in Germany, 10 in Spain, 9 in Italy and 7 in Canada. For countries culturally and economically closer to Ukraine, Poland registered 7; Czech and Slovakia came close to 10 and Romania 8 liters per capita.

Most of the alcohol consumed in Ukraine is drunk by men, who generally drink vodka and spirits; women in general drink moderately and on special occasions, and then typically wine and liqueur.

POLICY IMPLICATIONS AND CHALLENGES AHEAD FOR UKRAINE

There are many skeptics among Ukrainians. "Nothing can be done," is by now almost second nature to the Ukrainian personality, because in the past the promises of public officials and the political elite turned utterly deceptive. On the other hand, those with more liberal views feel it is not the government's business to involve itself in what is perceived to be the private matter of the individual; to them democracy is equated with *laissez faire* and social engineering is seen as the business of the totalitarian state. In my case, the Ukrainian state does not have the means today to undertake a meaningful, effective, large scale, preventive, therapeutic and curative campaign.

Table 10. 13
Recorded and Unrecorded Alcohol Consumption in Ukraine by Expert Estimates (in Liters of Pure Alcohol per Capita)

	1980	1981	1982	1983	1984	1985	1986	1987	1988	1989	1990	1991	1992	1993	1994
Recorded alcohol sale	6.3	6.2	5.7	5.7	5.7	5.2	3.4	2.9	3.2	3.8	4.1	4.1	3.6	3.3	2.0
Unrecorded alcohoi consumption	5.5	5.5	6.0	6.0	6.0	3.0	2.0	3.0	3.5	4.5	5.0	6.0	7.0	8.0	9.5
Total alcohol consumption	11.8	11.7	11.7	11.7	11.7	8.2	5.4	5.9	6.7	8.3	9.1	10.1	10.6	11.3	11.5

Source: Data courtesy of Alcohol and Drug Information Center, Kiev.

I argue that both the skepticism and the perception of a liberal state are the results of misunderstanding and, as of yet, little knowledge of democracy. According to the experience of many liberal, generally wealthy countries, a well-organized and systematic campaign to fight tobacco and alcohol can be mounted and yield successes, and it does not negate freedom and democracy. Canada, for instance, has declared a total war on smoking by banning it from public places, offices, public transportation and restaurants. As a result of this policy implementation, smoking among males has decreased from almost 60 percent in the 1960s to 30 percent in 1990s. There is evidence that it has been effective in reducing smoking-related illnesses such as lung cancer and heart diseases. Less smoking, a more active lifestyle and a more balanced diet greatly account for the reduction in mortality and the gains in longevity in Canada and in other modern, democratic states.

Even Gorbachev's much derided anti-alcohol campaign from 1985 to 1989 has had some positive results, regardless of its clumsiness, for example, the uprooting of entire vineyards. Soviet and some non-Soviet (Meslé, Shkolnikov, Hertrich & Vallin 1996) demographers and epidemiologists have indeed attributed the large drop in mortality in 1986 and 1987 in the USSR to the anti-alcohol campaign. According to Barbara Anderson and Brian Silver (1990: 240), Shkolnikov and Vallin "show convincingly, based on a month-by-month study of mortality trends by cause of death among provinces in European Russia, that the decline in mortality beginning in the middle of 1985 was related to changes in the pattern of causes of death that are consistent with a reduction in alcohol abuse." Of particular significance in this regard is the evidence pointing to the reduction in the number of deaths due to accidents.

Moreover, there are models to be followed: the Swedish and Canadian experience could serve as models of inspiration for Ukrainian policymakers. A vigorous, comprehensive anti-smoking campaign could be effective in Ukraine where culture provides fertile grounds for anti-smoking and anti-drinking education targeted at women and girls in particular. In Ukraine women smokers constitute only a minority. In rural areas, smoking among women is very low, and there is still strong public disapproval of female smoking. Therefore, in spite of the rather heavy smoking and drinking among men, and probably their resistance to be swayed from such habits, the fight against smoking among women and youth in general may provide rewarding opportunities. Women of all ages and young men should therefore be the prime targets.

Emphasis should be on public education, primarily in schools. The army should be targeted as well. It is in the army that young recruits are often initiated to alcohol and tobacco, being pressured by their peers or their superiors. Mothers of army recruits have already united and spoken out against *didivchena* (abuse of army freshmen by veterans) and could do the same regarding tobacco and alcohol abuse. This is an opportunity and challenge for women. While Ukrainian women may not be given a prominent role in politics, they are traditionally prominent at the workplace, in the community and most importantly in their own families, influencing the behavior of their partner and of youth.

CONCLUDING REMARKS

Traditionally, Ukrainian society has two different standards for men and women as far as smoking and alcohol consumption is concerned. Smoking and drinking by men is traditionally not only tolerated, but to some extent is a manly hallmark. Smoking and drinking by women is met with social disapproval except when the drinking is done relatively moderately and on special occasions (weddings and annual village festivities, such as *khram*). Ukrainian folklore is full of metaphors for this double standard in gender roles. For instance, Repin's story *Kozak z Liulkoiu Huliaye* portrays Kozaks sitting around a barrel, drinking and writing a menacing letter to the Turkish Sultan. Gogol's *Sorochinski Yarmarok* and Hulak-Artemovsky's opera *Zaporozhia za Dunayem* vividly portray women not only as abstaining from tobacco and excessive drinking but also as censuring the drunkenness of their husband's.

This division between male and female traditions regarding smoking and drinking is, however, eroding in the post-communist westernization of society. Greater social freedom and slackening public control over individual behavior, impoverishment and every day stress contribute to a higher rate of substance abuse among the general population. Moreover, the quasi elimination of domestic tobacco growers and manufacturers, and their replacement by multinational tobacco industries with more appealing, higher quality products, accompanied by sophisticated advertisement targeted particularly at youth, has raised the number of young smokers both male and female. Thus, were there to be in post-communist Ukraine a policy aimed at achieving the maximum benefits in terms of people's health at an affordable cost, such policy would most likely need to involve a comprehensive anti-alcohol and anti-tobacco campaign.

NOTE

I would like to acknowledge generous assistance in the form of professional advice and data analysis from various quarters. I am particularly thankful to Dr. Konstantin Krasovsky, Director of the Alcohol and Drug Information Center in Kiev and to Dr. Valentyna Steshenko, Head of the Center of Demography and Human Resource Development at the Institute of Economics, National Academy of Sciences. Serhiy Piskunov was helpful in guiding me through the statistical data maze, as was Yuri Subotine from the World Health Organization in Kiev. I benefited from my discussions with Oksana Kuts, Iryna Ignatova and Dr. Larysa Kobelianska from the UN Gender in Development Program; I am grateful for their encouragement. The United Nations Office, Gender in Development Program in Kiev was most generous in providing me with institutional support. I am, however, solely responsible for any of the paper's shortcomings. This research was partly supported by funding from the Michael and Daria Kowalsky Endowment Fund, Canadian Institute of Ukrainian Studies, University of Alberta.

REFERENCES

Alcohol and Drug Information Center (ADIC-Ukraine) (Informatsiynyi tsentr z problem al'koholiu ta narkotykiv). 1997. *Tobacco or health in Ukraine (Tiutiun abo zdorov'ia v Ukraini)*. Kiev: ADIC-Ukraine.

Anderson, Barbara A. & Brian D. Silver. 1990. *Trends in Mortality of the Soviet Population*. Report no. 348, Population Studies Center, The University of Michigan.

Binyon, Michael. 1983. *Life in Russia*. New York: Pantheon Books.

Canadian Center on Substance Abuse. 1997. *Canadian Profile— Alcohol, Tobacco and Drugs.* Ottawa: Canadian Center on Substance Abuse.

Kurylo, Iryna & Omeljan, Rudnitsky. 1996. Mortality from accidents and external actions and its influence on life expectation in Ukraine (in Ukrainian). *Demographichni Doslidzhennia, 18,* Kyiv: National Academy of Sciences, Economic Institute.

Meslé, France, Vladimir M.Shkolnikov, Véronique Hertrich & Jacques Vallin. 1996. *Tendances récentes de la mortalité par cause en Russie 1965-1994.* Paris: Institut National de Démographie.

Piskunov, Serhiy. 1996. *Ethnic peculiarities of mortality and life expectancy in Ukraine, 1958-1989* (in Ukrainian). *Demografichni Doslidzhennia, 18.* Kiev: National Academy of Sciences, Institute of Economics.

Riabov, Igor. 1999 *Ecologichnyj factor u vidtvorenni naselennya Ukrainy (Ecological Factors in Population Reproduction of Ukraine).* Ph.D. Dissertation, National Academy of Sciences: Institute of Economics.

Statistics Canada. 1997 (June). *Heart disease and stroke in Canada,* Ottawa.

Steshenko, Valentyna, et al. 1999. *Demografichni perspektyvy Ukrainy do 2026 roku. (Ukraine's Demographic Perspectives to 2026).* Kiev: National Academy of Sciences, Institute of Economics.

United Nations Development Program (UNDP). 1995. *Ukraine Human Development Report 1995.* Kiev: United Nations.

_____. 1996. *Ukraine Human Development Report 1996.* Kiev: United Nations.

_____. 1997. *The Health of Women and Children in Ukraine 1997.* Kiev: United Nations.

World Health Organization. 1996. *Tobacco Alert.* Geneva: World Health Organization.

11

Polish Women During Transition to Democracy: A Preliminary Research Report

J. Mayone Stycos, Barbara Wejnert and Zbigniew Tyszka

All of the Soviet Union's erstwhile satellites...have moved definitely away from communism. But the touchstone of progress has long since become not moving away from communism, but moving toward democracy. The goal of a Western-type liberal democracy had looked relatively simple as communism was being overturned, but in the following months the Eastern Europeans were to learn how difficult and apparently thankless their chosen task was to be (Brown 1992: 16).

The current democratic transformation taking place in the former communist states, and the transition toward a capitalistic market economy, have brought substantial changes in the lives of residents of prior countries of the USSR (Czapinski 1994; Reboud & Chu 1997; Stephenson 1998). Among these changes are the establishment of political freedom, free elections, elimination of censorship, an opening of opportunities for private entrepreneurs and, in the more economically advanced countries, availability of both food and quality consumer products. Moreover, the ongoing political and economic unification with Western Europe has exposed former Soviet-bloc societies to the lifestyle of Western democracies and presumably to a higher standard of living (Brown 1992; Dabrowski & Antczak 1996; Wejnert 1996b, 1996c; Wejnert & Spencer 1996). But democratization and transition toward a market economy have also been associated with changes in employment levels, family relationships, redistribution of financial resources, the restructuring of individual lifestyles and the emergence of a new class system. Though democracy was perceived as a system that would guarantee an equally high standard of living for all citizens, the connectedness of democratic freedom with economic liberty has led to social inequality and social discomfort, a problem that has been broadly discussed by scholars studying democratic transitions (e.g., Dahl 1971; DeSoto & Anderson 1993; Held 1990; Sandel 1996).

Pervasive changes in economic and political systems experienced over the last decade by Polish society and free market practices have generated disparity in socioeconomic conditions among various segments of the general population (Wejnert & Spencer 1996). This disparity could lead to a sense of unfairness and social inequality in all except the very top economic groups; thus lowering perceived quality of life. While the communist system constrained the expression of individual incentives, and hence aspirations were generally low, with the democratic and free market transformation, incentives and aspirations were kindled. For some groups, progress has been much slower than people had hoped, which could lead to a persistent state of deprivation relative to a new goal of success.

Vulnerability and sensitivity to such changes are likely to vary by gender, socioeconomic status, age and urban/rural residence (Funk & Mueller 1993; International Labor Office 1985; Wejnert 1996a). Women are particularly disadvantaged, especially those who live in rural communities (Wejnert 1996c; Wejnert & Spencer 1996). Although many of the contemporary trends have been commonly assumed to have enriched women's lives and increased their opportunities, the costs to them may have been substantial (Funk 1996; Wejnert 1996b). Rising unemployment has been a particular threat to women's sense of security. Further, the growth of social and economic inequality may have caused women's status to decline vis-à-vis that of men and other reference groups commonly targeted for self-evaluation (Issraelyan 1996; Lissyutkina 1993; Wejnert & Spencer 1996).

In short, objective measures of "progress" are easier to identify and collect than are subjective measures. Although political freedoms and economic well-being have improved for many Polish women over the past decade, it is less certain that there has been a commensurate increase in psychological well-being.

RESEARCH ON QUALITY OF LIFE IN POLAND

Reports on quality of life (QOL) for the general Polish population go back as far as the 1960s, when Hadley Cantril (1965) found that the medium evaluation score on general well-being on an 11-point scale was 5. Such studies are useful for cross-national comparisons and assessing overall change over time, but have two major limitations: first, they fail to report findings for sub-groups (e.g., scores by gender, region, social class, age or rural-urban residence); second, they fail to assess satisfaction with different sub-categories of life (e.g., family, economy, environment, and so forth) (Campbell, Converse & Rogers 1976; Gallup 1976).

Our study was intended to help fill in these gaps by designing a survey that would include various sub-categories of the population, and contain questions on satisfaction with a variety of life domains.[1] In essence, the research questions were: Have improvements in health, wealth, life and liberty led to greater achievement in the pursuit of happiness? and, To what extent have different groups in the population shared gains or losses in satisfaction with various aspects of life? A conceptual model generating hypotheses concerning the determinants of QOL, followed by a large-scale survey to test the hypotheses, would enhance answering such questions.

Conceptual Model

Based on the pioneering work of Andrews and others, we have selected fifteen life "domains" (Andrews & Inglehart 1979; Andrews & McKennel 1980; Andrews & Robinson 1991).[2] Micro-type domains that have proven to be especially important in other countries include satisfaction with work, marriage, standard of living, health and environment. We also included satisfaction with family size and contraception because of their special significance to women. Macro domains include satisfaction with government, church and the general economy. Respondents were also asked for their degree of general satisfaction with life as a whole.

Figure 11. 1
Model of Determinants of QOL in Study Conducted by Stycos, Wejnert and Tyszka in Poland, in 1995

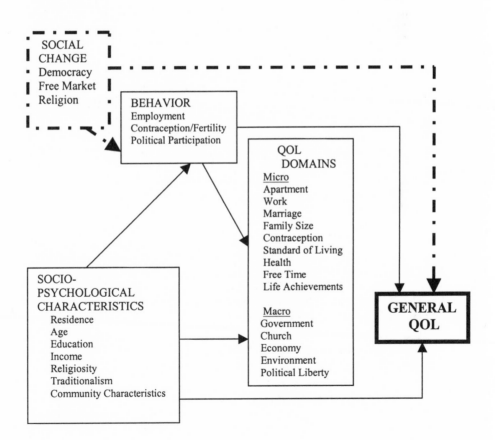

Figure 11.1 shows the overall model that drives the study design, the questionnaire content, and the mode of analysis. We divided the hypothesized determinants of QOL into two sets of variables: (1) behavioral histories of employment, fertility and political participation and (2) social psychological characteristics. These latter include familiar demographic and social variables—age, education, residence, income—that have been known to explain at least some of the variance in QOL, along with at least three less common measures—religiosity, traditionalism, and community characteristics.

Research Site

We selected the region of Konin near Poznan as our research side. Konin is an area (wojewodztwo) that over the past three decades has undergone historical changes that were typical of other Polish regions. Due to the communist policy of rapid industrialization and urbanization toward end of the 1960s, the government constructed an industrial city in the agricultural hinterland of Konin, an effort similar to those made in Brazil and India, but with more effective job creation. In addition to massive infrastructure development in the town of Konin, the government located several new industries in the region—aluminum production, electricity generation and coal mining/processing. Urbanization, industrialization and a surge of male and female employment in the service and industrial sectors came to the area almost overnight. At the same time, similar economic, demographic and social restructuring took place in other Polish rural regions, where substantial industrial centers were built in the midst of agricultural areas (e.g., a petrochemical industry in the Plock region, and the largest Polish metallurgy factory, Nowa Huta, near Krakow). Moreover, by its social, economic and demographic characteristics, Konin is representative of many other regions in Poland. It is a medium-sized region with a population of 476,000, where, despite the inputs of industry and infrastructure, 56 percent of the population still resides in villages, compared to 39 percent for all of Poland (GUS 1993:LXVI; WUS 1993:25).

Konin has the same proportion of working-age people as the nation (56 percent compared to 57 percent), a similar proportion of the labor force is female (43 percent in Konin compared with 46 percent in Poland), and a similar rising unemployment rate. Marriage rates and age at marriage are virtually identical for Konin and Poland (GUS 1995: 62; GUS 1994:34).

The attractiveness of Konin as a research side was further enhanced by data from research conducted in this region at the end of the 1960s by our Polish co-investigator Zbigniew Tyszka (Tyszka, 1970).

The Questionnaire and Sample

We devised a questionnaire of approximately 45 minutes duration (see Appendix) that was administered by interviewers to fifty women in urban and rural areas near Poznan and Konin. Fieldwork was carried out in 1995 by the survey organization ANKIETER, under the direction of Professor Krzysztof Podemski. About four-fifths of the women were married, three-quarters had completed high school and two thirds were employed outside the home.

Preliminary Results

Although a large-scale survey would be required to answer the questions we have raised, at this stage we can report the preliminary results of the pretest. Our first objective concerned:

"Your satisfaction with life. I will show you a card asking you to choose the number which best matches your opinion, where 1 means the most satisfaction and 7 the least satisfaction." Fifteen dimensions of life were queried, along with an overall appraisal of life in general. Table 11.1, which divides the domains into four levels of satisfaction, shows that the lowest degree of satisfaction refers to the environment, the government and the economy.

Table 11.1
Mean Score for Fifteen Quality of Life Domains

Satisfaction Level	Mean Scores (Range)	Domain
Low	4.8-4.9	Environment Governance Economy
Moderately Low	3.7-4.1	Church, Income, Free time, How free time is spent
Moderately High	2.9-3.3	Health, Neighborhood, Apartment, Political liberties, Work Self-Achievement
High	1.9-2.1	Family life, How treated by others

Source: Pre-test Research on Quality of Life of Polish Women, conducted by Stycos, Wejnert and Tyszka in Poland, in 1995.

The highest satisfaction concerns one's family and social life (how others treat you). In between these extremes but on the high side are political liberties, health, work, personal achievements, political freedom, housing and the neighborhood, while income, free time, how the free time is spent, and the Church are relatively low in satisfaction. About half of the fifteen items are classified in the higher and half in the lower categories.

"Life in general" received a mean score of 2.6, on the high side, but lower than family and social life. Thus, despite the generally low level of satisfaction with many particular aspects of life, a satisfactory family and social life may be crucial to the relatively high evaluation of "life in general."

Our second objective was to assess that impact of the political and economic changes since 1989 on women's satisfaction with life. To determine this, respondents were asked to compare their current situation to their situation prior to 1989. Were they "better, worse or about the same?" Responses demonstrated little enthusiasm for the current situation. According to just over half of the sample, the situation of women had worsened, while only one-third thought it had improved. Asked about employment opportunities for women, 82 percent said they had declined, and no one thought they had increased. One-half felt the environment[3] had worsened and only 12 percent thought it had improved. While just over half felt that their current income was better than before, two-thirds felt *less* secure financially, and half said they could buy less now *than before*. Regarding politics, only one-fifth feel the country is better governed now, and one-third regard it as worse governed. Moreover, while three-quarters said that there was greater freedom to express oneself now, only about one-third said their ability to criticize the local government had improved (56 percent said it had weakened). Only one-fifth said their influence on decisions of local government had increased, while a quarter said it decreased. Thus, the data point to considerable disillusion with the changes—in politics, economics and the environment. However, when asked "generally speaking how is your life now?" half say life is better than before the changes and only 10 percent said life is worse. Moreover, asked about their level of happiness six years ago, 80 percent said they were happy or very happy then—similar to the 82 percent that rated themselves as currently happy. These data not only suggest a general high level of satisfaction with life, but suggest no deterioration (or improvements) in *general* happiness over the decade. Indeed, there is considerable optimism about the future. In response to the question, "In five years do you think you will be very happy...etc.," 86 percent said happy, only 2 percent said unhappy and the balance gave "Don't know" responses.

CONCLUSION

How does our study compare with QOL research conducted by others, and can any hypotheses be derived for future research? First, other studies of the Polish population suggest long-range stability in levels of general happiness. Veenhaven and Ehrhardt (1995) and Veenhaven (1996) report a mean of 7.0, on a 10 point scale, in Polish happiness both prior to transition (1989) and in 1996. However, there were significant short-term changes, since the same measures taken in 1992 and 1993 dropped to 6.1 and 6.2, respectively, before rebounding to 7 in the latter part of the 1990s. These shifts may indicate that only powerful macro-changes in the society (like Polish "shock therapy") can effect substantial change in a relatively stable level of general happiness.

Second, although Veenhaven (1996) does not report differences by sex, his mean level for the general Polish population (7.0) exceeds our mean for women of 6.6 (adjusted to a 10-point scale). American studies have also found lower levels of life satisfaction among women (Andrews & Withey, 1976), who were also more likely than men to recall negative aspects of their lives (Campbell, 1981). Our findings that marriage and family are the strongest determinants of life satisfaction also has been confirmed by American studies (Andrews & Whithey, 1979; Andrews & Robinson, 1991; Campbell 1981). But why should women report lower levels of life satisfaction? One possibility is increasing dissatisfaction with male contributions to household tasks. Elina Haavio-Mannila (1992:105) concluded that "women were happier . . . the more the spouse participated in domestic work." Only half of our respondents reported that their husbands often help with household chores, data consistent with earlier World Bank studies carried out in five European countries including Poland (World Bank 1994).

Clearly two major areas for future research are indicated: First, what kinds of macro-changes affect which domains of life satisfaction? Second, what accounts for consistently lower female evaluations of quality of life?

APPENDIX

Questionnaire For the Quality of Life of Women Research

1. Have you ever lived in another location?
   1 – yes   2 – no (If no, go to question 5)
2. If yes, then
   a)   in a village or farmstead
   b)   in a small town
   c)   in a large town
3. In which county did you live before?........................
4. Why did you move here? (more answers possible)

	Main reason	Additional reason
- Move required by job (employer)	01	02
- No work in previous area	01	02
- Better housing conditions	01	02
- Better job opportunities	01	02
- Purchased/inherited/gained through compensation for farming	01	02
- Higher income	01	02
- Marriage	01	02
- Family moved	01	02
- Wanted to be closer to relatives and friends	01	02
- Other	01	02
- Do not know	01	02
X- No answer	0 – do not know	

5. Please list those family members who are in the same household as you (live and eat with you and with whom you share the expenses). Tell us their age, highest degree of education and their salary in their job. (The first row is for the respondent.)

first name	age	relation to the head of the household	education	income (monthly, net)

0 – do not know   X – no answer

6. How many rooms are in your flat (excluding the kitchen and the bathroom)?
.... rooms

7. Is there in the house/flat...

	yes	no
pipeline water-supply	1	2
hot water supply	1	2
water flush toilet	1	2
gas supply	1	2
electricity	1	2

8. Do you live in your first marriage?
   1 – yes   2 – no

9. If not, how old were you when you separated? ....
10. How old were you when you first got married? ....
11. How old were you when you remarried? ....
12. How old were you when your first child was born? ....
13. How old were you when you finished schools? ....
14. Have you ever had a job?
   1 – yes   2 – no

15. How old were you when you started to work? ....
16. Do you have a job now? (If yes, go to question 26)
   1 – yes   2 – no
17. If not,
   1 – would like to have a job   0 – do not know
   2 – would prefer to stay home   X – no answer

18. If you had someone to help in the household and around the house, then
   1 – would like to have a job   0 – do not know
   2 – would prefer to stay home   X – no answer

19. If you work at your own farm and you had an opportunity to take a job, which would you choose?

     1 – would work on own farm   0 – do not know

     2 – would take a job somewhere else   X – no answer

20. Are you looking for a job now?

     1 – yes   2 – no

21. Have you ever held a job?

     1 – yes   2 – no

22. If yes, then

     when did you start working........................(year) and

     when did you stop working........................(year)?

23. What do you do now?

     1   full time worker, not in own enterprise

     2   work in own enterprsie

     3   retired

     4   disabled retired

     5   unemployed (registered)

     6   unemployed (not registered)

     7   maternity aid

     8   housewife

     9.   student

     10   other

     0   do not know

     X   no answer

24. What was the main reason you got a job?

     1   Income   4   makes no sense

     2   Job satisfaction   0   do not know

     4   Increased opportunities   X   no answer

     3   Opportunity to spend time with others

25. Why did you stop working?

     1   lost the job   6. the question makes no sense

     2   had to take care of children   0   do not know

     3   did not like the job   X   no answer

     4   husband did not want me to work

     5   other reason...........................

QUESTIONS FOR A PERSON CURRENTLY EMPLOYED:

26. If you had the opportunity to choose (because you had enough money for living expenses), what would you prefer to do?

     1   continue at the present job   0   do not know

     2   change job   X   no answer

     3   stay at home

27. What is the main reason you are working?

     1   Income   0   do not know

     2   Job satisfaction   X   no answer

     3   Opportunity to spend time with others

28. How secure do you think your job is?

     4   completely secure   0   do not know

     3   fairly secure   X   no answer

     2   partially secure

     1   not secure

29. How many hours a week do you work?
    1   Job................hours   0   do not know
    2   Housework.........hours   X   no answer
    3   rural household, farming..........hours
30. People have different attitudes towards housework (not only child care, but also cooking, cleaning, sewing). How much do you like housework?
    5   like very much   0   do not know
    4   like somewhat   X   no answer
    3   dislike somewhat
    2   do not like at all
31. Are you a member of any organizations?

Organization	Now			Before 1990		
	yes	no	no answer	yes	no	no answer
church groups						
trade unions						
women organizations						
political organizations						
others, please specify						

32. Does any of the political parties represent and express your views?
    1   yes   0   do not know
    2   no   X   no answer
         If yes, please specify.......................................
33. Did you vote at the last parliamentary elections?
    1   yes   0   do not know
    2   no   X   no answer
34. Did you vote at the last municipal elections?
    1   yes   0   do not know
    2   no   X   no answer

ONLY FOR THOSE WHO VOTED

35. Can you list some politicians who were running in the last parliamentary elections?

....

36. How interested are you in political issues?
    1   very interested   0   do not know
    2   somewhat interested   X   no answer
    3   not too interested
    4   not interested at all
37. Can you tell us the name of the current president?
    1   yes...............................   2   no

38. Can you tell us the name of the current prime minister?
   1   yes...............................   2   no

I WOULD LIKE TO ASK YOU SOME QUESTIONS ABOUT THE POLITICAL CHANGE IN POLAND.

39. Compared to the period before the nineties how much are you interested in politics?
   1   more interested   X   no answer
   2   as interested as before
   3   less interested

40. Compared to the period before 1990 do you think that your influence on the decisions of the municipality is:
   1   much greater   5 much smaller than earlier
   2   greater   0   no answer
   3   unchanged   X   no answer
   4   smaller

41. Compared to the situation before 1990 is your ability to criticize the municipality:
   1   much greater   0   do not know
   2   greater   X   no answer
   3   unchanged
   4   smaller
   4   much smaller than earlier

42. Let's consider the past. Ten years ago everyone had a little but secure income with few shopping opportunities. Today very few people have the opportunity to earn a lot. Which of the following statements do you think is true?
   5   I definitely prefer the situation before 1990
   4   I think I prefer the situation before 1990
   3   I think I prefer the current situation
   2   I definitely prefer the current situation
   1   There is no difference
   0   do not know
   X   no answer

43. Compared to the situation before the political change can you buy in the stores
   5   much more   0   do not know
   4   more   X   no answer
   3   just as much
   2   less
   1   much less

44. Compared to the situation before the political change do you feel
   5   much more secure financially today   0   do not know
   4   more secure   X   no answer
   3   just as much secure
   2   less secure
   1   much less secure

45. Compared to the situation before the political change do you think that women's situation in general
   5   was much better   0   do not know
   4   was better   X   no answer
   3   is unchanged
   2   was worse
   1   was much worse

46. Compared to the situation before the political change do you think that employment opportunities for women

      5   increased significantly   0   do not know
      4   somewhat increased   X   no answer
      3   remained unchanged
      2   decreased
      1   decreased significantly

47. Compared to the situation before the freedom to express your own opinion has

      5   increased significantly   0   do not know
      4   somewhat increased   X   no answer
      3   remained unchanged
      2   decreased
      1   decreased significantly

48. Do you think that a person's life depends on chance/fate or on the person?

      1   more on chance/fate   0   do not know
      2   more on the person   X   no answer

49. How often did you go to church before 1990?

      1   more than once a week   0   do not know
      2   once a week   X   no answer
      4   once a month
      5   less than once a month
      6   not at all

50. Was your upbringing

      1   very religious   0   do not know
      2   religious   X   no answer
      3   not religious

51. If it was not religious, would you have liked to be brought up as a religious person?

      1   yes   0   do not know
      2   no   X   no answer

52. How would you describe yourself?

      1   very religious
      2   somewhat religious
      3   not religious
      X   no answer

53. Which religion do you belong to?

      2   Catholic   0   do not know
      3   Calvinist   X   no answer
      4   Lutheran
      6   other

54. Do you think that people should respect the norms of the church

	yes	no
concerning faith	1	2
concerning the upbringing of children	1	2
concerning issues of marriage	1	2
concerning politics	1	2
concerning family planning	1	2

55. Now I am going to read you different people's different opinions. Please indicate how do you feel about the following statements.

	strongly agree				strongly disagree		
Women are as intelligent as men.	1	2	3	4	5	0	X
Marriage is necessary for happiness.	1	2	3	4	5	0	X
Women and men should get equal pay for equal work.	1	2	3	4	5	0	X
Some jobs suit for men and some for women.	1	2	3	4	5	0	X
A man should have a job, and a woman should take care of the household and the family.	1	2	3	4	5	0	X
A man should make decisions and a woman should obey.	1	2	3	4	5	0	X
A woman respects a husband who does not dominate her.	1	2	3	4	5	0	X
Unmarried people can be happy.	1	2	3	4	5	0	X
The birth of a child cements a marriage.	1	2	3	4	5	0	X
Children have an obligation to take care of their elderly parents.	1	2	3	4	5	0	X
Large families are the happiest.	1	2	3	4	5	0	X
Sex education is an important school subject for young people.	1	2	3	4	5	0	X

56. I would like to ask you now who makes decisions on different family matters in your household. Who decides

	me	husband	both	do not know	no answer
when and where to go on vacation	1	2	3	4	5
your getting a job	1	2	3	4	5
borrowing money	1	2	3	4	5
buying a new TV or refrigerator	1	2	3	4	5
children's level of education	1	2	3	4	5
having another child	1	2	3	4	5

57. Do you talk to your husband before you buy
a) clothing for yourself   1 yes   2 no   0   do not know
b) clothing for the children   1 yes   2 no   0   do not know
c) furniture 1 yes   2 no   0   do not know

58. Does your husband help with the child-care, for example:

	often	occasionally	never	do not know	no answer
putting children to bed	1	2	3	4	5
playing with children	1	2	3	4	5
helping with the homework	1	2	3	4	5

59. Does your husband help with the housework?
1 a lot   2 a little   3 not at all   0 do not know   X no answer

60. On average, how many hours a week does your husband spend taking care of the household and the children?..............................hours   0 do not know   X no answer

61. How much does your husband help in your household generally?
    1   very often   0 do not know
    2   often   X no answer
    3   rarely
    4   very rarely
    5   not at all

62. Couples sometimes argue when they disagree about something.
    a) Has your husband ever pushed you or made fun of you during arguments? (underlined)
    1 very often   4 very rarely   0 do not know
    2 often   5 never   X no answer
    3 rarely

63. Now I would like to talk with you about your satisfaction with your life. The following table shows a scale of 1-7. Please choose the number which best matches your opinion. Number 1 means the least satisfaction, and 7 the most satisfaction.

	not satisfied at all					completely satisfied			
How would you rate your apartment?	1	2	3	4	5	6	7	0	X
How would you rate the area you live in?	1	2	3	4	5	6	7	0	X
How would you rate your work as a housewife?	1	2	3	4	5	6	7	0	X
How would you rate your family life? (your husband, marriage, children)	1	2	3	4	5	6	7	0	X
How would you rate your household income?	1	2	3	4	5	6	7	0	X
How would you rate how you spend your own free time?	1	2	3	4	5	6	7	0	X
How much are you satisfied with the way others treat you?	1	2	3	4	5	6	7	0	X
How much are you satisfied with the amount of your free time?	1	2	3	4	5	6	7	0	X

63. Continued

How much are you satisfied with your achievements in life and with the way you react to problems?	1	2	3	4	5	6	7	0	X
How would you rate your health and fitness?	1	2	3	4	5	6	7	0	X
How much are you satisfied with what the government is doing?	1	2	3	4	5	6	7	0	X
How much are you satisfied with the number of your children?	1	2	3	4	5	6	7	0	X
How much are you satisfied with the age difference between your children?	1	2	3	4	5	6	7	0	X
How would you rate what the church is doing?	1	2	3	4	5	6	7	0	X
How much are you satisfied with the Hungarian economic development?	1	2	3	4	5	6	7	0	X
How much are you satisfied with the political liberties you have?	1	2	3	4	5	6	7	0	X
How would you rate your environment (air quality, quality of drinking water)?	1	2	3	4	5	6	7	0	X
In general how would you rate your life?	1	2	3	4	5	6	7	0	X

0 do not know   X no answer

64. Let's now go back to the eighties, before the political changes. I would like to know how much did the situation change since then.
a) Is your job better than before?
        1 better   2 as good as before   3 worse
        0 do not know   X no answer
b) Is your family life better than before?
        1 better   2 as good as before   3 worse
        0 do not know   X no answer
c) Do you have more time for yourself than before?
        1 more   2 as much as before   3 less
        0 do not know   X no answer
d) Is the work of the church better than before?
        1 better   2 as good as before   3 worse
        0 do not know   X no answer
e) Is the condition of the environment today
        1 better   2 as good as before   3 worse
        0 do not know   X no answer
f) Is your current income
        1 higher   2 as high as before   3 lower
        0 do not know   X no answer
g) Is the way the country is governed today
        1 better   2 as good as before   3 worse
        0 do not know   X no answer
h) Generally speaking is the situation in Hungary today
        1 better   2 unchanged   3 worse
        0 do not know   X no answer

i) Is the ability to plan the number of children now

1 increased	2 unchanged	3 decreased
0 do not know	X no answer	

j) Generally speaking is your life now

1 better	2 as good as before	3 worse
0 do not know	X no answer	

k) Generally speaking is your life now

1 very happy	2 happy	3 fairly happy
4 not too happy		
0 do not know	X no answer	

l) Generally speaking was your life eight years ago

1 very happy	2 happy	3 fairly happy
4 not too happy		
0 do not know	X no answer	

m) In 5 years do you think you will be

1 very happy	2 happy	3 fairly happy
4 not too happy		
0 do not know	X no answer	

65. Now I would like to talk with you about some intimate issues which influence the lives of women.

a) How many times were you pregnant?...............................

b) How many times did you give birth?...............................

c) Are you doing anything to prevent pregnancy?

1 yes	2 no	0 do not know	X no answer

d) If not, do you plan to do anything to control the number of children?

1 yes	2 no	0 do not know	X no answer

e) Is your husband taking any steps to prevent pregnancy?

1 yes	2 no	0 do not know	X no answer

f) Do you want to have more children?

1 yes	2 no	0 do not know	X no answer

g) How many children would you like to have if you could choose freely?........................

i) In your view compared to the period before the political change women's ability to control the number of children

1 increased	2 remained unchanged	3 decreased
0 do not know	X no answer	

j) Compared to the period before the political change, is family planning today

1 increased	2 remained unchanged	3 decreased
0 do not know	X no answer	

k) There has been a lot of discussion about abortion recently. In your opinion:

1 it should be permitted to anyone whenever desired

2 it should be permitted to anyone whenever desired, but after consulting a doctor

3 it should only be permitted when the life/health of the mother or the child is in danger

4 it should be prohibited under all circumstances

0 do not know

X no answer

FINALLY I WOULD LIKE TO ASK YOU ABOUT YOUR HUSBAND

66. Does your husband have a job?   1 yes   2 no

67. What is his employment category?
1   full time worker, not in own enterprise
2   work in own enterprise
3   retired
4   disabled retired
5   unemployed (registered)
6   unemployed (not registered)
7   maternity aid
8   househusband
9   student
10   other (what does he do?)...
11   makes no sense
0   do not know
X   no answer

68. Did your husband vote at the parliamentary elections?
1 yes 2 no   0 do not know   X no answer
69. Does your husband go to church?
1 regularly   3 occasionally   4 not at all
0 do not know   X no answer
70. Was your husband born in the town/village you live now?
1 yes 2 no
71. If not, where was he born?

72. How many household members have moved out of the household since the political change?

relation to the head of the household	sex	age	to where	when

FOR THE INTERVIEWER

	poor						affluent
neighborhood evaluation	1	2	3	4	5	6	7
housing evaluation	1	2	3	4	5	6	7

NOTES

1. This research constitutes the first part of our large study on the quality of life of Polish women during post-communist period. We gratefully acknowledge the support of the IREX Foundation, the Polish Committee of Sciences, and a Cornell University Innovative Research Grant, which provided the funds for the preliminary data collection in 1995 and survey studies in 1999. We gratefully acknowledge Krzysztof Podemski's help in preparation of the interviews questionnaire and his advice on the preliminary stages of this research.

2. For each of these domains the respondent was asked for her current degree of satisfaction, and for satisfaction prior to the political changes a decade ago. A scale of seven points from extreme satisfaction to dissatisfaction was used.

3. The question was, "How would you rate your environment, I mean air quality, the quality of drinking water, etc.?"

REFERENCES

Andrews, Frank & Ronald Inglehard. 1979. The Structure of Well-Being in Nine Western Countries. *Social Indicators Research, 6,* 73-90.

Andrews, Frank & Aubrey McKennell. 1980. Measures of Self-Reported Well-Being: Their Affective, Cognitive, and Other Components. *Social Indicators Research, 8,* 127-155.

Andrews, Frank & John Robinson, 1991. Measures of Well-Being. In J. Robinson, P. Shaver & L. Wrighstman, *Measures of Personality and Social Psychological Attitudes* (pp. 1-115). San Diego, CA: Academic Press.

Andrews, Frank & Stephen Withey. 1976. *Social Indicators of Well-Being. Americans' Perception of Life Quality.* New York: Plenum Press.

Brown, J. F. 1992. The East European Agenda. In I. J. Lederer (Ed.). *Western Approaches to Eastern Europe.* New York: Council on Foreign Relations Press.

Campbell, Angus, Phillip Converse & Williard Rogers. 1976. *The Quality of American Life.* New York: Russell Sage Foundation.

Campbell, Angus, 1981. *The Sense of Well-being in America. Recent Patterns and Trends.* New York: McGraw Hill.

Cantril, Hadley, 1965. *The Pattern of Human Concern.* New Brunswick, NJ: Rutgers University Press.

Czapinski, Janusz, 1994. Uziemnienie Duszy Polskiej. *Kultura i Spoleczenstwo [Culture and Society], 1,* 19-37.

Dahl, Robert. 1971. *Polyarchy: Participation and Opposition.* New Haven: Yale University.

Dabrowski, Marek & Rafal Antczak (Eds.). 1996. *Ukrainska Droga do Gospodarki Rynkowej 1991-1995. [Ukrainian Road Toward Market Economy].* Warszawa: Wydawnictwo Naukowe, PWN.

DeSoto, Hermine & David Anderson. 1993. *The Curtain Rises.* Atlantic Highlands, NJ: Humanities Press.

Funk, Nanette. 1996. Patriarchal Morality Versus Democracy: The 1993 German Constitutional Court Decision on Abortion. In: B. Wejnert & M. Spencer, *Women in Post-Communism.* Greenwich, CT: JAI Press.

Funk, Nanette & Magda Mueller. 1993. *Gender Politics and Post-Communism.* New York: Routledge Press.

Gallup, George H. 1976. Human Needs and Satisfactions: A Global Survey. *Public Opinion Quarterly, 40,* 459-467.

Glowny Urzad Statystyczny (GUS). 1993. *Rocznik Statystyczny [Statistical Annual].* Warsaw: GUS.

Glowny Urzad Statystyczny (GUS). 1994. *Rocznik Statystyczny Wojewodztw [Annual Statistics of Regional].* Warsaw: GUS.

Glowny Urzad Statystyczny (GUS). 1995. *Rocznik Statystyczny [StatisticalAnnual].* Warsaw: Glowny Urzad Statystyczny.

Haavio-Mannila, Elina. 1992. *Work, Family and Well-Being in Five North and East European Capitals.* Helsinki: Suomalainen Tiedeakatemia.

Held, David. 1990. *Models of Democracy.* Palo Alto, CA: Stanford University Press.

International Labor Office (ILO). 1985. *Working Women in Socialist Countries: The Fertility Connection*. Geneva: ILO.

Issraelyan, Yevgenia. 1996. Russian Women: Challenges of the Modern World. In B. Wejnert & M. Spencer, *Women in Post-Communism*. Greenwich, CT: JAI Press.

Lissyutkina, Larissa. 1993. Soviet Women at the Crossroad of Perestroika. In N. Funk & M. Mueller, *Gender Politics and Post-Communism*. New York: Routledge.

Reboud, Michelle & Hoaquan Chu. 1997. *Pension Reforms and Growth in Ukraine: An Analysis Focusing on Labor Market Constraints*. Washington, D. C.: World Bank.

Sandel, J. Michael. 1996. *Democracy's Discontent*. Cambridge, MA: Harvard University Press.

Spencer, Metta. 1996. Post-Communist Patriarchy. In B. Wejnert & M. Spencer, *Women in Post-Communism*. Greenwich, CT: JAI Press

Stephenson, Patricia (Ed.). 1998. *Improving Women's Health Services in the Russian Federation: Results of a Pilot Project*. Washington, D.C.: World Bank.

Titkov, Anna. 1993. Poland: Let,s Pull Down the Bastilles Before They Are Built. In R. Morgan (Ed.). *Sisterhood is Global*, New York: Doubleday.

Tyszka, Zbigniew. 1970. *Przeobrazenia Rodziny Robotniczej w Warunkach Uprzemyslowienia i Urbanizacji.*[Changes in Workers Families During Urbanization and Industrialization Period]. Warsaw: PWN.

Veenhaven, R. 1996. Happy Life-Expectancy: A Comprehensive Measure of Quality-of-Life in Nations. *Social Indicators Research, 39*, 1-58.

Veenhaven, R. & J. Ehrhardt. 1995. The Cross-National Pattern of Happiness: Test of Predictions Implied in Three Theories of Happiness. *Social Indicators Research, 34*, 33-68.

United Nations. 1991. *The World of Women 1970-1990: Trends and Statistics*. New York: United Nations.

Wejnert, Barbara, 1996a. Political Transition and Gender Transformation in the Communist and Post-Communist Periods. In B. Wejnert & M. Spencer, *Women in Post-Communism* (pp. 3-19). Greenwich, CT: JAI Press.

_____. 1996b. The Dynamics of Societal Macro-Changes: Implications for the Life of Women. In B. Wejnert & M. Spencer, *Women in Post-Communism* (pp. xii-xvii). Greenwich, CT: JAI Press.

_____. 1996c. The Quality of Life in Post-Communist Poland: A Gender Perspective. In B. Wejnert & M. Spencer, *Women in Post-Communism* (pp. 169-184). Greenwich, CT: JAI Press

Wejnert, Barbara & Metta Spencer (Eds.). 1996. *Women in Post-Communism*. Greenwich, CT: JAI Press.

Wojewodzki Urzad Statystyczny (WUS). 1993. Rocznik Statystyczny Wojewodztwo Koninskiego [Statistical Annual of Konin Region]. Konin: WUS.

World Bank. 1994. *World Development Report 1994*. Oxford, UK: Oxford University Press.

V

Impact on Culture

12

Cultural and Civic Movements Prefiguring the Breakdown of the Socialist Regime in Yugoslavia

Stjepan Gredelj

The bicentenary of the French Revolution was followed by the domino effect of the breakdowns of the Communist regimes in Central and Eastern Europe (C/E Europe). A wave of triumph splashed the minds of the ordinary people and the temples of "Sovietology" and similar scientific disciplines involved in the analysis of the communist systems and regimes.

The removal of the Iron Curtain, symbolically expressed by pulling down the Berlin Wall, suddenly opened a clear opportunity for ordinary people to fulfill their dreams of relief from pressure and fear, prosperity, personal and social progress, and the opening of many possibilities. Numerous scholars, no matter how deeply aware of the complexity of these societies, also fell into the trap of optimistic wishful thinking. Only a few were somewhat reluctant to predict a one-way direction toward the political and economical modernization of C/E Europe.

The former Yugoslavia made the very best example of such delusions. Namely, the most prevailing optimistic prediction was that Yugoslavia, which seemed to differ from the majority of other C/E European countries,[1] had significant advantages to painlessly bridge the transitional gap and carry out rapid post-communist modernization. These predictions were not based so much on the wrong arguments as they were put forward too globally (Table 12.1).

POST-COMMUNISM AND THE CASE OF YUGOSLAVIA: SELF-DENIED PROPHECY

As Susan Woodward in her book entitled *The Balkan Tragedy* wrote: "On the eve of 1989 revolutions in eastern and central Europe, Yugoslavia was better poised to make a successful transition to a market economy and to the West than any other socialist country" (Woodward 1995: 1). Numerous analysts of transition grounded their optimistic estimations for the Yugoslav transformation on a number of significant advantages former Yugoslavia had had when compared to other countries of Eastern and Central Europe.

Table 12.1
GDP per capita—Federal Republic of Yugoslavia and East-Central European Countries in Transition

	1989		1994	
	$US	%	$US	%
FR of Yugoslavia	2.920	100.0	1100*	100.0
Czechoslovakia	3.450	135.8	-	-
Czech Republic	-	-	3.200	290.9
Slovakia	-	-	2.250	204.5
Hungary	2.590	88.7	3.840	349.0
Bulgaria	2.320	91.3	1.250	113.6
Poland	1.790	70.4	2.410	219.0
Romania	-	-	1.270	115.4
Albania	-	-	380	34.5

Source: The World Bank 1991, 1994. Federal Statistic Office of Yugoslavia , 1994.

Those well-meant prognoses failed and Yugoslavia disintegrated in a bloody nightmare of the mutual massacre of its citizens, instead of entering the transition painlessly. The unexpected outcome does not reveal so much the incorrectness of these prognoses as the need to examine the smoldering mechanism, which turned latent under the circumstances, and transformed the minority structures into the dominant disintegrating forces.

The advantages of Yugoslavia primarily reflected on certain structural shifts historically built-in, which made the Yugoslav system a softer type of totalitarianism. Although, there was not much harm done to the formal network of the totalitarian power, the system managed to postpone the threat of severe social conflicts and commotion, reducing its own aspirations to the total control.

The first stage of this reduction lay in permitting the co-existence of private property, not only in otherwise very important segments of socialist economy (such as agriculture), but also in some service activities and production (however small-scale and fiscally controlled they may have been). This resulted in the creating of a market, albeit a limited one, and certain freedom of economic agents who sought to widen the boundaries of that freedom by initiating numerous, mostly ill-fated economic reforms.

The second stage was a partial and, in time, increasingly important decentralization of political and economic decisionmaking, which, following the introduction of self-management, favored the sprouting germs of economic and therefore, political liberalization. The third and most important level of reduction was the inauguration of the *ideology of self-management*, as a shift from rigid communist universalism or its more moderate variant.

Finally, the fourth level and often compared advantage was the idea of the Yugoslav melting-pot, based on the affective-value role of "brotherhood and unity" as a patriotic value pattern. Despite the semblance of a successful lobotomy which erased the historical memory of the brutal ethnic, religious and civil clashes during World War II, this idea survived the collapse of the Communist and self-management model only in the short run. Indeed, this fell apart when the *supra-institutional dome* embodied in the (late) leader, Josip Broz Tito, disappeared from the historical scene.

This new ideology of self-management, even in its rudimentary form, flirted with other universalistic ideas, primarily those of individual rights and social participation (although of producers rather than citizens!). Self-management as a model of state organization was never truly functional, either on the micro or especially on the macro level.[2] Self-management on the micro level first served to contain the industrial conflict in a class conflict of the class-divided society— (through the feigned, ritual participation of workers), and preserve its interest and political articulation (through the so-called trade-unions). Moreover, the farce of the micro-self-management formed a conservative coalition between the ruling oligarchies and, primarily, manual workers corrupted by excessive consumption (granted on behalf of foreign petrodollar loans during the seventies).

On the macro level, the legal-state farce was institutionalized by proclaiming self-management a state-grounding principle and Utopian attempt to turn the state into a self-management community. Deprofessionalization and loosening of the elementary administrative functions of the common state reduced them to the agreement negotiations (i.e., quarreling, haggling and mutual blackmailing in the oligarchy top ranks). This actually weakened the already fragile foundations of the federal state on behalf of the fluid (unlimited) meta-political/power monopoly of sects (cliques, castes, whatsoever) at the top of the multiplied one-party hierarchical pyramids.

Tito had allowed the obedient majority a certain increase in the standard of living and consumption (higher then anywhere in Eastern Europe), travelling discounts, and narrowed freedom of self-expression. In exchange, he got social peace and the consent to his permanent rule. The most important article of this social contract was a tacit *conservative coalition* between the regime and the broadest working class strata. The latter were awarded with ever-increasing income and benefits for their less and less productive contribution to the society. The immediate costs of this were covered by the foreign loans that piled up and became the main source of both investment and consumption during the 1970s. These long-term expenses came due for payment later, not only because of the dubious foreign currency debt (about US $20 billion) but also because of the total dependence on the investments in further development supported by (expensive) short-term foreign loans. But that was the inevitable baggage of Tito's authoritarianism behind the human face and velvet gloves instead of boxing ones. Unfortunately, he left this heritage to his less skilled successors after his death.

These crucial points explain why the stability of Tito's regime was not seriously challenged during his long-term rule (43 years) and why he easily and rather softly managed to foil the rare and weak attempts toward resistance without the excessive use of violence. (The same applies even to one of the most open rebellions during his rule—the 1968 Students' Movement—which had the same ideological background as the self-management. The students only appealed for the regime's turnover but not for its change. Yugoslavia's relatively peaceful existence was unusual in the Soviet bloc, both in the field of industrial conflict (such as Solidarity movement in Poland), and serious anti-systemic political demands (such as the Charter '77 in Czechoslovakia). Massive resistance to the regime never occured in Tito's Yugoslavia. Even a consistent and strong cultural movement which could gradually build a parallel society did not appear in Yugoslavia, as was the case with the underground *Samizdat* literature and culture in the USSR, Poland, Czechoslovakia and Hungary. Finally, Yugoslavia was neither affected by massive post-war economic and intellectual emigration of people who had not been discredited by previous, open or tacit, collaboration with Nazits, nor were a number of its most outstanding dissidents forced out of a universities and sent to filling-stations (as, for example, Karel Kosik), or forced into the internal exile (as this was the case with Andrew Sacharov).

Up to the mid-1960s, Yugoslavia had been reaching very high rates of economic growth, especially in industry and trade (Table 12.2). However, this proved to be a disbalanced development strategy, which, at the same time, kept exhausting the natural resources (both row materials and human assets) and failed to achieve the balanced development of all the regions in the country (Table 12. 3).

Table 12.2
Average Annual GDP Growth in (former) SFR of Yugoslavia

Period	Total economy	Industry and mining	Agriculture and fishing	Trade
1953-1956	6.6	11.3	6.6	7.3
1957-1960	11.3	14.1	9.2	14.0
1961-1965	6.8	10.9	- 0.1	10.1
1966-1970	5.8	5.4	3.1	8.0
1971-1975	5.9	7.9	3.2	6.1
1976-1980	5.6	6.8	2.4	5.2
1981-1988	0.5	2.2	0.7	- 1.8
Total 1953-1988	5.4	7.5	3.1	5.9

Source: Statistical Yearbook, Federal Statistical Office of Yugoslavia, 1990 –reduced table.

Table 12.3
Regional (Republic) Developmental Differences

Country	Income per capita in $US		Relative level	Yugoslavia= 100
	1950	1986	1950	1986
Yugoslavia	469	2,300	100.0	100.0
Serbia	407	2,075	86.8	90.2
Croatia	532	2,873	113.4	124.9
Slovenia	820	4,664	174.8	202.8
Voyvodina	387	2,714	82.5	118.0
Serbia proper	450	2,291	96.0	99.6

Source: Statistical Yearbook, Federal Statistical Office, 1990 –reduced table

The 1970s ended with the series of external shocks. An economic crisis originating from the foreign trade deficit balance could no longer be averted by minor adjustments, and society started to seek fundamental reforms. Instead, unemployment and impoverishment started to sharply intensify. In 1979, the total unemployment growth rate was below 14 percent and, in 1988, it rose up to nearly 17 percent At the same time, by the end of 1984, the average income amounted to approximately 70 percent of the bare life necessities for a family of four. The population living below the poverty line showed an increase from 17 to 25 percent. Above all, the annual economic growth had dropped to the lowest rate ever recorded after the World War II (in the period of 1981-1988 it was only 0.5 percent). During the 1980s, the former newly industrialized and promising Yugoslavia was again turned into stagnant and underdeveloped country with a politically unstable society and peripheral economy (Schierup 1991). But this shift was ideologically rationalized through the discourse of nationalist rhetoric aimed at preserving the leading positions of a weakened (Communist) nomenclature in all the federal units which made it possible to deliver the bill of its devastating policy to the neighbors' door. Despite the official rhetoric on national inequality, the primary social divisions and inequalities in Yugoslav societies were not defined by ethnicity but by job status and mounting unemployment. In terms of how people saw themselves, ethnicity was less important than an occupation, social status, or a place of residence (urban or rural) along with the corresponding culture.[3]

Most of the energy generated from rising social conflicts poured into the ideologically lower and prima-rily cultural sectors of the superstructure. These sectors were gradually (or deliberately?) left to the bards of the national(istic) intelligentsia. This added one more detrimental effect to the social structure: crushed and nondifferentiated as it had been, the deficiency in social structuring and stratification was offset by the primordial (ethnic) homogenization.

For a decade or more, the opposite minor cultural and civic movements, devoted to the ideas of establishment and development of a civil society and modern citizenry, somehow managed to exist behind the shadow of this major nationalist stream in the collective mind (i. e., social consciousness) in Yugoslavia, regardless of their marginality and eventual defeat by the main stream. In the beginning of the 1990s, these initiatives failed but they deserve to be recognized as having offered a different answer to the solution of the society crisis.

SOCIALIST COUNTER-CULTURE

Science and Ideology: Converging or Diverging?

As in other socialist countries, the initial questioning of Yugoslav social conditions started in the most autonomous social subsystem, the cultural sphere— in the broadest sense of the word. The first criticism came from the least reliable companion of any regime, the intelligentsia. Their experiences in Yugoslavia were most similar to other socialist experiences throughout the world, as well as specific to Yugoslavia itself, arising from the distinctive characteristics of the Yugoslav road to socialism.

During the 1950s and 1960s the intelligentsia in Yugoslavia played an important role in providing legitimacy for the regime, wittingly or otherwise. That was the case not only with the technical intelligentsia (which by the very nature of its social position and role readily fits into the system) and the party intelligentsia (which is loyal by its nature), but also the creative intellectuals in the social sciences who did not seriously endanger the dominant ideological project of self-management, while occasionally displaying a somewhat critical attitude towards the proponents of power. The creative intellectuals were deeply imbued with the same monistic Marxism as the ruling elite was. However, the intellectuals did claim (and rightfully so) a deeper knowledge of the multiple meaning of Marxism, considering its official interpretation a reductionistic one. The *sanctification of self-management* was the key feature of the intellectual climate of that time. In their narcissistic enchantment by this epochal innovation in the Marxist theory, intellectuals were really convinced that self-management offered a concrete Utopia, that is, the global emancipation of the mankind.

Even so, in the 1960s, the critical intellectuals were the first to challenge not the concept of self-management as such, but rather its practical implementation. With mounting unemployment, a decline in standard of living, and growing dissatisfaction of the population, the faith of the intellectuals was shaken. They began to recognize the ideological manipulation of self-management by the regime's elite. This consciousness-raising, coupled with growing manifestations of social problems, was the source of the first open social conflict in the post-war Yugoslav society (the intellectuals' and students' rebellion in June 1968). The students' demands were not directed against the system; they only asked for the *rectification of deviations from the generally correct course of development.* However, the movement was judged as so antithetical to the regime, that no scientific study of it could published, even fifteen years after.[4] The movement obtained insignificant and mostly symbolic and sporadic support from other social strata, including from workers whose historical rather than empirical interests the students sought to promote. Being isolated from a wider social support, and, most of all, politically naive, the student movement was pacified at first, and then suppressed by the regime, which selectively repressed prominent individual students and intellectuals. The disintegration of the student movement did not entirely eradi-cate its spirit. Indeed, its very occurrence showed that the decades of social peace had gone and that the Yugoslav community entered an unstable period of social conflicts. In addition, the fate of the students' and youth movement was clear proof that under existing circumstances any autonomous civilian arrangement had no chance of success, including even one which invoked the official ideology of self-management, unless it deve-loped separately from that ideology and the existing power structure.

Awareness of the necessity for challenging the government increased together with each subsequent effort to forcibly pacify the internal relations. A kind of vicious circle was formed. A growing resistance to the regime provoked its increasingly nervous and repressive reactions which, in turn, precipitated the *functional* differentiation of critics who had been homogenous until then. The regime reacted harshly, finding it increasingly complicated to control such a dispersed network of parallel and relatively autonomous anti-regime activities.

In the early 1970s, a classical state-party *coup d'etat was* carried out, especially targeting three groups: the advancing counter-elites, the reformist liberals within the party, and the remnants of the youth and students' movements.

One of these dangerous counter-elites was the so-called technocracy, which increasingly demanded economy modernization on market principles and the limitation of the Party's control over the economy, in favor of an expanded role in decisionmaking by skilled economic experts. The second counter-elite was the huma-nistic intelligentsia, whose hair splitting and boring nagging often disturbed the complacent conviction of the ruling elite that it had created the best of all possible worlds.

In "reward" for their ingratitude, the regime presented both counter-elites with the gifts they hardly wanted to receive. The significance of the technocrats was diminished and thousands of economic managers were replaced by less capable but more loyal experts. The humanistic intelligentsia (the so-called new leftists) found its wings clipped by the abolition of universities' autonomy and the abridgement of the academic freedom. Some university professors and their assistants were dismissed and prosecuted. The loyal intelligentsia launched a repressive cultural policy against the critical groups that threatened its own selfish interests. Actually, it is unlikely the repression would have reached anywhere near the proportions it assumed had it not been for that echelon acting as the executor of the punitive policy.

Punishments imposed on the "ungrateful" youth varied in their sophistication, but were all painful and far reaching. They were directed against present and future generations of youth. Students' organizations lost their autonomy and the rebellious student leaders were denied employment or even indicted and sentenced to prison for such offenses as "anarcho-liberalism" or "Trotskyism." Future generations were punished in advance by the Party's decision on education reform, passed solely for the purpose of producing semi-educated specialists in only one line of business, who could easily be blackmailed, prevented from changing their specialist vocation, and thereby silenced for good.

The effects of the coup penetrated all spheres of social life, with the main intention of restoring the Party's leading role. All other fields of culture took on an ideological coloring, while self-management Marxism was promoted as the only acceptable world view. Finally, the regime, incapable of turning its conspira-torial perception of social conflicts into a rational resolution of the conflict, developed a collective paranoia by multiplying the alleged "enemies of the people". Previously expressed as a soft form of Stalinism, Titoism now struck out against the autonomy of society. Although this produced some momentary stabilizing effects, it also had some unexpected consequences that were disturbing for the regime. This caused the political maturation of the critical intelligentsia and fostered a diversification and pluralization of the parallel social institutions. The critical intelligentsia gradually adopted a wide spectrum of resistance to the regime and especially its crude methods of repression and manipulation. All ideological restrictions of free artistic expression were attacked by the counter-cultural reactions in art. The autonomy of the university and academic freedom were also revoked, and this provoked responses such as: the reaffirmation of professional academic responsibility through the revival of professional associations, scientific and cultural journals, academic gatherings, publications, and even the setting up of a so called *parallel university* not under the control of the communist government. Part of the critical intelligentsia moved toward permanent political and civil disobedience. They objected to the incrimination of expression of opinion as an offence, the limitation of freedom of speech and expression, and the restriction of civil rights and personal freedoms. Thus, a powerful petition campaign started, which become the core of the future movement for the protection of human rights and liberties. During the 1980s such activities grew into a public force aiming to end the one-party monopoly in the political and social sphere. Requests for the introduction of political pluralism as a necessary precondition for democracy grew stronger. In contrast, the youth and students' movements of the 1960s had produced a classical anti-movement with a nationalist, chauvinist program, *The Movement of the Croatian Universitarians*. By doing this, the regime opened a Pandora's box and let one of its evil but legitimate children— nationalism—out into the public social stage, rejecting the requests for modernization and democratization. The anti-movement was pushed aside (but not definitely crushed) and it had a consequential influence on the social consciousness in the later events in Yugoslavia.

Most of the other movements by students and intellectuals were the legitimate heirs to their predecessors of the sixties. The most outstanding were the counter-cultural movements in painting, theater, literature and, especially, the film industry; youth subcultures in music; the youth and student media, which had a significant role in challenging the entire official public; and alternative lifestyle groups (punks, squatters, communes, feminists and homosexuals, new spiritualists, and other groups). These forms of opposition were nonviolent and often nonpolitical, but they decisively fought against the ruling values and norms of the regime during the 1970s, gradually forming the initial core of alternative movements in the 1980s. They emerged, disappeared, intertwined and supported each other. At first, they appeared spontaneously as a means of protecting the freedom and dignity of individuals from selective repression by the state, and then steadily developed into effective advocates of an autonomous civil society.

Unlike the expectations and intended goals of the *coup d'etat* designers, Yugoslav more repressive times did not bring about a massive withdrawal into social autism and internal emigration (from political life) during 1970s. Regardless of that partially achieved effect for the first year or two. Just the opposite, after the first shock among the "criticists," new capacities for alternatives were gradually revived. (Of course, while speaking of criticists, I do not have in mind the same persons placed in new conditions, but rather widely spreading and recognizable rejection attitudes by new persons which inclined them towards deeply controlled and significant subsystems such as journalism.

Due to the limited volume of this paper one cannot extensively present each form of the resistance. I shall highlight only the most authentic and less frequently reflected ones, and thus, maybe, the less familiar.

Artistic Dilemmas and Criticism of the Past

Once the emancipating attempts in the meta-cultural sphere had been crushed, the *anti-cultural* conflict focus shifted onto everyday cultural life. The everlasting dispute between art and revo-lution, that is, the criticism of recent history presented in the works of art, served as a pretext for the conflict. Opposing views appeared concerning the limits of artistic expression and led to controversies over the "Black Wave" in art. Officially, this period lasted about five years, but its consequences stretched into the early 1980s. This undesirable label—the Black Wave—initially referred to the basic tone of discussions on painting of that time. However, it is primarily remembered as an official evaluation of surely the most important period of development in Yugoslav cinematography, between 1960 and 1970. The Black Wave began with *Rani radovi (Early Works)*, a film directed by Zelimir Zilnik. The film was invited to represent Yugoslav cinematography at the Berlin Film Festival. However, on the request of the District Public Prosecutor in Belgrade, it was temporarily banned for public screening on the grounds of its negative portrayal of the political and social attitudes and achievements of Yugoslav communism. The indictment did not evaluate the aesthetic or artistic value of the film. The District Court in Belgrade passed an exonerating judgment explaining that although the film was obsessed by obscure circumstances, social misery and apathy, and could be used for ill-meant purposes, the public was mature enough to critically evaluate an artistic creation, and therefore, this particular film. The fact that films like at one are made and shown, reflects the strength of that society.

With this acquittal, Zilnik went to Berlin only to be given the Golden Bear, the top award of the film festival, for being provocatively sharp in confronting ideology with reality. The reactions were quite different at home. The local public was quite immune to the film and demonstrated their attitude by leaving the cinema theatres in the middle of the film's screenings. Early Works was a prologue to further analyses carried out in Yugoslav films, which became a trend defined as the Black Wave. In the first round of social criticism to Black Wave films, negative attention was drawn to the film *Zaseda (The Ambush)* by Zivojin Pavlovic, *Vrane (The Craws)* by Mihiz and Kozomara, and *Uzrok smrti ne pominjati (The Cause of Death is Not to Be Mentioned)* by Jovan Zivanovic.

The second round of ciritcism lasted until 1973 and included a larger number of films made by the most prominent directors in Yugoslav cinematography. To mention a few: *Lisice (The Foxes)* and *Predstava Hamleta u Mrdusi Donjoj (Playing Hamlet in the Village of Mrdusa Donja)* by Krsto Papic; *Uloga moje porodice u svetskoj revoluciji (The Role of My Family in the World Revolution)* by Bata Cengic; *The Maestro and Margaret,* by Aleksandar Popovic and the three films (*Dvojnik [The Double], Budjenje pacova [The Awakening of Rats]* and *Crveno klasje [The Red Ears of Wheat]* by Zivojin Pavlovic whose films also were included in this group. The third method of criticism and repression was demonstrated through the stirring up of audiences against a film that was synonymous to the Black Wave: *WR—Mysteries of Organism* by Dusan Makavejev. Citizens, who wanted to stay anonymous in their complaints, objected with rage, claiming that the director insulted the memory of Joseph Vissarionovich Stalin. Provoked by the anti-totalitarian and especially anti-Stalinist message of the film, the audience readily identified Stalinism with the socialist revolution in the Soviet Union. The Moscow journal, *Literaturnaya Gazeta (The Literary Gazette)*, made the case completely bizarre (as reported by the Yugoslav official news agency Tanjug) by condemning Makavejev's film, as well as the entire situation in Yugoslav cinematography, and, among other things, blaming the director for the hatred toward Communist ethics. The District Attorney, who denied the film a censor's card and thereby prevented it from participating in the national Pula Film Festival in 1971, sealed its fate.

The last act of the Black Wave drama took the form of shelving an incomplete film by Zelimir Zilnik, entitled *Freedom or Strip.* This had drastic consequences for Zilnik's Belgrade Academy for Theater, Film, Radio and Television tutor, the director Zivojin Pavlovic, who was proclaimed morally and politically unfit and expelled as a lecturer from the Academy. In 1973, director Lazar Stojanovic was sentenced to three years in prison for his graduation project, a film entitled *The Plastic Jesus* (which was never screened publicly before 1994). Eventually, directors Zilnik, Makavejev and Petrovic went abroad and numerous film artists discontinued their creative work for years. Yugoslav cinematography was overflown by the so-called "White Wave," which did not represent a return to the innocence of the revolutionary poetics, but instead, in most cases, to worthless films ranging from war and Western-type films to epic films such as *The Neretva River* and *The Sutjeska River,* which were the mythologized interpretations of the communist resistance during the Second World War.

Culture Withdraws to the Margins: Perseverance of Subcultural Challenges

The youth subcultures most successfully tested the White Wave that was splashing against the shore of culture. These were marginal groups far from the traditional movement. This enabled them to avoid the dominant cinematographic current. Their plurality and multimedial approach enabled them to shift from one sector to another, which ensured their vitality. During the 1970s, youth subcultures helped revive the badly damaged elite culture. Youth subcultures opened an underground communication channel for elite artists when all other channels were blocked. These subcultures were also the sources of new, fresh ideas.

The most important were the rock culture and its subspecie—the punk. There were also artistic subcultural groups, alternative lifestyle groups, and finally, youth journalism, which acted as a communicational network between other subcultural groups.

Rock culture was the mass, global culture of youth, which penetrated Yugoslav society by the end of the 1950s, gradually dimming the influence of jazz, the only music culture officially recognized. Communication possibilities were limited and thus, the reception of rock culture was chaotic. The first rock fans were mostly students, but rock music attracted even younger and less educated followers over the next decade. The rise in the standard of living introduced symbolic products into everyday life, such as jeans, plastic raincoats, soft-soled slippers, tights, checked shirts and pointed shoes. Relevant values and meanings were also imported, producing authentic subcultural effects. However, the different look, lifestyle and demeanor of the youth were often regarded as scandalous, prompting the resistance of traditionalists as well as their condemnation and even repression, ranging from insults and public humiliations (e.g., forcible hair-cutting) to physical assaults and expulsion from schools. In contrast, to the combative, deeply ingrained mentality was the appearance of hippies during the late sixties, whose counter-culture brought the exotic aroma of the East and a philosophy of peace, which was especially irritating for a society imbued with patriarchal and epically belligerent traditions. Unexpectedly, the resistance only strengthened the symbolic importance of music for the separation rituals of youth. Their music became a major source of satisfaction and identity.

By the early 1970s, the domestic rock-stage had already been formed. Korni-grupa, Time and a super-band of changeable ensemble members, called September, dominated it. That was also the period of complete liberalization of consumers' rock' n' roll. The legendary Radio Luxembourg ceased to be the single source of information on the latest hits and trends in rock music of the West. As the market opened up for the import of entertainment products and equipment, the suppression of rock was abandoned. The state made its own calculation that these products paid off, at least from the sales tax on music equipment and records. In the mid-1970s most of the current trends were mastered—hard rock, acoustic music, heavy metal, reggae and hard-core. In this breakthrough, the characteristic style of the Sarajevo rock school soon became dominant with the first really domestic cult-band Bjelo dugme (The White Button) as its trademark. This music met the needs of the first generation born and raised in an urban environment where newly composed folk music dominated, and yet presented an attempt to appeal to the satisfaction of their parents.

The White Button band did not imitate the image and behavior of foreign bands. The band was supported by domestic record companies and entertainment industry, which finally realized that rock' n' roll could be a good and profitable business even in socialism. Furthermore, the Buttons easily fitted into the imposed stereotype of the mischievous but essentially good and cheerful youngsters who conveyed the message you can count on us.

Having been ideologically fit (the leader of the band, Goran Bregovic, was a member of the Party and took part in several voluntary youth labor campaigns), The White Button became a success with its emphasis on genuine Yugoslav patriotism which was still recognized as an official value. Ideological criticism against the rock culture rarely came from the Party or state officials, but more often from the cultural sphere run on the princi-ples of self-management, especially from leaders of the official youth organization, the Socialist Youth League (SSO). This artificial organization, created as an ideological counterpart to the dispersed rebellious youth and students' organizations, no longer had the image of the war and post-war Yugoslav Communist Youth League (SKOJ). The SSO was only a pigeon hole for the dissemination of ruling political values to the youngsters, but it still occasionally tried to pass judgments on issues which were considered to be within its competence. Such arbitration granted or denied the individual styles of rock' n' roll the right to exist. Thus, the artificial pink mist covering the White Button fans (and other performers of the suitable, soft rock and pop music) with veils of ignorance, for a time concealed several new streams in domestic rock. These streams emerged in the late 1970s in the form of punk music and the New Wave, as a rockers' response to the social crisis.

Silent (Symbolic) Resistance: Punk and the New Wave

The appearance of punk was marked by the urban protest of previously happy robots of socialism, who were dumbfounded by the sudden deprivations during the 1980s. Excessive consumption had created needs which, as a result of discovery of the external financial liabilities of the country, would not be satisfied for a long time to come. Schools for vocational education started to send the disoriented gene-rations of the reserve labor army straight into the streets. Former social deals began to crumble, along with the foundations of ideology of permanent economic growth and progressive social development. All values had to be reassessed in the view of the new circumstances of the crisis. This new predicament called for different ways of musical expression, artistic perception and a conscious feeling of the crisis within a segment of the youth population, along with its iconography—unemployment, lack of perspective, discrepancy between public promises and deeds, dissatisfaction and revolt.

The appearance of punk in the former Yugoslavia coincides with that in its homeland, Great Britain. Within a year, the punk scene was made official since the first performance of the Pankrti (Bastards) band. It was the first time that a new music style had reached Yugoslavia without the already proverbial historical distance. The new bands, which were mushrooming everywhere, were a direct part of the new trend and its creation. In Yugoslavia, punk started in the small creative groups of young people following a similar line of development elsewhere in the world.

A punk rocker opnely revealed his or her interests in music, books, song words, behavior and style of clothing, all of which strikingly, almost grotesquely, disclosed to society its own distorted picture. Politically, punks in Yugoslavia were neither left-nor right-oriented. They were rather close to anarchism, denying institutionalized political power. In addition to musical expression, punk was quickly transformed into the world view, dominated by nihilism. Punk pronounced a refusal of any engagement in changing the world, mostly insisting on a recognizable lifestyle. The main characteristic of this style was the subcultural division into the individual informal groups, meeting in territories specially marked by punk rockers. Thus, in addition to a few disco clubs in Ljubljana, they also created their own "Johnny Rotten Square" as an acknowledged cult meeting place. Regardless of the misgivings in their wider surroundings, the pioneers of punk in Slovenia got substantial support from students institutions such as Radio-Student, which broadcasted punk-music, and SKUC (Student Cultural Center), which produced the first single record of the Pankrti band in Ljubljana.

The second punk generation demonstrated a wider heterogeneity in style and, more importantly, started to separate from the basic ideological characteristic of a genuine substyle of noninvolvement. Sociological surveys carried out among this generation of punk rockers provided a wide range of responses which confirmed that their group identification was much more externally oriented, that is, intended to impress outside observers, while inwardly it appeared as much more democratic and did not fully limit the individuality of its fans. Thus, in Yugoslavia, punk never created illusions of being excluded or separated from everyday social life, but it represented an active response to society, at the level of a spontaneous politicization of the lifestyle. Punks open outgrowth into a specific social movement[5] through socially undesirable artistic expression, as well as the convincing and vigorous addressing of immediate and actual problems of everyday life, strongly challenged the establishment, which reacted in the usual manner (by repression).

This repression was selective and did not equally affect all subjects of the punk stage. Punk rockers of the city of Ljubljana suffered the most. This unevenness could be explained by the fact that in the cities of Belgrade and Zagreb punk did not manifest such subversive tendencies. These wider cultural surroundings had better possibilities for absorption and assimilation of the punk energy and also the ability to cushion and re-channel it into the ritual and repetitive consumption of an unusual appearance and music. In the instances where punk managed to escape ghettoization as just another fashionable style, attempting its own affirmation within an alternative social project, the response was more aggressive. The severity of repression imposed on punk in Slovenia was due to the fact that for the first time in fifty years, the society was faced that a socially critical subculture which was seriously recognized as a threat to the existing establishment.

The severity of repression was reinforced and intensified by the social crisis. From the paranoid perspective of the regime, punk became dangerous because of its two tendencies: first, it advocated and practiced the right to be different; and second, it appeared to be a growing alternative movement to the establishment with permanent meeting places where things did happen differently. Whereas the subcultural rebels of the 1950s were educated city marginals of a modest social background, and the politicized hippies of the 1960s were limited circles of students and secondary school youngsters, the punk movement encompassed and poisoned a substantial part of the elemen-tary school pupils and employed youth. Their rejection of dominant cultural values threatened to gradually grow into a powerful center of opposition. The subversive radiation had to be prevented, which is why the ferocity of the reaction had to be as intense as possible.

Persecution of punk rockers and getting even with punk fans began in the media, which staged the so-called Nazi-punk affair. During the summer of 1981, three punk rockers were arrested and accused of launching a National Socialist party of Slovenia. Almost at the same time, a few young men organized a sadistic session for their schoolmates in a part of town far away from the usual meeting place of punks. The newspapers merged the two unrelated events and provided an appropriate graphic setting—a rigged photograph of a young man in Nazi uniform and a graffito displaying PUNK. Press articles set off a time bomb which, briefly, blew the punk scene apart and revived almost forgotten models of repression.

Not only were punk rockers banished from downtown and premises frequently visited by them rearranged in an acceptable manner, but a wave of shutting down numerous discos followed, along with censorship of radio, TV programs and records, as well as the *Punk Problemi* (*Punk Problems*) magazine. These effects also included police raids, interrogation, ID inspections in restaurants, bringing young people in for "informative interrogation," raids of the private apartments and harassment of pupils at schools. Ordinary people exploded in outbursts of uncontrolled hostility and hatred toward anyone who caused suspicion by style of clothing or behavior. The hunt for the scribblers of graffiti became one of the popular entertainments of citizens. Faced with overheated social actions they could hardly comprehend, the punks withdrew from the streets into a ghetto of less conspicuous socialization and isolation.

Thus the political clash with punks achieved its short-term goal: the elimination of new-coming *Weltanschauung*. The fact that the Nazi-punk affair was a staged fabrication aroused little concern. But this onslaught also had unpredictable long-term effects, transforming dispersed punk energy into a more purified form of the *neue Slowenische kunst* (New Slovenian Art) and promoting a subcultural rejection of the established cultural values based on the parody of socialism. Furthermore, the repression fostered the development of a new youth subpolitical theory focused on the concept of civil society and the practice of alternative social movements.

The *neue Slowenische kunst* was a multimedia aesthetic project involving writers, architects, applied artists, musicians and local theater. It gathered the avant-garde group of painters called the *Irwin*, the cosmo-kinetic theater called Crveni pilot (The Red Pilot), an independent group of students of applied arts under the name of Novi kolektivizem (The New Collectivism) and a punk band called the Laibach.

The project was profoundly ironic and provocative. Its participants presented themselves as the ones searching for the roots of the Slovenian tradition and seeking the revival of the original Slovenian spirit. However, that should be taken *cum grano salis*, since the very choice of terms from the German language indicated that this reference to the long-term Slovenian dependence on Austria was rather a provocation and toying with the ethnic feelings. Still more complicated and subtle was the message conveyed by the spectacular image and performance of the Laibach band. In addition to the name of the band (the German name for Ljubljana, the Slovenian capital), there were also other elements: brown shirts and a series of other Nazi symbols (like totalitarian speeches, the project of building a new man and a new world, glorification of collectivism, demonstration of anti-individualism and verbal rejection of the decadent Western culture) that seemed to offer evidence of pro-Nazi orien-tation. However, those well acquainted with this band held that the Laibach iconography on was a delibe-rate and shocking expression of deeper messages. This provocation was intended to have a sobering effect and make the audience think. The question asked was whether the symbols and iconography were really the only elements that Nazism and Communism had in common.

In the early 1980s, a new wave in rock-pop music emerged. It was rather more dispersed than punk and covered Slovenia, Croatia and Serbia, respectively. It is hard to deny punk's distinct influence on the New Wave sound when it comes to its image and means of musical expression: sharp, almost irritating sound, an even more pronounced effort in "marginalyzing" the melodic and especially harmonic line and finally, the reciting form of singing which puts an emphasis on the text.

However, the role attached to the verbatims in songs precisely indicated the liberation of New Wave from the influence of punk. The initially adopted values of punk: anarchy, surrender, downfall rhetoric soaked in irony and, above all, refusal of an taking active political stand, were abandoned in favor of the diagnosis and criticism of the social environment and its diseases. The texts of songs revealed that this music was recognized and accepted as a tool for change because it proclaimed that people could turn around or upside down, and point the way to a different order of things.

DIRECT REJECTIONS

Alternative Social Movements

Alternative social movements presented a different response to the violence toward punk. They were created as an expression of a mature awareness of the necessity for self-protection against the voluntarism and uncontrolled violence. The establishment of new social groupings that would develop into the instruments for the limitation of the state through the strengthening of the public sphere and selforganization of the society became necessary. The idea of the civil society was discovered.

Alternative Way of Life: Communes. In 1968, communes were thought of as a concept of social change that could spread to wider surroundings in the future. Undoubtedly, this hippie philosophy inspired some types of communes, at least the earliest ones. Second form had more moderate aspirations; the spontaneous association of kindred spirits who shared a similar way of thinking and wanted to share modest urban apartments, in order to reduce costs. A third type was inspired by the Rousseauian motivation of an escape from the dominant and repressive civilization into the natural environment, combined with a sensitivity for the detrimental consequences of the philosophy of growth. The fourth type combined the needs for inner peace and personal freedom with a nonmaterial search for artistic and creative expression.

Of course, these provisional "types" were not the only communes. The first commune was organized in the Slovenian village of Tacen in 1970. Eight art students, six boys and two girls, lived together in a rented house. The chores (shopping, cooking and cleaning) were shared among all members, and common expenses were initially financed from a joint fund. The commune's manifesto defined itself as a community of people permanently living together and seeking to establish a new way of life, and, above all, closer human relations. As an experiment, it wanted to demonstrate the possibility of introducing an essentially different model of living. The social life of the commune was fairly intensive. Part-time members, including some foreigners, joined the hard-core. Their neighbors were suspicious and kept a close watch on the new Robinsons from a distance. The members followed a variety of philosophical standpoints, ranging from oriental traditions and active involvement in the industrial society, to an emphasis on the importance of a healthy life in concordance with a nature. Through contacts with their guests from the Netherlands, they became aware of environmental problems and started to get more familiar with these issues. The sympathetic youth media tried to provide correct coverage on the commune and mitigate the pervasive prejudice against its members.

In the same year that the first commune fell apart, a second one appeared. On the basis of mutual agreement, its members (two couples and one single) moved into a rearranged wooden village house. In terms of their doctrine, they tried to merge together the political principles of the 1968 Students' Movement and a more extensive knowledge of communalism, expressed in the views of Wilhelm Reich and cultural action. The commune lasted for two years in a much more intolerant environment than the Tacen group. The police frequently raided them searching for drugs, harassing their visitors and seizing their travel documents.

Third commune lasted the longest from 1976 to 1980. Three couples with children bought a house together and tried to survive under less-than-enviable conditions, on the verge of austerity. Their income came from their own agricultural and textile production (growing vegetables, sheep breeding, sewing, and knitting), as well as from sources outside the commune—fellowships, employment and occasional participation in field surveys. Expenses were born equally by all members. The couples lived separately, but there was a joint room for socializing, where they could talk, listen to music, dance and entertain guests. They had no major problems with the authorities or their neighbors until they were reported by an anonymous citizen as being involved in drug trafficking. Apparently, this had only been a pretext, since the police in their searches showed much less diligence in looking for narcotics and were much more interested in "spiritual drugs,"—the objectionable political publications.

A group of some twenty students from the city of Ljubljana chose a different way of establishing a housing community in the best tradition of the Dutch, German and Italian squatters. By the end of 1977, they took hold of an old villa at the outskirts of the city. Apart from the permanent tenants, numerous visitors started calling at the villa, especially a couple of weeks after the intruders had been served an eviction order, which they ignored. Since a forcible eviction by the police was expected at any minute, numerous citizens stopped by just to express their solidarity with the squatters, who organized numerous literary meetings and discussions explaining the motives for their action as a protest against the current housing policy. Due to a blockade of the media and biased coverage of the issue, the squatters tried to reach the audience by publishing own bulletin and distributing it to visitors. However, the lack of confidence and fear on the part of the wider society was too powerful. About a month after they took over the villa, an armed policeman broke in and moved its tenants out under the threat of physical violence. This put an end to the first squatting attempt.

Rural communes showed a greater stability and durability than urban ones. Perhaps this was because their aspirations and philosophy of life shifted from social pedagogy, self-construction and self-adjustment to natural way of life. Another reason was that these communes were smaller. They were usually formed by separate couples and perhaps should not even be called communes. In common with authentic communalism was the concept of nonprofit economy restricted to meet the fairly modest personal needs of its members.

Cultural Subversion. During the 1970s, communes were established by dozens throughout Yugoslavia. In addition to a social experiment, they also represented the oases of an alternative artistic and spiritual expression and new sensibility. Some of them were a complex mixture of commune, artistic colony, and the private charity missions which sponsored both the alternative creativity and the underground, uncensored cultures. Some were also the centers of alternative medicine and aid to the poor or socially deprived.

One of the most interesting aspects of the creative cultural rebellion was the appearance of the so-called Household literature which was not largely known. This Household literature was a patchwork of various genres, activities, and forms of a voluntary cultural isolation. Thus, it extended the usual concept of literature as a cultural phenomenon. The motive for self-isolation was derived not so much from a particular social doctrine, but more from an actual situation following the crush of the 1968 Belgrade Students' Movement. The Household art, (perhaps a more appropriate name) remained mostly unavailable to the public since it was predominantly verbal and singled out. The isolation from the outside world was compensated by the complete openness inward. This renaissance group constantly gave home multimedia performances, within the authentic code of happening.

The writings of the household literature seem to be somewhat intentionally coded. Its basics were imaginative puns and witty associations, which easily turned into mocking exaggerations and generalizations. This became increasingly irritating for censors as it turned into the more sophisticated expression. The manner of immediate creation was twofold: first it involved the reading of an already written text, followed by a speech with improvisations on the text, all of which were subsequently recorded. In both cases, comments and suggestions of the audience were incorporated into the initial text, so the creation itself was essentially a joint act, which is why the final result often differed from the initial idea, while the artistic action itself became a dialogue with friends.

Of greater importance, in addition to this kind of creative association which had its own value, householders sowed the seeds which swept through various realms of serious social and, especially, cultural actions. This included giving support to the distribution and popularization of particular books and ideas, spreading cultural and other prophylaxis and recruiting people for free creativity and promotion of sophisticated and non-utilitarian intellectual disciplines.

THE SCOPE AND LIMITS OF 'POST-TITO'S' TITOISM

The basic concept of household literature was revived a few years later in a somewhat different form and in more comfortable environment. Since the public platforms were out of reach, there were a series of discussions, organized in private apartments under the title of the Free University, which were similar to the Flying Universities created in Poland in 1970s (Wejnert 1988). This effort represents the best known form of the so-called dissident intellectual subculture.

The very term *dissident* here is used entirely as a technical term and, therefore, should be understood more as a radical disapproval of the prevailing social values and the search for extra-institutional possibilities, than as a developed dissident movement, typical for other countries in Central and Eastern Europe. Nothing of the kind has ever been seriously established in Yugoslavia. In Yugoslavia, these differences came from specific conditions, that made the dissident situation much less uncomfortable than this was the case with their fellow suffe-rers in other parts of the socialist world. This first characteristic was due to the efforts of the regime to preserve its image of being a soft one, which is why its opponents were not widely and severely repressed. This was especially true for the more prominent opposition members who were rarely denied individual rights such as the right to work or to be free to travel abroad. The monitoring of self-management proved to be a more efficient way of control, along with the restriction of access to official public channels.

By the end of 1978, the Free University was established, the idea for it had naturally occurred at a time when all over the world an increased quest for alternative forms of parallel institutions started under the influence of new social movements, reflecting the dissatisfaction with existing official institutions. Undoubtedly the idea was inspired by the Flying University, which was active in the period of 1976-1980 in Poland, and expressed political disobedience (Wejnert 1988). The first organizers and participants of the Free University were professors of the faculty of Philosophy in Belgrade who were expelled from the university under a special law (*Lex specialis*) passed in 1975. Thus, the political disobedience shifted from the individual act toward a group action and was thereby distinguished from civil disobedience as a personal act. It became a branch of the different oppositional activities aimed at the annulment or modification of the contested order. In the case of the Free University there was a tacit modification. The law, which forbade lecturing for a group of professors, was not revoked. However, an alternative form of university lectures emerged and continued, rarely disturbed by authorities. Officially, it did not exist, although the number of lecturers and their audience gradually increased, transforming it into an important institution of a parallel cultural elite, with an unquestionable influence on the public scene.

The associates and students of the Free University were the initial core of numerous disturbing initiatives for the regime ranging from human and civic rights movement (petition movement), through complaints, requests, open letters to legislative and juridical bodies, up to the attempt of starting an independent newspaper under the name of *Javnost* (*The Public*) in 1990. On 20 April 1984, when Belgrade police broke into a session dedicated to the national question in Yugoslavia, the activities of the university were abruptly. Twenty eight people from the audience were arrested. One of the arrested, Radomir Radovic, died under unknown circumstances during an inquiry. A group of six persons (V. Mijanovic, G. Jovanovic, P. Imsirovic, M. Nikolic, M. Milic and D. Olujic) was charged with the criminal offence of associating for the purpose of a hostile activity.

Spectacularly staged proceedings produced meager results in 1984. After about one hundred witnesses had paraded before the board of judges and the indictment had been changed several times, people's justice befell only Milic for publishing the book titled *The Birth of Tito's Despotism,* published in the emigrant publishing house Nasa rec (Our Word) in London. He was sentenced to spend a year and a half in prison, while the others were acquitted due to lack of evidence. Putting aside the assumption that in Belgrade this almost forgotten technology of repression was caused by the appearance of the most prominent Yugoslav dissident Milovan Djilas, all the cases demonstrated that a new ideological struggle was underway. This reflected the impotence of the authorities to cope with the growing identity crisis in any other way but by nonselective repression, political trials and ideological condemnations.

Not only books, but also a significant portion of intellectual and artistic works were under ideological scrutiny. In October 1983, a year before the Belgrade affair, a symposium was organized by the Center for Ideological and Theoretical Work of the Central Committee of the League of Communists of Croatia, discussing the *White Book*. This document was probably unprecedented in the entire post-war history of Communist rule in Yugoslavia. It represented a detailed and systematic index of banned ideas, books and persons. Over two hundred creative individuals from the country (but also from abroad: Milan Kundera, Czeslaw Milosz, Josef Skvorecki, etc.) were blacklisted and records were made of almost every public word freely spoken, while a number of works from the spiritual sphere were declared reactionary. This symposium met with a highly unfavorable response in the cultural circles of Belgrade, because nine-tenths of the unsuitable titles and authors were discovered in this city. The repressive measures were strengthened following the appearance of the *White Book*, which facilitated the identification of "evil sprouts."

All these are only a surface demonstration of the deeply rooted social and political crises in the Yugoslav society and the state. Its strongest manifestations appeared in the mid-1980s. This was in the first half of the decade after Tito's death (1980), when the flustered regime, composed from mostly second-rate party executives, was faced with the difficulty of remaining in existing positions with privileges gaine under the umbrella of Tito's charisma. The regime was incapable (and unwilling) to deal with the necessity of reconsidering the legitimate grounds for holding and exercising the power on a society deeply shaken. This was due to two facts inherited from the period of Tito's rule.

The first one has been already mentioned—the preservation of second-rate politicians on the political stage. During the 1960s and 1970s Tito successfully purged the majority of capable and creative members of the Party from his surroundings, as potentially opponent to his unlimited rule. While doing this, the former president installed an institutional framework of assumed/shared power that prevented any one in particular from emerging as his successor (i.e., to become "Tito" instead of the genuine Tito).

According to the 1974 Federal Constitution, the supreme authority delegated to lead the country was the collective state Presidency, the head of which was to be rotated every year (after Tito's death). The Presidency was constituted of the representatives of all the federal units (six republics and two autonomous provinces) and the decisionmaking was supposed to be carried out by consensus rather than by execution of the will of the majority. After Tito's death, this structure of supreme power division gradually created tension in an atmosphere of growing dissatisfaction with existing conditions and relations within the Yugoslav Federation. This atmosphere brought about the formation of different concrete and *ad hoc* coalitions. The institutional blockades of the collective state Presidency functions were transferred to the lower levels of the institutional system. Still, attempts were made to plant the roots of the crisis and the quests for its resolution into the shadow of Tito's spirit through some kind of perverse post-mortal spiritism of the dead leader.

That is why even the spreading of the nationalistic secession in a minor fraction of the League of the Communists of Serbia (gathered around, up to that moment, an almost anonymous *aparatchik* Slobodan Milosevic) started in the name of protection of Tito's name and spirit. Serious questioning began to appear on the cover pages of the less and less controlled press. Thus, the first appearance of Milosevic's secessionists on the public stage was closely connected with the attempt to hush the public criticism of Titoism, particularly in the youth press.

FROM PASSIVE RESISTANCE TO CONFRONTATION: LOBBIES AGAINST PRESSURE

The ferocity, diversity and wide scope of the repressive wave precipitated the resistance against the institutionalized violence: ranging from hunger strikes by the accused, through complaints and petitions to state officials, up to public protest gatherings and the setting up of influential pressure groups comprising public figures. Despite the systematic demonization in media controlled by the regime and primarily due to the youth media and numerous renegades from the official public sphere, these activities grew increasingly difficult to conceal from the local and foreign public. The repressive attacks were mainly focused on intellectuals and artists. Therefore, self-defense organization was yeasting mainly in the cultural sphere. Soon it expanded into a wide movement for the protection of human and civic rights.

Since the most intense pressure on creative and personal freedom was in Belgrade, the main bastions of the resistance movement were located in the capital as well. The first significant instance of repression was the imprisonment of the poet Gojko Djogo, accused for publishing his collection of poems, *The Woolen Times*. The authorities overestimated their ability to control the situation the only way they had known. The establishment of the Board for the Protection of the Artistic Freedoms within the Writers' Association of Serbia took them by utter surprise, as did the mass support and popularity of the protest evenings organized in the Writers' Club. Having spent some time in prison, Gojko Djogo was released without serving his time in full. The 1984 trial of the Group of Six, conceived as a spectacular event, not only turned out a poorly staged fiasco, but also initiated a more serious and influential pressure group on the opposition stage. This was the establishment of the Board for the Protection of the Free Thought and Expression, which got a special rating due to the participation of thirteen members of the Serbian Academy of Sciences and Arts, headed by the writer Dobrica Cosic.

Although the Board was never officially recognized, the reputation of its members shielded them against persecution. During the first two years of its activity, the Board issued over thirty documents and appeals addressed to the domestic and foreign institutions, as well as to domestic and foreign public opinion, with an aim of creating democratic public pressure for the promotion of democratic political culture, individual freedom and civil rights. Another significant expression of the stronger self-defense against repression was the revival of professional institutions and associations like the philosophical and sociological societies of Serbia and Croatia and the Yugoslav Association of Sociology. The media gave the appropriate publicity to these events, but with substantial differences in their approach, reflecting the controversy between the essentially complementary roles of the media when it comes to presenting and creating public opinion.

Untill the second half of the 1980s it seemed that the "peripheral field of social representation" in Yugoslavia, in the sense of support for individualism and civic initiatives, was going to prevail against the predominant and up-to-then central field, in the sense of retrograde collectivism (Abric 1995). This was only an illusory, wishful hope of the marginal minority. The capacities of the vanishing (and divided) Communist party-state for the destruction of positive trends were obviously underestimated. Incapable of confronting the growing demands for its own political democratization and economic liberalization, the Party-state responded by activating the last available mechanism for its survival in the new circumstances: self-destruction as a mode for its posthumous continuation.

TURNING FUKUYAMA'S PARADIGM UPSIDE DOWN: REVIVAL RATHER THAN THE END OF HISTORY

Regardless of Francis Fukuyama's (1992) questionable and controversial conclusion that the end of communism in Europe represents the end of history and a triumph of the liberal-democratic model of society, the great impact of Fucuyama's paradigm on the ongoing (pre)transitional discussions on capitalism versus socialism all around former C/E Europe (except in Yugoslavia) cannot be denied. I will stress the consequences of this practical rejection in the Balkans.

In the sense of transitional preconditions, Yugoslavia still had several important advantages in comparison with the rest of C/E Europe by the end of 1980s. It still showed a satisfactory level of economic development (being close to semi-developed European countries, such as Spain, Portugal, Greece, etc.); it had fairly open trade, cultural and communicational links with the majority of Europe and other countries; and it maintained a stable geo-political position in Europe and the rest of the world. The ideological shift to socialism had already been done. So the process of privatization, according to federal law, was put on the agenda. Furthermore, the modern-oriented federal government brought the country to the doors of the European Community by bringing high inflation down through resolute monetary reform and cranking down the inflation which the huge (and inefficient) socialist enterprises benefited from. But such direction toward the successful development of the Federation was not in concordance with the political will of the leaders of the re-feudalized Yugoslav Federal Units,[6] who were able to remain in power only by the support of the loyal majority. The attention of the majority was thereby permanently diverted from modernization toward the nationalization of the society. A big swindle was on the agenda in the form of the nationalism as a counter-movement against modernization.

The strongest resistance came from Serbia, where President Slobodan Milosevic and the group under his patronage seized power in autumn 1987. Presenting themselves as the leaders of change, the members of the Milosevic's patronage group proclaimed themselves forerunners of the "transition" in Eastern Europe. Therefore, any further discussions on the post-socialist political and economic reform were permanently struck from the agenda. Indeed, the experience represented the formation of an autarkic national economy. This economy was more or less closed within the boundaries of the Republic of Serbia. Its purpose was both the destruction of Federal Government policy by imposing internal taxes for the import of goods and the nationalization of enterprises from the other republics on Serbian territory.[7] This violent and aggressive behavior of the Serbian leadership reached its climax in the illegal break-in to the federal budget in autumn 1990. The stolen money (about US $ 2 billions) was used for buying social peace and investment in the pre-election campaign for Milosevics' Socialist Party on the eve of the first free elections held in November 1990.[8]

In this manner, demands for the inevitable political and economic reforms were neutralized and de-legitimized with a sudden invention from the establishment of a new legitimacy source, that is, the re-building of the post-communist nation-state. Thus, the South-Slavonic peoples were encouraged and pressured to return to their respective eternal tribal identities and embrace regressive self-identification with refreshed ethno-collectiv patterns of the past. This was, of course, headed by the post(?)-communist elite. The brotherhood and unity ideal and civic initiatives were turned into ashes over night. The representatives of the peripheral field, who did not have a change of heart and become genuine nationalists (and a lot of them did!), were labeled as the new internal enemies, and furthermore, as national traitors, the popular term in those times.

This way, Tito's successors and political clones, genetically handicapped through the long-lasting negative selection of suitable members, chose the struggle for smaller but stronger rule in their own satrapies, instead of preserving his achievements, that is, the continuity of the common state (preferred by the majority of people). The *coup de grâce* to the dome came as a desperate attempt to modernize the entire country. This attempt was made in 1990 by the last federal prime minister, Ante Markovic, who was wiped out from the political scene through the joined efforts of the new satraps (for the first and for the last time).[9] Belated economic reform (without a serious political one) was an inefficient attempt to prevent the falling apart of the common state, and the disillusionment with the famous Yugoslav experiment was very painful. Two years after the period called by T. G. Ash the "refolution" in C/E Europe (Ash 1990), Yugoslavia ceased to exist, and devastating local wars were being waged for the creation of new nation-states.

After the misplacement of the real problems and pressures against the non-Albanian population in the autonomous province of Kosovo, the Serbian post-communist elite took the leading role in the disintegration and destruction of Yugoslavia. Officially, Serbia and Montenegro (the current, shorter Yugoslavia), did not take part in these disintegration processes: they "were not involved" in the local wars in the former Yugoslavia as state(s), but costs of the wars were transferred to the Serbian and Montenegrin population to be paid through different accounts.

Now, let me come back to Fukuyama. One should take Fucuyama's (Marxist-like) optimism about the *end of history* rather relatively when faced with the imposed anti-modern consciousness and surplus of violent and destructive energies which emerged from the re-traditionalization of the particular national histories. In the Balkans, those histories put into operation the pre-modern (barbarian) know-how of turning the national state into actual banana-states. Maybe another, less optimistic thinker was closer to the truth when he wrote that "history is an everlasting return of the same" (Nietzsche 1966). This especially goes for the Balkans!

INSTEAD OF A CONCLUSION—CONSEQUENCES OF THE SERBIAN MODEL OF TRANSITION

What are the consequences of this turnover in which the structural advancement in the modernization of the society switched into stagnation and underdevelopment and why the current Serbia/Yugoslavia suffers the transition blockade and retrograde trends in economic and political development?

The caving in (implosion) of the majority of the Real-Socialist systems was initiated from the top as an introduction to the transition processes (after Gorbachev's switch in the Soviet Union). The ruling Communist elite's was aware of the complete loss of legitimacy and, therefore, lost self-confidence and the will to rule.

This process took the opposite course in Serbia. The Serbian communist elite demonstrated a different behavior. In 1987, through internal political clashes between the two fractions, the winning fraction (headed by Slobodan Milosevic) was revitalized with the new disciples eager to rule and obtain political affirmation and meta-political benefits. Thus, this new elite did not meet the 1989 "refolution" unprepared. The Serbian regime (and its ideologists) proclaimed that the transition in Serbia was successfully completed through this seizure of power.[10] And it was, indeed, but in a peculiar direction. The regime had really redefined the grounds for its legitimacy. It was not communism any more but ethnic nationalism. Milosevic and his followers managed to eradicate the people's will for transition toward the modernization of society, and turned it into the recruitment of the masses for nationalism. They focused those changes' on the creation of not so much a civil society and political community of modern citizenry, but rather a homogeneous and ethnically based one. This recruiting was focused on the idea of the "Great Serbia" meaning the establishment of a majority Serbian nation-state at all costs, including war with the neighboring peoples of the former Yugoslavia for their territories. This way, both simultaneous tasks of dual transition from the authoritarian system—the liberalization of the economy and the democratization of the political order— were postponed, in fact, pushed aside *ad callendas graecas.*

Now, after a decade of this development strategy, Serbia has been devastated and destroyed with a paralyzed society. Part of it (Kosovo) is under UN (read: NATO) protectorate. The ongoing process of exhausting the economic resources (bankruptcy of almost all unprofitable socialist industrial giants) and incompetent economic management (with the simultaneous criminal privatization of profitable national economic sources) lead to the extreme poverty of a majority of the people. By the end of 1990s, the distinct society gap between the masses of poor (96 percent) and the tiny nouveau riche minority (Milosevic's political capitalists and war profiteers), was getting bigger. In comparison with 1990, in 1994 the number of poor increased 5.75 times. In 1996, 70.5 percent of the poor people lived in towns.

In 1989, the annual GDP per capita dropped from almost US $3.000 (a level of semi-developed European countries). In 1998 t dropped to $1.500, then to less than $ 900 (estimated) at the end of 1999, which is the level of the poorest countries of the Third World. The average monthly income in the state-commanded economy is about 80 DEM (US $45), which is sufficient for about 30 percent of the minimum elementary needs for a family of four. The miracle of survival is owing to the informal, illegal, grey economy (e.g., smuggling oil and cigarettes, tax-free small trading on the open-markets, etc.) that was introduced due to the drop in quality of life. The share of this informal economy sector was officially estimated at 54 percent of the national economy in 1996! Social services—the back-bone of the previous socialist welfare free health care, care for children, education, science, etc.)—are in a disastrous state. This lead to the reappearance of some almost forgotten diseases of poverty (such as tuberculosis); no day care services; a return of children's socialization to the broader family network provided by grandmothers; the weakening impact of education on youth's values; and the irreversible technological regress of industry. A further impact of the devastation in education and science is the huge brain drain of highly educated and mostly young people.[11]

In a word, the consequences of the Serbian model of *(anti)transition* are devastating. Serbia is now economically on the level of the former Yugoslavia of early the 1950s. Even if the current devastating processes could be reversed immediately, with a significant influx of foreign capital (of at least US $ 5 billions), Yugoslav economists estimate that Serbia would need a decade or two to return to the 1989 economic level, and three decades or more to reach the level of some post-communist countries of today, like the Czech Republic and Slovenia. Without foreign loans, Serbia will need almost a century (80 years) to return to the 1989 level of economic development on its own! The bill for Milosevic's *adventure* against modernization has already been delivered for the next five to eight generations of Serbian people to pay.

NOTES

1. Since the 1970s Yugoslavia was offered as a good example of successful industrialization, specific and different to those implemented in other East European socialist countries. Due to the introduction of workers' control in state-owned enterprises in the Yugoslav model of socialism, it was considered as opposite to the Soviet type of model (Griffin 1989). Another foreign observer, Paul Lendvai (1991), emphasized three

main reasons why Yugoslavia deserved different treatment in comparison with other Central/East European countries. First, it was independent from Soviet control. Second, it was involved in the creation of a new kind of international policy, through the movement of non-aligned countries. Finally, its social and economic system was neither orthodox state socialism, nor western free market economy, but a sort of economic democracy (self-management) in economy and federalism in politics.

2. Two crucial causes of the fateful Yugoslav crisis during the 1990s— "decentralization bereft of democratization and conflicting principles of self-management and dictatorship of the proletariat—were from the outset woven into the very foundations of the self-management system" (Sekelj 1993: 3-4).

3. In the first and last national sociological research on a representative sample of about 13,000 respondents across former Yugoslavia, conducted by the Consortium of Yugoslav Sociological Institutes in 1989-1990, when asked whether each ethnic group in Yugoslavia should have its own state, two thirds (over 66 precent) of respondents answered negative, while only about 13 percent responded positive. Obviously this 13 percent was powerful enough to realize nationalistic desires!

4. In 1983, the request of the public prosecutor, the court in Belgrade passed a decision prohibiting publication of Dr. Nebojsa Popov's Ph. D. thesis titled, *Social Conflicts - a Challenge to Sociology* and the book, which had been already printed, was shred.

5. This could be illustrated by the statement from one of the sociological surveys conducted at that time, which denies the stereotype about the apolitical nature of Yugo-punk. From the very outset, punk meant a movement to me, as it did not assume only music but also an attack on institutions, the system. Punk has very sharply indicated the mistakes of our society. It does not seem to me to be a copy of the West, although it may be so in terms of music, but our punk is largely its own, since it deals with our problems bothering us for days on end.

6. Indeed, "without a fundamental political shift in Yugoslavia the establishment of a system of divided power, the eradication of party monopoly, the establishment of civil society and the construction of economic relations as non-political ones, the economic crisis could only deepen" (Sekelj 1993: 163).

7. As formation of a national economy in this partisan manner presupposes growth of state ownership rather then privatization of previous "social ownership," it is interesting to point out the economic results of this "statization," a few years later: "in the first 1994 semi-annual, 11 of the biggest 'state-owned' enterprises in Serbia had 'produced' about 4 billion DEM losses. That is more than 60% of losses of [the] entire economy and equal to half of the semi-annual national product *per capita*!" (Belgrade weekly *Vreme* (*Time*), 10 October 1994).

8. Nevertheless, behavior of other members of the Yugoslav (quasi)federation— Slovenia and Croatia especially—was oriented in the same direction. Although their behavior was more or less reactive and performed as a response to challenges coming from Serbia, similar to Serbia, it was oriented toward the disintegration of a common state.

9. During 1990 the federal government reform program was permanently obstructed and attacked on behalf of "protection" or "endangered national interest" until the government was overturned.

10. This way both corner-stones of post-communist transformation— political democratization and establishment of a free market economy—were resolutely rejected by Serbian (and Montenegran) post-communists. Resistance to transformation of the ownership model from social (state-controlled) to private ownership was justified with hypocritical arguments. The first argument explained the "deep care" of the nation-state

for employees (mainly manual workers) in inefficient former socialist industrial "dinosaurs." This care by the state for industrial workers was expressed through sending hundred of thousands of them on endless "obligatory leaves" (with payment 60 percent of average salary) and, in fact, pushing them to illegal economy. Before the clash with NATO, there were 800,000 unemployed in Serbia (Gredelj 1996); now it is expected to be doubled. What is worst, 47 percent of unemployed are young people, age 15 to 24, applying for their first jobs, while another 35.7percent are in the 25 to 34 age group. The second argument was even worse: allegedly, capitalism was not appropriate model for Serbian economic development, because it could lead to dramatic social inequalities and poverty! Of course, this did not apply to the patronage group of Milosevic's "political capitalists" including his family. This "more equal" group was not limited with any barriers to illegal privatization of profitable firms and branches (such as the oil and tobacco industries, agriculture monopolies, or the post and telephone systems), robbery of state financial funds or from transferring currency to secret private accounts abroad.

11. The 1979-1994 data indicate disturbing trends: in that period 1,256 researchers from scientific and research institutions in Serbia emigrated abroad, three-quarters of them (918) left in the most intensive period of emigration (1990-1994). Their academic and educational structure was as follows: 329 Ph. D, 261 MA and 666 BA, mainly in the fields of electronics, physics, mathematics, chemistry and health care. Fifty could be considered as top experts by international standards: they had published articles and are quoted in prestigious international scientific journals, they have registered intellectual property (patents and models) and they taught in some of the most prestigious universities in the world.

REFERENCES

Abric, J. C. 1995. L'organisation interne des representations sociales. In C. Guimelli (Ed.), *Structures et transformations des representations sociales*. Lausanne: Delachaux et Niestle

Ash, T. G. 1990. *We People of the Revolution of '89*. London: Grant Books.

Fukuyama, Francis. 1992. *The End of History and the Last Man*. New York: Avon Books.

Gredelj, S. 1996. Gewerkshaften als Spiegel der Parteien (Trade Unions as Mirrors of the Parties). *Ost-WestGegen Informationen*. Austria: Graz.

Griffin, K.1989. *Alternative Strategies for Economic Development*. London: Macmillan, OECD Development Centre.

Lendvai, P. 1991. Yugoslavia without Yugoslavs. The Roots of the Crisis. *International Affairs, 67, 2.*

Nietzsche, F. 1966. *Beyond Good and Evil: Prelude to a Philosophy of the Future*. New York: Vintage Books.

Schierup, C. U. 1991. The Post-Communism Enigma—Ethnic Mobilization in Yugoslavia. *New Community, 18,* 1.

Sekelj, L. 1993. *Yugoslavia: The Process of Disintegration*. Social Science Monographs. Highland Lakes, NJ: Atlantic Research and Publications (distributed by Columbia University Press).

Wejnert, B. 1988. The Student Movement in Poland, 1980-1981. *Research in Social Movements, Conflict and Change, 10,* 173-183.

Woodward, S. 1995. *Balkan Tragedy*. Washington DC: The Brookings Institution.

13

The Artist's Freedom and Democracy

Maria Nowakowska Stycos and Grazyna Borkowska

The relationship between political freedom and the realm of art is not an easy one. Democratic transitions affect the themes and style of writing and create opportunities for new journals or literary centers. The decade (1990s) of democratization in Poland has witnessed the appearance of new magazines, new stars and new bestsellers. The centrality of Warsaw with its established literary journals, *Dialog (Dialogue)* and *Tworczosc (Creative Writing)*, has been broken by new, regional publications such as *Tytul (Title)* in Gdansk, *Kresy (Border-lands)* in Lublin, *Dekada Literacka (The Literary Decade)* in Krakow, *Fraza (The Phrase)* in Rzeszow, and *Topos (Topos)* in Lodz. Young Polish writers have clearly marked their distinctiveness by overlooking Poland's history and provocatively turning away from traditional myths. Instead, they treat taboo subjects such as German-Polish relations, but present a more personal aspect of historical experience.

But, did democracy change the writing practices of mature artists, those who made their debut twenty or thirty years ago and who have been continually widening the scope of their artistic work in communist Poland? Take, for example, Wislawa Szymborska, a subtle poet, outside of the mainstream, who first entered the literary scene in Stalinist times, or Ewa Lipska, who debuted during the student movement in 1968: Do they write differently now? Did they need a lesson in democracy at all? Do not Szymborska's receipt of the Nobel Prize in 1996, and Lipska's growing international recognition testify that one can be a great writer under any conditions? Does this not suggest that a poet's freedom is not directly dependent on political freedom? We, two critics from East and West will consider the poetry of Wislawa Szymborska and Ewa Lipska written before and after 1989, during the communist years and after the return to democracy.

WISLAWA SZYMBORSKA

I (Borkowska) think[1] that the answers to these questions lie not in the creative act itself, but in the esthetics of reception, via different modes of reading, and in the perception of new possibilities of understanding and interpreting artistic works. Szymborska writes as she always has, but today we read her differently. In a country deprived of sovereignty, literature is treated as the voice of truth, both solemn and definitive. Poetry is combed for profound ideas, new directions and ethical norms. In the time of freedom, literature returns to its main functions: It is again a mirror of the world, a reservoir of existential experiences, and an art of life. Szymborska's poetry has undergone various schools of reading: The poet has been seen as a moralist, philosopher and re-inventor of poetic language.[2] Today, Szymborska's anti-speculative, ironic and ostentatiously "ordinary" artistic stance is also interpreted as distinctly feminine.

Naturally, this femininity is experienced by Szymborska and manifested in her poetry in a very specific way. Distrustful toward various ideologies, Szymborska is also at times moderately suspicious of the body, which she sees as deceitful, but all the same one's own; we know more or less what to expect from it. It is limited, but homely. The poet never displays a need for unbounded artistic freedom. To the contrary, she hides the independence of her beliefs and her thinking under a mask of naiveté and astonishment. She is known not only for her aversion to pathos, but also for her reluctance for simplified self-definitions, self-categorizations and declarations; and her disinclination toward personifying extreme attitudes, which from her perspective look inhuman. A romantic belief in the power of poetry is also foreign to her. The poet communicates her complex, difficult to interpret artistic credo in a poem "The Joy of Writing" ["Radosc pisania"]. Szymborska, as *an equal of gods* speaks, about the territory of her poems with Olympic pride:

> Other laws, black on white, here hold sway.
> The twinkling of an eye will last as long as I wish,
> will consent to be divided into small eternities
> full of bullets stopped in flight.
> Forever, if I command it, nothing will happen here.
> Against my will no leaf will fall
> nor blade of grass bend under the full stop of the hoof
> (Szymborska, "The Joy of Writing" 19-25, in Krynski & Maguire, p. 59)

But immediately afterwards, a different Szymborska, a mistress of ink, will destroy the illusion of the reliability of her created world. The act of creation does take place, but is limited to a very small, intimate space coincident with a sheet of paper. "This is not real life," says the poet in "The Joy of Writing" (Szymborska 1981: 19). The joy of writing is necessarily the joy of play, doubt, and imperfect imitation; it is the joy of producing a crippled recreation of actual fears and nebulous anxiety.

Yet the game does not end here. If it did, we might conclude that Szymborska values life above all, that she is fascinated by its might, its ferocity and the irrevocable factuality of events. But here we encounter an intriguing triplet:

> The joy of writing.
> The power of preserving.

The revenge of a mortal hand
(Szymborska, "The Joy of Writing" 30-33, in Krynski & Maguire, p. 59)

Let us start our interpretation from the end, from this "hand." Wladyslaw Kopalinski, in his *Dictionary of Myths and Cultural Traditions* [*Slownik mitow i tradycji kultury*], under the entry "hand" writes:

faithfulness; in Zeno of Elea, a clenched fist symbolizes dialectics, and an open fist— oratorical skills. [. . .] In Medieval art the hand was a symbol of dialectics. In ancient Egypt it was a symbol of courage, in ancient Rome, a symbol of commanding power and of dexterity: God was portrayed as a hand emerging from clouds. It was a sign of order (hebr. "iad": "hand" or "authority"), a blessing (with two extended fingers and with rays beaming from them) or a threat hanging over humanity. The king's hand represents judicial power, an imparting onto the king one of the most important attributes of godliness. The hand of *Homo Faber* (lat. "man-creator," "manufacturer") differentiates him from animals. (Kopalinski 1985: 977-978)

It seems that Szymborska's poem confirms and realizes all of the above archetypal meanings of the word "hand." That an intelligent author knows a great deal about history and her own culture would not be surprising if it was not for a certain circumstance. Meanings enumerated by Kopalinski do not form a singular semantic group; they either contradict one another or simply lack a clear connection. After all, what connection is there between a hand as a symbol of dialectics and a hand as an allegoric representation of dexterity and courage?

If anyone finds himself lost in a meander of Kopalinski's references, Szymborska may be of help. "The Joy of Writing" states precisely that a man daring to engage in creative work transcends the boundaries of space allotted to him; that he breaks the principles of God's order, faith and obedience, and finally, that he is a usurper without any chances to succeed, yet not without courage. What about Zeno of Elea? What about dialectics and all the rest? In the excerpt quoted above, Szymborska states clearly:

The twinkling of an eye will last as long as I wish,
will consent to be divided into small eternities
full of bullets stopped in flight.
(Szymborska, "The Joy of Writing" 20-21, in Krynski & Maguire, p. 59)

It is here that we have the eleatic paradox of movement broken down to its irreducible elements, to inert particles suspended in space. Through this paradox Szymborska expresses her view of the nature of art, and the problem of art's reliability which directs us simultaneously to truth and falsehood, lie and invention. Szymborska repeatedly refers to eleatic tradition (e.g., in poems such as: "Frozen Motion," "Motion," "Laughter" ["Znieruchomienie," "Ruch," "Smiech"]. Similarly, the poem analyzed here outlines a dialectic space formed in between contradictions: creativity and the illusion of thereof, seriousness and joke, obviousness and paradox, movement and inertia, true activity and the uselessness of an empty gesture. The poem is built on the semantic opposition of two images, which shatters Kopalinski's explanation as well: a hand extended towards the absolute, mediating between human and divine orders, and a clenched fist—rebellious, dangerous and threatening.

Let us put aside "The Joy of Writing." It is time to draw preliminary conclusions. My impression is that in Szymborska's case we cannot reconcile two issues: The issue of freedom understood as the basis of existence, and artistic freedom understood as the lightness of writing and the fluctuations of tone, which in Szymborska's work leans toward wit, play and the release of tension.

Szymborska as an Ex-Centric

The specific positioning of the lyrical subject within the poetic space, at least at first glance, marks Szymborska's poetry as original. The poet's voice often catches us off guard for it comes from unexpected places: from the corner of a hall, from backstage, from the inside of the museum showcase, from the sewers of a big city, from within a dream or depths of the sea. Szymborska's poetry is a mark on a margin of the great book of the world, the sixth act of a drama, the back side of a painting. What can be seen "from the back door" or in a "low gap" created between a stage and a lowering curtain?

> here one hand hastily reaches for a flower,
> there a second snatches up a dropped sword.
> Only then does a third, invisible,
> perform its duty:
> it clutches at my throat.
> (Szymborska, "Theater Impressions" 28-32, in Krynski & Maguire, p. 115)

Szymborska answers: The essence of things makes itself immanent in twilight, at the boundary between realms. It is instantaneous and revelatory. It lights up for an instant, like a match illuminating darkness; a ray of light falling on the stage from underneath the half-drawn curtain. It enables us to discern the human countenance of art: the sweat and awkwardness that mean truth.

The poet does not trust artistic conventions; she searches for truth beyond them, underneath the lining of art. Looking at the baroque presentation of bodies exuding satiety and lust, she shares with us following reflection:

> O meloned, O excessive ones,
> doubled by the flinging off of shifts,
> trebled by the violence of posture,
> you lavish dishes of love!
>
> Their slender sisters had risen earlier,
> before dawn broke in the picture.
> No one noticed how, single file, they
> had moved to the canvas's unpainted side.
>
> Exiles of style. Their ribs all showing,
> their feet and hands of birdlike nature.
> Trying to take wing on bony shoulder blades.
> (Szymborska, "The women of Rubens" 12-22, in Krynski & Maguire, p.51)

On the unpainted side of the canvas one can clearly see what the lining of Ruben's art is really made of. Sensuality hides a fear of death. Angelic figures seemingly pushed outside the artistic frame in spite of the artist are reminiscent of dying.

Szymborska's poems contain an important pattern: The poet looks at the world "ex-centrically," she moves her gaze to the periphery, to the very verge of the frame. She uses this method of description repeatedly, as in "Medieval Illumination" ["Miniatura sredniowieczna"] and "Rest" ["Reszta"], just to name a couple. Looking at the sugary picture from a distant past, she speculates about its author: "He however took care to strike a balance: /the hell he prepared for them in the next picture" (Szymborska, "Medieval Illumination" 36-37, in Krynski & Maguire, p.170).

In the poem "Rest" the poet perversely comforts Ophelia: "Non omnis moriar from love" (Szymborska, "Rest" 10, in Kwiatkowski 1997: 62).[3] Wherever Szymborska appears the unimportant becomes important. In Paris, the poet looks not at the cathedrals, but at the local vagrant (in "Clochard"). At the author's poetry reading, she notices an old man sleeping soundly, dreaming perhaps about a plum pie (in "Poetry Reading"). Entering a museum the poet asks: "There is a fan—where are the rosy cheeks?" (Szymborska, "The Museum" ["Muzeum"] 4, in: Krynski & Maguire, p. 37).

One can hear laughter, joking inquiry and gaiety in her questions and observations. Clearly, the poet is able to look at herself from a distance, from the side, and also not without a smile. The existence of self seems to her the surprising realization of a fortuitous accident. Szymborska says: "It could have happened./It had to happen." (Szymborska, "There But for the Grace" [Wszelki wypadek] 1-2, in Krynski & Maguire, p. 113). But this understanding of the essence of being influences her understanding of the essence of freedom. According to Szymborska, absolute freedom is not available to men. Our freedom is exercised in a sphere of certain minute and not always fundamental choices:

I prefer movies.
I prefer cats.
I prefer oaks by the Warta River .
I prefer Dickens to Dostoevsky
(Szymborska , "Possibilities" ["Mozliwosci"] 1-4, in Szymborska 1996: 78-79).[4]

Szymborska does not fetishize freedom. She enjoys her existence fully aware of its limitations and of the accidental nature of being. She does it in the same way that she experiences the joy of writing— aware of being subject to cultural models and the limits of the poetic imagination.

Three Strategies of Survival

Oftentimes though, the inherent *relativity* of happiness and joy of writing brings about fear and depression. Szymborska's poetry suggests at least three strategies of surviving this ontological and existential crisis. She activates these strategies therapeutically by thoroughly identifying with her biological and social roles. She becomes a woman and speaks as a woman. The first strategy is one of regression. Szymborska announces a wish to throw in the towel. She is ready to sacrifice the joy of being for unflinching perseverance. Female characters in her poems do the same: During a crisis, they "retreat into themselves," they lock themselves inside their own microcosm of being. Szymborska wants to include her accidental existence in the universal order without conflict. These visions are realized in the poem "Landscape" ["Pejzaz"]:

> In the old master's landscape,
> the trees have roots beneath the oil paint,
> the path undoubtedly reaches its goal,
> the signature is replaced by a stately blade of grass,
> it's a persuasive five in the afternoon,
> May has been gently, yet firmly, detained,
> so I've lingered too. Why, of course, my dear,
> I am the woman there, under the ash tree.
> (Szymborska, "Landscape" 1-8, in Baranczak & Cavanagh 1995: 37)

A second source of salvation lies in eroticism—and we will see just how permanent that will turn out to be. Love in Szymborska's poetry (as with two other great Polish poets, Pawlikowska and Poswiatowska) allows an internal cohesion: "Created in his image/I am a reflection in his eyes," says the poet in the poem "Drinking Wine" ["Przy winie"] (Szymborska 1997: 78). Loss of love has a final dimension; it threatens one with a fall into nonexistence:

> When he is not looking at me,
> I search for my reflection
> on the wall. And I see only
> the nail, left after the picture was taken down.
> (Szymborska, "Przy winie" 27-30, Szymborska 1977: 79)

Szymborska cannot find peace on so unstable ground. Her love stories are dramas that are framed in literary models which means that they have already been consciously aestheticized by the writer (e.g., in "Ballad" ["Ballada"]). They also take the form of confessions of impotency and lack of fulfillment (e.g., in "The Tower of Babel" ["Na wiezy Babel"]).

The poet invents a third measure to ease her feeling the internal split and anxiety. This crisis strategy is again characteristic for all currents of feminist literature. Szymborska seeks contact with other women; she weaves a delicate thread of female solidarity. Stubbornly, she attempts to persuade us and herself that she is just like other women, and perhaps even worse:

> In my sister's desk there are no old poems
> nor any new ones in her handbag.
> And when my sister invites me to dinner,
> I know she has no intention of reading me poems.
> She makes superb soups without half trying,
> and her coffee does not spill on manuscripts.

(Szymborska, "In Praise of My Sister" ["Pochwala siostry"] 9-14, in Krynski & Maguire, p. 173)

Her portrait of the "other" woman does not bear aristocratic traces or needless consistency. She says about her female character: "Reads Jaspers and ladies' magazines" (Szymborska, "Portrait of a Woman" ["Portret kobiecy"] 12, in Krynski & Maguire, p. 177). This statement can be applied to Szymborska herself, an author of reviews published at one time in *Zycie Literackie*, the most widely read literary journal, and now in *Gazeta Wyborcza*, a new daily newspaper. In the latter, the poet writes about great works and popular publications meant for a broad audience, such as guide books, atlases and cook books. This choice testifies not only to her sense of humor, but to her solidarity with the reading public as well.

For Szymborska commonality means more then we might suspect. In "Lot's Wife" ["Zona Lota"] Szymborska wonderfully rehabilitates commonality as it is frozen in a myth with a mistreated heroine:

They say I looked back from curiosity.
But I could have had reasons other then curiosity.
I looked back from regret for a silver bowl.
From distraction while fastening the latchet of my sandal.
To avoid looking longer at the righteous neck
of Lot my husband.
From sudden certainty that had I died
he would not even have slowed his step.
(Szymborska, "Lot's Wife" 1-8, in Krynski & Maguire, p. 159)

Poems praising feminine tenderness (e.g., "Returns" ["Powroty"]), women's attachment to life (e.g., "Into the Arc" ["Do arki"]), and femininity itself do not dominate Szymborska's poetry. She confesses in "Under a Certain Little Star" ["Pod jedna gwiazdka"]: I apologize to everything that I cannot be everywhere. I apologize to everyone that I cannot be every man and woman. (Szymborska, "Under a Certain Little Star" 28-29, in Krynski & Maguire, p. 147)

Szymborska rejected feminism's make-shift strategies. She could not be satisfied with the "idiocy of perfection" and "perseverance for the sake of perseverance" as she expresses in "The Onion" ["Cebula"]). She remains cautious in love, dividing herself into "body and soul" in "Autotomy" ["Autotomia"]). In her striving for solidarity with similar men, "she herself is an obstacle to herself"(Szymborska, "Under a Certain little Star" 31, in Krynski & Maguire, p. 147).

Beyond Fashions and Ideologies

Szymborska's poetic offering is astonishing. It is a dedicated critique of abstract, generalizing thinking imposed by the restrictive, "patriarchal" order. In this sense Szymborska remains close to deconstructivist, and feminist, practices. Yet no single formula, be it deconstructivism or feminism, can encompass the entirety of Szymborska's poetic wealth. Szymborska is faithful to herself despite changes in history, fashions, and regimes. Nowadays one can openly admit to this, without fearing that existential reading can throw the poet on the pedestal of great art.

EWA LIPSKA

When Wislawa Szymborska was awarded the Nobel Prize in 1996, she modestly announced to the Polish press that the honor was due to Polish poetry rather than her own achievements.[5] No doubt Szymborska was thinking of her generation, born between the two world wars, which includes such luminaries as Zbigniew Herbert and Tadeusz Rozewicz.[6] Sixteen years earlier, the prize was also awarded to Czeslaw Milosz,—a poet of the preceding generation, who chose freedom and settled at Berkeley,—attesting to the vitality of Polish poetry of the second half of the twentieth century and the high esteem in which it is held by world readers. These poets, deeply rooted in classicism, had to reinvent poetry after the destruction caused by World War II, the holocaust and the imposition of the Soviet-dominated communist regime. The poetry that grew out of disillusionment and repression of the Cold War, was profound, steeped in irony and stripped of ornamentation. It found a way to address individual and national losses, avoid entrapment by political slogans and become the conscience/consciousness of a people.[7] In its ability to pose serious existential questions, it remains, a poetry of universal appeal.

Even more surprising to readers from the West was the rise of another brilliant generation of post World War II poets, who have come to be known as The New Wave or The Generation of 1968. Their poetry is characterized by a sense of "timelessness, syncretism, and a variation of neoclacissim" (Lipska 1996:5).[8] Ewa Lipska, born in 1945, is often included in this group. However, in a recent anthology, *A Specific Period: The New Wave 1968-1993* (Nyczek 1995), she was placed in the appendix at her own request, to mark her independence from any movement or group. Her constant probing of accepted values embedded in customs and language set her apart from members of her generation, with whom she nonetheless, admits ties of friendship, generational experiences and literary traditions. Her poetry shows her independence from imposed norms, expectations and political restrictions. She does respond to the times she lives in but in a style that has continued to evolve, regardless of prevailing political norms, from communism to democracy.

Lipska's career and writings illustrate that women have entered the public forum in Poland today. Lipska lives in Krakow, as does Szymborska, and has reputedly received the senior poet's encouragement. By 1998, she had authored seventeen volumes of poetry and anthologies (Lipska 1996: 19).[9] She has worked as the poetry editor for the publishing house Wydawnictwo Literackie (1970-1980), served on the editorial boards of literary journals such as *Arka* and *Dekada Literacka* (1990-92) and worked in various capacities at the Polish embassy in Vienna, where she also directed the Polish Institute. She has received numerous literary awards, including a grant from the Iowa International Writing Program (1975/76), the prize of the "Ring" from the city of Gdansk (1978), from the Polish PEN Club (1992) and from the Jurzykowski Foundation of New York (1993). Of her poetry, Stanislaw Baranczak—himself a member of the

1968 generation—has said that until her publication of *Check-room for Darkness* (1985), Lipska had been "a poet drawing distant analogies between an individual existence and the state of civilization," but that this volume marked a new direction, defining "the experience of a specific community in a specific historic moment" (Baranczak 1985).[10] The historic moment was the 1980s when Solidarity raised new hopes for a democratic government and freedom in Poland. *Check-room for Darkness* was published clandestinely during the state of siege declared by General Jaruzelski in an effort to stem the political changes sought by Solidarity.

In this chapter, through a close reading of selected poems, I intend to show Lipska's engagement with questions of historic memory, national identity and democracy, both in the context "of a specific community" and impinging on "the state of civilization," as she perceives it in the course of some thirty years of writing (1968-98). I will also briefly analyze aspects of her style, emphasizing on her use of humor and wit, as well as her poetics, intimately linked to her subject matter and mode of communication. "Citizen of a Small Nation" ["Obywatel malego kraju"], a poem from the collection commented by Baranczak, is indicative of Lipska's thematics and style.

> A citizen of a small nation
> Born imprudently at the edge of Europe
> Is called upon to reflect on freedom.
> As a reservist, he has never given it any thought
> He interrupts his morning feeding of the whale
> And leafs through dictionaries.
> A few times in his life
> He crossed freedom in transit.
> Sometimes he even had *lunch*
> And drank a small glass of orange juice.
> Sometimes they were
> underground stations.
> Tunnels' black sleeves.
> Small carriages over precipices.
> Still, he always returned
> To his collection of whales.
> To his personal spaces of freedom
> Through which he took walks
> In a safety jacket
> And slung over his shoulder,
> A first-aid kit.[11]
> ("Citizen of a Small Nation," in Lipska 1985)

Clearly, the poetic speaker (the implied author?) distances him/her/self from the protagonist of the poem, represented as an average person, the man in the street, whose "prudent" precautions—as indicated by his safety jacket, the first-aid kit and the feeding of the whale—secure his survival and a modicum of personal freedom. If the metaphor of "the collection of whales" suggests the hierarchy imposed by the Big Brother to the east, our everyman has learned how to co-exist with the whales. Hiding behind a mask of irony, the poetic speaker raises the broader issues of Poland's survival on the eastern frontier of Europe, and her precarious membership in the Western world. From the West's perspective, Poles may seem *imprudent* rather than *heroic,* and Poland marginal to the West's interests or simply *a buffer* zone. Poland, unlike Russia, chose the Roman Church at the dawn of its history as a nation (966), thus aligning herself with the West. Today, Poland's entry into the European Union is scheduled for the year 2002. The subtle manipulation of the point of view through the transposition of the qualifier, "imprudent" (for how can anyone choose where to be born prudently or imprudently) oblige Polish readers to reconsider treasured notions of their place in the family of nations and especially how they are viewed by the West.

Characteristically, Lipska uses humor to underscore serious themes. Poland's brief existence as an independent nation in this century (1918-1939) and the forty years of Soviet-imposed communist rule are evoked by the witty phrase, "he crossed freedom in transit." To the Polish reader there are obvious allusions to visits to the U.S. ("lunch," given in English in the text and "orange juice"), and perhaps to England (the London underground). The citizen's recourse to the dictionary exposes his poor knowledge of freedom. Historically, the Poles' motto had been to fight "for our freedom and yours." For example, Kosciuszko and Pulaski fought in the American Revolutionary War and Polish pilots fought in the Battle of Britain in World War II. But Lipska questions whether the struggle against foreign powers has prepared average citizens for the exercise of freedom in a democracy. As elsewhere in her poetry, the light-hearted tone and colloquial language mask a multi-level play on words and concepts.

Lipska's awareness of the importance of history and her use of unexpected, often incongruous juxtapositions—Sartre and telephone books, in the next poem—are already evident in her first collection, named simply *Poems* (*Wiersze,* published in 1967). The poem "We", sometimes considered a statement on the 1968 generation, illustrates its struggle to create a new vision for the future out of the grey reality, contrasting with a more glorious wartime past.

> We—the post-war generation wide open—
> in the full comfort of our bodies
> read Sartre and telephone books.
> We consider carefully all earthquakes.
> We. The post-war generation, from peaceful flower pots.
> . . . .
> We envy those
> who in high lace-up boots
> went through war.
>
> With our birth, they honored the dead.
> But the bullet ridden memory
> We must bear. We.[12]
> ("We", in Lipska 1967: 5-6)

Lipska continues her exploration of the meaning of freedom and democracy in her 1990 collection, *Restricted Parking Zone (Strefa ograniczonego postoju)*, written after Poles voted for a democratic government. Poems such as "We choose freedom" ["Wybieramy wolnosc"] (p. 152), or "Service Manual" ["Instrukcja obslugi"] (p. 153) expose the unpreparedness of ordinary citizens for the new democratic freedoms. Instead of expressing euphoria, Lipska calls the nation *dead* or unresponsive. "Service Manual" is conceived as an attempt on the part of the first-person speaker to get a new machine (the nation) to work. The reader constantly has to make connections between phrases with a concrete, mechanical content ("replacement parts") and abstract concepts and historical events engraved on the national consciousness ("uprisings"). In addition, some expressions, such as "revolutions," can have a concrete or an abstract meaning depending on the context. Other expressions, such as "ambushes," are out of context at the literal level of a service manual but serve as a bridge between a serious and a humorous reading of the poem. Readers must constantly be on the alert and operate on two wavelengths. According to Arthur Koestler (1964), a theorist of humor, the moment when the connection between the two separate spheres of discourse is perceived by the reader or when s/he *gets it*, a jolt of energy thus produced is then dispelled in laughter.[13] I would argue that Lipska's text creates a framework allowing the readers to perceive the incongruities between the present, dominated by technology, and national historical memory. Then, with the stimulus of the text, the readers are spurred on to assume an active role and to imagine the future. The excess energy is redirected to ignite a new project. The gender-marked first-person feminine verbs—Lipska uses masculine forms when they suit her purpose—tempt us to identify the speaker as the implied and ultimately "real" author of the text. The poem may then be read as a statement of Lipska's poetics: It is the role of the poet to mobilize the nation's inner mechanisms, to awaken its historical memory and to mine its deposits of vital energy, for the nation to re-create itself. She declares:

> I attempt to get the nation to work.
> I read carefully the service instructions.
> I turn the nation to the left.
> I turn the nation to the right.
> But the nation doesn't respond.
> The nation is dead.
> I choose revolutions. Uprisings. Codes.
> I set up ambushes exactly according to the description
> but the nation does't work.
> The nation is dead.
> The old battlefields are overgrown by grass.
> ("Service Manual," in Lipska 1990: 153)

In her most recent collection, *People for Beginners* [*Ludzie dla poczatkujacych*], (Lipska 1997), inspired no doubt by Lipska's stay in Austria, the attitudes and contexts of average citizens in a Western democracy are exposed in a series of poems centering on "Mr. Schmetterling." In a further stylistic development, these poems seem to be brief narratives, similar to photographic snapshots, although at times, the verbal juxtapositions are hermetic or surreal, the language is colloquial and the disposition of the text on the page resembles prose.

> Mr. Schmetterling thinks skeptically
> about United Europe. He treats the idea as a failed
> tourist offer. Europe of the end-of-the-century
> reminds him of a skyscraper. There's a bigger and bigger crowd on
> the staircase. From the hands of the librarian loaning
> registration books, a handbag falls down. An abandoned first
> edition of someone's joint autobiography. Tatoos of metaphors
> on the building's walls. Democracy for Mr.
> Schmetterling is like a stomach medication; bitter, tart
> drops. They help and they disagree with you. Mr. Schmetterling
> unites with his own solitude. The New Europe is
> useless to him. Just in case, he perfumes
> his bed and puts two trout into his micro-
> wave oven. Around him, a transparent landscape of Gösser
> beer. A culinary hippopotamus of history. Mr. Schmetterling
> stands on the right side and sets his alarm clock
> for seven a.m.
> ("Mr. Schmetterling Ponders the European Union," in Lipska 1997: 202-203)

In this poem, the speaker is almost invisible and his/her voice restricted to reporting facts and observable details, with a minimum of commentary. Nevertheless, the speaker's role is only deceptively simple. As a photographer behind a camera, s/he is responsible for selecting the field of vision: the subject and the details of the story. Unlike a snapshot, however, a narrative can easily juxtapose moments in time that are out of chronological order. As part of Mr. Schmetterling's story, we learn that "as a child he stood/between the thighs of his parents applauding Hitler"—his first political experience. The adult protagonist's perception of democracy as bitter-tasting medication for indigestion and his self-absorption in the routines and comforts of daily life—the setting of the alarm clock, the trout in the microwave oven—expose the limitations of citizens at the grass-roots level in the "free West" (Austria). In addition, Mr. Schmetterling's biography evokes the threatening past of those whose parents supported Hitler, still haunting us today. But the speaker does not say that. The readers must consider the un/importance of those memories in the making of the European Union. Lipska exposes difficult problems and poses hard questions. Ultimately, the readers wonder where are the model citizens, "the people for beginners" in newly established democracies? What are the differences between the citizens of Western and Eastern European democracies?

I have chosen to focus on the theme of national consciousness in Lipska's work,[14] of particular interest as we consider the place of women in Polish society and the impact of the change to democracy. It seems clear that in all of Lipska's poetic enterprise there is a visionary whose voice, like Cassandra's, calls out to those who would listen. (Lipska anticipates this view of the poet's role, in a poem titled "Poet? Criminal? Madman?" ["Poeta? Zbrodniarz? Szaleniec?"] in Lipska 1998: 150). If she does not write feminist manifestos to claim women's rights, she has assumed the role to which those who fight for equal rights aspire.[15] A close reading of her poems demonstrates that behind the play of masks, a voice addressing the nation may be heard. Poles have a long tradition of looking to their writers to preserve their sense of national selfhood and to *tell the truth*. In the nineteenth century when Poland was partitioned, and again during the forty years of communist rule, it was the writers and other creative artists who kept national memory alive and offered views of reality independent of prevailing politics and propaganda. (This tradition of course is not unique to Poland. Latin Americans living under political dictatorships have also traditionally looked to their writers to tell the truth [Riffaterre 1978)]). Lipska's poems discussed here reveal that she is passionately absorbed in the fate of the nation and the survival of Western values. Ultimately, however, her colloquial language, word play and the oppositional tension between the protagonists and the poetic speakers requiring the participation of complicit readers, transform the role of the poet as visionary into that of a catalyst. Although Lipska's persistent word games call attention to language itself, her work is not art for art's sake. Her poetry beguiles the readers through its wit and verbal play but, as in any form of humor, it also allows them to rise above the naïve protagonists and serves as a stimulus to critical thinking. Lipska leads her readers to assume the responsibility for co-creating of the poems' meanings, transforming readers into active participants in the flow of ideas and the creation of culture.

CONCLUSIONS

Although Lipska's poetic voice is very different from Szymborska's, the two poets share some techniques: the use of multiple points of view, ironic use of naïve protagonists, and colloquial language, manipulated to expose its clichés and mined for ambiguities and hidden meanings. Both poets oblige their readers to make an intellectual effort: to compare, invert, reflect, and draw conclusions. With few exceptions, their poetry is unsentimental, far removed from the confessional poetry often associated with women poets. They uphold Western values despite relentlessly questioning them. In a broad sense, the place from which both Szymborska and Lipska speak as poets remains constant before and after democracy, even when their specific subjects vary.

While the Polish economy is committed to capitalism, and a great many professional and working-class Poles have turned their energies to closing the economic divide between Eastern and Western Europe, Polish poets have concerned themselves with enduring values. A recent *New Yorker* article illustrates the changes in Polish society in a feature on Helena Luczywo, with the following subtitle: "Eighteen years ago, Helena Luczywo was a revolutionary. Now she's about to become one of Eastern Europe's most powerful media moguls" (Ash 1999: 32). The newspaper Helena Luczywo started in her kitchen during the Solidarity period has been transformed into a conglomerate whose shares will be sold at world exchanges. The bemused author, Timothy Garton Ash, who once called Luczywo "Solidarity's Rosa Luxemburg," quotes her as saying, "I'm Margaret Thatcher now." Our reading of Szymborska's and Lipska's poetry demonstrates that their poetic voices have *not* undergone the same volte-face as the economy.

Neither Szymborska nor Lipska withdraw from the broad themes of Western culture and values. By addressing the major themes of our time, they assume a place in the public forum, a place where democracy was born but where, until now, few women were able to speak during two millenia of Western history. Perched precariously on the eastern, exposed flank of Europe, Poles have a unique vantage point for viewing the hard-fought-for Western values as both *insiders* and *outsiders*. They write with the diffidence of those who often feel betrayed by the West but yet are passionate in the defense of Western values. Both poets assume multiple masks, and explode language from the inside, exposing the inconsistencies, the traps and shortcomings of our common Western (patriarchal) norms. They set up unexpected juxtapositions and probe themes essential to Western culture, committing the readers to "hard mental work."[16]

NOTES

1. The section on Szymborska was written by Grazyna Borkowska. For Borkowska's earlier work on this author, published in Polish see Borkowska (1991).

2. For a sample of these readings of Szymborska's poetry see, Stanislaw Balbus (1996); Malgorzata Baranowska.(1996); Anna Legezynska (1996); Tadeusz Nyczek (1997).

3. "Reszta," in Wislawa Szymborska, *Poezje* (1997: 62). All translations from this edition are by the co-author (Nowakowska Stycos) of this chapter in cooperation with Elzbieta Kosakowska.

4. " Mozliwosci," in Wislawa Szymborska (1996: 78-79). Translation by the co-author (Nowakowska Stycos) of this chapter in cooperation with Elzbieta Kossakowska.

5. The text on Ewa Lipska was written by Maria Nowakowska Stycos.

6. Anna Swirszczynska had died by that time.

7. Literature has been the source of *truth* for Polish readers since the time of the partitions by Russia, Prussia and Austria (1772, 1793, 1795), when Poland was wiped from the map of Europe until independence in 1918.

8. Krzysztof Lisowski, editor of Lipska *(*1996: 5).

9. Lisowski, (Lipska 1996: 19; see note 3) mentions sixteen. *Godziny poza godzinami* (Lipska 1998) appeared two years later.

10. The translation is mine (Nowakowska Stycos). Baranczak teaches Polish Literature at Harvard University.

11. The whale ["wieloryb"] is a composite word in Polish made up of the adjective "big" and the noun "fish." Lipska plays on the word at different levels. There is a popular expression, "a fat fish" ["gruba ryba"], which indicates an influential person in the power structure. Baranczak aptly connects it with the Biblical leviathan which, according to the *Columbia Encyclopedia* (1963), is "a symbol of evil to be ultimately defeated by the power of good."

12. All translations are done by the co-author, Maria Nowakowska Stycos. Here she has consulted the translation by Barbara Plebanek and Tony Howard (1991).

13. For a synthetic theory of humor and its interrelation with art and discovery, see Arthur Koestler (1964).

14. For a discussion of Lipska's work in English, see Lidia Stefanowska (1996).

15. For those who may wonder, Lipska is divorced and has a daughter.

16. Wislawa Szymborska,."Landscape", in Stanislaw Baranczak and Clare Cavanagh (1995: 37).

REFERENCES

Ash, Timothy Garton. 1999. Helena's Kitchen. *The New Yorker* (13 February): 32-38.
Balbus, Stanislaw. 1996. *Swiat ze wszystkich stron swiata. [The World from All Sides of the World]*. Krakow: Wydawnictwo Literackie.
Baranczak, Stanislaw. 1985; Dec. Kwit z "Przechowalni ciemnosci" [A Ticket from the "Check-room for Darkness"] *Kultura, 12*, no. 459, 132-35.
Baranczak, Stanislaw & Clare Cavanagh (Trans.). 1995. *View with a Grain of Sand: Selected Poems.* New York: Harcourt Brace & Company.
Baranowska, Malgorzata. 1996. *Tak lekko bylo o tym wiedziec...Szymborska i swiat.* Wroclaw: Wydawnictwo Dolnoslaskie.
Borkowska, Grazyna. 1991. Szymborska ex-centryczna [Szymborska Ex-Centric]. *Teksty drugie [Secondary Texts]*; no. 4, 45-58.
Koestler, Arthur. 1964. *The Act of Creation.* New York: Macmillan.
Kopalinski, Wladyslaw. 1985. S*lownik mitow i tradycji kultury [Dictionary of Myths and Cultural Traditions]. Vol.* 2. Warsaw: Panstwowy Instytut Wydawniczy.
Krynski, Magnus J. & Robert A. Maguire (Trans. 1981). *Sounds, Feelings, Thoughts: Seventy Poems by Wislawa Szymborska.* Princeton, NJ: Princeton University Press.
Kwiatkowski, Jerzy. (Ed.). 1997. *Poezje by Wislawa Szymborska.* Warsaw: Panstwowy Instytut Wydawniczy.
Lipska, Ewa. 1967. *Wiersze [Poems].* Warsaw: Panstwowy Instytut Wydawniczy.
Lipska, Ewa. 1985. *Przechowalnia ciemnosci. [Check-room for Darkness].* Warsaw: Wydawnictwo "Przedswit."
_____. 1990. *Strefa ograniczonego postoju [Restricted Parking Zone].* Warsaw: Panstwowy Instytut Wydawniczy.
Legezynska, Anna. 1996. *Wislawa Szymborska.* Poznan: Dom Wydawniczy Rebis.
_____. 1998. *Godziny poza godzinami [Hours after Hours].* Warsaw: Panstwowy Instytut Wydawniczy.
_____. 1996. *Wspolnicy zielonego wiatraczka. Lekcja Literatury z Krzysztofem Lisowkim [Co-owners of a Green Windmill. Literature Lesson with Krzysztof Lisowki].* Krakow: Wydawnictwo Literackie.
_____. 1997. *Ludzie dla poczatkujacych [People for Beginners].* Krakow: Wydawnictwo Literackie.
Nyczek, Tadeusz (Ed.) 1995. *Okreslona epoka. Nowa Fala 1968-1993: Wiersze i Komentarze.* Krakow: Oficyna Literacka
_____. 1997. *22x Szymborska [22 times Szymborska].* Poznan: Wydawnictwo a5.
Plebanek, Barbara & Tony Howard (Trans.). 1991. *Poet? Criminal? Madman. Poems by Ewa Lipska.* Intro by Adam Czerniawski. London & Boston: Forest Books.
Riffaterre, Michel. 1978. *Semiotics of Poetry.* Bloomington: Indiana University Press.
Stefanowska, Lidia. 1996. To Behold the Missing Part of the World: The Poetic Vision of Ewa Lipska. *The Polish Review, 41*, no. 4, 383-400.
Szymborska, Wislawa. 1981. *Sounds, Feelings, Thoughts: Seventy Poems by Wislawa Szymborska.* Princeton, NJ: Princeton University Press.
_____. 1997. *Poezje [Poems].* Warsaw: Panstwowy Instytut Wydawniczy.
_____. 1996. *Widok z ziarnkiem piasku.* Poznan: Wydawnictwo a5.

14

The Politics of Architecture and the Architecture of Politics

Sergei Zherebkin and Barbara Wejnert

The role of culture for the appraisal of social reality has attained far-reaching importance. Proceeding beyond denoting the specificity of configuration of human society as a culture product, many have attributed a dynamism to culture in the name of 'culture change' as complementary to, or equal with, "social change." Culture has also been conceived as a process distinct from but related to the social processes. And, from the 1980s, attempts have been made to assert the fundamental or unique role of culture in appraising social reality (Mukherjee 1998: 45).

The architecture and monuments that are one of the products of existing culture clearly reflect and define the social reality of the communist and post-communist periods throughout the regions encompassed by the former Soviet Union. This chapter explores the ideological and political meaning of such architectural forms, an exploration that supports, in conceptual terms, much recent systematic analysis of the interconnectedness rather than the particularities of the three basic social components of polity, economy and culture. In this sense, the discussion supports the post-Marxist viewpoint, embedded in post-modernism, that conceives a unique role for culture in the appraisal of social reality (Lyotard 1984). This perspective directly contradicts the theoretical approaches that prevailed from the 1950s through the 1970s, which analytically distinguished culture as distinct from other societal structures (Mukherjee 1998).

In this framework, the architectural forms of the communist and post-communist periods in the Soviet Union operated as articulated segments of societal structures, and thus, played a significant role in holding together configurations of Soviet-type societies. As Jameson vividly explains, "No satisfactory model of a given mode of production can exist without a theory of the historically and dialectically specific and unique role of 'culture' within it" (1984: XV).

Therefore, this chapter offers an analysis of how architectural forms and monuments can be understood as artifacts that articulate and portray the social, economic and political reality of the developing communist society of the Soviet

Union from its establishment in 1917 to its rupture in 1990. We first provide an analysis of the diversified architectural styles in *appendage* to their personification and reflection of social reality of different stages of communist system's development. We then offer some conclusions about the impact of democracy and market economy ideology on social reality of post-communism as mirrored by architectural forms.

IDEOLOGY, MONUMENTS, AND ARCHITECTURE: RELATIONAL IDIOMS OF THE SOVIET ERA

One of the most visible reminders of the communist epoch is undoubtedly the architecture which accentuated the appearance of Soviet cities for so many years. Regardless of post-communist societal demand for the immediate destruction of such monuments, most citizens of the former Soviet Union still live surrounded by communist architectural forms.

Since the 1917 revolution, the Soviet power, striving to realize communist utopian ideas of cooperative living arrangements and collectivism, supported artistic trends that elaborately glorified the happiness of the masses in drawings, painting, sculpture, artistic posters, films, architecture and monuments. In so doing, the regime intentionally promoted desire among the proletariat to be represented in fine art and other forms of artistic expression. Architectural forms and monuments constructed at that time strongly represented contrasts between the happiness of communist society and the enormity of grief from battles lost to enemies of the people. The category of *enemy of the people* was defined both in economic terms as any property owners, and in human rights terms as those who advocate individualism, human rights, civil liberties and exclusivity of private life. In simple terms, enemies were all those groups that did not want to conform to communist ideological guidance of to communalism, state control and planned living.

One of the initial strategic goals of the Soviet power was to eliminate privacy in social, individual and economic life. Thus, during the first stage of the communist revolution (1917 through the early 1920s), the destructive energy of the proletarian masses was channeled mainly against the policies of the pre-Revolutionary regime and its social institutions. These new post-revolutionary masses were conceptualized as a potency of energy, often represented in art and public monuments as super-productive females that, like the mythological images of sacred Mother Earth, were steadily giving birth to Gods and titans.

Graphic images celebrating this archetypal female potential for bringing new masses to birth were complemented by monuments suggesting the phallic, impregnating male, which, like the mythological Father/Creator, represented how the revolutionary leaders were guiding communist ideology and the collective mind of the Party. As a result, Soviet architecture and public monuments acquired a character of gender asymmetry: women representing the masses; men representing the political power and leadership of the Communist party.

By the late 1920s, as architects began to promote the notion that proletarian power could be only expressed and represented by the masses, this elemental approach to form began to give way to a new movement now called Soviet

Modernism. Directly portraying working people rather than archetypes, this movement coincided with the first five-year plan for rebuilding the Soviet industrial centers, and intentionally linked architecture/monument design style with ideological shifts.

By way of example, in the late 1920s Kharkov, the capital of the Ukraine and one of the biggest industrial and military cities lacking academic or cultural traditions, was selected to serve as a model city that would demonstrate how workers were not only to be organized but to be presented to others as organized by the Soviet power. To underscore this political message, alongside tractor and tank-building plants, the biggest construction works of the first 5-year plan, the government built colossal architectural constructions of iron, concrete and glass in the Bauhaus modernist style (ironically borrowed from socialists in noncommunist Europe). Among the most sizeable of these was the famous Gosprom—the State Industry Management Office Building, constructed between 1925 to 1929—which Romen Rolan, the famous French writer who visited Kharkov early in the 1930s, called an *organized mountain*. Gosprom, representing the new trend in architecture, was at the time of its construction the biggest Ferro-concrete building in Europe. Its shape is that of a rising stepped figure, with many assorted verges and surfaces symbolizing rational organization of the masses. The mountain-ridge is reinforced by the descending contours of the university and military academy buildings located in a semi-circle on the right and left of the Gosprom building itself.

Soviet architectural styles changed again in the 1930s, this time to accommodate new groups of communist hard-liners and their political guidance. It was this period that saw the culmination of mass repression in the USSR, including the continuation of forced collectivization of farms, and, as a result, great famine. The first evidence of corresponding change in the architecture of the time was a visible rupture with the avant-garde and modernist style of the previous direct representations of the masses. Second, most of the new monuments were devoted to the one theme of massive statues portraying the leader of the communist masses—Joseph Stalin. Third, a tendency emerged to connect art with functionalism in the architectural styles expressed in the construction of such buildings as the Moscow Metro, the Communist Party and military headquarters, and high buildings in both the center of Moscow and the capitals of other USSR republics. Each of these buildings was designed to serve not only an administrative or production function but also as a massive public monument, crowned with large-sized figures whose very mass and power would imprint the readiness of working masses to sacrifice themselves to phallic communist utopia.

A good example of this style is the well-known Kharkov monument of Taras Shevchenko (build in 1935), which presents a figure of the poet on a pedestal, surrounded by a spirally-arranged sculptural ensemble that includes three female and thirteen male figures. The characters of the ensemble symbolize the history of the struggle of the Ukrainian people, women and men alike, against oppression (see Photo 14.1).

Photo 14.1
Monument of Taras Shevchenko, built in Kharkov, in 1935. Photo courtesy of Sergei
Zherebkin.

The three female figures, who represent the various stages of the process of radical transformation for Ukrainian woman, are particularly prominent. Two of them are placed below the pedestal, where they eloquently speak for the sufferings of Ukrainian people in pre-Revolutionary times. The first figure is the "mother-pokrytka" (covering/hiding) with her illegally borne child, a frequent female image found in Taras Shevchenko's poetry. The second is a woman-peasant doing her serf obligation work at panschina. The third female image, prominently figured at the top of the monument, represents the new generation of Ukrainian women: the Soviet woman, worker and Komsomol member. Her position at the pinnacle of the monument symbolizes the feeling of joy and happiness of Ukrainian workers within the new socialist society. The mimicry and poses of female images in the Shevchenko monument, like other sculptures of Stalinist times, thus illuminate by juxtaposition the division between, on one hand, the deepest of people's sufferings, the torments caused by oppression and aggression prior to the communist period, and on the other, the feelings of supreme joy and enthusiasm of the communist masses.

The male figures in the ensemble serve as links between woman's terrible past with her promising future. These thirteen figures are massively male, positioned physically between the women, as if to fill in the gaps between the past and present of woman's status, and to express through their bodily postures their determination to sacrifice themselves for the new political system.

Interruption of Soviet societal life by the Second World War, post-war involvement in border disputes and discourse regarding internal political structures of neighboring countries diverted Soviet leaders' attention away from internal politics and toward external affairs. One of the consequences of this political turmoil was relative stability in architectural trends of that time. During the 1950s through 1980s, the period following Stalin's death and subsequent softening of the communist regime, Soviet architecture reflects the ideological shifts that characterized that time. In the earlier period, the focus had been the dictatorship of workers initially presumed essential for establishing a communist system. Now, the dominant ideology called for emphasizing the achievement of the communist regime in terms of developed rather than emergent socialism. The images of the proletariat, the joyful victims, sacrificing themselves for the good of others gave way to a festive style expressive of an epoch of fully-developed socialism. The main theme portrayed in architecture and monuments of this time was that of workers not only desiring to support of the programs and policies of the communist leaders but also courageously withstanding all failures to realize the new regime's full potential.

It was at this time, in the end of 1970s, that Soviet architecture created its apotheosis in the most significant Kharkov monument of the Soviet period: the monument to Lenin, constructed in Svoboda Square. From the ground level one sees, on the right and left of the monument's base, a bas-relief depicting the contours of one female and five male figures. The details of faces and clothing are not as precise as those of the figures of the Shevchenko monument, but the figures themselves similarly symbolize the people's struggle against capitalistic oppression prior to the communist revolution. In the Lenin monument's case, however, their primary purpose lies less in what they themselves symbolize but in how they serve as a foundation for the phallic figures of the leaders of the communist revolution, embodied here in Lenin himself.

Ironically, at the same time that the Lenin monument celebrated communist leadership built on the committed backs of the people, other artists began to privilege attention to the base itself as significant in its own right. In a monument built about the same time—the Heroes of the Ukrainian Revolution of 1917—for example, it is the base in itself that expresses communist ideology. This monument, one of the last large monuments of the Soviet era, was built in the central part of Kharkov, in Sovietskaia Square (now Constitution Square). It consists entirely of a granite block base in the shape of an irregular parallel-piped. Around this base are five figures representing the heroes of the Ukrainian revolution—three workers (including a farm worker), a soldier and a sales-man—but no leader: the space above the base is empty. The monument is thus in actuality, and powerfully, an empty pedestal, which contemporary Khark-ovites describe ironically, with characteristic post-Soviet humor as *Five of them are carrying a refrigerator* (see Photo 14. 2).

At this same time, when leaderless pedestals suggested a shift in perception about the relationship of the people to the state, some Soviet architecture focused more specifically on representing issues of the people's rights. One example of this is a set of monuments (in Tibilissi, for example, which portrays a powerful Mother Georgia looking protectively out over the city) supposedly celebrating women's political rights and their participation in social, economic and political structures such as people's councils, committees of trade unions and congresses of the Communist party. Like the empty pedestal, however, such monuments speak more of irony than reality. While it was true that the overall representation of Soviet women in political institutions was much higher than that of women in Western parliamentary structures, very few women actually held positions at the highest levels of the decision-making political structures, such as the Politburo, the Central Committee of the Communist Party or Minis-tries. Most of the women representatives served only on the lowest levels of the nomenclature, where they reached up to 30 percent of the total number of mem-bers of the lower administration. Thus, while public monuments might try to praise the progress of women toward equality, such representations of gender equality were more façade than real—just as publicly promoted strategies of gender equality were more democratic-appearing facades of an otherwise totali-tarian regime than real attempts to establish or promote equality, civil and de-mocratic rights, or to include a broader spectrum of society's representatives into local and national governing assemblies.

ARCHITECTURE OF THE POST-SOVIET ERA

Since the collapse of the USSR no new monuments that symbolize general communist ideology have been constructed. On the contrary, in many Soviet cities communist monuments have been demolished.

Photo 14.2
Monument of the Heroes of the Ukrainian Revolution of 1917. Photo courtesy of Sergei
Zherebkin.

The scope of the destruction of monuments varies between republics and their cities. For example, in general in the Ukraine most remaining Soviet-period monuments have been destroyed, but in Kharkov, site of so many of the previous regime's symbolic monuments, only one has been shattered: that of Dzerzhinskiy, the first chief of the Extraordinary Committee that proceeded the Soviet Security Forces (KGB), located in front of the Metro Station. Furthermore, also in Kharkov, the post-perestroika period saw the construction of a huge, communist-style monument of Marshal Zhukov, a famous Soviet commander in the Second World War, in one of city's central squares, [the Prospect of 50th Anniversary of the USSR]. This construction raises questions about whether the state authorities may remain more ambivalent with respect to the former Soviet traditions than more recently proclaimed desires to gain a new *democratic* image of the independent nation state would suggest.

Since this last monument of Zhukov, no monuments have been constructed for or about the masses in any other Ukrainian city. This reflects the very real changes that have occurred in the character of the proletariat, who—no longer blindly following the communist leaders, relying on their help in every aspect of life—are now independent, self-organized survivors in the initiated market economy system. The new masses have gone through proletariat dictatorship, developed socialism and the collapse of the USSR. They are no longer killed, nor put in prisons, camps or psychiatric clinics. They may often be impoverished, but they are also victorious over the former monopoly of a totalitarian communist regime that had unlimited control and hegemonic decision-making power over all issues of life and death for its citizens.

The new masses no longer desire to be glorified in monuments or to accommodate themselves to communist ideology. Their primary concern is participation in and adaptation to new economic structures (Baev 1995). Hence, the role of public monuments is being replaced by functional architectural constructions designated to serve *consumer needs* of the people living in the post-perestroika period of transition to the market economy.

Since the early 1990s, architectural developments no longer emphasize construction of the large-size industrial plants and Party headquarters or other political institutions' buildings, which typified the architecture of the Soviet period. Rather than embodying the previous ideological propaganda about the greatness of communist society, the focus of post-Soviet architecture now emphasizes consumerism, commercialism, private ownership and societal wealth. New commercial buildings, such as banks, private offices and small luxury shops for the newly rich post-Soviet societies, are copies of contemporary Western European and American architectural styles. Moreover, many of the old residences that used to belong to aristocratic families prior to the revolution are being renovated in central cities of the former Soviet Union (e.g., Moscow, St. Petersburg, Kiev and Kharkov).

But most visible of all, especially during the first years of the post-communist period, are new shopping places, geared to accommodating new consumers' needs. Along with exclusive, luxury shops are mushrooming market places for the working masses, the bazaars. Unlike the luxurious stores mirroring Western cultural images, these bazaars have a distinct style that is worth serious attention.

Initially, just after the collapse of the communist regime, bazaars consisted of miniature trading posts or booths where tradesmen, placing clothes, cosmetics or other consumer or food products directly on pavements on blankets, small portable tables or on chairs, tried to sell their goods to passers-by. Most such bazaars were located on main streets and squares, or in front of public places with heavy pedestrian traffic, such as train, metro and bus stations or large stores. The most common architectural forms prevailing in every city's central streets and traffic arteries, the functional purpose of bazaars was to provide public spaces for non-formal business transactions. Given their enormous numbers, however, such bazaars can be also been seen as a kind of architectural monument that functions similarly to those of the Soviet years, redecorating cities to reflect the changing ideologies and values of the new era.

Initially, after the collapse of the Soviet state, the bazaars sprang up spontaneously, when a lot of people who had lost state jobs started to sell food and second-hand goods wherever it was possible to find potential buyers. By the mid-1990s, city authorities began to take control over bazaar activity and development, regulating their spread and controlling income acquired from sales by its taxation. As part of such new regulations, bazaar owners were now required to get permission, or a formal license, to establish a bazaar, and hence to be registered as a bazaar owner. The registered bazaars were allowed to be placed in cities as more permanent constructions, characterized by roofs, walls and counters similar to newsstands. Sometimes they were separated from the street or sidewalk by a fence. Atypical in communist countries, these new architectural forms now widely decorate post-communist cities.

As more permissions were issued, creating more such structures taking up more space within cities themselves, some bazaars were moved outside the city limits to specially designated fenced-off squares. These new spaces, similar to American flea-markets, are characterized by rows of trading booths arranged in geometrical order with on office building designated for city managers of the property, and for militia that execute control over sales' taxation and can confiscate goods or issue fines if proof of paid taxes is not presented.

From a distance, these bazaars, as presented in Photo 14.3, resemble besieged forts, an image which in actuality comes close to a kind of truth. In fact, due to an atmosphere of fear, the uncertainty of tax inspections, militia, and the possibility of fines and confiscations, bazaars have indeed become kinds of forts, not keeping danger out but containing it by providing parameters that can be more readily controlled.

Photo 14.3

A bazaar in Kharkov in 1999. Rows of trading booths in geometrical order. Photo courtesy of Sergei Zherebkin.

In other words, bazaars are forts where the enemies do not stand outside the walls but rather penetrate inside, fueling an atmosphere of threat and fear. Within the limited space that the newly-constructed bazaars provide, executing control over non-formal trade transactions is easier and quicker for the new state regime.

An extension of bazaars particularly worth noting are trading posts operated by shuttles, or Chelnocks in Russian (Morvant 1995). The name is a slang word for a person who is working as a seller at a big market (a post-Soviet outdoor shopping center) who at times travels to neighboring countries such as Turkey or Poland to purchase more goods. The shuttles' posts are similar to the initial bazaars that emerged within cities, with goods exposed on blankets and a trade person standing by, but with a difference: Rather than respected entrepreneurs, shuttle sellers carry a negative image of an impoverished, dishonest beggar more than that of an honest salesman, and most of them are women. The shuttles are legally permitted to sell goods only within the limits of bazaars, and are prime targets for taxation.

On the radio, tradesmen are constantly reminded about their liability for breaking the rules of trade and tax legislation which, with time, have become more rigid and often confusing, as double tax systems and regulations reversing prior rules become more frequent. In other words, the bazaars that were spontaneously established to the secure financial needs of workers released from work within the Soviet controlled economy—and which are spontaneous expressions of adaptation to the new market economy—are now becoming targets of local government control. In Michel Foucault's words, the totalitarian repression has acquired a form of bio-power of biological survival finally beyond gender codes of "phallic" and/or "female" (in Rabinow 1991: 257).

The harsher restrictions placed on shuttle operators as compared to bazaar operators take the form of more parsimonious scrutiny (and control) of their trading activities, and more frequent control of their tax liabilities. Such discriminatory treatment reinforces the negative image of shuttles, vividly portraying the role that gender plays in acceptance of entrepreneurial pursuits. In contrast to bazaar operators, who are predominantly male, the shuttles are mostly women, and this gender distinction fuels differential images, of men's and women's entrepreneurial skills and abilities.

The post-communist symbolic portrayal of women has changed a great deal since communist times. In architectural iconography she is no longer referred to as a Motherland, a hero Woman-Worker and a hero Woman-Peasant. Two emerging symbolic presentations of women include the historical symbol of Bereginia, the *feminine* keeper of Ukrainian hearth and home, as now the owners of the marginal, publicly criticized shuttles. These new female symbols bear little or no relation to the mystery of femininity so glorified by pre-communist as well as communist iconography. They also suggest, particularly in the social architecture of the shuttle, that the social-economic status of post-Soviet women, who receive scanty pensions or eke out livings through shuttle management, represent the highest percentage of those suffering the severest financial deprivation.

CONCLUDING COMMENTS

As noted, the politics of architecture and the architecture of politics within the communist period went through a number of transformations with respect to the relationships of style, form and functionality to ideological messages intended to convince both Soviet citizens and the outside Western world that Soviet communism embodied great *Truths*—particularly about the revered role of proletariat in a communist society. Such old symbolic representations of proletariat power, replete with obedience to the guidance of the Communist party and political leaders, no longer hold in the post-communist time, but no new politic of architecture has yet emerged to take its place.

The visible architectural forms of newly built banks, shops and commercial places, trading booths and bazaars, however, may play a disturbingly similar role to that played by architectural monuments during communism. On one hand, they symbolically deliver a message to former Soviet citizens and to the outside world that post-Soviet society is indeed changing its priorities and values. But, just as the previous era's monuments symbolized proletarian obedience to communist political power, so the commercialized architectural forms of post-communist society may embody a new set of Westernized values, such as individualism, materialism and consumerism. If so, the new politics of architecture may represent less an engagement with democracy than a shift of proletarian obedience from one master to another: from communist political power to the new macro-structures of a market economy.

Regardless of political connotations and the impact of diverse systems of communism and post-communism, the description of the politic of architecture provides vital evidence that "the evaluation of the cardinal valuation of humankind in any configuration of human society, at any point in time, is internalized and registered by its culture" (Mukherjee 1998: 40). But it also suggests the importance of broader structural relations between institutional structures of polity, economy and culture, and an exegetic expression of biases toward minorities that protrude ideological statements communicated within, and through, cultural artifacts and political ideology.

The latter points to the interconnectedness of culture with political and economic spheres, and to the interaction of new cultural images with the social stratification system, an argument that has received insufficient attention in studies on post-communist transitions. Although much more research on this theoretical proposition is needed, this discussion illustrates that a broad array of variables can significantly influence the societal internalization of reality, and calls potential researchers to further investigate this problem. If future analyses are conducted, such an integrated view will add to the understanding and measurement of democratization processes, and potentially lead to parsimonious accounts of their outcomes.

REFERENCES

Baev, Pavel. 1995. Drifting Away From Europe. In *Transition: Events and Issues in the Former Soviet Union and East Central Europe and Southern Europe* (No. 11, pp. 30-36). Czech Republic: Open Media Research Institute.

Jameson, F. 1984. Foreword. In J. Lyotard, *The Postmodern Conditions: A Report on Knowledge*. Minneapolis: University of Minnesota Press.

Lyotard, J. 1984. *The Postmodern Conditions: A Report on Knowledge*. Minneapolis: University of Minnesota Press.

Morvant, Penny. 1995. The Beleagured Coal-Mining Industry Strikes Back (No. 11, pp. 58-61). In *Transition: Events and Issues in the Former Soviet Union and East Central Europe and Southern Europe*. Czech Republic: Open Media Research Institute.

Mukherjee, Ramkrishna. 1998 (April). Social Reality and Culture. *Current Sociology, 46,* 39-50.

Rabinow, Paul. 1991. *The Foucault Reader*. Harmondsworth: Penguin Books.

VI

Concluding Remarks

15

The Impact of Democratic Transitions on Politics, Economy and Culture: Lessons from Eastern Europe and Russia

Barbara Wejnert

Based on the material covered in this book, three important lessons can be drawn from Eastern European and Russian transition to democracy. The first is that the transition did not take place in the political and economic sphere alone, as it is often presented (Lederer 1992), but transpired simultaneously in all major spheres of societal life. Furthermore, because all social institutions are interconnected, the initiation of political reforms caused enormous, multilevel changes in all social strata and affected the performance of all essential institutions, from governments and political institutions to the banking and trade systems, industry and arts.

The second lesson develops from an understanding of democratic transitions as processes that started long before the democratic elections of 1989 and the 1990s. Social dissatisfaction and economic and political tensions within each of the states were expressed in civil protests and the rise of alternative culture well before the 1990s, as well as in progressive economic strategies implemented by communist reformers, for example, the Hungarian and Yugoslavian economic reforms (Bruszt & Stark 1991; Putnam 1990; Stark 1990; Szelényi 1990; Szelényi & Kostello 1998). Thus, regardless of individual pathways that each country selected for their political and economic reforms (Stark & Bruszt 1998), the history of transition from communism to democracy in East-Central Europe and the former USSR should begin with the first organized citizens' rebellion against totalitarianism, communist rule, or the first economic reforms oriented toward the market economy.

Considering existing literature, we can assume that the same trend was exhibited by democratic transitions that took place in other countries in the 1970s and 1980s, for example, in Latin America (Higley & Gunther 1992; Przeworski 1991) and Southern Europe (Pridham 1990; Tarrow 1989).

The third lesson refers to the specific type of material that this book encompasses. This book is a collection of articles written by political leaders and scholars that presents a variety of perspectives on selected issues, strategies and political events that directly reflect this complex process of democratic transition. These events and strategies were chosen as a focus of the study because of their critical nature in assessing the transition. The editor of this volume believes that such an approach could benefit potential investigations by (1) providing fertile material for future heuristic and ideographic scholarly analysis of democratization processes and their practical implementation; (2) providing knowledge that could be transferred, in the form of informative data on the complex matter of these transitions, to political advisors, policy practitioners and government members; and (3) providing information that could be disseminated to a broader public interested in democratization processes.

In other words, the material presented about democratic transitions in former communist states drawn from the *political, economic, policy* and *culture-centered* analyses, could be utilized in future studies on democratic transitions as well as in practical attempts at adoption of a democratic system by nondemocratic states. We now briefly turn to the contents of each type of analysis.

THE POLITICAL-CENTERED ANALYSIS

During the years prior to democratic transition, the communist countries began a journey toward developed communist systems on what seemed to be an even road. If they met occasionally with twists and turns, this was only part of the process of exploring the different paths that communist governments and ruling elites might devise for public regulation to buffer its citizens against political rights and material wants. In an era when many industrialized nations were developing competitive market economies and democratic rights for their citizens, the communist regimes sought to help not working people, but small ruling elites secretly covering this political strategy with ideological propaganda.

Such ideological manipulation and unfair economic and political maneuvering culminated in the illegitimacy of ruling regimes, and their eventual collapse. Within this perspective, Wejnert's chapter explicates the issue of civil resistance to communist rule in the light of civil movements and dissatisfaction which eventually led to administrative replacements within the communist regimes. Examination of workers' dissatisfaction with communist regime is the topic of Bloom's paper, which recounts the strikes and collective protest actions against the communist regime organized by Polish shipyard workers. Bloom draws on interviews with eyewitnesses and protestors to offer a general overview of the impact of these historical events on the future development of nationwide Solidarity movements and the breaking of the communist regime in 1989. These chapters offer explicit examples of the power of social movements in weakening nondemocratic governments.

In a similar vein, Gredelj's paper investigates public reactions to the Yugoslavian regime's communist propaganda and its strategy of manipulation, nationalist promotion and lies, which act to divert societal attention from the problems of extended privileges toward ruling elites and growing poverty, social inequalities and potential unemployment among the masses. Yugoslavian society, discontented with the propaganda and the politics of ruling groups, organized cultural protest movements as the safest form of political protest actions.

Collective protests that were spreading through the Soviet-bloc states eventually culminated in the collapse of communist rule and the introduction of democratic transition. But the newly implemented democratic system brought with it new policies and laws. Among them was the policy of legal and financial retributions paid to victims of communist economic and political oppressions (e.g., victims of the forced collectivization of farms, nationalization of industry and private property, and political persecution). Jan Kavan's analysis of the *lustration* policy in the former Czechoslovakia at the time of Vaclav Havel's presidency—the first popularly elected presidency in the post-communist period—provides a personal recounting of post-communist retributive justice initiated by newly democratic governments. Here the goals and mistakes made in the implementation of the *lustration* policy, and their impact on a societal sense of justice and fairness are discussed in great detail. Kavan also briefly compares the Czechoslovakian situation to other forms of retroactive justice in former communist states.

It is possible to draw two conclusions from these politically-centered discussions. Firstly, civilian opposition and protests action was a response to the authoritarian, anti-democratic rule of communist regimes. The growing dissatisfaction with communist elites that was expressed through such collective protest actions became the *corner stone* and *precipitating* factor, that resulted in the eventual downfall of nondemocratic regimes. Secondly, the early post-communist community was characterized by innovative, sometimes drastic changes, including implementation of new policies and laws. The new policies were not always perceived as the most just and fair by citizens, and were sometimes associated with turmoil and political mistakes. Such situations created dissonance between the social expectation of equality consistent with the image of a democratic system, and the social reality of injustice. Thus, the introduction of free democratic elections, and other forms of democratic political participation, were not equivalent with the establishment of democracy, but rather the first steps on the long road to the institutionalization of democracy.

THE ECONOMY-CENTERED ANALYSIS

In a continuation of the road metaphor, the former communist states were lagging on the otherwise universally traveled road toward modernity, high quality of production and a competitive market economy. They also lagged in the creation of suitable economic living standards comparable to Western democracies. A centrally-organized economy and a tendency toward self-sufficiency cut communist states off from the fast-developing Western world and its technological innovations. Strategies of mutual economic assistance within the communist bloc inhibited exposure to the principles of global markets, international investments and international finances. It is true that exposure to global corporatism is not always the most beneficial to local national economies in the developing world, because it often produces large economic disparities and social inequalities (Bornschier, Chase-Dunn & Rubinson, 1992). However, in most cases it provides higher living standards and a better quality and greater quantity of consumer goods. Because of this, most developing countries strive to be incorporated into Western markets. As a result, in most of the former communist countries, demands to improve living conditions led to protest confrontations, loss of legitimacy within ruling regimes, reforms of centrally-organized communist economic systems (e.g., in Hungary and Yugoslavia) and requests for privatization and market competition. Mirroring the economic opportunities of Western democracies, market competition was assumed to constitute the ultimate key to the overall improvement of living conditions and quality of life.

However, as several chapters of this book address, the market re-orientation of post-communist states has resulted in the emergence of a large income gap, social inequality, need for state fiscal reform, complex financial problems due to the reconstruction of banking systems and subsequent difficulties typically experienced by transitional economies in the formation of new capital. The chapter written by former Polish Finance Minister Grzegorz Kolodko, for example, comprehensively and comparatively analyzes fiscal policies and capital formation in transitional economies across former communist states. Nancy Tuma, Mikk Titma and Rein Murakas, who emphasize the transitional economy of Estonia, focus on income inequality, the primary contributor to social inequalities. Alexei Makeshin in turn discuses the complexity of privatization politics in Russia, which as Piccone observed, made the dismantling of the Soviet system inevitable:

the Soviet system cannot be readily marketized without first being dismantled. Its future prospects are in at least one respect even worse that those of other Third World societies attempting to industrialize: unlike in the latter where it is merely a matter of standard industrialization, the USSR will have to first, deindustrialize, i.e., dismantle most of the existing industrial system, before even beginning to re-industrialize on the basis of a de-politicized instrumental rationality. (Piccone 1990: 20)

The complicated problems of economic reconstruction and prevailing social inequality in new democracies frequently led to societal disappointment and dissatisfaction, leading in some instances to a return to semi-communist societies (e.g., in Belarus or Albania).

By presenting the interconnectedness of new political institutions with new economic developments, this book allows readers to see the sustainability and success of democratization as highly dependent on many preexisting domestic economic conditions of the formerly communist states. In any future analysis of a post-communist, new democratic system and the economic restructuring associated with these systems, the consideration of such pre-existing economic conditions might be an essential component of dialectic, analytic scholarly debates regarding the success potential of newly implemented policies in the transitional economies of democratizing nations.

THE POLICY-CENTERED ANALYSIS

It is easy to understand why former Soviet-bloc states developed distinct social policies during communist times, but only if the politics of such policymaking are situated within a broader, organizationally grounded analysis of communist political development. In the same vein, to understand post-communist policies, one needs to consider a broad spectrum of conditions within the political and economic environment during the years of the post-communist transition. Theda Skocpol correctly explains that:

Social policies in the United States (and elsewhere) have not developed simply in tandem with capitalistic industrialization or urbanization; they have not been straightforward responses to the demands that emerging social classes place upon governments. Governmental institutions, electoral rules, political parties, and prior public policies—all of these, and their transformations over time, create many of the limits and opportunities within which social policies are devised and changed by politically involved actors over the course of a nation's history. (Skocpol 1992: 527)

In former communist countries, the formation and standardization of post-communist governments and the governing entities supporting them were the main focus of post-communist ruling elites, which created barriers for the implementation of numerous social policies. Hence, until recently democratized governments did not respond to many societal demands concerning citizens' well-being and emerging social problems. The policy-oriented chapters by Lara Romaniuk, Mayone Stycos, Barbara Wejnert and Zbigniew Tyszka, Juliusz Gardawski, and Grzegorz Kolodko examine some problems relevant to policy. The list of such problems is long and diverse, and includes issues such as poverty, emergence of the underclass, change in worker attitude toward the market economy, uncontrolled alcohol and tobacco sales, rapidly increasing gaps in income and living conditions, and disparities in the economic development of rural and urban communities. Romaniuk's paper considers the problems of health policy, with specific emphasis on tobacco and alcohol addictions and their impact on the mortality rate and health complications. Stycos, Wejnert and Tyszka address issues related to the welfare and well-being of women living in rural communities. Finally, Kolodko explores social security and social equality policies incorporated in the presented strategy for economic development that, by emphasizing economic justice, could serve as a potential solution to the attitude of workers toward market competition, as analyzed by Gardawski. The central message of all these analyses is that new democratic governments need to respond to many quickly evolving social problems. Hence, in the near future, a concentration on domestic policy and the domestic problems of social security and societal quality of life inevitably ought to be on the political agenda of the democratic governments and need the immediate attention of policymakers if democratization processes are to continue.

THE CULTURE-CENTERED ANALYSIS

The emphasis on changes in culture assisting political and economic transformations represents examples of a new conceptual trend to re-focus theoretical analysis on the interconnectedness of the three basic elements of societal life: politics, economics and culture. Maria Nowakowska Stycos and Grazyna Borkowska, for example, discusses the impact of political transitions on poetry and artistic freedom by analyzing the literary output of two Polish writers, Nobel prize winner Wislawa Szymborska and the younger, promising poet Ewa Wolska. Trends and changes in artistic expressions within music and film are the main focus of Stjepan Gredelj's chapter on cultural movements as political protest. In "Politics of Architecture and Architecture of Politics," Sergei Zherebkin and Barbara Wejnert offer an analysis of changes in architectural forms and monuments as a function of political and economic reforms.

These concluding chapters, which discuss the formation of culture as a function of political and economic conditions, provide an empirical groundwork for the developing scholarly dispute regarding the connectedness of the products of culture with political and economic decisions. In the past, this topic had been a focal issue for many major thinkers in sociology. Thus, these papers tie the end of the book to the theme introduced in the first section, which articulated macro- (political and economic) and micro- (cultural) interrelations in social reality. In the most general terms, *Transition to Democracy in Eastern Europe and Russia: Impact on Politics, Economy and Culture* illustrates what has happened in societies during the transition from communism to democracy; what accounted for the formation of the resulting political, economic, policy and cultural realities; and what were the processes influencing such results.

This volume does not intend to take a stance in the popular dispute regarding democracy as the ultimate dream and the end of history and the last men (Fukuyama 1990). However, it adds valuable information to an understanding of the complex and multifaceted processes of democratic transition. It also informs the reader that the success of democratization depends highly on precursory factors such as the preexisting economic and political conditions, the development of political leadership, and the organization of civil society.

REFERENCES

Bornschier, Volker, Christopher Chase-Dunn & Richard Rubinson. 1992. Cross-National Evidence of the Effects of Foreign Investment and Aid on Economic Growth and Inequality: A Survey of Findings and a Reanalysis. *American Journal of Sociology*, *84*, 3, 651-683.

Bruszt, Laszlo & David Stark. 1991. Remaking the Political Field in Hungary: From the Politics of Confrontation to the Politics of Competition. *Journal of International Affairs*, *45*, 1, 201-245.

Fukuyama, Francis. 1992. *The End of History and the Last Man*. New York: Avon Books.

Higley, John & Richard Gunther. 1992. *Elites and Democratic Consolidation in Latin America and Southern Europe*. Cambridge, UK: Cambridge University Press.

Lederer, Ivo John (Ed.). 1992. *Western Approaches to Eastern Europe*. New York: Council on Foreign Relations Press.

Piccone, Paul. 1990. Paradoxes of Perestroika. *Telos*, *84*, 3-33.

Pridham, Geoffrey (Ed.). 1990. *Securing Democracy: Political Parties and Democratic Consolidation in Southern Europe*. New York: Routledge Press.

Przeworski, Adam. 1991. *Democracy and Market*. Cambridge, UK: Cambridge University Press.

Putnam, George W. 1990. Occupational Sex segregation and Economic Inequality under Socialism: Earnings Attainment and Earnings Decomposition in Yugoslavia. *Sociological Quarterly, 31*, 1, 59-75.

Skocpol, Theda. 1992. *Protecting Soldiers and Mothers*. Cambridge, MA: Harvard University Press.

Stark, David. 1990. Privatization in Hungary: From Plan to Market or From Plan to Clan? *East European Politics and Societies, 4*, 3, 351-392.

Stark, David & Laszlo Bruszt. 1998. *Postsocialist Pathways: Transforming Politics and Property in East Central Europe*. Cambridge, UK: Cambridge University Press.

Szelényi, Ivan. 1990. *Socialist Entrepreneurs: Embourgeoisement in Rural Hungary*. Madison, Wisconsin: The University of Wisconsin Press.

Szelényi, Ivan & Eric Kostello. 1998. The Market Transition Debate: Toward a Synthesis. *American Journal of Sociology, 101*, 1082-1096.

Tarrow, Sidney. 1989. *Democracy and Disorder*. New York: Oxford University Press.

Selected Bibliography

Andeweg, Rudy B. 2000. Consociational Democracy. *Annual Review of Political Science, 3,* 509-536.

Banac, Ivo (Ed.). 1992. *Eastern Europe in Revolution.* Ithaca, NY: Cornell University Press.

Beissinger, Mark. 1990 (August). *Protest Mobilization among Soviet Nationalities.* Report submitted to the National Council for Soviet and Eastern European Research.

Bermeo, Nancy (Ed.). 1992. *Liberalization and Democratization: Change in the Soviet Union and Eastern Europe.* Baltimore: John Hopkins University Press.

_____. 1992 (April). Democracy and Lessons of Dictatorship. *Comparative Politics,* 273-291.

Berger, Suzanne. 2000. Globalization and Politics. *Annual Review of Political Science, 3,* 43-62.

Bollen, Kenneth A. 1998. *Cross-Nation Indicators of Liberal Democracy, 1950-1990.* Chapel Hill: University of North Carolina Press.

Bornschier, Volker, Christopher Chase-Dunn & Richard Rubinson. 1992. Cross-National Evidence of the Effects of Foreign Investment and Aid on Economic Growth and Inequality: A Survey of Findings and a Reanalysis. *American Journal of Sociology, 84,* 3, 651-683.

Brown, J. E. 1992. The East European Agenda. In I. J. Lederer (Ed.), *Western Approaches to Eastern Europe.* New York: Council on Foreign Relations Press.

Bruszt, Laszlo & David Stark. 1991. Remaking the Political Field in Hungary: From the Politics of Confrontation to the Politics of Competition. *Journal of International Affairs, 45,* 1, 201-245.

Bunce, Valerie. 1989. Soviet Decline as a Regional Hegemon: Gorbachev and Eastern Europe. *Eastern European Politics and Society, 3,* 235-267.

_____. 1990 (Summer). The Struggle for Liberal Democracy in Eastern Europe. *World Policy Journal, 7.*

Burawoy, Michael. 1997. The Soviet Descent into Capitalism. *American Journal of Sociology, 102,* 1430-1444.

Centeno, Miguel Angel. 1994. Between Rocky Democracies and Hard Markets: Dilemmas of the Double Transition. *Annual Review of Sociology, 20,* 125-147.

Clemens, Elisabeth S. & James M. Cook. 1999. Politics and Institutionalism: Explaining Durability and Change. *Annual Review of Sociology, 25*, 441-466.

Crenshaw, Edward M. 1995. Democracy and Demographic Inheritance: The Influence of Modernity and Proto-Modernity on Political and Civil Rights, 1965 to 1980. *American Sociological Review, 60*, 702-718.

Dahl, A. Robert. 1982. *Dilemmas of Pluralist Democracy*. New Haven: Yale University Press.

_____. 1989. *Polyarchy: Participation and Opposition*. New Haven: Yale University Press.

_____. 1990. *After the Revolution? Authority in Good Society*. New Haven: Yale University Press.

_____. 1998. *On Democracy*. New Haven: Yale University Press.

Deacon, Bob. (Ed.). 1992. *The New Eastern Europe: Social Policy Past, Present and Future*. London, UK: Sage Publications.

DeSoto, Hermine G. & David G. Anderson. 1993. *The Curtain Rises: Rethinking Culture, Ideology and the State in Eastern Europe*. Atlantic Highlands, NJ: Humanities Press International.

DeSoto, Hermine G., David Anderson, Joni Lovenduski & Jean Woodall. 1987. *Politics and Society in Eastern Europe*. Bloomington, IN: Indiana University Press.

DeSoto, Hernando. 2000. *The Mystery of Capital*. New York: Basic Books.

Doyle, Michael. 1983. Kant, Liberal Legacies and Foreign Affairs. *Philosophy and Public Affairs, 12*, 205-236.

Evens, Peter, Dietrich Rueschemeyer & Theda Skocpol (Eds.) 1990. *Bringing the State Back In*. Cambridge, UK: Cambridge University Press.

Fligstein, Neil. 1996. The Economic Sociology of the Transitions from Socialism. *American Journal of Sociology, 101*, 4, 1074-1081.

Fukuyama, Francis. 1992. *The End of History and the Last Man*. New York: Avon Books.

Gamson, William. 1990. *The Strategy of Social Protest*. Belmont, CA: Wadsworth Publishing Company.

Geddes, Barbara. 1999. What Do We Know About Democratization after Twenty Years? *Annual Review of Political Science, 2*, 115-144.

Gerber, Theodore P., & Michael Hout. 1998. More Shock than Therapy: Market Transition in Russia. *American Journal of Sociology, 104*, 1-50.

Glenny, Misha. 1991. *The Rebirth of History: Eastern Europe in the Age of Democracy*. New York: Penguin Books.

Gligorov, Vladimir. 1992. Balkanization: A Theory of Constitution Failure. *East European Politics and Societies, 6*, 283-303.

Goldfarb, Jeffrey C. 1991. *Beyond Glasnost: The Post-Totalitarian Mind*. Chicago, IL: University of Chicago Press.

Gurr, Ted Robert. 1995. Persistence and Change in Political Systems, 1800-1971. *American Political Science Review, 68*, 1482-1504.

Gurr, Ted Robert, Keith Jaggers & Will H. Moore. 1990, Spring. The Transformation of the Western State: The Growth of Democracy, Autocracy, and State Power Since 1800. *Studies in Comparative International Development, 25*, 1, 73-108

Gwertzman, Bernard & Michael Kaufman (Eds.). 1988. *The Collapse of Communism, the Correspondents of New The York Times*. New York: Times Books.

Havel, Vaclav. 1985. The Power of the Powerless. In V. Havel et al., *The Power of the Powerless: Citizens against the State in Central-Eastern Europe*. Edited by John Keane and translated by Paul Wilson. Armonk, N.Y: M.E. Sharpe.

Headey, Bruce, Peter Krause & Roland Habich. 1995. East Germany: Rising Incomes, Unchanged Inequality and the Impact of Redistributive Government 1990-92. *British Journal of Sociology, 46,* 225-243.

Held, David. 1996. *Models of Democracy.* Palo Alto, CA: Stanford University Press.

Higley, John & Richard Gunther. 1992. *Elites and Democratic Consolidation in Latin America and Southern Europe.* Cambridge, UK: Cambridge University Press.

Holmes, L. 1997. *Post-Communism.* Oxford: Oxford University Press.

Huntington, Samuel. 1991. *The Third Wave: Democratization in the Late Twentieth Century.* Norman: University of Oklahoma Press.

Jagger, Keith & Ted Robert Gurr. 1995. Tracking Democracy's Third Wave with the Polity III Data. *Journal of Peace Research, 32,* 4, 469-482.

Karatnycky, Adrian. 1995 (February). Democracies on the Rise, Democracies at Risk. *Freedom Review,* 5-10.

Karnoouh, Claude. 1991. The End of National Culture in Eastern Europe. *Telos, 89,* 133-140.

Kolodko, Grzegorz W. 1996. *Poland 2000. The New Economic Strategy* Warszawa: Poltext Press.

_____. 2001. *From Shock to Therapy. The Political Economy of Postsocialist Transformation.* Oxford: Oxford University Press.

Kornai, Janos. 1992. The Postsocialist Transition and the State. *American Economic Review, 82,* 1-21.

Kriesberg, Louis. 1998. *Constructive Conflicts: From Escalation to Resolution.* Lanham, MD: Rowman & Littlefield Publishers.

Laba, Roman. 1991. *The Roots of Solidarity.* Princeton, NJ: Princeton University Press.

Laitin, David D. 2000. Post-Soviet Politics. *Annual Review of Political Science, 3,* 117-148.

Lederer, I. J. (Ed.). 1992. *Western Approaches to Eastern Europe.* New York: Council on Foreign Relations Press.

Leibfried, Stephan & Paul Pierson. 1992. Prospect for Social Europe. *Politics & Society, 20,* 333-367.

Lipset, Seymour Martin. 1960. Some Social Requisites of Democracy: Economic Development and Political Legitimacy. *American Political Science Review,* 69-105.

Lovenduski, Joni & Jean Woodall. 1987. *Politics and Society in Eastern Europe.* Bloomington: Indiana University Press.

Lowenthal, Richard. 1976. Social Transformation and Democratic Legitimacy. *Social Research, 43,* 246-275.

Markoff, J. 1996. *Waves of Democracy.* Thousands Oaks, CA: Pine Forge.

Marody, Mira. 1991. New Possibilities and Old Habits. *Sisyphus, 7,* 33-40.

Mouffe, Chantal. 2000. *The Democratic Paradox.* London, UK: Verso.

Nee, Victor & David Stark (Eds.). 1989. *Remaking the Economic Institutions of Socialism. China and Eastern Europe.* Palo Alto, CA: Stanford University Press.

Neubauer, Deane E. 1967. Some Conditions of Democracy. *American Political Science Review, 61,* 4, 1002-1009.

Nielsen, Niels C. 1991. *Revolutions in Eastern Europe: Religious Roots.* Maryknoll, NY: Orbis Books.

Oberschal, Anthony. 1996. The Great Transition: China, Hungary and Sociology Exit Socialism into Market. *American Journal of Sociology, 101,* 4, 1028-1041.

O'Donnell, Guillermo, Philippe C. Schmitter & Laurence Whitehead. 1988. *Transitions from Authoritarian Rule: Comparative Perspective.* Baltimore: John Hopkins University Press.

Offe, Claus. 1991. Capitalism by Democratic Design? Democratic Theory Facing the Triple Transition in East Central Europe. *Social Research, 58,* 4, 865-892.

_____. 1997. *Varieties of Transition: The East Europe and East German Experience.* Cambridge, MA: MIT Press.

Opp, Karl-Dieter & Christiane Gern. 1993. Dissident Groups, Personal Networks, and Spontaneous Cooperation: The East German Revolution of 1989. *American Sociological Review, 58,* 59-681.

Ost, David. 1990. *Solidarity and the Politics of Anti-Politics.* Philadelphia: Temple University Press.

Parish, William L. & Ethan Michelson. 1996. Politics and Markets: Dual Transformations. *American Journal of Sociology, 101,* 4, 1042-1059.

Pellicani, Luciano & Florindo Volpacchio. 1991. The Cultural War Between East and West. *Telos, 8,* 127-132.

Pridham, Geoffrey (Ed.). 1990. *Securing Democracy: Political Parties and Democratic Consolidation in Southern Europe.* New York: Routledge Press.

Przeworski, Adam. 1991. *Democracy and Market.* Cambridge, UK: Cambridge University Press.

Putnam, George W. 1990. Occupational Sex Segregation and Economic Inequality under Socialism: Earnings Attainment and Earnings Decomposition in Yugoslavia. *Sociological Quarterly, 31,* 1, 59-75.

Quigley, Kevin F.F. 1997. *For Democracy's Sake: Foundation and Democracy Assistance in Central Europe.* Baltimore, Maryland: John Hopkins University Press.

Raina, Peter. 1999. *Droga do Okraglego Stolu. [The Road to the Round-Table Talks].* Warsaw: EFEKT Press.

Rawls, John. 1971. A *Theory of Justice.* Cambridge, MA: Harvard University Press.

Ray, James Lee. 1998. Does Democracy Cause Peace? *Annual Review of Political Science, 1,* 27-46.

Rueschemeyer, Dietrich, Evelyn Stephens & John Stephens. 1989. *Capitalist Development and Democracy.* Chicago, Ill.: University of Chicago Press.

Rueschemeyer, Marilyn. 1998. *Women in the Politics of Postcommunist Eastern Europe.* Armonk, N.Y.: M.E. Sharpe.

Rustow, Dankwart A. 1970. Transitions to Democracy: Toward a Dynamic Model. *Comparative Politics, 2,* 337-364.

Sandel, Michael J. 1996. *Democracy's Discontent.* Cambridge, MA: Harvard University Press.

Sanford, George (Ed.). 1992. *Democratization in Poland, 1989-1990.* New York: San Martin's Press.

Schwartzman, Kathleen. 1998. Globalization and Democracy. *Annual Review of Sociology, 24,* 159-181.

Sedatis, Judith & Jim Butterfield (Eds.). 1991. *Perestroika from Below.* Boulder, CO: Westview Press.

Skocpol, Theda. 1992. *Protecting Soldiers and Mothers: The Political Origin of Social Policy in the United States.* Cambridge, MA: Harvard University Press.

_____ (Ed.). 1998. *Democracy, Revolution, and History.* Ithaca, NY: Cornell University Press.

Skocpol, Theda & Morris P. Fiorina. 1999. *Civic Engagement in American Democracy.* Washington, D.C.: Brookings Institutions Press.

Sommers, Margaret. 1993. Citizenship and the Place of the Public Sphere: Law, Community, and Political Culture in the Transition to Democracy. *American Sociological Review, 58,* 587-620.

Sørensen, Annemette & Heike Trappe. 1995. The Persistence of Gender Inequality in Earnings in the German Democratic Republic. *American Sociological Review, 60,* 3, 398-406.

Stark, David. 1990. Privatization in Hungary: From Plan to Market or From Plan to Clan? *East European Politics and Societies, 4,* 3, 351-392.

_____.1992. Path Dependence and Privatization Strategies in East Central Europe. *Eastern European Politics and Societies, 6,* 6, 17-53.

_____.1996. Recombinant Property in East European Capitalism. *American Journal of Sociology, 101,* 993-1027.

Stark, David & László Bruszt. 1998. *Postsocialist Pathways: Transforming Politics and Property in East Central Europe.* Cambridge, UK: Cambridge University Press.

Starr, Harvey. 1991. Democratic Dominoes. Diffusion Approaches to the Spread of Democracy in the International System. *Journal of Conflict Resolution, 35,* 356-381.

Stephens, John D. 1989. Democratic Transition and Breakdown in Western Europe, 1870-1939: A Test of the Moore Thesis. *American Journal of Sociology, 94,* 1019-1077.

Stokes, S. C. 1999. Political Parties and Democracy. *Annual Review of Political Science, 2,* 243-267.

Stone, Richard. 2000. Stress: The Invisible Hand in Eastern Europe's Death Rates. *Science,* vol. 288, pp. 1732-1733.

Szelényi, Ivan. 1990. *Socialist Entrepreneurs: Embourgeoisement in Rural Hungary.* Madison: The University of Wisconsin Press.

Szelényi, Ivan & Eric Kostello. 1996. The Market Transition Debate: Toward a Synthesis. *American Journal of Sociology, 101,* 1082-1096.

Tarrow, Sidney. 1989. *Democracy and Disorder.* New York: Oxford University Press.

_____. 1991a. "Aiming at the Moving Target:" Social Science and the Recent Rebellions in Eastern Europe. *Political Science and Politics, 3,* 9-10.

_____. 1991b. Understanding Political Change in Eastern Europe. *Political Science and Politics, 3,* 12-20.

Titma, Mikk, Nancy Brandon Tuma & Brian D. Silver. 1998. Winners and Losers in the Post-Communist Transition: New Evidence from Estonia. *Post-Soviet Affairs, 14,* 2, 114-136.

Touraine, Alain. 1997. *What Is Democracy?* Boulder, CO: Westview Press.

Uhlin, Anders. 1993. Indonesian Democracy Discourses in a Global Context. The Transnational Diffusion of Democratic Ideas. *The Center of Southeast Asian Studies Working Paper, 83,* Monash University, Clayton, Australia.

_____. 1995. *Democracy and Diffusion: Transnational Lesson-Drawing Among Indonesian Pro-Democracy Actors.* Lund Political Studies Working Paper 87, Lund University, Sweden.

Vodopivec, Peter. 1992. Slovens and Yugoslavia, 1918-1991. *East European Politics and Societies, 6,* 220- 242.

Vladislav, Jan (Ed.). 1987. *Vaclav Havel: or Living in Truth.* London: Faber and Faber.

Wallerstein, Immanuel. 1995. *After Liberalism.* New York: New Press.

Wejnert, Barbara. 1988. Student Movement in Poland in 1980-1981. *Social Movements, Conflict and Change, 10,* 173-183. Greenwich: Connecticut: JAI Press.

_____. 1993, August. *Did Democracy Diffuse in Eastern Europe?* Paper presented at the Annual Meeting of the American Sociological Association, Miami.

_____. 1996. Family Studies and Politics: The Case of Polish Sociology. *Marriage and Family Review, 22,* 233-257.

_____. 2002 (in press). A Conceptual Framework for Integrating Diffusion Models. *Annual Review of Sociology, 28.*

Wejnert, Barbara & Metta Spencer (Eds.). 1996. *Women in Post-Communism.* Greenwich, CT: JAI Press.

Wesolowski, Wlodzimierz. 1990. Transition from Authoritarianism to Democracy. *Social Research, 57,* 2, 435-461.

White, Stephen (Ed.). 1991. *Handbook of Reconstruction in Eastern Europe & the Soviet Union.* New York, NY: Longman Current Affairs.

Whitehead, Laurence (Ed.). 1996. *The International Dimensions of Democratization: Europe and the Americas.* Oxford, NY: Oxford University Press.

Woodward, S. 1995. *Balkan Tragedy.* Washington D.C.: The Brookings Institution.

Zakowski, Bronislaw. 1991. *Zakowski Pyta Geremek Odpowiada,* Warsaw: PWN.

Index

Agricultural sector, poverty and, 210

Albania: democratic mobilization in, 73, 80; pyramid schemes in, 210

All-Poland Trade Union Federation (OPZZ), 224

Architecture, Soviet, 326-36; bazaars and trading posts and, 332-35; and communist society, 21, 325-36; contemporary and commercialized Western styles in, 332, 336; destruction of, 331-32; elemental approach to form in, 326; functional constructions in, 332; gender and, 326, 330, 335; ideology and, 326-30; Lenin monument, 329-30; modernist movement in, 326-27; post-communism, 330-35; of Stalinist times, 328-29

Artistic expression: and Black Wave cinematography, 20-21, 289-90; communism and, 20-21, 289-90, 292-95, 301-2; in counter-culture of Yugoslavian youth, 286-95; impact of po-

litical transitions on, 20, 309. *See also* Architecture, Soviet; Polish poetry

Asset redistribution policy, 187, 195-97, 200-201

Baluka, Edmund, 104

Basta, Jaroslav, 49, 50, 51, 52, 53

Belarus, income distribution in, 189

Birth of Tito's Despotism, The (Milic), 299

Black Wave cinematography, 20-21, 289-90; Bloom, Jack M., 91

Bogacz, Zbigniew, 105, 106

Borkowska, Grazyna, 309

Borusewicz, Bodgan, 101, 106

Budgets, transitional, 150-51, 156

Bulgaria: democratic mobilization in, 73, 80; income distribution in, 190

Calfa, Marian, 47

Capital formation, 205-6; in centrally planned economy, 162; contraction, in transition economies, 162-63; fiscal policy and, 142, 143, 152-71; as function of level of income, 153; and government size, 154; recovery and, 164-67; savings and, 153, 154; in transition economies, 205-6

Capital gains preference policy, 205-207

Celejewska, Malgorzata, 94, 95-97, `106

Central European University, 179

Charter 77 (Czechoslavkia), 33-34, 36, 42, 44, 47

Check-room for Darkness (Lipska), 317

Christian Science World Monitor, 43

Chubaise, Anatoly, 175

"Citizen of a Small Nation" (Lipska), 317

Civic Democratic Party (Czechoslovakia), 41-42

Civic Forum (Czechoslovakia), 33, 34, 36

Civic Movement (Czechoslovakia), 41, 42, 46-46

Civilian opposition movements. *See* Political mobilization

Class, entrepreneurial, 211-12

Communication technology, 7, 14-15

Communist regimes: and acceptance of reforms, 69; executive adjustments in, 73-74, 82-83; liberalization and softening of, 68-69, 70-71; strength of, democratization and, 70-71, 72, 80

Communist system: disintegration of, 304; marketization and, 191, 344

Corporate governance structure, privatization and, 174-76

Cosic, Dobrica, 301

Council of Mutual Economic Assistance (CMEA), 13

Cultural images, social stratification and, 336. *See also* Arhitecture, Soviet

Culture, 345-46; as function of political conditions, 20-21, 345-46; post-Marxist view of, 325; and social change, 325; and Socialist counter-cultures, 286-95; Western influence on, 12, 21, 332, 336

Culture-polity-economy interconnectedness, 325, 346

Czechoslovakia: anticommunist laws in, 55-56, 57; Communist party reforms in, 67; democratic mobilization in, 73, 80; discrediting of former dissidents in, 36-45; executive adjustment in, 80; former Communist officials in, 30, 35; human rights movement in, 31-34; income distribution in, 189; Prague Spring reforms in, 32, 39, 56; privatization in, 187; Secret Service, 29

Czechoslovakian lustration law, 36-58; aims of, 30, 47-48; and alleged collaborators, 29, 36-40; bureaucrats and, 56-57; denazification and, 30-32; Havel's attitudes toward, 54, 55, 57; and high-ranking Communists, 48-49, 53; Independent Commission of the Ministry of Interior and, 49-55; international criticism of, 41; and international human rights laws, 58; legal framework for, 45-50; media and, 40-45; Parliament and, 45-47; and Secret Service files, 39, 43, 55, 57; supporters of, 29-30, 45, 48, 56

Democratic transitions: culture and cultural effects in, 20-21, 345-46; diffusion effects in, 11-15;

domestic factors in, 9-11, 69-70; dual-level conceptual framework of, 3-4, 5*f*; economic variables in, 10-11, 18-20, 70, 343-44; education's role in, 10-11; historical roots of, 341; implementation of new policies in, 343; international influences in, 6-9; literacy and, 7, 10; multilevel changes in, 341; political determinants of, 9-10, 342-43; polity-centered entity in, 16-18; social impacts of, 259; social processes of, 6-15; socio-economic and demographic crises and, 241; spatial effects in, 12-13; structural entities of, 15-21; urbanization's role in, 7-8; waves, 11. *See also specific country*; East Central European transition; Transitional economies

Devaty, Stanislav, 43, 44

Dienstbier, Jiri, 47

Diffusion theory, 11-15

Dissident movements 16-17, 31-34, 343. *See also* Political mobilization

Djilas, Milovan, 299

Djogo, Gojko, 301

Dubcek, Alexander, 48-49

Early Works (Rani radovi), 289

East Eurpean Reporter, The, 33

East Germany, democratic mobilization in, 73, 80, 83

East Central European transition, 65-86; global hegemonic changes and, 66; n, 68, 69, 70, 71-72, 73, 80; domestic conditions for, 68-70; and executive regime adjustments, 73-74, 82-83; Gorbachev era opportunity structure and, 67; internal socio-political structure and, 68-70; and international political and economic trends, 65, 66-68; political processes in, 68-69; and political mobilization, 68-73, 80; regime's liberalism and, 68-69; regime's strength in, 70-71, 72; social and economic processes in, 69-70

Economic consciousness: notion of, 221; theoretical dichotomy and, 222. *See also* Polish workers' economic views

Economic development, democratic movements and, 69-70

Economic policymaking: asset distribution in, 196-97, 200-201; capital formation in, 205-6; equity issues in, 185; income and wages in, 193-97, 204; pensions and disabled benefits in, 204-5; savings and taxation in, 205, 206-7; subsidy reductions in, 193; wealth accumulation in, 197-98, 200-201

Economies, centrally planned: failures of, 173; fiscal policies of, 152-53. *See also specific country*; Transition economies

Economy, global, and democratic transition, 7-9, 67

Economy-culture-polity interconnectedness, 325, 346

Entrepreneurship, in transitional economies, 191-92

Estonia: economy of, 113; education and income in, 128, 130-33; and European Union negotiations, 113; gender/ethnic differences in income in, 116, 127, 133-34, 136; gross domestic product of, 113; income attainment factors in, 115, 130-35; income differentiation in, 113-37; income distribution in, 190; income inequality in, 114,

126-28; locality's effect on income in, 133; migration and income in, 116, 133; income mobility in, 114, 128-30, 135-36; move to market economy in, 112-13; nationality as predictor of income in, 116, 134; occupational structure and income in, 137; private versus state sector income in, 115-16; rural-urban income inequality in, 127-28, 136-37

European Community (EC), 67

European Union: membership, 19, 113, 186; trade with, 142

Fiscal policy, 150-71, 204; asset depreciation and, 158-59; budgets and, 150-51, 156; and capital flight, 152; of centrally planned economies, 152-53; and current account liberalization, 159; during early transition, 150; and fiscal deficit, 150; and foreign direct investment, 159; human capital and, 151-52, 169; illusory prudence in, 210; inflation and, 145, 150-51; and institutional arrangements, 150, 168; political compromise in, 197; and public finance system overhaul, 141; and short-term capital flow, 150-60; savings and, 156-57; systemic reforms and, 152; taxation in, 141, 142, 150, 168, 169

Flying University (Poland), 299

Foreign capital, and democratic change, 9

Foucault, Michel, 335

Frasyniuk, Wladyslaw, 107

Free University (Yugoslavia), 298-98

Fukuyama, Francis, 302, 304, 346

Gdansk Shipyard strikes, 93

Gierek, Edward, 102, 105-6

GKI (State Committee for Property of the Russian Federation), 175, 176-77, 180

Global communication systems, democratization and, 7

Global economy, and democratic transition, 7-9, 67

Gomulka, Wladyslaw, 91-93, 101, 105, 106

Gorbachev effect, 7

Gorbachev, Mikhail, 66, 174, 255

Gorecki, Winicjusz, 107

Gredelj, Stjepan, 281

Gross domestic product (GDP), of transitional economies, 141, 142, 145, 187, 198, 208-12

Havel, Vaclav, 33, 35, 42, 54, 55, 57, 58

Hegemonic powers, global shift in, 9

Health, in former Soviet Union, 241-56

Helsinki Watch, 46

Human capital: capital gains preference policy and, 207; formation, and government size, 154; government investment in, 151-52; realignment of wages with, 195

Hungary: Communist party reforms in, 67; democratic mobilization in, 73, 80; goulash communism in, 83; income distribution in, 188-89

Income attainment, predictors of, 115, 130-35

Income distribution: asset transfers and, 196-97; change mechanisms in, 193-97; parallel economy and, 191-92; shifts, 1987-88 and 1993-95, 188-90. *See also specific country*

Income inequality: and income mobility and, 114; increase in, 145; as obstacle to growth, 212; in post-communist countries, 10, 114. *See also specific country*

Inflation, in transitional economies, 145, 150-51, 193-94

Informal sector, 191-92, 194, 332-35

International Monetary Fund (IMF), 146, 159, 193

Javnost (The Public) newspaper, 299

"Joy of Writing, The" (Szymborska), 310-12

Kasprzyk, Krzystof, 107

Kavan, Jan, 29. *See also* Czechoslovakian lustration law

Kharkov monument, 327-28

Klimova, Rita, 40

Kociolek, Stanislaw, 93

Kolodko, Grzegorz W., 141, 185

Krystosiak, Aleksander, 94, 99-101, 103, 104-5, 107

Kuron, Jacek, 93

Laber, Jeri, 46

Langos, Jan, 50

Latvia: income distribution in, 189; life expectancy in, 210-11

Life expectancy, transitional countries, 210-11

Lipska, Ewa, poetry of, 309, 316-21

Literature and journalism, prevailing political norms and, 309, 310, 316. *See also* Artistic freedom; Polish poetry

Lithuania, income distribution in, 190

Luczywo, Helena, 321-22

Makavejev, Dusan, 290

Makeshin, Alexei, 173

Mandela, Nelson, 57

Market-oriented economy: Polish workers' expectations of, 223; push for transition to, 186, 344; transition processes in, 142. *See also* Transition economies

Markovic, Ante, 303

Marxism, 105, 286

Matuszewska, Alicja, 94, 97-99, 107

McNeil, Don, 43

Media, and diffusion of democracy, 14-15

Michnik, Adam, 43, 47, 54

Middle and upper class, creation of, 197

Milic, M., 299

Milosz, Czeslaw, 316

Mlodzik, Krysztof, 103, 107

Moldova, income distribution in, 190

Molosevic, Slobodan, 301, 303, 304, 305

Muller, Jiri, 31, 33

Murakas, Rein, 111

Nobel Prize, 316

Organization for Economic Cooperation and Development (OECD), 142, 174

Palach, Jan, 32

Palach Press, 33

Paths of a Generation study, 111, 116-20, 135

Patocka, Jan, 53-54

Pithart, Petr, 42

Plawinski, Tadeusz, 93, 102, 107

Poland, communist: economic stagnation and income inequality in, 91-92, 93; Gomulka regime in, 91-93, 101, 105

Poland, post-transition: agricultural sector, 210; capital formation policy in, 206; democratic mobilization in, 73, 80; economic contraction in, 198; economic policy in, 187, 200; Gini coefficient in, 201, 203, 212; gross domestic product (GDP), 141; income distribution in, 189, 201, 202-4; life satisfaction of women in, 263-65; Package 2000 growth program, 206-7; poverty in, 210, 211; quality of life in, 260-65, 201; socioeconomic disparities in, 260; taxation system in, 206-7; unemployment in, 200; wage inequality in, 204

Polish Communist Party, 67

Polish poetry, 309-22; acclaim for, 316; deconstructivist and feminist practices in, 315; engagement with national identity and democracy in, 317-21; of Ewa Lipska, 316-21; historical experience in, 309, 316, 318, 320; New Wave, 316; of Wislawa Szymborska, 309-16; and Western values and culture, 321-22

Polish workers' economic views, 221-38; ambivalence effect in, 237-38; communist orientation of, 226-27; corporatist system and, 229; egalitarian and etatist, 228; enterprise autonomy/competition in, 226; income egalitarianism in, 226; justice-oriented capitalism and competition in, 229; liberal orientation of, 226-27, 229, 232; market expectations of, 223; modernization in, 231-32, 238; petty bourgeois capitalism and, 227, 228, 229; privatization and, 228, 234-37; state ownership and, 234; support of efficiency-oriented principles, 224-26; trade unions and, 224

Polish workers' strikes, 91, 92-101; ideal of unity and, 104-5; impact and lessons, 101-6; and independent trade unions, 103-4; injuries and deaths in, 94, 96-97, 101; police and, 98, 99-100, 102

Political freedom, artistic freedom and, 20-21, 309, 310, 312, 313, 316

Political mobilization, 16-17, 68, 69, 70-73, 343; and regime strength, 80; and state's use of deadly force, 102; temporal rate of, 81-82, 83

Polity, in transition to democracy, 16-18

Polity-economy-culture interconnectedness, 325, 346

Poverty, post-communist, 113; contributing factors in, 210; democratic movements and, 69-70; as result of declining income equality, 208

Price liberalization, income distribution and, 187

Privatization: corporate governance structure and, 174; mass, through free asset distribution, 106, 187; obstacles to, in former communist countries, 173; and "people's capitalism," 188; Polish workers' views of, 228, 234-37. *See also* Russian privatization

Quality of life research model, 261-62

Radio Luxembourg, 291

Role modeling, in democratic transitions, 12

Romania: Ceausescu regime in, 69; democratic mobilization in, 73, 80; income distribution in, 189

Romaniuk, Lara A., 241

Russia: corruption and "crony capitalism" in, 201; economic policy, 187; gross domestic product (GDP), 141; income distribution in, 190; life expectancy in, 210-11; MMM schemes in, 210; Yeltsin's policies in, 174-76. *See also* Former Soviet Union; Ukraine

Russian privatization, 19, 174-82; buy-out option in, 174, 180; and corporate governance, 176-82; economic goals and problems of, 180-81; formed on economic principles, 176-77; implementation options, 174-75; mass entrepreneurial consciousness and, 174; monitoring of, 178-80; and standards of living decline, 176; State Program for, 175; trends and scenarios for future development, 180-82; voucher scheme and passive proprietary ownership, 175-76, 179

Sabata, Jaroslav, 53, 55-56

Savings: capital formation and, 153, 155; capital gains preference policy and, 205-7; erosion of, 210; and general government revenue, 156-57; propensity, and fiscal policy, 156-57

Serbia: economy, 305; transition, ethnic nationalism in, 304-5

Shawcross, William, 51

Shevchenko, Taras, 328-29

Slovenia: income distribution in, 188-89; New Lovenian Art project in, 294-95

Social consciousness, "transition to democracy" paradigm and, 222

Social inequality: democratization and, 69-70; Gini index of inequality, 10, 188-90, 145, 146

Social policy implementation, 345

Social problems, post-communist, 17-18

Socialist Youth League (Yugoslavia), 292

Solidarity movement, 105, 186, 224, 317

Soviet Union, 66, 174; Breznev regime in, 69; health policies, 248, 255; income levels and living standards in, 188; life expectancy in, 210-11

Stalin, Joseph, 290

Structural adjustment policies, 193, 194

Structural equivalence, in diffusion theory, 13-14

Stycos, J. Mayone, 259

Stycos, Maria Nowakowska, 309

Sucharski, Adam (pseudonym), 92, 107

Szymborska, Wislawa, poetry of, 309-16

Tax evasion, 191-92

Taxation: income distribution mechanism and, 197; post-transition, 141, 142, 150, 206-7; savings and, 205; in transition economies, 155, 156, 158, 168, 169

Titma, Mikk, 111

Tito, Josip Broz, 283-84

Transition economies: asset ownership and distribution in, 195-97, 200-201; capital formation policy in, 205-6; contraction and recovery in, 162-63, 198; estimates of growth in, 198-200; expectation-achievement gap in, 186-88; first decade outcomes, 142-49; foreign trade, 142; gross domestic

product (GDP), 141, 142, 145, 187, 198, 208-12; income attainment in, 115; income differentiation in, 111, 112, 113; income distribution/redistribution in, 187, 188-92, 193-97; income inequality in, 114, 141, 145, 146, 112; inflation in, 145, 150-51, 193-94; institutional and development gaps in, 186-87; *nouveaux riches* in, 211-12; policymaking in, 185-213; poverty in, 207-12; price liberalization impacts in, 187, 193; privatization in, 112, 188, 195, 196; regional differences in, 188; shadow (parallel) economy in, 191-92, 194, 332-35; social and political tensions in, 187; recession in, 198; stabilization programs in, 194-95; subsidies in, 193; unemployment in, 210; wages in, 195, 204. *See also specific country*; Fiscal policy
"Transition to democracy" paradigm, 222
Tuma, Nancy Brandon, 111
Tyszka, Zbigniew, 259

Uhl, Petr, 35, 38, 46, 47, 50
Ukraine: demographic crisis in, 241; economic contraction in, 198; gross domestic product, 141; income distribution in, 190
Ukraine health crisis, 241-56; alcohol and tobacco consumption in, 246-48, 250-52; and leading causes of death, 244-46; and life expectancy, 210-11, 242-44; major threats in, 242, 248-49; mortality/morbidity patterns and, 242; policy implications and models, 253-55; social freedom and, 256
Unemployment, in transition countries, 210
Urban, Jan, 44
Urbanization, 7-8

Walentynowicz, Anna, 105
Walesa, Lech, 92, 96, 101, 103, 105
Wealth accumulation, 197-98, 200-201
Wejnert, Barbara, 3, 65, 259, 325, 341
Western culture, adoption and influence of, 12, 21, 321-22, 332, 336
White Book, 300
Women, post-communist; morbidity/mortality and, 243-48; symbolic portrayal of, 335; well-being and life satisfaction of, 263-65
Woodward, Susan, 281
World Bank, 179, 198
World system cycles, concept of, 8
WR—Mysteries of Organism, 290

Yalta agreement, 9
Yeltsin, Boris, 174
Yugoslav Communist Youth League (SKOJ), 292
Yugoslavia, 281-305; alternative social movements in, 296-98; Black Wave art movement in, 20-21, 289-90; civil society and, 295, 298, 302; communalism in, 296-97; counterculture in, 286-95; decentralized decisionmaking in, 282; democratic mobilization in, 73, 80; destruction of, Serbian post-communist elite in, 303; economy, 284-85, 302; global oil crises and, 8; Household literature in, 294; idea of melting

pot in, 283; income levels and living standards in, 188; intelligentsia in, 286, 287, 288; market economy and economic reforms in, 282; nationalism, 285, 288, 302-303; political disobedience in, 298-300; punk and New Wave as symbolic resistance in, 292-95; repression of artists and intellectuals in, 301-2; self-management ideology in, 282, 283, 286, 288; source of social conflicts in, 284, 285; state-party *coup d'etat* (1970s'), 287-88, 289; students' and intellecturals' movement in, 284, 286-287, 288; Tito's regime and Titoism in, 283-284, 299-301, 303; youth subculture in, 291-95

Zajicek, Frantisek, 32, 38, 39, 51, 52, 53
Zeman, Milos, 35, 47
Zherebkin, Sergei, 325
ZIL Company (Russian), privatization of, 177-78
Zilnik, Zelimir, 289, 290

About the Editor and Contributors

Barbara Wejnert is an associate professor of sociology. She is currently teaching and is a faculty research associate at Cornell University. The former director of the East European Academic Program at Cornell, she has been a consultant to many public and governmental agencies dealing with transition to democracy in former communist states. Among her book publications are *Women in Post-Communism* (1996) and *Theoretical and Empirical Approaches to Quality of Life* (2001). She has published numerous papers in peer-reviewed American and European journals including *Annual Review of Sociology; Research on Social Movements, Conflict and Change* and *Marriage and Family Review*; in English and many Eastern European languages. Her research interests in political sociology, social movements and gender include recent empirical studies on quality of life in post-communist countries and analysis of diffusion of democracy in the world.

Jack M. Bloom is an associate professor of sociology and Academic Director of the Polish Studies Center at Indiana University Northwest, as well as a former activist in social movements. He is the author of books and articles on race, social inequality and social movements in the United States, Poland and Africa. His book, *Class, Race and the Civil Rights Movement* won second prize in the C. Wright Mills competition given by the Society for the Study of Social Problems and was named by G. Meyer Center as an outstanding book on race and inequality. He is presently working on a book about Polish workers movements during the communist period and their implications for the 1989 democratic transition.

Grazyna Borkowska, a professor at the Polish Academy of Science in Warsaw and editor of the journal, *Pamietnik Literacki,* has published extensively on Polish women writers of the nineteenth and twentieth centuries: *Dialog powi-*

esciowy, [Dialogue in Novels] based on the work of Eliza Orzeszkowa and *Pozytywisci i inni, [Positivists and Others]*. Her book, *Cudzoziemki [The Alien Ones]* is widely accepted as a feminist reading of nineteenth-century Polish women writers. Her latest book, M*aria Dabrowska i Stanislaw Stempowski* (1999) studies the relationship between these two well known authors.

Juliusz Gardawski is an associate professor of economics at the Warsaw School of Economics. He is the author of numerous papers and books. Among his published books are *Poland's Industrial Workers on the Return to Democracy and Market Economy* (1998) and *Politics and Economy as Seen by Employees* (1999). Since 1991, based on funds received from the Friedrich Ebert Foundation, he has conducted a series of research survey on Polish workers' attitudes toward the market economy. These surveys constitute the most extensive series of research on the subject of Polish workers in the 1990s.

Stjepan Gredelj, is an associate professor at the Institute for Philosophy and Social Theory in Belgrade. He is the author and co-author of six books, among them *Behind the Mirror* (1986), discussing Yugoslav media as the "Alice in the Wanderland" of Titoism; and *Cleaning the Decks* (1998), analyzing the ideological and nationalistic purges of journalists in Radio Belgrade (1989-1993). He also published over fourthly articles in domestic and international scientific journals. His primary interests are political sociology, global sociological theory and social movements.

Jan Kavan is presently vice premier for foreign affairs, defense and security and foreign minister of the Czech Republic. The son of a Czechoslovak diplomat and British mother he had to leave Czechoslovakia as a student leader after the 1968 Soviet-led invasion and studied at London School of Economics and St.Antony's College (Oxford). For 20 years he was helping Czechoslovak opposition by supplying them with literature and duplicators. Through his London press agency, Palach Press, he published dissident's papers and samizdat books. In the 1980s he also founded two charities—Jan Palach Information and Research Trust and East European Cultural Foundation, which acted as a liaison center for Czechoslovak, Polish, Hungarian, East German, Slovinian and Bulgarian opposition groups. He was a founder and an editor of the East European Reporter, a quarterly with renowned subscribers, including United States State Department, Hoover Institution and Harvard University. On returning to Prague in November 1989 he was elected to the Federal Assembly (Parliament) 1990-1992. In 1996 he was elected Senator and in June 1998 was appointed foreign minister in the new social democratic government.

Grzegorz W. Kolodko is a key architect of Polish economic reforms. In 1994-97 he was first deputy premier and minister of Finance, and led his country to the OECD in 1996. he is an advisor to the president of Poland and an expert on international organizations. Professor at Warsaw School of Economics (SGH), in 1999-2000 he was a visiting scholar at the International Monetary Fund and in 1998 a consultant to the World Bank. In 1997-98, Kolodko held distinguished Sasakawa Chair and Research Professor in Development Economics at the United Nations University, World Institute for Development Economics Research (WIDER) in Helsinki. He is an author of twenty books and over 300 articles and research papers published in twenty languages worldwide, of which over eighty are in English. He contributed comments and editorials to *The New York Times, Financial Times, International Herald Tribune, Journal of Commerce* and *The Economist.* His newest book, *From Shock to Therapy. The Political Economy of Postsocialist Transformation* (2000) has been just published by the Oxford University Press.

Alexei Makeshin lives in Moscow, Russia, working as an independent consultant in executive recruitment and organization development. He also represents Ray & Berndtson, a major international search firm, as a project consultant in Russia/CIS. Currently is conducting research on organization development and management change in Russia with the support of ECA/USIA Alumni Small Grants Program of Year 2000. He is a former fellow of R. F. Wagner School of Public Administration, at New York University.

Rein Murakas is a researcher in the Department of Sociology at Tartu University in Estonia and Head of the Estonian Social Science Data Archive (ESSDA). His main research interests concern income inequality in post-socialist societies, economic well-being of young adults, problems of youth, the use of computers and information technology in sociological research, and problems in archiving of social science data. He is the author or co-author of several articles, mainly focusing on market reforms and rising income inequalities in transitional societies. He is a member of several scientific organizations. In the last few years he has been an active participant in the cross-national, longitudinal research project, "Paths of a Generation."

Maria Nowakowska Stycos teaches modern Spanish and Spanish American literature at Cornell University. Her Ph.D. dissertation on the Argentine feminist poet Alfonsina Storni established her interest in twentieth-century Hispanic poetry and women's writing. She has edited a special issue of *Revista/Review* on "New Approaches to Twentieth-Century Hispanic Women Poets." More recently, she has published a comparative study of Anna Swirszczynska, Gioconda Belli and Rosario Castellanos (*Letras Femeninas).*

Lara A. Romaniuk wrote her paper while an intern at the U. N. Development Program (Gender in Development) in Kiev, Ukraine. Currently, she is completing a master's degree at the London School of Economics, and is specializing in Central and Eastern European Affairs. Recently, she has written about forecasting in international affairs, specifically forecasting methods and their application to the Soviet Union and the future of Russian transition. Her next research project will base her in Skopje, where she will research transition in the former Yugoslavia, with a focus on Macedonia.

J. Mayone Stycos is professor of rural sociology and former director of the Population and Development Program at Cornell University. He has been a consultant to many private and public agencies dealing with population. Among his nearly twenty book publications are *Human Fertility in Latin America*; *Community Development and Family Planning*; and *Demography as an Inter-discipline*.

Mikk Titma is a professor of sociology at Tartu University in Estonia and a senior researcher at Stanford University. He lived in the Soviet Union until 1991 and has traveled widely through the region. He has authored or edited more than twenty books and 200 articles. He served as the elected vice president of the Soviet Sociological Association from 1988-1990. He is especially known for his longitudinal studies of the career paths of young adults in the Soviet Union and its successor states. In 1983 he founded the "Paths of a Generation" (PG) project, which began with a survey of secondary school graduates in fifteen regions of the Soviet Union. He and Nancy Tuma are currently analyzing data from the fourth PG survey, which was conducted in 1997-1998 in Russia, Ukraine, Belarus, Moldova, Estonia, Latvia, Kazakhstan and Tajikistan.

Nancy Brandon Tuma is a professor of sociology at Stanford University. She has authored numerous articles on life careers, social inequality, and research methods; edited several books; and co-authored Social Dynamics: Models and Methods (1984), a pioneering and widely cited book on event history analysis. Following her doctoral study of life careers of Mexican-Americans, she examined the impacts of welfare policies on the lives of low-income American families. Around 1980 she began to study social inequality and life careers of people in other countries: Poland, Germany, China and, eventually, the former Soviet Union. She and Mikk Titma are currently analyzing data from the fourth PG survey, which was conducted in 1997-1998 in Russia, Ukraine, Belarus, Moldova, Estonia, Latvia, Kazakhstan and Tajikistan.

Zbigniew Tyszka is a professor of sociology and director of the Institute of Sociology of the Family at the Adam Mickiewicz University in Poznan, Poland. From the 1970's until mid-1990s, after receiving two large center grants from the Polish Ministry of Education, he directed a field research team of over 100 Polish social scientists studying the transition in Polish families under changing historical conditions. He is an author of nearly thirty books and numerous research articles. He is an editor of one of the leading Polish sociological journals, the *Annals of the Sociology of Family*. His recent book *Z Metodologii Badan Socjologicznych nad Rodzina [From the Methodology of Sociology of Family Research]* (1991) was awarded first prize by the Polish ministry of Science and Education.

Sergei Zherebkin is an associate professor of philosophy at The Academy of Sciences of the Ukraine and co-director of Gender Studies at Kharkov University. He is an author of many articles on gender politics, and on the impact of politics on the arts. In the 1990s, as an IREX visiting scholar, he visited many American universities, including Cornell. In addition to teaching, he also serves as an editor of the Gender Studies Journal (Ukraine) and as co-director of the Summer Institute on Gender Studies in Foros.